HISTORY OF MODERN CREATIONISM

By

Henry M. Morris

INSTITUTE FOR CREATION RESEARCH

SANTEE, CALIFORNIA 92071

HISTORY OF MODERN CREATIONISM

Copyright, Second Edition, 1993
Henry M. Morris

INSTITUTE FOR CREATION RESEARCH,
10946 Woodside Ave. North
Santee, California, 92071

First Edition, 1984
Master Book Publishers

Library of Congress Catalog Card Number 84-60865
Paperback, ISBN 0-89051-102-0
Cloth, ISBN 0-89051-107-1

Cataloging in Publication Data
Morris, Henry Madison, 1918-
    A history of modern creationism.

      1. Creation. 2. Evolution. 1. Title.

213
ISBN 0-89051-102-0, Paper   84-60865
ISBN 0-89051-107-1, Cloth

Printed in the United States of America

Table of Contents

Appendices

ILLUSTRATIONS

Foreword

One of the truly remarkable phenomena of the late twentieth century has been the "resurrection" of biblical and scientific creationism. It was at the infamous Scopes Trial in Dayton, Tennessee, in the month of July, 1925 , that the scientific credibility of the early chapters of Genesis was effectively killed and buried by the secular (and even religious) establishment.

Or so it seemed! But God's Word cannot even be imprisoned (II Timothy 2:9), to say nothing of being killed and buried! For centuries, seeds had been sown by the Spirit of God in human hearts concerning the absolute truth of Creation, the Fall, and the Genesis Flood, as recorded in the first book of the Bible and authenticated by the Lord Jesus Christ (Matthew 5:18, 19:4, 24:37–39; John 5:44–47, 10:35, etc.). It would take more than a Scopes Trial or even a Darwin Centennial Celebration (University of Chicago, November, 1959) to destroy those seeds. They were not dead; they were underground and actively germinating, ready to sprout forth in a tremendous display of heart commitment to the literal truth of Genesis 1–11, in the 1960s and 1970s, all over the world.

Henry M. Morris is uniquely qualified, by God's grace, to write *History of Modern Creationism*. He has not only been a contemporary to this great movement, but also one of its prime movers, under God. No history of biblical and scientific creationism in this century would be complete or even valid without careful attention to the brilliant and tireless efforts of this man of God. It has been one of my special privileges to have known him now for over forty years and to have had a small part with him in God's work, marvelous in our eyes, of drawing His Church back to a renewed appreciation of its foundations in Christ as *Creator* and sovereign *Ruler* of the universe.

My acquaintance with Henry Morris began at Princeton University in February, 1947, through reading his excellent book, *That You Might Believe*. Six years later we met at Grace Theological Seminary in Winona Lake, Indiana, and began a correspondence and a series of editorial discussions that eventuated in the publication of *The Genesis Flood* in 1961. How this came about, in God's mysterious providence, is told in Chapter 5.

Using this publishing event in 1961 as the pivotal point, Dr. Morris devotes the first four chapters to a fascinating analysis of the early history of creationism, from distant antiquity to Darwin; the vast influence of the theory of evolution climaxing in the Darwinian Centennial Celebration of 1959; some of the isolated and apparently futile "voices in the wilderness" who struggled against this evil influence in the name of the living God; and the various attempts to launch creationist associations, all of which failed because of doctrinal and spiritual compromise. These well documented facts, hardly known even in the Christian world, are rich with lessons for the present hour.

The final chapters of the book trace God's use of *The Genesis Flood* to bring into visibility and coordination the creationist convictions of thousands of people around the world, including many scientists of high academic standing and respect. Thus, such organizations as the Creation Research Society and the Bible-Science Association were launched in the early 1960s, and ultimately the Institute for Creation Research in 1970. Similar groups, with their own publications, have appeared in England, Germany, Holland, Australia, Russia and other countries. Many readers will be fascinated by the discussion of creation/evolution debates in major universities, directly or indirectly observed by over 5,000,000 people, and the basic failure of "the Arkansas trial" together with other efforts to legislate creationism in public schools.

The final chapter, "The Coming Battle for Creation," is outstanding. Who can remain indifferent in the presence of such topics as "Creation and Public Opinion," "Evolutionists Sound the

Alarm," "Organized Anti-Creationism," or "The Problem of Christian Compromise?" But for any of God's people who might sink into despair at the very thought of organized and Satanic opposition to biblical truth or, even worse, widespread compromise among Christian leaders with such enemies of God, the book ends with a tremendously uplifting spectrum of scriptural assurances of **the final victory of the Creator.** Surely all who name His name in faith anticipate the infinite joy of joining that ultimate heavenly chorus of praise to our Lord Jesus Christ: "Thou art worthy, 0 Lord, to receive glory and honor and power: for thou has created all things, and for thy pleasure they are and were created" (Revelation 4:11).

I am now very thankful to see an updated edition of this important book. May our gracious God be pleased to use it for His glory around the world.

Winona Lake, Indiana   John C. Whitcomb
October, 1992

Acknowledgments

A number of creationist friends and colleagues have been kind enough to read the manuscript for this book, and I have profited greatly from their corrections and suggestions. These have included Dr. Walter Lammerts, first president of the Creation Research Society, Rev. Walter Lang, founder and long-time director of the Bible Science Association, creationist attorney Wendell Bird, and two ICR scientists, Dr. Duane Gish and Dr. Richard Bliss.

A special word of thanks must go to my long-time friend, co-author of *The Genesis Flood,* Dr. John C. Whitcomb. Dr. Whitcomb took valuable time from his heavy teaching, administrative, and speaking responsibilities at Grace Theological Seminary, where he was Director of Doctoral Studies, not only to provide a thorough review of the manuscript, but also to write the Foreword for the Book. His kind remarks in the latter are deeply appreciated.

I am also grateful to Mrs. Becky Nichols for typing the original manuscript, to Mrs. Rebecca Barber for typing and preparing the updated manuscript for printing, and to many others who have contributed in various ways.

Most of all, I thank my wonderful wife, Mary Louise, who has been such a patient companion and prayer supporter, as well as loving wife and mother, through over 50 years of my own intense involvement in the many activities reported in this history of modern creationism.

Introduction

One of the most surprising phenomena of the second half of the twentieth century has been the resurgence of creationism—not a compromising amalgamation of evolutionary thought with theistic overtones, but a clear-cut, Bible-centered, literalistic, young-earth special creationism. Accompanying this has been the concurrent development of a clear-cut, non-religious, non-evolutionary scientific creationism. Furthermore—all the more unexpected—this has been a movement led, not by churchmen, but by scientists—scientists with Ph.D. degrees from recognized universities, holding responsible scientific positions, and using cogent scientific data and argumentation.

Unlike previous creationist revivals, the current movement has had great impact among groups largely untouched by those earlier revivals. Young people on secular campuses have been affected by the scores of thousands, and its impact has spread overseas, with creationist organizations springing up not only in every American state and Canadian province, but also in at least 20 other countries around the world. Even the scientific and educational establishments, while bitterly resisting the movement, have been profoundly affected by it.

Although it has only been three decades since evolutionists were widely proclaiming the complete victory and universal acceptance of evolution, nationwide polls have recently shown the amazing fact that over half the American people now reject evolution, and most of the rest at least want creation to be taught as an alternative in the public schools. Whatever the future may hold for the present complex of creationist organizations, we can be sure that things will not go back like they were before. Creation will continue to be recognized by multitudes as a truly viable model of origins.

Such a remarkable phenomenon could not, of course, have sprung into existence overnight out of nowhere. It has to have a history, and that history can hardly help being instructive in various ways. It must involve many concerned and dedicated people, battling against strongly entrenched opposition, and, of course, it must be based on solid evidence, not on mere emotional rhetoric. Most of all, it must ultimately be spiritual in nature, reflecting the unseen hand of the Creator Himself, guiding the history of the world and its nations, and moving in response to the prayers of His people.

Despite the intrinsic importance and interest involved in such a history, very few people have so far attempted to record it. The movement has been so new and unexpected, with so many ramifications, that it has been difficult to put it into historical perspective up to this point. This is still the case today, with the movement still growing and changing so rapidly.

Nevertheless, I believe that the time has come for at least a preliminary outline of this significant historical development. As one who has been actively involved in it for almost fifty years, I cannot, of course, claim the objectivity which should characterize a historian. No writer is ever *really* objective, however, particularly when he deals with subjects which impinge upon the very meanings and goals of life, as this one does. My own commitment to creationism, both as a movement and as Biblical and scientific truth, is freely expressed right at the start, so the reader may certainly wish to evaluate the narrative with that perspective in mind. A few evolutionist writers have also recently tried to write histories of creationism, and their biases (against creationism) are quite evident, too![1]

In any case, I have made every attempt to be factual. My files are bulging with correspondence and other materials relating to

---

1. The most extensive of these is *The Creationists*, by Dr. Ronald Numbers, Professor of History of Science at the University of Wisconsin (New York: Alfred A. Knopf, 1992), 458 pp. Dr. Numbers, although an evolutionist, has made a conscientious effort to appear to be objective, and has treated creationists more gently and fairly than most other anti-creationists have done.

this topic, not to mention an extensive library collection of creationist and evolutionist publications, so a great deal of judgment has been necessary in selecting what to include and what to omit. Admittedly, these decisions have been subjective in some degree, but at least I have written as a sympathetic "insider," not as an outside critic who really has very limited first-hand knowledge of the relevant facts. The book is written in the first person (unlike most of my other books) and is frequently autobiographical. This is because I have been closely associated with the creation movement for a long time, and much of its history connects at various points with my own experiences. I have naturally written more regarding those aspects of the movement which I know best from my own personal experience, but I do have the greatest appreciation for all the others who have been involved in modern creationism, as well as all our predecessors. Although many people have been, and are, active in the creation movement, its dimensions have become far too broad to be credited to any one person or any group. My own conviction is that: "This is the Lord's doing; it is marvelous in our eyes" (Psalm 118:23).

The first edition, published in 1984, was very favorably received, with excellent reviews in many significant journals. The succeeding decade has seen many further victories and advances in the creation movement, and these now need to be added to the record of the history of modern creationism. I hope that, as more and more people learn of the deep roots and vital importance of scientific Biblical Creationism, it will make a real difference in the world, and help to "make ready a people prepared for the Lord" (Luke 1:17) when He returns.

Chapter I

The Background of Modern Creationism

Creationism is not a sort of cultic or fringe movement of these latter days, as its enemies try to represent it. It is the most ancient of all cosmogonies and has been the belief of orthodox Christians, as well as orthodox Jews and Muslims, all down through the centuries. It is based specifically on the very first verse of the Bible, the first revelation from God Himself. "In the beginning God created the heaven and the earth" (Genesis 1:1).[1]

These primeval words—possibly the first words ever written down, perhaps even transcribed by Adam himself—do not attempt to argue that God exists, or to prove that He created all things in the beginning. They simply assume that God is, and that without Him there could be nothing else. When the words were first written, no one doubted them, so there was no occasion to argue them. Then, in the rest of the marvelous first chapter of Genesis, the writer (ultimately God Himself) simply narrates the events that took place as God created and made all things in that unique first week of earth history. The account concludes by repeatedly stressing (Genesis 2:1–3) that God had finished all His work of creating and making all things, thus conclusively refuting all those future evolutionary concepts of origins and development which would allege that God's works of creating and developing things were still being used in the ongoing process of evolution.

Thus the creationist view of origins, stressing God's unique,

---

1. Unless otherwise noted, Biblical references used in this book are from the Authorized (King James) Version.

special, completed acts of creation in the beginning, is not new at all, but is the original, primeval revelation from God Himself!

The Creation/Evolution Conflict in Antiquity

On the other hand, the evolutionary philosophy is also very ancient, almost as old as creationism. Men from the very earliest days have, naturally enough, wanted to know about the origin and meaning of things, and so they tried to understand and explain these things as best they could. If, for whatever reasons, they did not want to believe God's revelation of special creation, then the only alternative was evolution. That is, if the universe was not created by a transcendent Creator God, then it must always have existed in some form or another. Thus, the space/mass/time universe would be the ultimate reality, and all things must be derived from the systems and energies of this cosmos, not from God.

According to the Bible, however, the cosmos did not even exist at all, until God created it. He created time and space, as well as matter and energy, so that the universe is now a marvelous continuum of space and time and mass/energy.

Thus, the ultimate choice is between God and the cosmos as the ultimate reality from which all other things derive their existence. In one form or another, this choice has confronted all men through the ages. It is the choice between creation and evolution, between theism and atheism, between supernaturalism and naturalism, between monotheism and polytheistic pantheism, between divine revelation and humanistic philosophy, between God's Word and man's speculations, between Biblical Christianity and paganism.

Consequently, the most ancient human records (apart from the Bible) show the very early apostasy of primeval man from belief in an omnipotent God to belief in a polytheistic pantheism, attributing the development of the universe from some primeval chaotic state to the work of various gods and goddesses (actually mere personifications of the various systems and energies of the cosmos), who over long ages had organized it into its present very complex state.

This decline from creationism to evolutionism is graphically outlined in Romans 1:18–32 and is the testimony of the history of all ancient nations. It is also the testimony of the decline of the nations of "Christendom" in the present era from belief in Biblical creationism to modern evolutionary humanism and all its bitter fruits. Darwin did not, as his disciples like to claim, bring in an age of scientific enlightenment. He merely revived ancient paganism, clothing it in apparently sophisticated modern apparel, but underneath there was still the same old pantheistic materialism of antiquity.

> *"Because that, when they knew God, they glorified Him not as God, neither were thankful; but became vain in their imaginations, and their foolish heart was darkened. Professing themselves to be wise, they became fools, and changed the glory of the uncorruptible God into an image made like to corruptible man, and to birds, and four footed beasts, and creeping things. Wherefore God also gave them up to uncleanness through the lusts of their own hearts, to dishonor their own bodies between themselves: Who changed the truth of God into a lie, and worshiped and served the creation more than the Creator, Who is blessed for ever. Amen" (Romans 1:21–25).*

Evolutionism is, thus, merely worshiping the forces and systems of nature instead of their Creator.

In this sense, the evolutionary system has been arrayed against creationism since the dawn of history. The evolutionistic basis of the religions of the ancient Greeks, Romans, Babylonians, Chinese, and others has been documented in two of my own books,[1]

---

1. Henry M. Morris, *The Troubled Waters of Evolution* (San Diego: Creation-Life Publishers, 1974), pp. 50–76. See especially, Henry M. Morris, *The Long War against God* (Grand Rapids: Baker Book House, 1989), pp. 207–260.

but is actually a fact generally recognized by evolutionists anyhow. Many evolutionary historians have themselves pointed this out, contending that the great antiquity of evolutionary thought is an argument in its favor.[1]

But creationism is even more ancient, as noted above. Even those early nations which drifted quickly into pagan polytheism after the great Flood and the confusion of tongues at Babel did retain for some time a vague knowledge of the true God and His primeval creation. This fact is noted, for example, in several instances in the book of Genesis. God spoke to Abimelech, king of the Philistines, in the matter of Sarah, Abraham's wife (Genesis 20:3). A later Abimelech acknowledged that God had blessed Isaac (Genesis 26:28,29). Potiphar saw that the Lord was with Joseph (Genesis 39:3), and Pharaoh acknowledged that the Spirit of God was in Joseph (Genesis 41:38). Both the Philistines and Egyptians worshiped many gods, but they still realized there was a higher God than these. "For all the gods of the nations are idols; but the Lord made the heavens" (Psalm 96:5).

There are many other Biblical references to pagan rulers who, for one reason or another, were forced to acknowledge the true God of creation. The great Nebuchadnezzar, king of Babylon, said: "Now I Nebuchadnezzar praise and extol and honor the King of heaven, all whose works are truth, and His ways judgment; and those that walk in pride He is able to abase" (Daniel 4:37). The mighty Cyrus of Persia acknowledged that: "The Lord God of heaven hath given me all the kingdoms of the earth" (Ezra 1:2).

But for the most part, it was not long after Babel before the various peoples of the world, with their rulers, were worshiping all the pantheon of gods and goddesses with which the heathen world abounded, and this was essentially, as explained above, merely a form of evolutionism. This Biblical teaching has been

---

1. See, for example, Henry F. Osborne, From *the Greeks to Darwin* (New York: Charles Scribners Sons, 1929).

abundantly confirmed by archaeologists and ethnologists in their researches in all parts of the world.

At the same time, these researches have also shown that there is often an indication of a primitive monotheism among the various early tribes and nations. A great Roman Catholic scholar, Dr. Wilhelm Schmidt,[1] for many years Professor of Primitive Ethnology and Philology in the University of Vienna, long ago demonstrated this ubiquitous tradition of a primitive "high god" among the world's primeval tribes. Many other ethnologists have come to the same conclusion. A great wealth of evidence to this effect was marshaled and documented by Dr. Samuel M. Zwemer, Professor of History of Religion and Christian Missions at Princeton Theological Seminary.[2]

More recently, a missionary scholar, Don Richardson, has documented a similar phenomenon among modern-day tribes living in remote areas.[3] That is, even though all these tribes now follow an animistic religion, worshiping nature and unseen spirits, they still are aware of the very remote, but nevertheless real, God of creation. In fact, Richardson argues effectively that the best way to reach these tribes with the gospel of salvation is to approach them first of all on the common ground of their awareness of primeval creation. This, of course, was exactly the approach used by the Apostle Paul when he first preached to the pagan polytheists of Lystra and at Athens (Acts 14:11–17; 17:22–31).

For the most part, the great ethnic religions of both past and present—ancient polytheism and animism, as well as Shintoism, Buddhism, Hinduism, Taoism, Confucianism, etc., not to mention

---

1. Wilhelm Schmidt, *The Origin and Growth of Religion: Facts and Theories*, trans. H. J. Rose (London: Methuen, 1931). Schmidt wrote numerous other scholarly volumes on this and related themes.

2. S. M. Zwemer, *The Origin of Religion: Evolution or Revelation*, rev. 3d ed. (New York: Loiseaux Brothers, 1945), 256 pp.

3. Don Richardson, *Eternity in Their Hearts* (Ventura, CA: Regal Books, 1981), 176 pp.

overtly atheistic religions such as communism—have all been fundamentally evolutionary systems in that they deny the fact of primeval creation and the existence of an omnipotent Creator. In contrast, there has always existed a remnant who knew and believed in the true Creator. Finally, God's remnant nation, Israel, was specially called to preserve the knowledge of God in the world until He would come back into the world as its Savior. But there would always be a continuing conflict, both before and after the coming of Christ, between the nature-gods of the heathen and the true God of creation.

The Creationist Origins of Modern Science

A new dimension was added to this conflict of the ages with the rise of modern science. The evolutionary concept of the world's origin, which for millennia had been promoted mainly by pagan priests, witch doctors, and pantheistic philosophers, is now being pushed as a proven fact of modern science. In a day and age which almost worships at the shrine of science (and the standard of living supposedly created by modern science), this assertion has been tremendously persuasive and intimidating.

Evolutionists now even have the arrogance to claim that all modern scientists must believe in evolution in order even to be considered as scientists. For example, a graduate student in geology at Rice University (no doubt resentful of the fact that I was also once on the Rice engineering faculty, since Rice prides itself on being a very "intellectual" school, the "Harvard of the south") reacted in the following manner against my claim that thousands of scientists are now creationists:

> I dispute Henry Morris's claim that thousands of scientists are creationists. No scientist today questions the past and present occurrence of evolution in the organic world . . . Those "thousands of creationists" with legitimate post-graduate degrees and other appropriate credentials are not scientists, precisely be-

cause they have abandoned the scientific method and the scientific attitude, criteria far more crucial to the definition of scientist than the location or duration of one's training or the identity of one's employer.[1]

Thus, modern creationists are conveniently excluded as scientists merely by definition! Science no longer means "knowledge" or "truth" or "facts," as we once were taught, but "naturalism" or "materialism," according to this new article of evolutionary faith. The very possibility of a Creator is prohibited by majority vote of the scientific priesthood, and one who still wishes to believe in God as Creator must be excommunicated.

This absurd and arbitrary proclamation is currently being spread far and wide over the land by modern anti-creationist reactionaries. For example, entomologist Stanley Beck, of the University of Wisconsin, says:

> Is scientific creationism scientific? Obviously, it is not. Creationism involves acceptance of a premise that lies outside of science.[2]

The premise to which he refers, of course, is that God just might exist, after all. Such a notion must be banned from science! To the contention of creationist scientists that they can teach creationism with no reference to religion, he replies:

> If separated from its origin in a religious tradition, might not the creationist view of life on earth be offered as a scientific theory? . . . The answer is an unequivocal "no," because the creationist theory requires that some force, some factor, has created and, in so doing, has bypassed the natural forces and

---

1. Steven Schafersman, Geotimes, Aug. 198 1, p. 11. Schafersman was then head of the evolutionists' "Committee of Correspondence" for Texas.

2. Stanley D. Beck, "Natural Science and Creationist Theology," *Bioscience* (Oct. 1982), p. 740. This article was actually a special Sigma Xi-sponsored lecture at Virginia Tech, an institution which may also be embarrassed by the fact that I was for many years chairman of one of its engineering departments.

mechanisms by which the physical universe operates.[1]

Dr. Beck professes belief in Christianity, but it is obvious that he does not believe in an inerrant Bible, nor in Christ as He is revealed in the Bible. He does believe, apparently, in the necessity for a Christian to pay due allegiance to naturalistic science if he is to fit into the scientific establishment today.

Well, no matter. At least we creationist scientists can take comfort in the fact that many of the greatest scientists of the past were creationists and, for that matter, were also Bible-believing Christians, men who believed in the inspiration and authority of the Bible, as well as in the deity and saving work of the Lord Jesus Christ. They believed that God had supernaturally created all things, each with its own complex structure for its own unique purpose. They believed that, as scientists, they were "thinking God's thoughts after Him," learning to understand and control the laws and processes of nature for God's glory and man's good. They believed and practiced science in exactly the same way that modern creationist scientists do.

Beck, in fact, practically admits as much. First, he tries to delineate the basic premises of science, as follows:

> The first of the unprovable premises on which science has been based is the belief that the world is real and the human mind is capable of knowing its real nature. . . . The second and best known postulate underlying the structure of scientific knowledge is that of cause and effect. . . . The third basic scientific premise is that nature is unified. [2]

Now it should be obvious that no creationist, especially a Bible-believing Christian, could object to any of these premises. They are specifically affirmed in Scripture and are the basic premises of scientific creationism (there is nothing at all in evolutionism, on the other hand, that requires such premises). Beck goes on to make

---

1. *Ibid.*

2. *Ibid,.* p. 739.

the following remarkable admission:

> These scientific premises define and limit the scientific mode of thought. It should be pointed out, however, that each of these postulates had its origin in, or was consistent with, Christian theology. . . . Scientific thought soon parted from theology, because no assumption is made concerning any force outside of or beyond natural measurable forces.[1]

Thus, one could as well say that scientific thought has now departed from its own scientific premises!

Science once was recognized as the organized body of known truth, or at least as a search for truth. It dealt with facts, demonstrated facts. The essence of the scientific method was considered to be experimentation and observation, involving factual predictions which could be tested and, at least in principle, either falsified or confirmed by measurement.

Evolution, of course, cannot be falsified—or even tested—in its broad scope, and thus is not real science. While the same is true of creation, this very fact is itself a prediction of creationism—namely, that creation was completed in the past and therefore cannot possibly be observed taking place in the present. This stricture should not apply to evolution, however, since it presumably is still going on at present, and therefore should be observable. When it is not observed, then the evolutionist has to impose an arbitrary modification on the concept, claiming that it proceeds too slowly to be observed. This sophisticated device is itself an implicit admission that evolution is not as scientific as creation.

It is interesting to note the definition of science in the first edition of Webster's Dictionary, published originally in 1828. At that time, the primary definition of science was as follows:

> *Science:* In a general sense, knowledge or certain knowledge, the comprehension or understanding of truth or facts by the mind. The science of God must be perfect.

---

1. *Ibid.*

Figure 1.   Great Creationist Scientists of the Past

Many of the founding fathers of modern science were Bible-believing creationists. Among these were: (upper left) Francis Bacon, originator of the scientific method; (upper right) Johann Kepler, the father of astronomy; (lower left) Isaac Newton, considered by most to be the greatest of all scientists; and (lower right) Robert Boyle, the father of chemistry.

Thus God, who indeed is the true Creator of heaven and earth, and who also created the very forces and mechanisms which now operate His created universe, is today being denied admission to that universe by the very people whose own professional activities were made possible by the creationist world view out of which modern science was born.

That modern science is, indeed, an outgrowth of the creationist world view, particularly as developed and propagated during and following the Protestant reformation, has been documented by numerous writers.[1] Of even more direct interest is the fact that, as noted previously, so many of the great founders of modern science were themselves devout creationists and Bible-believing Christians.

Somehow this attitude did not hinder *them* in their commitment to the scientific method! In fact, one of them, Sir Francis Bacon (1561–1626), is credited with formulating and establishing the scientific method! They seem also to have been able to maintain a proper "scientific attitude," for it was men such as these whose researches and analyses led to the very laws and concepts of science which brought about our modern scientific age. The mechanistic scientists of the present are dwarfed in comparison to these intellectual giants of the past. The real breakthroughs, the new fields, the most beneficial discoveries of science were certainly not delayed (in fact, were probably hastened) by the creationist motivations of these great founders of modern science.

For example, consider Robert Boyle (1627–1691), universally acknowledged as the "father of chemistry" and Johann Kepler (1571–1630), the founder of physical astronomy. There was Blaise Pascal (1623–1662), the father of hydrostatics and analytical ge-

---

1. For example, Charles Raven, *Science and Religion* (London: Cambridge Univ. Press, 1953); R. J. Hooykaas, *Religion and the Rise of Modern Science* (Grand Rapids: Eerdmans Pub. Co., 1972); Eugene M. Klaaren, *Religious Origins of Modern Science* (Grand Rapids: Eerdmans Pub. Co., 1977); A. N. Whitehead, *Science in the Modern World* (New York: Macmillan. 1926).

ometry; John Ray (1627–1705), who is considered the founder of natural history; Nicholas Steno (1631–1686), the father of stratigraphy; and William Harvey (1578–1657), who discovered the circulation of the blood. All these men were devout Christian creationists.

Or consider Sir Isaac Newton (1642–1727), who is generally regarded as the greatest scientist of all time. He discovered the law of gravity, laid the foundation of the discipline of dynamics, invented the calculus, and made innumerable other key scientific discoveries. He also wrote books on Bible chronology (defending the "short" chronology of Bishop Ussher) and on Biblical prophecies, defending the literal accuracy of Scripture.

The list can go on and on. It would include John Woodward (1665–1728), founder of paleontology, and Carolus Linnaeus (1707–1778), whose biological taxonomy is still followed today. Michael Faraday (1791–1867) developed the disciplines of electromagnetics and field theory. Samuel F. B. Morse (1791–1872) invented the telegraph, and Charles Babbage (1792–1871) developed the first true computer system. Matthew Maury (1806–1873) is regarded as the father of the sciences of hydrography and oceanography.

The most eminent scientists of the nineteenth century were the great physicists, Lord Kelvin (1824–1907) and Clerk Maxwell (1831–1879), along with the great biochemist and bacteriologist Louis Pasteur (1822–1895). In addition to their numerous key scientific contributions, they were vigorous opponents of evolutionism, as were such great scientists as the mineralogist David Brewster (1781–1868), the geologist Louis Agassiz (1807–1873), the German pathologist Rudolph Virchow (1821–1902), the entomologist Henri Fabre (1823–1915), and many others.

All of these men were believers in God, Christ, the Bible, and creation, and yet they were each able to make contributions in science of unique importance and lasting influence. There are many, many others. I have given brief biographies and testimonies

Figure 2.   Creationist Scientists Contemporary with Darwin

Although many of the scientists who were contemporary with Darwin quickly became evolutionists, many of the greatest did not. These included: (upper left) Michael Faraday, the great experimentalist in electricity and magnetism; (upper right) Matthew Maury, the "pathfinder of the seas"; (lower left) Louis Pasteur, the real father of bacteriology; (lower right) William Thompson, Lord Kelvin, the outstanding physicist.

of over 100 such scientists in another place.[1]

Thus, whether or not evolutionists are willing to recognize it, the fact is that modern science grew originally not out of Greek philosophy or the Enlightenment associated with Renaissance humanism, or some other source, but out of Biblical creationism.

It is a strange sign of the times that, like an ungrateful child, "modern science" now denies and repudiates its own heritage.

Creationism of America's Founding Fathers

Just as modern science was nurtured in a creationist cradle, so was the fledgling nation of America. Although there was a wide spectrum of religious beliefs among the colonists and, later, among the citizens of the new Union, practically all believed in God and special creation.

> The American nation had been founded by intellectuals who had accepted a world view that was based upon Biblical authority as well as Newtonian science. They had assumed that God created the earth and all life upon it at the time of creation and that these forms of life had continued without change thereafter. Adam and Eve were God's final creations, and all of mankind had descended from them. When Jefferson, in his old age, was confronted with the newly developing science of geology, he rejected its evolutionary concept of the creation of the earth on the grounds that no all-wise and all-powerful Creator would have gone about the job in such a slow and inefficient way.[2]

The creationist premises of the founding fathers are implicit in the very words of the Declaration of Independence:

> . . . the Laws of Nature and of Nature's God. . . . We hold these truths to be self-evident, that all men are created equal,

---

1. Henry Morris, *Men of Science—Men of God* (San Diego: Creation-Life Publishers), 1988, 106 pp.

2. Gilman M. Ostrander, *The Evolutionary Outlook*, 1875–1900 (Clio, MI: Marston Press, 1971), p. 1.

that they are endowed by their Creator with certain unalienable rights, that among these are Life, Liberty, and the pursuit of Happiness.

... appealing to the Supreme Judge of the world. ...

... with a firm reliance on the protection of divine Providence. ...

One of the early presidents of the Continental Congress, Dr. Elias Boudinot, in an Independence Day address soon after the winning of American Independence, drew a remarkable parallel between the Sabbath Day, as commemorating the completion of God's work of creating the world, along with the Jewish passover, as a remembrance of their deliverance from Egypt, and the Fourth of July, as commemorating American freedom:

> The history of the world, as well sacred as profane, bears witness to the use and importance of setting apart a day as a memorial of great events whether of a religious or a political nature.
>
> No sooner had the great Creator of the heavens and the earth finished His almighty work, and pronounced all very good, but He set apart (not an anniversary, or one day in a year, but) one day in seven, for the commemoration of His inimitable power in producing all things out of nothing.
>
> The deliverance of the children of Israel from a state of bondage to an unreasonable tyrant was perpetuated by the Paschal Lamb, and enjoining it on their posterity as an annual festival forever, with a "remembrance this day, in which ye came out of Egypt, out of the house of bondage." The resurrection of the Savior of mankind is commemorated by keeping the first day of the week, not only as a certain memorial of His first coming in a state of humiliation but the positive evidence of His future coming in glory. Let us then, my friends and fellow citizens, unite all our endeavors this day to remember with reverential gratitude to our supreme Benefactor, all the wonderful things He has done for us, in our miraculous deliverance

from a second Egypt . . . another house of bondage.[1]

This extended quotation is given to illustrate the commitment of many of the early leaders of our country, not only to genuine Biblical Christianity (Dr. Boudinot was also the first president of the American Bible Society), but also to a literal six-day creation of all things, *ex nihilo*.

Even those leaders who were not Bible-believing Christians, such as Thomas Jefferson and Benjamin Franklin, did believe in God and in special creation, as well as the Creator's sovereignty in the affairs of men and nations. Real atheism and evolutionism, though fairly common in Europe (the French revolution was imminent) were very rare in America at this time.

The schools in those days were almost all private schools; in fact, most of them were Christian schools. However, the strongly Biblical orientation of the colonial churches, and especially the colleges which they had formed (Harvard, Yale, and others) had already become strongly diluted by deism and unitarianism, and it would not be long before these entrenched heresies would be yielding to two even more deadly British imports—the uniformitarianism of Charles Lyell and then later the evolutionism of Charles Darwin. In the meantime, the Unitarian, Horace Mann, would lead in getting American education shifted to a system of public schools. The latter would still have a nominal commitment to creationism and Christianity for a while, but would eventually be subverted to a full-blown evolutionary humanism through the baleful influence of John Dewey and his disciples.

It is a strange and sad phenomenon in American life that the scientific establishment, though originally founded on creationism, now denies the right of scientists to believe in creation at all, and the educational system, also founded on creationism, now won't allow students even to consider it as an alternative. The founding

---

1. Elias Boudinot, "Address to the New Jersey Society of the Cincinnati," July 4, 1783. Cited in *Foundation for Christian Self-Government* July 1982, p. 3.

fathers certainly never intended any such thing, but "while men slept, an Enemy came and sowed tares among the wheat" (Matthew 13:25). An apathetic and compromising Christian church has allowed these two invaluable gifts of God—science and education—to be stolen away while it was busy at rest and play. It is high time for revival of true creationism, especially in our churches.

The Apparent Triumph of Evolutionism

The life and times of Charles Darwin and his famous book have been told and retold so often that it would be superfluous to include much of this familiar history here. Those who have read only the "official" narrative, however, may not realize that it "ain't necessarily so." Darwin was not the brilliant scientist he is portrayed to be, and his "discoveries" were not original with him anyhow.

The only college degree he ever earned was in theology, not biology, and he did poorly in that. His grandfather, Erasmus Darwin, had written a number of influential books on evolution even before Charles was born. Many writers[1] have commented on the fact that Erasmus Darwin, especially in his book *Zoonomia,* formulated most of the standard arguments for evolution that are still being parroted today, as well as proposing that new species are developed by natural selection. Comparison of Charles' book, *The Origin of Species*, with that of his grandfather makes it obvious that he owed a great many of his ideas and arguments to him, but he never acknowledged this fact at all, preferring to pass them off to those of his own generation as original with himself.

There were also a number of other evolutionary scientists before Charles Darwin, the most influential of whom was Jean Lamarck,

---

1. See for example, C. D. Darlington, "The Origin of Darwinism," *Scientific American*, 201 (May 1959), pp. 62–66. Also note the summary in "Erasmus Darwin: the True Father of Evolution," by A. G. Tilney, *Evolution Protest Movement*, 88, July 1971.

best known for his theory of evolution by acquired characteristics. However, most of the evolutionists of the time were among the political radicals and liberal social philosophers rather than the scientists. As a result, in a society increasingly enamored of modern science, the evolution concept was not very influential among the general British population, and even less so in America.

Therefore, those who were desirous of destroying Christianity and the general theistic world view, as well as the existing social order built on it, realized that a general return to atheism or humanistic pantheism, which necessarily must be grounded on evolutionism, would have to be preceded by the popularization of some system which would make evolution appear scientific to the general public. The scientists had, for the most part, with their elucidation of the marvelous order and complexity in natural systems, effectively confirmed the theological argument from design, especially as set forth by the widely read works of the great Christian apologist William Paley. If a watch required a watchmaker, then the infinitely more complex universe, especially the living things in it, would have required an infinitely intelligent and skilled Universe-Maker. Somehow this persuasive teleological argument of the scientists would have to be overcome by some seemingly scientific argument that would eliminate this need for a Designer.

Lamarckianism was thought to be a prime candidate for a while. Lamarck himself hated the Bible and Christianity, and his ideas became popular with communists and other radicals. However, his theory of evolution through inherited environmental effects turned out to be contrary to observed scientific data and it was never accepted by most scientists.

With Darwin's theory of evolution by natural selection, however, it was altogether different. Even though it was not original with Darwin (not only his grandfather but many others had advocated this idea long before he did), it was quickly accepted when *The Origin of Species* was published in 1859, not only by scientists,

tists, but also by most other people. It seemed to be confirmed in principle by common experience with artificial selection in breeding plants and animals, and it did not require any mathematical proficiency to understand it, as in the physical sciences. Most of all, it appealed to the innate desire of man to escape from his responsibility to God, and it did so by persuading him that this escape was supported by science.

The main reason it was accepted so readily in Charles' time, rather than in his grandfather's time, was undoubtedly because of the development of uniformitarian geology and the geological-age system in the intervening period. Erasmus Darwin's *Zoonomia* was published in 1794 and Charles Darwin's *The Origin of Species* in 1859. The French scientist, Pierre Maupertuis, in fact, had vigorously promoted his own theory of evolution by mutations, natural selection, and survival of the fittest almost an entire century before the *Origin*.

During that period, however, most scientists still believed in the Bible, in literal six-day creation, and in the worldwide Flood of the Bible as the cause of the geological strata. Before evolution by natural selection could be feasible for the production of more than mere new varieties of basic kinds, much more time was needed in earth history than the six thousand years or so allowed by the Bible. And since none of the world's ancient nations possessed historical records going back any earlier, the only hope of finding more time to support evolution would have to depend on the new sciences of geology and paleontology.

The founding fathers of these sciences of earth history had been men like John Woodward (1665–1728), Nicholas Steno (1631–1686), Thomas Burnet (1635–1715), and William Whiston (1667–1752), all of whom believed that the geological strata had been formed mainly by the Noachian Deluge. There had been a few writers proposing a very old earth, such as Georges Louis de Buffon (1707–1788), a lawyer who wrote a 15-volume treatise on natural history, in which he rejected the Biblical record and insisted the earth must be very old in order to provide time for evolution. For the most part, however, it was not until the nineteenth century that the old pagan idea of an ancient earth began to take solid root again in scientific thinking.

The father of uniformitarian geology is generally recognized to be James Hutton (1726–1797), an agriculturalist and medical doctor who turned to geology. He laid down the dogma that "the present is the key to the past" and thus that the great geological formations of the earth must be explained in terms of the ordinary processes of nature (e.g., erosion and sedimentation) operating slowly over vast ages.

However, the uniformitarian concept and its geological-age system (with the different ages recognized in terms of index fossils supposedly characterizing those ages) did not really become widely known and accepted until the epochal work of Sir Charles Lyell (1797–1875), who published the first edition of his famous *Principles of Geology* in 1830. It was this work that finally provided all the vast aeons of time which the idea of natural selection required to make evolution feasible, and which thus prepared the way for Charles Darwin. In fact, Darwin freely acknowledged his debt to Lyell, even though he was never willing to recognize his similar debt to his grandfather and others.

Lyell is thus a figure of key importance in the sudden conversion of the world from creationism to evolutionism, probably even more important than Darwin himself. Yet he is also a very enigmatic figure. He was educated as a lawyer, rather than in geology, and thus skilled at argumentation. In fact, his *Principles* in many respects reads like a legal brief, attacking Biblical catastrophism and promoting uniformitarianism, rather than merely expounding geological principles.

Lyell also happened to come from a wealthy family, so never had to earn his living. Like Darwin, he could devote all his time to pursuing his own research, spreading his dogma of uniformitarianism and refuting the Bible.

There has been some difference of opinion as to whether Lyell was originally an evolutionist, though all agree that he acknowledged his evolutionary beliefs after evolution became popular. He occasionally wrote as though he believed in God and in what would now be known as progressive creation over the geological ages. In his private correspondence, however, he seems to come through as, at best, an uncertain theistic evolutionist. To whatever extent he may have believed in God, he certainly did not believe in the God of the Bible, for he was highly critical of the Biblical account, considering one of his chief contributions to have been the refutation of the Mosaic records.

A recent British creationist writer, Malcolm Bowden, who has done much research on the life and times of Darwin and his contemporaries, was forced to conclude, after examining all the evidence that:

> . . . it was Lyell's deliberate intention to prepare the ground for evolution by publishing his *Principles of Geology*, leaving the theory itself to be promoted by someone else at a later stage.[1]

That "someone" would turn out to be Charles Darwin, who read Lyell's book while on the famous voyage of the Beagle in 1832. The book profoundly influenced him, and he soon became a convinced uniformitarian. However, according to Himmelfarb,[2] he remained a creationist until some time after he had returned from his five year voyage.

He did become close friends with Lyell and was also well acquainted with the other leading geologists, philosophers, historians, and literary figures of the age. He began to speculate and write notes on evolution soon after his Beagle experiences, but did not do any serious writing on the subject until he was prodded to

---

1. Malcolm Bowden, *The Rise of the Evolution Fraud* (San Diego: Creation-Life Publishers, 1982), 227 pp.

2. Gertrude Himmelfarb, *Darwin and the Darwinian Revolution* (London: Chatto and Windus, 1959), pp. 90–103.

do so by Lyell and then suddenly goaded into action when he found out that Alfred R. Wallace was about to publish an almost identical theory. When the book was finally published in 1859, the times were right for it.

Even then, however, its rapid acceptance was largely stimulated by the strenuous efforts of Thomas H. Huxley, who soon became known as "Darwin's bulldog." Huxley was a biologist who called himself an "agnostic," and he held a bitter hatred of the Anglican establishment and the clergy in general. He was an exceedingly capable protagonist, both in verbal discourse and in print. His famous exchange with Bishop Wilberforce at the Oxford meeting of the British Association in 1860 is still being used as a club against creationists, in spite of the fact that various historians have shown that the popular accounts of the incident were badly distorted in Huxley's favor. It is interesting also that Huxley acknowledged toward the end of his life that he had never been personally convinced that Darwin's theory was right. He fought so vigorously for it, evidently, for two main reasons: first, he saw it as an effective club he could use against the religious establishment he hated; second, he was very ambitious and saw this as a great opportunity of achieving fame for himself.

It is the enigmatic role of Charles Lyell, however, which is especially intriguing. Why would he try to keep his own evolutionary beliefs hidden for so long, while he well understood that his uniformitarian geological treatise would be the very weapon needed for evolution to triumph? Bowden[1] and others have shown that he realized this approach (which is equivalent to advocating progressive creationism instead of straightforward evolutionism) would be far more effective in the long run. An open espousal of both uniformitarianism and evolutionism by the same man would have produced too great a reaction from both the clergy and the Christian people of England at the time, not even to mention the

---

1. Malcolm Bowden, *op. cit.*, pp. 92–99.

Americans. It was better to get the geological ages accepted first in a creationist framework and then to get someone else to take the lead in destroying creationism itself. As a matter of fact, this technique worked perfectly, and it has worked many, many times since—in Christian colleges, churches, and other institutions, as well as in the thinking of multitudes of individual Christians. It is still working today.

There were many other people and movements involved in this drama, but this is intended to be a history of creationism, not of Darwinism. There were many besides Lyell, Darwin, and Huxley, of course, who helped to maneuver this sudden and almost complete capitulation of nineteenth-century British science to evolutionism. It was not too much longer before the scientists of continental Europe and then those of the United States also were converted to Darwinism.

Once the scientists became evolutionists, other intellectuals hastened to adjust their own disciplines as well, to conform to this new secular and humanistic world view. The colleges and universities, and then all the public schools were soon fully committed to evolutionism. For those who would like a more complete discussion of the history of evolutionary thought, written from a creationist point of view, a number of good treatments are available.[1] In addition, there are numerous such histories written by evolutionists, and almost any library would have several in its collections.

---

1. Bert Thompson, *The History of Evolutionary Thought* (Fort Worth: Star Bible and Tract Co., 1981), 192 pp.; Bolton Davidheiser, *Evolution and Christian Faith* (Nutley, NJ: Presbyterian and Reformed Pub. Co., 1969), pp. 38–138; Harold W. Clark, *The Battle Over Genesis* (Washington, D.C.: Review and Herald Pub. Co., 1977), pp. 1–92; Robert E. D. Clark, *Darwin: Before and After* (London: Paternoster Press, 1972); 192 pp.; Malcolm Bowden, *The Rise of the Evolution Fraud* (San Diego: Creation-Life Publishers, 1982), pp. 1–143. Ian T. Taylor, *In the Minds of Men* (Toronto, TFE Publishing, 1987), pp. 1–137. See especially Henry M. Morris, *The Long War against God* (Grand Rapids: Baker Book House, 1989), 344 pp.

To me, however, the saddest aspect of this whole dismal history is not the fact that scientists and sociologists so quickly capitulated to evolution. The worst feature is the inexcusable behavior of the theologians. As long as the scientists believed in creation, Christian leaders were quite content to believe in the inerrancy of Scripture and the literal historicity of the Biblical accounts of Creation and the Flood. For almost 300 years, following the Reformation, the hoary pagan philosophies of evolution and the eternity of matter had been rejected, and pure Biblical creationism was believed and taught almost everywhere. But, as soon as the scientists turned to evolution, theologians and church leaders in almost every denomination scurried in a hasty retreat to the old compromising types of exegesis used by early theologians, such as Origen and Augustine, in order to accommodate evolution and the geological ages in Genesis. Instead of standing on the plain, clear teaching of the Word of God, which they professed to believe and were paid to uphold, they allowed these evolutionary scientists, who had no real scientific proof of evolution at all, to stampede them into either a compromising pietism or overt religious liberalism. No wonder Thomas Huxley and other nineteenth century evolutionists expressed such disdain for the religious establishment.

In England, the Anglican clergy almost immediately went over to theistic evolution, or at least to progressive creationism, as well as to higher criticism in Biblical studies. The same was true in most of the other "main-line" denominations, with a few notable exceptions (e.g., Charles Haddon Spurgeon, and his Metropolitan Baptist Tabernacle in London). The smaller fundamentalist churches, such as the so-called Plymouth Brethren and various independent churches, for the most part retreated to the "gap theory," inserting the geological ages in an imaginary gap between the first two verses of Genesis, hoping they could thereby ignore the whole problem.

Certain very popular religious leaders of the day who were believed to be orthodox Bible-believers, such as Frederick Farrar,

James Orr, Charles Kingsley, and Henry Drummond, were tremendously influential in persuading rank-and-file Christians to accept theistic evolution. The same was true in the United States, where even such stalwarts as B. B. Warfield and A. H. Strong—known as strong defenders of the faith—capitulated to evolution. With so many of the conservative theologians becoming theistic evolutionists, it is almost redundant to mention that all the more liberal theologians quickly accepted evolution. The most popular and eloquent preacher of the day was Henry Ward Beecher, pastor of the nation's largest congregation, Plymouth Congregational in Brooklyn, and he exerted enormous influence. Advocating the "double-revelation" theory (one in Scripture, the other in nature, the first dealing with religious matters to be expounded by clerics, the second with physical questions to be decided by scientists), Beecher proclaimed:

> In every view of it, I think we are to expect great practical fruit from the application of the truths that flow now from the application of Evolution. . . . Old men may be charitably permitted to die in peace, but young men and men in their prime are by God's providence laid under the most solemn obligations to thus discern the signs of the times, and to make themselves acquainted with the knowledge which science is laying before them.[1]

There were, of course, a few great American preachers (e.g., D. L. Moody) and theologians (e.g., Charles Hodge, of Princeton) who refused to compromise with evolution, but these were exceptions. The chronicle of this pervasive theological apostasy has been recently rather smugly detailed by evolutionist James Moore.[2]

---

1. H. W. Beecher, "The Two Revelations," in his book *Evolution and Religion* (1885), as included in the anthology, G. M. Ostrander, ed., *The Evolutionary Outlook, 1875–1900*, (Clio, MI: Marston Press, 1971), p. 43.

2. J. R. Moore, *The Post-Darwinian Controversies: A Story of the Protestant Struggle to Come to Terms with Darwin in Great Britain and America, 1870–1900.* (Cambridge: Cambridge Univ. Press, 1979), 502 pp. Cf. review article by John Whitcomb, Grace Theological Journal, Vol. 2, No. 1 (Spring,

Early Scientific Opponents of Darwinism

It is significant that the most vigorous opposition to Darwinism in the nineteenth century came, not from theologians, but from creationist scientists. The latter were, of course, in the minority among the scientists—at least so far as those willing to go on record were concerned—but they did make a strong and legitimate scientific case against evolution.

In the first place, the physical scientists of the time were almost unanimously skeptical of—if not downright opposed to—evolutionism. These included some of the greatest scientists of all time, men such as Michael Faraday, James Clerk Maxwell, David Brewster, Matthew Maury, and William Thompson (Lord Kelvin). Many leading biologists also opposed Darwinism, including such outstanding scientists as Louis Pasteur, Henri Fabre, Rudolph Virchow, and Gregor Mendel. Creationist geologists who fought evolutionism included such leading scientists as Benjamin Silliman, Edward Hitchcock, and John William Dawson.

It is interesting to note that a number of scientists were creationists and opposed to Darwin for strictly scientific reasons, not for Biblical reasons, since they did not believe the Bible. They were either deists or (like Cuvier) believers in multiple catastrophes and re-creations, but in any case opposed evolution. One of these was Sir Richard Owen, probably the most important biologist and paleontologist of Darwin's own generation, and a vigorous opponent of Darwin and Huxley. In America, probably the leading anti-evolutionist was Harvard's Louis Agassiz, especially famous as the chief authority on ichthyology and the founder of glacial geology. The leading catastrophist of the day was Sir Henry Howorth, another man who did not believe the Bible, but who insisted that all the data of geology and archaeology refuted uniformitarianism.

1981), pp. 131–137.

The names cited above are only a few of the best known scientists of the last half of the nineteenth century who continued to oppose Darwinism and evolutionism. There were a host of others, fully competent scientists, though not as well known. A "scientists' declaration" in support of the authority of Scripture, and the necessary harmony of science with Scripture, was published in 1865,[1] containing 717 signatures of scientists.[2] The "declaration" did not specifically mention Darwinism or evolutionism, however, so the signers may have included some theistic evolutionists. Some of the best-known signatures were Adam Sedgwick, England's leading geologist, James Joule, the chief founder of thermodynamics, Philip Gosse, a prominent zoologist and ornithologist, and Sir Henry Rawlinson, the great archaeologist and Assyriologist. There were 86 Fellows of the Royal Society on the list.

However, even this impressive number of Bible-believing scientists represented only a small percentage of the total number of British scientists at the time (estimated at around 5,000), and the Declaration quickly became the object of intense ridicule and self-righteous indignation on the part of the scientific establishment. The theological establishment, for the most part, treated it with disdain. (This was over a hundred years ago, and things have not changed very much!) The text of this declaration is given in Appendix A.

One outgrowth, however, was the formation in 1865 of the Victoria Institute, also called the Philosophical Society of Great Britain. By the end of 1866, the Institute had 200 members, and it has continued active to the present day. Its purpose was stated as follows:

> . . . to investigate fully and impartially the most important

---

1. W. H. Brock and R. M. Macleod, "The Scientists' Declaration: Reflections on Science and Belief in the Wake of *Essays and Reviews,* 1864–65." *The British Journal of the History of Science,* 9 (Mar. 1976), pp. 39–66.

2. *Ibid.,* p. 45.

questions of Philosophy and Science, but more especially those
that bear upon the great truths revealed in the Holy Scriptures,
with the view of defending those truths against the opposition
of science, falsely so-called.[1]

Although membership in the Victoria Institute was not limited
to scientists, or even to creationists, and although its journal articles
represented a wide range of viewpoints, it has published over the
years a great many valuable articles in defense of Biblical creationism and catastrophism.

During this period, even such creationist scientists as mentioned
above were, for the most part, willing to accept the geological ages.
Uniformitarian geology, as promoted by Sir Charles Lyell and his
disciples, had made such an impression on the world that almost
everyone had accepted it, even those who still resisted evolution.
Consequently, the creationists of this period—at least among the
scientists and also among the main theological spokesmen—were,
for the most part, what we would now call "progressive creationists," advocating the "day/age" interpretation of Genesis and trying
to find a concordance between the creative acts of the six days of
creation and the succession of life-forms in the geological ages.
Many great geologists, such as Adam Sedgwick, J. W. Dawson,
and Louis Agassiz, took this approach. Dawson, especially, wrote
a number of widely read books attacking evolution, but nevertheless still adhering to the geological ages.

The gap theory, with the geological ages inserted in a supposed
gap between the first two verses of Genesis, was advocated by few
scientists, but was widely taught by fundamentalist Bible teachers.
Although it had been suggested by certain ancient writers,[2] it had
only been reintroduced in 1814 by the Scottish theologian Thomas
Chalmers in order to deal with the geological-ages concept. It was

---

1. Transactions of the Victoria Institute, Vol. 1, Pref., 1866.

2. See the book by Arthur Custance, *Without Form and Void* (Brockville,
   Ontario: Dorway Press, 1970), 211 pp., for a historical review and spirited
   exegetical defense of the gap theory.

later popularized especially by M. A. Pember's famous book *Earth's Earliest Ages,* published in 1885, as well as by many books by Plymouth Brethren writers. So far as I have been able to find, however, no geologist of note has ever accepted the gap theory which, by its very nature, requires a world-wide cataclysm terminating the geological ages. The latter, of course, are completely based on the assumed continuity of present processes with those of the geological past, and thus cannot allow such a cataclysm.

For the most part, however, the Christian geologists became, first, progressive creationists and, then eventually, full-fledged theistic evolutionists. Several of the most prominent American geologists were in this category. James Dana, of Yale, at first opposed Darwinism, but eventually accepted evolution. Nevertheless, he continued to be a firm believer in Biblical Christianity. The same type of experience was true of Joseph Le Conte, of the University of California, and George Frederick Wright of Oberlin.

An interesting development of this period was the publication of evidence by Lord Kelvin that the earth could not possibly have been old enough for evolution to be true. He based his argument on accurate physical measurements and a precise mathematical analysis of the earth's internal heat flow and cooling. This greatly troubled the evolutionists for a long time, because they could not refute his case. The nineteenth century evolutionists, as noted before, were generally weak in physics and mathematics. In fact, many writers have attributed as one cause of the great popular rise in interest in Darwinism the fact that this was a "science" which could be understood without mathematics. Modern evolutionists delight in telling how the discovery of radioactivity finally solved this problem for them, but not even the radioactive heat sources in the earth can make the age of the earth anywhere near old enough to allow for evolution.

Although they could hardly be classed among the scientific leaders of the period, there were a few geologists and other scientists of the late nineteenth century, as well as some theologians, who did continue to defend recent creation and flood geology, as taught in the Bible when taken literally. Philip Gosse, a Fellow of the Royal Society and prominent zoologist, as well as a member of the Plymouth Brethren, tried to resolve the problem by a rather extreme exposition of the Biblical doctrine of creation of apparent age, even involving the creation of fossils in the rocks. This idea was itself unBiblical and attracted few followers.

There was still a remnant, however, who wrote in support of the straight-forward Biblical chronology, literal six-day creation and the world-wide cataclysmic deluge as the main cause of the geologic strata and great fossil beds. Byron Nelson has given us a fascinating survey of these "flood geologists" and their books.[1] Some of the writers in this category included General George Twemlow, of the British army, who wrote *Facts and Fossils*, and the Jesuit, Athanasius Bosizio, who wrote *Geology and the Flood*.

These could hardly be considered as more than a feeble remnant, however. Within two or three decades after Darwin, it is not too much to say that science and education world-wide had been completely taken over by evolutionism. Even the religious world had capitulated, and the churches and religious schools had almost all seriously compromised their stand.

---

1. Byron Nelson, *The Deluge Story in Stone* (Minneapolis: Augsburg Pub. Co., 1931), 204 pp.

Chapter II

One Hundred Years of Darwinism

The dawning of the twentieth century saw a world that had been vastly changed by the Darwinian revolution. The previous chapter has outlined the conflict that ensued among the scientists, but its effects were felt even more in society as a whole.

Racism, Imperialism, and Social Darwinism

Modern evolutionists would like for people today to forget the devastating sociological effects of the evolutionary philosophy in the post-Darwinian century. Creationists, of course, don't want them to forget, since these bitter fruits were only naturally to be expected from such bitter roots. To keep the weeds out of the garden, one must dig the seeds out of the ground. It does little good to cut off the fruits without also cutting out the roots.

The fact is that the waves of imperialism, revolutionism, and racism which took such deadly toll in the wake of Darwin can be traced directly to the spread of evolutionary philosophy in society, a complex of doctrine and practice known as social Darwinism. The supposed law of the jungle—struggle for existence and survival of the fittest-was assumed to apply in human societies, as well, and so was applied to competition between corporations, between capital and labor, between races, between classes, and between nations.

Evolutionism in the form of social Darwinism was applied with a vengeance in the laissez-faire capitalism of the great period of American economic growth after the Civil War. Many of the captains of industry pursued the Darwinian ideal ruthlessly. James Hill, the railroad tycoon, John D. Rockefeller, the oil baron, and Andrew Carnegie, the steel magnate, are typical examples. All of these men and many of their associates consciously and systematically applied the survival-of-the-fittest philosophy in their business dealings, convinced as they were by Darwinian philosophy that this was the natural law which assured optimum benefit over the ages.[1]

Probably the chief theoreticians of Social Darwinism were Herbert Spencer in England (1820–1903) and William Grant Sumner (1840–1910) in America. Spencer, who had used the term "survival of the fittest" in his own books even before Darwin did, was a great popularizer of evolution. He specifically applied Darwinian principles to society and insisted that civil laws should never contribute to the artificial preservation of those people who were least able to take care of themselves.

Sumner was Professor of Political Economics at Yale, where he was the teacher of many of the future leaders of American business and industry. According to Ostrander:

> America's own leading social Darwinist was William Grant Sumner of Yale, who vigorously fought programs of government control and public welfare as so much obstructive interference with the law of the survival of the fittest. . . . To help the unfit was to injure the fit and accomplish nothing for society.[2]

The laissez-faire capitalism of the American industrialists was only one of the deadly fruits of evolutionary theory. Perhaps even more devastating was the growth of imperialism, first in the Euro-

---

1. Richard Hofstadter, *Social Darwinism and American Thought* (Boston: Beacon Press, 1955), pp. 32, 45.

2. Gilman M. Ostrander, *The Evolutionary Outlook, 1875–1900* (Clio, MI: Marston Press, 1971), p. 5. See especially Sumner's essay on "Sociology," reprinted by Ostrander *(Ibid.,* pp. 18–21).

pean nations, then in America.[1] This was associated also with racism, the growing belief that the white race (some even narrowed this to the Teutonic race) had demonstrated its superiority in the struggle for existence and was thus destined to control or eliminate the other races.

Neither imperialism nor racism originated with Darwinism, of course, as both have been present in one form or another throughout history. For that matter, so has the evolutionary, materialistic, pantheistic, humanistic philosophy been present throughout history, and careful study will show that this has always been the root that supports these bitter fruits. However, Darwinism finally provided racist imperialism with an apparent scientific justification.

Darwin's books were quickly translated into all the earth's main languages, and the political leaders of the various nations began using the Darwinian catchwords to justify their expansionist ambitions. The influence in Germany was especially profound. There, the atheistic biologist Ernst Haeckel embarked on a popularization campaign fully comparable to that of Huxley in England. The philosopher Nietzsche, with his doctrine of the "super-man," was also greatly influenced by Darwin, though he thought Darwin did not go far enough in promoting the militaristic and racist implications of his theories. Darwinistic imperialism had great impact on the policies of Bismarck and even more so on those of Adolph Hitler:

> Along with his social Darwinist followers, [Haeckel] set about to demonstrate the "aristocratic" and nondemocratic aspect of the laws of nature. . . . up to his death in 1919, Haeckel contributed to that special variety of German thought which served as the seed-bed for National Socialism. He became one of Germany's main ideologists for racism, nationalism, and imperialism.[2]

1. *Ibid.*, pp. 60–62.

2. Daniel Gasman, *The Scientific Origins of National Socialism: Social Darwinism in Ernst Haeckel and the German Monist League* (New York:

> [Hitler] stressed and singled out the idea of biological evo-
> lution as the most forceful weapon against traditional religion,
> and he repeatedly condemned Christianity for its opposition to
> the teachings of evolution. . . . For Hitler, evolution was the
> hallmark of modern science and culture, and he defended its
> veracity as tenaciously as Haeckel.[1]

The eventual outgrowth of Darwinian evolutionary racism is
measured both in terms of the multitudes killed in Africa during
the European conquest of that continent and, finally, the Jewish
holocaust in Germany. A Jewish biology professor at Purdue University, writing for the Association of Orthodox Jewish Scientists,
has discussed this subject in light of the *Torah* (that is, the books
of Moses):

> I don't claim that Darwin and his theory of evolution brought
> on the holocaust; but I cannot deny that the theory of evolution,
> and the atheism it engendered, led to the moral climate that made
> a holocaust possible.

> But there is another, equally sinister, side to this argument.
> *Consider*—if life has evolved, by chance alone, then no creature
> is qualitatively different from any other. If it is morally repre-
> hensible to kill a man, then it is equally odious to kill our
> "brother," the chimpanzee. By the same token, how can we kill
> cows for food, or dogs or mice for research? And mosquitoes?

> *The Torah* teaches us a different approach. . . . Man was also
> given dominion over all animals on land, sea, and air, as well
> as a moral code to live by. Therefore, he cannot be compared to
> animals and treated as such, nor can the animals be compared
> to man and accorded his rights.[2]

Without such a divinely ordained moral code, of course, then
the law of the jungle prevails for man as well as animals, might

---

American Elsevier, 1971), P. xvi.

1. *Ibid.*, P. 168.

2. Edward Simon, "Another Side to the Evolution Problem," *Jewish Press,* Jan.
   7, 1983, p. 248.

makes right, and let the fittest survive!

The study of human origins by anthropologists was particularly influenced by racist considerations, and this situation extended well into the first half of the twentieth century. It is well known that Darwin and Huxley, as well as Haeckel, believed in white supremacy, as did practically all the nineteenth century evolutionary scientists,[1] but it is not as widely known that the leading twentieth century physical anthropologists also shared such opinions. This list would include such luminaries as Sir Arthur Keith, the eminent British anthropologist,[2] Ales Hrdlicka, at the American Museum of Natural History,[3] E. A. Hooton, under whom most of the second generation of American anthropologists studied at Harvard University,[4] and Henry Fairfield Osborn, president of the American Museum of Natural History. The latter actually taught that members of the Negroid race were of some other species than *Homo sapiens!*

> This is the recognition that the genus *Homo* is subdivided into three absolutely distinct stocks, which in zoology would be given the rank of species, if not of genera, stocks popularly known as the Caucasian, the Mongolian, and the Negroid. . . . The standard of intelligence of the average adult Negro is similar to that of the eleven-year old youth of the species *Homo sapiens.*[5]

---

1. John Haller, Jr., *Outcasts from Evolution* (Urbana: Univ. of Illinois Press, 1971), 280 pp.

2. Arthur Keith, *Evolution and Ethics* (New York: G. P. Putnam's Sons, 1947). In this book Sir Arthur also defended imperialism and even Hitler, on the ground of sound evolutionary thinking. Keith is also famous as the co-discoverer of Piltdown Man.

3. Loring Brace, "The Roots of the Race Concept in American Physical Anthropology," Chapter I in *A History of American Physical Anthropology,* Frank Spencer, ed. (New York: Academic Press, 1982), 496 pp.

4. *Ibid.*

5. Henry Fairfield Osborn, "The Evolution of Human Races," *Natural History,* Jan./Feb., 1926, reprinted in *Natural History,* 89 (Apr. 1980), p. 129.

Osborn was considered at the time as possibly the leading American anthropologist and paleontologist. Yet it was he who was mainly responsible for promoting the ridiculous *Hesperopithecus haroldcookii* (a single tooth, later identified as belonging to an extinct peccary) as a very significant ape-man[1] and also for promoting the Piltdown Man (later shown to be a hoax) as the oldest human. Evidently evolutionary thinking can easily lead to self-delusion, as well as dangerous and arrogant sociological presumptions.

Associated with the Darwin Centennial Year (1959), two very important books were published which took a very different approach than that of the spirit of adulation with which Darwin was being effusively honored that year. Though neither author was a creationist, they were both clear thinkers and historians who discerned clearly the tremendous scourge of evil which the publication and promotion of Darwinism had let loose upon a world still deluding itself with dreams of evolutionary progress.

One was by Gertrude Himmelfarb, who held a doctorate from the University of Chicago and many other honors, and was later Professor of History at the City University of New York. After first noting that the subtitle to Darwin's *Origin of Species* was *The Preservation of Favored Races in the Struggle for Life,* Dr. Himmelfarb then went on to draw the obvious inference that,

> ... it was a short step to the preservation of favored individuals, classes, or nations—and from their preservation to their glorification. Social Darwinism has often been understood in this sense: as a philosophy exalting competition, power, and violence over convention, ethics, and religion. Thus it has become a portmanteau of nationalism, imperialism, militarism, and dictatorship, of the cults of the hero, the superman, and the master race.[2]

---

1. Henry Fairfield Osborn, *"Hesperopithecus,* the First Anthropoid Primate Found in America," *American Museum Noviates,* No. 37, (1922), p. 2.

2. Gertrude Himmelfarb, *Darwin and the Darwinian Revolution* (London:

The second was by Jacques Barzun, Professor of History and Dean of the Graduate Faculties at Columbia University. After discussing this unique period of man's intellectual history, he concluded:

> No one who has not waded through some sizable part of the literature of the period 1870 to 1914 has any conception of the extent to which it is one long call for blood.[1]

The older-style Darwinian racist imperialism and social Darwinism have now—after two world wars, many revolutions of so-called "liberation," and the American civil rights movement—fallen into disfavor with evolutionists. They tend now to regard these concepts, once so popular with their intellectual forebears, as merely unfortunate misunderstandings, not as legitimate extensions of evolutionary thought. For example, it is interesting to creationists that evolutionists are now saying what creationists have been insisting all along with respect to the (completely non-Biblical) evolutionary idea of "race."

> [Brace] reiterates the modern view that we should abandon the concept of race altogether and instead record the gene frequencies and traits of populations that are identified simply by their geographic localities. This genotypic and phenotypic information is to be interpreted in terms of historical and proximate selective forces.[2]

Creationist writers have also stressed for many years the fact

---

Chatto and Windus, 1959), p. 343.

1. Jacques Barzun, Darwin, Marx, Wagner (New York: Doubleday, 1958). The Centennial Edition was re-issued and updated from the 1942 edition, with the statement cited above given on p. 100.

2. Russel H Tuttle, "Five Decades of Anthropology," Science, 220 (1983), p. 832. Tuttle, an anthropologist at the University of Chicago, calls this the "modern view." However, I said essentially the same thing 15 years earlier in my column in The Montgomery Messenger on June 26, 1969, later incorporated in my book The Bible Has The Answer (Nutley, NJ: Craig Press, 1971), pp. 69–71, 110–113.

that evolutionism has led to wars of imperialism and aggression, a fact now reluctantly acknowledged by evolutionists. See especially the books *Evolution the Root of all Isms*, by Dan Gilbert (Grand Rapids: Zondervan, 1942), and *Darwin-Before and After*, by R.E.D. Clark (London: Paternoster, 1948), 192 pp.

Marxism, Modernism, and the Social Gospel

But if so-called "right-wing Darwinism" (e.g., laissez-faire capitalism, imperialism, racism, nazism) has fallen out of favor with modern intellectuals, its counterpart at the supposedly opposite end of the political spectrum continued alive and well. By the 1980s, almost half the world was enslaved by communism, and most of the free countries had socialist style governments. Marxism of one variety or another was enthusiastically studied and quoted in the colleges of most of the others, including the United States. Even the recent collapse of many communist governments has not led to true freedom but merely another variety of socialism, along with much occultism.

These systems are all, of course, based on evolutionary humanism to even a greater degree, if possible, than the various systems involved in social Darwinism.

> Defending Darwin is nothing new for socialists. The socialist movement recognized Darwinism as an important element in its general world outlook right from the start. When Darwin published his *Origin of Species* in 1859, Karl Marx wrote a letter to Frederick Engels in which he said: ". . . this is the book which contains the basis in natural history for our view. . . ." By defending Darwinism, working people strengthen their defenses against the attacks of these reactionary outfits, and prepare the way for the transformation of the social order.[1]

1. Cliff Conner, "Evolution vs. Creationism: In Defense of Scientific Thinking" *International Socialist Review* (Monthly Magazine Supplement to the *Militant*), (Nov. 1980). By "reactionary outfits," this communist publication was, of course, referring to the modem scientific creationist movement, which it

These two forms of evolution have been, to some degree, at odds with each other almost from the start. The one believes in gradual evolution resulting from natural law, with species (and then nations and races) struggling with one another for existence, with only the fittest surviving and thus advancing the over-all cause of biological (and then human) life. The other believes in rapid evolution resulting from catastrophic environmental changes brought about either naturally or (in modern human societies) artificially by social planners and/or revolutionaries. The first tends to favor traditional Darwinism or neo-Darwinism, the second tends to favor either Lamarckianism or modern punctuationism or both. The first is slow evolution, preferred by conservatives, the second is quick evolution (revolution) and appeals especially to radicals and "new-agers."

Both, however, are intrinsically evolutionist philosophies; therefore, they are both humanistic and ultimately atheistic philosophies. Instead of representing opposite ends of the spectrum (left-wing and right-wing), a better metaphor would call them two species of the same genus, both with the same ancestry. True theism, on the other hand, especially Biblical Christianity, is a different "kind" altogether.

Unfortunately, because Christians are basically theologically "conservative," believing as they do in the eternally unchanging verities of Scripture, they often tend to be aligned with political conservatives—that is, with slow-and-gradual evolutionists instead of revolutionary evolutionists. They *should,* however, be aligned with *neither!* Christians ought to stand without compromise on Biblical theistic creationism, rather than on *any* variety of humanism.

These relationships are complicated in the United States, of course, by the unique history of its people. Since most of the original colonies were founded for religious reasons, their entire

---

regarded as a serious threat to the great cause of "revolutionary socialism."

history and later fight for independence was a history of genuine belief in God as sovereign Creator and the desire to establish a nation governed by laws based on that belief. At the time of the new nation's establishment, although deism and unitarianism had become strongly represented among the nation's leadership, the great majority of the people still believed the Bible. Even the deists and unitarians still believed in God and special creation. Atheism and real evolutionism had few followers as yet, although their influence was rapidly growing in Europe.

Consequently, creationism and Christian theism continued strong in the young nation almost until the rise of Darwinism. There were, indeed, strong pockets of unbelief, especially in the colleges, from time to time, but these had been ephemeral exceptions, until Lyell and Darwin came along. Both political liberals and political conservatives tended to agree on Biblical creationism until this time. With the triumph of Darwinism, however, many among both liberals and conservatives became evolutionists; this even included many religious leaders, as noted before.

While the industrialists and political conservatives, led by such men as William Grant Sumner, made social Darwinism dominant in American life during the first half-century after Darwin, another form of Darwinism would eventually have even more sociological and political impact. This was evolutionary collectivism, or evolutionary socialism, stressing cooperation and planning in promoting social evolution, rather than a simple free-for-all struggle for existence. The first American leader in this field was Lester Frank Ward (1841–1913), who is considered the father of sociology in American thought. He strenuously opposed the system advocated by Spencer and Sumner. Christian historian Gregg Singer summarized Ward's teaching as follows:

> Ward admitted that in all lower forms of life environment was the determining factor in the evolutionary process, but that with man the case was quite different, for here the mind of man could, and should, exercise a determining influence on environ-

ment. . . . According to the concept of acquired characteristics, the characteristics that one generation consciously acquired for its own betterment would be transmitted to those which should follow it . . . the forces of evolution would be guided toward the realization of human happiness which, for Ward, was man's chief end in life.[1]

The idea of planned evolution of society corresponded closely with the teachings of various collectivist philosophers, including the socialists and communists.

Ward replaced the Darwinism of Sumner, which upheld individual action, with a Darwinism that was closely akin to Marx and Nietzsche. For Ward, a sociocratic state was the all-in-all.[2]

Ward, even more than Sumner, was an avowed opponent of creationism and of Biblical Christianity in general. He fought Biblically mandated institutions such as the home and the concept of an eternal moral law, as well as the church, believing that all of these were inimical to human happiness. Science, implementing controlled evolution, would be society's salvation, he taught, and he believed all this could be brought about through education.

Ward's teachings (at Brown University) and writings influenced many key people, but among the most significant were: psychologist William James (1842–1910), whose philosophy of "pragmatism" placed the study of human psychology on a thoroughly animalistic evolutionary basis; jurist Oliver Wendell Holmes, Jr. (1841–1935), whose 30-year tenure as supreme court justice contributed more than any other single factor to the now prevalent idea that the law is a product of evolution and should continue to evolve in accord with social policy; and, especially, John Dewey (1859–1952). The latter incorporated James' pragmatism into his own philosophy of "instrumentalism," along with a

---

1. C. Gregg Singer, *A Theological Interpretation of American History* (Nutley, NJ: Craig Press, 1964), pp. 113, 114.

2. *Ibid.*, p. 117.

thorough-going commitment to collectivist Darwinism, and became by any reckoning the most influential architect of governmental education, not only in America but throughout the world. He abundantly fulfilled Ward's goal of turning America's public schools into centers of indoctrination in evolution, humanism, and collectivism.

The effect of all this upon the theological world was profound. Although many rank-and-file Christians and their pastors remained true to the Bible and Biblical creationism, most of the theological leadership in the seminaries and major churches, as well as officials in the denominational hierarchies, felt they were intellectually required to incorporate evolutionism into their theologies and Biblical exegesis. Not only Darwinism, but also German higher criticism (which, of course, was also based on an evolutionary approach to the origin of the Scriptures) had given them, they thought, the right to take such liberties with the Word of God. In addition, there was the incentive of the grievous social conditions resulting from the industrial revolution, the Civil War, and the practice of social Darwinism by the captains of business and industry.

The result was the development and wide promulgation of the so-called "social gospel," with its corresponding theology, known for many years as "modernism." The social gospel was, by no means, merely the application of the Christian gospel to society and social needs. It was "another gospel" altogether, exactly the type of thing placed under divine anathema by the Apostle Paul in Galatians 1:6–9. It denied supernatural creation, the inerrancy and authority of Scripture, the deity of Christ, and salvation by the shed blood of Christ. It assumed an evolutionary origin of man and his social systems, the improvement of human nature through education, and the redemption of human society through collective action and governmental controls. Christ was said to be merely a great teacher, the highest pinnacle of the evolutionary process so far, whose vision of the kingdom of God and the brotherhood of man now needed to be implemented through the ecumenical action of his followers in the churches.

Rejecting the atheistic collectivist teachings of Ward, as well as those of Marx, the modernists accepted theistic evolution and went on from there to promote social evolution. The original leaders of this movement were such men as Washington Gladden (1836–1918) and Walter Rauschenbusch (1816–1918), but it soon became dominant in practically all the main Protestant denominations, as well as very strong in Roman Catholicism.

The Federal Council of Churches was formed in 1908, primarily to serve as the united voice of modernism and the social gospel. This entire movement not only had tremendous effect in the churches, but also in political life, with most of the nation's presidents and other political leaders following it in one degree or another. It really came into its own when much of the legislation it had long advocated finally was implemented under Franklin Roosevelt and his "New Deal."

As a matter of fact, with the passing of time and the increasing influence of John Dewey and his followers in the schools, the social gospel came more and more to resemble outright socialism, or even Marxist communism. But that is another story.

In any event, in one form or another, by the time of the first World War, evolutionism had thoroughly permeated American intellectual life. The influence of social Darwinism was still strong in business and industry, and among political conservatives. Collectivist Darwinism had all but captured the schools and churches, as well as socialists and other political liberals.

The Creationist Testimony Before 1925

During the first quarter of the twentieth century, a really virile creationist testimony was almost nowhere to be found in the United States. The great anti-Darwinian scientists of the nineteenth century (Pasteur, Kelvin, Maury, etc.) were gone, and the new generation of scientists (even those attending church schools) had been indoctrinated in evolutionism right from the start. There were still a number of evangelical scientists of importance, but unfortunately even most of these (e.g., Howard Kelly, the great Johns Hopkins surgeon) had accepted theistic evolution to a considerable degree.

Until the rise of the fundamentalist movement, only a handful of anti-evolutionist books appeared, and these were from rather obscure authors and publishers. One book that received a fairly wide reading was *The Other Side of Evolution*, written by Alexander Patterson (not a scientist) and published by The Moody Bible Institute in 1912.

Moody Bible Institute is the oldest of the nation's Bible institutes. It was founded in 1879 as an outgrowth of the great evangelistic campaigns of Dwight L. Moody (1837–1899), in the late nineteenth century. He held tremendous meetings, both in England and North America, just at the time when Darwinism was sweeping over the intellectual world. In particular, it is estimated that he preached to over 2,500,000 people in the British Isles alone, during the period 1873–1875. In his preaching, he never compromised with evolutionism at all, though many of the other great preachers of the day were doing just that. The latter included Henry Drummond, who was a coworker with Moody for a short time and, after his death, even wrote his biography.

Moody was an evangelist and simply preached salvation through Christ, winning multitudes to Him during this age of growing unbelief. He did not attempt to argue the scientific questions himself, since most of his audiences still retained a simple faith in the Bible, whether or not they practiced it, but he did realize the need to train young men who could stem the growing tide of apostasy in the churches. The seminaries and church colleges were no longer doing this, for the most part, and the result was the beginning of the Bible institute and Bible college movements, with Moody Bible Institute being the first such school, founded by Moody in 1879.

Moody's successor, R. A. Torrey (1856–1928), was also a highly successful evangelist but, in addition, he was well trained academically, so he vigorously fought evolutionism and other aspects of intellectual unbelief. After serving a period as president of Moody, he headed the Bible Institute of Los Angeles from 1912 to 1924. These two schools served as models for many other Bible colleges after them, and they continued to serve for many years as highly influential centers of Biblical Christianity in a time when modernism dominated the main denominations.

In addition to the Bible institutes and Bible colleges, however, the Biblical conservatives in these large denominations finally also began to organize in opposition to the modernistic and social gospel influences which were rapidly taking over their denominations. This situation eventually led to the famous fundamentalist/modernist controversy of the 1920s.

The "fundamentalist" revival of this period was so named because of a strong emphasis on a return to the fundamentals of the faith, which was especially crystallized by the publication beginning in 1909 of a series of 12 booklets called *The Fundamentals,* written by various conservative theological leaders of the time. Essentially five doctrines—the infallibility of Scripture, the deity of Christ, the substitutionary atonement, the bodily resurrection of Christ, and His future personal return—were taken as the basic doctrines, which were thought to be the irreducible fundamentals of the faith held in common by all Bible-believing Christians. *The Fundamentals* had been published by two laymen, Lyman and Milton Stewart, and then widely distributed. Torrey himself was one leading figure in this movement. Having been educated at Yale University and Yale Divinity School, followed by further study in Germany, he was well equipped to deal with the modernists on their own ground. In fact, he published a book in 1919[1] entitled

---

1. It is a matter of personal interest and satisfaction to me that I "met" Dr. Torrey early in 1919 in Dallas, Texas, where I had been born in October 1918. According to my mother, he was conducting a campaign in Dallas and

The Fundamental Doctrines of the Christian Faith, which was translated into many languages and which served as one of the key "textbooks" motivating the fundamentalist movement. His Bible Institute (along with Moody Bible Institute) and his worldwide evangelistic campaigns and Bible conferences were profoundly influential in this revival

Another key personage in the fundamentalist revival was Dr. William B. Riley (1861–1947), pastor of the First Baptist Church in Minneapolis, who founded the World's Christian Fundamentals Association in 1919. Dr. Riley carried on for years a battle with the evolutionist faculty at the University of Minnesota and elsewhere, including a number of formal creation/evolution debates, and his great church was one of the strongest conservative bulwarks in the Northern Baptist Convention. He was also founder and long-time president of the Northwestern Bible College.[1] By any accounting, Dr. Riley was one of the most outspoken fundamentalists and creationists of this period. Yet, oddly enough, he was an insistent advocate of the day/age theory, at one time even participating in a formal debate on the subject with Dr. Harry Rimmer, who was an equally vigorous proponent of the gap theory.

---

somehow called on our family in connection with it. In the process, as preachers are wont to do, he took the infant Henry Morris in his arms and prayed that God would save him and use him in the Lord's service. I am very thankful that God, in some measure at least, has graciously answered that prayer!

1. As another personal aside, I had an interesting meeting with Dr. Riley just a few months before his death. My first book, *That You Might Believe,* had been published in 1946, and he had been quite impressed with it. He was at that time searching for a young man to take over the presidency of his Northwestern Bible College. When he learned that I had just joined the University of Minnesota faculty, he called me to come meet with him, which I did. Unknown to me, this was to be an interview for the job. However, when I told him I had come to the University mainly to work on my Ph.D., in order thereby better to defend creationism, he agreed that this was better. Shortly afterward, Billy Graham was appointed president of Northwestern. Dr. Graham and I, incidentally, are essentially the same age.

In fact, these two compromising theories (as most scientific creationists would view them today) almost universally characterized the creationist testimony of the period. While anti-evolutionism was strong among the fundamentalists, almost none of their leaders questioned Lyellian uniformitarianism and the geological-age system. The Scofield Reference Bible, originally published in 1909, had actually incorporated both these theories in its notes, while at the same time ignoring the critically important question of the universality of the Flood, and it had a tremendous impact on fundamentalists in many denominations.

Another key leader of the fundamentalist movement was Dr. W. H. Griffith Thomas (1861–1924). With a Ph.D. from Oxford and several years of distinguished service as Principal of Oxford's Wycliffe Hall, he moved to Canada in 1910 to join the faculty of Wycliffe College. He became widely known in both Canada and the United States as a scholarly writer and speaker, publishing many outstanding volumes of Biblical and apologetics studies. Canon Dyson Hague said he was "without exaggeration among the first half-dozen of the foremost and strongest witnesses to the truth of the Bible and the Gospel in the twentieth century."[1] He was a key leader in the organizing of the great annual World Conferences on Christian Fundamentals, beginning in 1919. Finally, he and Dr. L. S. Chafer organized the school which would become Dallas Theological Seminary in 1924, but he died suddenly just before its classes began.

Like his friend Dr. Riley, although Dr. Thomas advocated the day/age theory, he was a strong and influential opponent of evolution. Although I never knew him, I had the privilege of receiving his file of miscellaneous notes on Genesis and science from his daughter, Mrs. Winifred Gillespie. I did get to know his wife, Mrs. Alice Thomas, who was living with her daughter and son-in-law

---

1. Rudolph A. Renfer, "Giant in the Church," *Sunday School Times,* Vol. 103, 23 Sep. 1961, p. 742.

(both of whom were serving as missionaries in southwest Louisiana), when I moved to Lafayette, Louisiana, in 1950. For several years I had frequent opportunities to fellowship with the Gillespies in evangelism among the "Cajun" people of the area.

Then, in 1967, I had the honor of being invited to give the W.H. Griffith Thomas Memorial Lectures at Dallas Seminary. My lectures had the title "Biblical Cosmology and Modern Science" and were later published in a book under that title, the book being

Figure 3.   George McCready Price

One of the most important creationist writers of the first half of the 20th century was a self-taught Seventh-Day Adventist geologist. Here Professor Price is shown both as a young man and then, with his wife, when he was 83 years of age.

dedicated to Mrs. Gillespie.

Almost the only writers to advocate literal recent creationism during this period, however, were to be found among the Lutherans and Seventh-Day Adventists—no doubt partly because their respective founders, Martin Luther and Ellen G. White, had taught six-day creationism and a worldwide flood. Even among the Lutherans, modernism had made great inroads, but there was a strong remnant of creationists, and many of these still adhered to a no-compromise position on the six days.

However, the only serious *geological* defense of the Biblical view came from an unlikely source, a self-taught Adventist geologist named George McCready Price (1870–1963). In 1906 Price published a small book entitled *Illogical Geology,* in which he stressed that the only really effective way to defeat evolution was to show that its geologic-age framework is invalid. This was the first of a long series of books, booklets, and articles by Price and his students advocating flood geology and refuting the supposed geological evidences of evolution. Although his initial impact was only in his own denomination, and he remained a strong Adventist throughout his long life, his books and articles were read by many people in every denomination and contributed significantly to the fundamentalist revival.

Nevertheless, the majority of the fundamentalist creationists continued to accept the geological ages, differing among themselves only as to whether they could be handled better in terms of the gap theory or the day-age theory. The argument against evolution focused primarily on the gaps in the fossil record and the harmful moral and sociological effects of evolutionism, in addition to the fact that the Bible contradicted it.

Interestingly enough, despite the strong emphasis on creationism in the fundamentalist/modernist controversy of the time, and the general awareness that modernism was based on evolution, creation was not even listed as one of the five "fundamentals" of the faith. Several of the *Fundamentals* booklets were actually written by men who were theistic evolutionists. This was even true of the booklet that dealt specifically with the evolution question, the author of which was the geologist George Frederick Wright, who seemed to equivocate between progressive creationism and theistic evolutionism. Whenever creation was stressed, it dealt primarily, if not exclusively, with man's creation. This characteristic is still observable today in the list of doctrinal tenets in the various fundamentalist missions and Bible colleges, most of which were organized during this time.

In any case, most of the fundamentalist preachers of the first quarter century did indeed fight evolution, as well as modernism and the social gospel which (whether they realized it or not) were squarely based on evolution. In addition to Torrey and Riley, some of the other leaders in this fight included Dr. A. C. Dixon, who edited *The Fundamentals,* Dr. John Roach Straton, pastor of New York City's famed Calvary Baptist Church, and Dr. J. Frank Norris, a Baptist pastor in Fort Worth who eventually led many churches out of the Southern Baptist Convention to form what eventually became the World Baptist Fellowship and the large body now known as the Baptist Bible Fellowship. There were many others, of course, some of whom will be discussed in the next chapter.

In the meantime, a few words about the situation in Europe during this period are in order. Although the Moody and Torrey evangelistic meetings in England had been very fruitful, and although Spurgeon and other British pastors continued strong in the faith, nothing comparable to the American situation developed. There were a number of British scientists who continued to defend creationism, and this was especially apparent in the published papers in the Journal of the Victoria Institute. This venerable organization, though not specifically anti-evolutionist, did publish excellent creationist articles from time to time, by eminent scientists who were creationists. One of the most outstanding of these was Sir Ambrose Fleming (1849–1945), whose discoveries and developments in electronics almost entitle him to be called the father of modern electronics. He was president of the Victoria Institute for a time and published many excellent articles in its journal, including a fine critique of radiometric dating, as well as at least one important book opposing evolution.

In continental Europe, there were also a number of outstanding creationist scientists writing in this period, especially in France. These included Professor Louis Vialleton, Professor of the Faculty of Medicine at Montpellier, and Paul LeMoine, Director of the National Museum in Paris, as well as President of the Geological Society of France. In Germany, there was Albert Fleischmann, Professor of Zoology and Comparative Anatomy at the University of Erlangen.

D. Carazzi, Professor of Zoology at the University of Padera, was an important creationist in Italy. And there were many others.

But our more direct concern at this point is with the developing creation/evolution conflict in the United States. With the establishment of fundamentalism as a more or less formal system, with creationism either explicitly or implicitly at its heart, a number of more ambitious books on creation began to be produced. One that had an exceedingly broad influence was a devastating critique of the ape-man fossils that were then in vogue (Java Man, Neanderthal Man, etc.). The book was by a Roman Catholic lawyer named Alfred Watterson McCann and had the provocative title *God or Gorilla,* published in 1922. There were a number of others, some of which will be mentioned in the next chapter.

Also it was realized more and more that Darwinian philosophy had been responsible in considerable part for the German aggression that had led to the Great War, as well as the pseudo-scientific rationale for Communistic atheism and the Russian revolution. Studies had also shown that the nation's colleges were having a devastating effect on the Christian faith of students educated in the colleges. Suddenly, the nation was aroused at the dangers implicit in the indoctrination in evolution which young people were receiving in the public schools. Many states began to consider anti-evolution laws. Very few actually passed such laws, but one of those which did was Tennessee, and this soon led to the famous "Monkey Trial. "

The Scopes Extravaganza

Never in the history of American jurisprudence was there ever such a court trial as the famous Scopes Trial, held in the Dayton, Tennessee, County Court House in July of 1925. This trial has been the theme of many books and almost innumerable articles, as well as at least one major motion picture (*Inherit The Wind*, starring Spencer Tracy as the "hero," the atheist lawyer Clarence Darrow). The current creationist revival has stimulated a new spurt of articles featuring this watershed event. The trial was covered by over 200 news reporters, writing about two million words, but much of this was highly biased reporting, specifically designed to destroy creationism and the fundamentalist revival which reached its climax in this media event. Chicago radio station WGN here produced the first national broadcast of an American trial. Sixty-five telegraph operators sent out more words to Europe and Australia than had ever before been cabled about any American event. A recent article published by the Tennessee Historical Society comments as follows:

> A stranger trial there probably never was. One or more of the jury were there primarily to get a good seat, but ironically they missed many proceedings because the jury was excluded from the lengthy, technical legal discussions. . . . Scientific experts were brought hundreds of miles to testify, but their statements were not accepted as evidence. . . . The chief counsel for the defense [Darrow] was cited for contempt of court, and the leader for the prosecution [Bryan] took the witness stand. The accused never was called to testify.
>
> . . . The proceedings were cut short by the judge partly to protect the chief prosecution and defense lawyers against threats on their safety. . . . Last in the list of trial oddities is the fact that

the defense did not claim the accused was innocent of the charges, but at the end asked that the jury return a verdict of guilty.[1]

As a matter of fact, the defendant John T. Scopes was probably not guilty of teaching evolution at all, as he later acknowledged,[2] but agreed to say that he had simply in order to help set up the scenario. The whole thing had been arranged as a sort of local conspiracy to attract attention and possibly industrial developers to Dayton.[3]

The local conspiracy, motivated by local economics, was of course merely a convenient tool utilized by a much more serious and far reaching group of "conspirators" in New York City. The Dayton group hatched the idea only as a result of reading an article in a Chattanooga newspaper in which the American Civil Liberties Union had offered to finance any Tennessee teacher who was willing to be tried for breaking the state's newly passed law banning the teaching of evolution. The A.C.L.U. leadership was justifiably concerned about the strong reaction that the fundamentalists were generating in the nation against the pervasive teaching of evolutionism and collectivist humanism in the schools. They saw this as a golden opportunity to destroy the fundamentalist movement through news media ridicule and were willing to pay whatever amount it might cost to accomplish this.

The A.C.L.U. contingent, and the nation's evolutionist establishment in general, were especially anxious to stop the strong Christian creationist testimony of William Jennings Bryan, who

---

1. R. M. Cornelius, "Their Stage Drew all the World: A New Look at the Scopes Evolution Trial." *Tennessee Historical Quarterly,* Vol. XL (Summer, 1981), pp. 133, 134.

2. John T. Scopes and James Presley, *Center of the Storm: Memoirs of John T. Scopes* (New York: Holt, Rinehart, and Winston, 1967), p. 60.

3. Warren Allem, "Backgrounds of the Scopes Trial at Dayton, Tennessee," M.A. Thesis (Univ. of Tennessee, Knoxville, 1959, pp. 55–61), as reported by Cornelius, in above reference.

Figure 4.   The Scopes Trial

The Scopes Trial in 1925 was a classic confrontation between evolutionists and creationists, resulting in an overwhelming news-media
victory for evolution. In this photograph, taken in the County Court
House at Dayton, Tennessee, are shown several of the leading figures
at the trial, including Assistant defense attorney Dudley Field Malone
(left foreground), William Jennings Bryan (center, with bow tie), and
Judge J. T. Raulston, shaking hands with Clarence Darrow (with sus-
penders, far right).

Photo courtesy of Bryan College, Robinson Photo Collection.

would undoubtedly be persuaded to serve as the main attorney for
the creationists. Bryan was a liberal Democrat politically, former
Secretary of State, three-time Democratic candidate for president,
and very popular with "commoners" (he was known popularly as
the "Great Commoner"). In spite of his liberal political associations, however, he was a Bible-believing Christian and had for
several years been greatly exercised about the deadly moral and
spiritual influences of evolutionary teaching in the world, especially its direct connection with German militarism in the Great
War, as well as its deadening spiritual effect on young people in
the schools. With his oratorical brilliance, he had become probably

the top spokesman for fundamentalism and creationism in the nation. He was not a scientist, however, nor was he devious, and he failed to realize he was walking into a deadly trap set by the A.C.L.U. and their lead attorney, the famous Clarence Darrow.

The story of the trial itself has been told and retold so many times that it seems redundant to repeat it again here. As anticipated and intended, the press had a field day and Bryan was made to appear ridiculous by the insulting sarcasm of Darrow. He foolishly allowed himself to be placed on the witness stand by Darrow, after being promised that Darrow would then take the stand himself, thus allowing Bryan to question him and also to give his own final address. Darrow, however, after mercilessly ridiculing Bryan on the stand with all sorts of irrelevant Bible questions, then maneuvered quickly to get the trial terminated by the judge without giving Bryan his own opportunity to question Darrow and to give his masterly summary address.

Probably the most serious mistake made by Bryan on the stand was to insist repeatedly that he had implicit confidence in the infallibility of Scripture, but then to hedge on the geological question, relying on the day/age theory. He had been warned against this very thing by George McCready Price. Darrow, of course, made the most of it, ridiculing the idea of people claiming to believe the Bible was inspired when its meaning was so flexible that one could make it say whatever he wished!

Technically, the case was won by the creationists, but Darrow, the A.C.L.U., and especially the news media created one of the most successful "stings" in the long, long history of humanistic intrigues. Dr. Fay-Cooper Cole, who had been Anthropology Department Chairman at the University of Chicago, and who had given one of the scientific depositions for the evolutionists at the trial, said:

> Where one person had been interested in evolution before the trial, scores were reading and inquiring at its close. Within a year the prohibitive bills which had been pending in other states

were dropped and killed. Tennessee had been made to appear so ridiculous in the eyes of the nation that other states did not care to follow its lead.[1]

Further than that, of course, the creationist revival of the 1920s was all but stopped dead in its tracks. Bryan himself died in his sleep just five days after the trial ended, at the age of 65, and there is no doubt that the emotional ordeal, as well as the physical exhaustion, associated with the trial contributed to this sad—perhaps symbolic—tragedy.

While evolutionists have complained that the Scopes trial resulted for some years in the dilution of evolutionary emphasis in school textbooks,[2] this complaint is hard to justify. There has certainly been nothing about *creation* in these books! From our point of view, they are literally saturated with evolutionary thinking, expressed either explicitly or implicitly, and this has been true ever since the trial. Except for occasional courageous Christian teachers here and there, the public educational institutions from kindergarten through graduate school have been strictly centers of evolutionist indoctrination for well over sixty years. Textbooks may not always have "evolution" listed in their indexes, but they are invariably permeated with evolutionary presuppositions and naturalistic, humanistic interpretations of all phenomena.

One of the most disappointing aspects of the Scopes trial was its intimidating effect on Christians. Multitudes of nominal Christians capitulated to theistic evolution, and even those who retained their belief in creation retreated from the arena of conflict, using the fiction that it was somehow unspiritual to be involved in such controversies and urging each other to concentrate instead on "soul-winning" and "personal Christianity," with a great emphasis also on the soon return of Christ. The schools and government and

---

1. Fay-Cooper Cole, "A Witness at the Scopes Trial," *Scientific American, Jan.* 1959, p. 130.

2. Judith Grabiner and P. D. Miller, "Effects of the Scopes Trial," *Science, 185,* 6 Sep. 1974, pp. 832–837.

society in general were, to all intents and purposes, simply abandoned to secular humanist control, and they have been firmly under that control ever since.

This did not happen over night, of course. Even though their champion had been downed, there continued to be a flurry of activity among fundamentalists and creationists for a couple of years or so. For a while, there were many who even thought the creationists had won, despite the continuing news media campaign of ridicule and vituperation. Even Bryan himself seems to have thought this, and he arranged to have his intended summary speech—which he had been prevented from delivering at the trial—printed for distribution to the papers.

This speech was reprinted by Bryan College on the 50th anniversary of the trial, in 1975, and is indeed an excellent message,[1] stressing the right of citizens to control their own schools, the misuse of scientific data by evolutionists, and especially the devastatingly harmful effects of evolutionary teaching. It concluded with a strong Christian testimony and exhortation. It might indeed have made a difference if it had been actually delivered and accurately reported, but it was soon forgotten, even by most Christians.

One good result from the trial was the establishment in Dayton of a fine Christian liberal arts college, paid for by friends of Bryan all over the nation as a memorial to him and to the great cause for which he had fought and died. Bryan College has remained true to the ideals and beliefs of its founder and is today a thriving accredited college with over 600 students,[2] at least 17 majors, a beautiful 100-acre campus, and over 3500 alumni.

Furthermore, the interest generated by the trial soon resulted in the publication of a number of significant anti-evolution books. The most important was a book by a physics professor at the

---

1. *The Last Message of William Jennings Bryan* (Dayton, TN: William Jennings Bryan College, 1975), 32 pp.

2. R. M. Cornelius, *op. cit.*, p. 139. I myself have had the privilege of speaking at Bryan College.

University of Cincinnati. Although the author, Louis T. More, indicated his basic faith to be in evolution, his book was a devastating scientific critique of evolution.[1] Two prominent Lutheran theologians, Leander S. Keyser and Theodore Graebner, published excellent volumes,[2] and a truly outstanding treatise was written by the Roman Catholic Professor of Animal Zoology at Seton Hall College.[3]

In spite of these and a few other significant efforts, however, the Scopes trial and the continual media bombardment of ridicule afterward proved so discouraging and intimidating to the Christian world that the whole fundamentalist movement seemed to wither away, at least as far as impact on the secular world was concerned. Introspective evangelism and pietistic separationism seemed henceforth to characterize most of the evangelical community.

The real poverty of the evolutionists' scientific position, however, could have been evident to anyone who would take the trouble to read the actual trial transcripts. The poverty of evolutionism has also been repeatedly reemphasized over the past half-century by the perpetual stream of books, articles, and other replays of the Scopes trial. It was evolution's great triumph (greater even than the famed Huxley-Wilberforce debate), and evolutionists never seem to have anything better to offer when there arises a need to defend evolution.

For instance, in 1973 I spent six weeks in New Zealand, speaking on scientific creationism in universities, schools, and churches all over that country. There was a great deal of interest and I think a real impact was made. But in city after city, either during my

---

1. Louis T. More, *The Dogma of Evolution* (Princeton, NJ: Princeton Univ. Press, 1925).

2. Leander S. Keyser, *The Problem of Origins* (Wartburg Press, 1925); Theodore Graebner, *Essays on Evolution* (St. Louis: Concordia Publishing House, 1925).

3. George Barry O'Toole, *The Case Against Evolution* (New York: Macmillan Publ. Co., 1926).

visit or immediately afterward, the government-controlled television channels kept showing the Scopes trial motion picture, *Inherit The Wind,* over and over.

Of course, maybe it was only a coincidence. But the picture was an old film, and there seemed no other reason for resurrecting it just at that time. At least, however, it helped focus the interest of one small nation on the creation-evolution issue, for a while.

The Great Darwinian Centennial Celebration

The hold of evolutionism on the educational system and the intellectual life of the nation grew stronger year by year after 1925. The rift between the fundamentalists and modernists continued in the great denominations, but the modernists and liberals continued to grow in relative power in all or most of them. In many cases, small conservative groups broke away to form new denominations, and many new evangelical schools and mission societies were formed. However, even though most of these had a nominal commitment to creationism, at least as far as the origin of man was concerned, the whole subject was largely deemphasized as too controversial and too specialized.

To a large degree, real scientific creationism seemed almost to disappear. No scientists, especially on the faculties of the great universities, seemed willing to admit to being creationists—or even evangelical Christians. Very few publications appeared advocating literal creationism or Biblical catastrophism.

Yet the evolutionists were still not satisfied. They still felt that evolutionary philosophy was not being applied as widely and thoroughly in society as they would like. The specter of theism was still inhibiting the publishers and the legislatures, preventing the full implementation of an evolution-based morality and sociology upon the people. Accordingly, more and more agitation began to be heard for still more evolutionism, especially in the schools and colleges.[1]

The great opportunity came as the key year 1959 approached, for this would be the 100th anniversary of the publication of Darwin's *Origin of Species.* This would focus the world's attention once again on evolutionism, and the point could be made strongly that, as the first century after Darwin was the time of evolutionary conquest, so the second century should be one of evolutionary reign.

And, indeed, as the great year approached, a veritable flood-tide of books and articles eulogizing Darwin and explaining and promoting evolutionary thought streamed from the scientific and educational presses. These, of course, included many reviews of the Scopes trial and its impact on American thought.

The same type of phenomenon was occurring in England and other countries, and many meetings and observances were scheduled in 1958 and 1959. The greatest of these, by far, however, was the Centennial Celebration held at the University of Chicago, for a week beginning on November 24, 1959, the exact Centennial of the publication of Darwin's book.

To this unique convocation were invited all the world's greatest leaders of evolutionary thought, representing many different fields and ten different nations. About fifty of these scientists prepared original papers dealing with the implications and applications of Darwinism (or better, by this time in history, "neo-Darwinism") in their own fields. These papers were submitted in advance, and then the participants took part in five panel discussions, one each day, on all the various topics, grouped under five divisions. Approximately 2500 people were in the audience to hear the discussions.

All of these papers and discussions were later published in a

---

1. One typical example is the book *The Unleashing of Evolutionary Thought* by the Princeton biologist Oscar Riddle (New York: Vantage, 1955), 414 pp. Another was a paper by the Indiana University geneticist H. J. Muller, "One Hundred Years without Darwin are Enough" *(The Humanist,* V. XIX, 1959, p. 139).

very influential three-volume set[1] of books. The most important of all the papers, however, was undoubtedly the Centennial Convocation Address, delivered (ironically enough) on Thanksgiving Day, November 26, 1959, by Sir Julian Huxley. This keynote address was entitled "The Evolutionary Vision," and could well be considered as a definitive Manifesto of the worldwide humanistic religion of evolution. A few of Sir Julian's pronouncements in this visionary message are excerpted below:

> Future historians will perhaps take this Centennial Week as epitomizing an important critical period in the history of this earth of ours—the period when the process of evolution, in the person of inquiring man, began to be truly conscious of itself. . . . This is one of the first public occasions on which it has been frankly faced that all aspects of reality are subject to evolution, from atoms and stars to fish and flowers, from fish and flowers to human societies and values—indeed, that all reality is a single process of evolution.[2]

> In 1859, Darwin opened the passage leading to a new psychosocial level, with a new pattern of ideological organization— an evolution-centered organization of thought and belief.[3]

> Man's destiny is to be the sole agent for the future evolution of this planet.[4]

> In the evolutionary pattern of thought there is no longer either need or room for the supernatural. The earth was not created, it evolved. So did all the animals and plants that inhabit it, including our human selves, mind and soul as well as brain and body.

---

1. Sol Tax, ed., *Evolution after Darwin:* Vol. I *The Evolution of Life,* 629 pp.; Vol. 2 *The Evolution of Man,* 473 pp.; Vol. 3 *Issues in Evolution,* 310 pp. (Chicago: Univ. of Chicago Press, 1960).

2. Julian Huxley, "The Evolutionary Vision," in *Issues in Evolution,* Vol. 3 of *Evolution after Darwin,* pp. 249–261. This paper largely echoed the infamous Humanist Manifesto of 1933, which had been strongly influenced by Huxley as one of its framers.

3. *Ibid.,* p. 251.

4. *Ibid.,* p. 252.

So did religion.[1]

Evolutionary man can no longer take refuge from his loneliness in the arms of a divinized father figure whom he has himself created, nor escape from the responsibility of making decisions by sheltering under the umbrella of Divine Authority, nor absolve himself from the hard task of meeting his present problems and planning his future by relying on the will of an omniscient, but unfortunately inscrutable, Providence.[2]

Finally, the evolutionary vision is enabling us to discern, however incompletely, the lineaments of the new religion that we can be sure will arise to serve the needs of the coming era.[3]

In this address, Huxley not only repudiated any vestige of creationism, he left no room even for theistic evolution. He would not even admit to being an agnostic, as his grandfather, Thomas Huxley, had been. When Harlow Shapley, the Harvard astronomer, suggested to him that he might really be only an agnostic, he replied:

I am an atheist, in the only correct sense, that I don't believe in the existence of a supernatural being who influences natural events.[4]

There are many apologists for evolution, however, who say that Huxley was not typical and, therefore, his comments should not be taken too seriously. But nothing could be further from the truth than this. Huxley was undoubtedly the world's most important living evolutionist, and that is precisely why he was chosen as the main speaker for this greatest of all Darwinian Centennial Celebrations.

Huxley's significance can hardly be overestimated. He was

---

1. *Ibid.,* p. 252–3.

2. *Ibid.,* p. 253.

3. *Ibid.,* p. 260.

4. Julian Huxley, in *Issues in Evolution* (Chicago: Univ. of Chicago Press, 1963), p. 46.

probably more responsible than any other single individual for the so-called "modern evolutionary synthesis," or "neo-Darwinism" (slow and-gradual evolution through random mutations and natural selection). He was best known to the lay public as the first Director-General of UNESCO, in which position he vigorously promoted humanism on a worldwide scale.[1] He was author of many important evolutionist books and countless articles.

One of Huxley's most significant "contributions" was his service as one of the chief co-founders, along with John Dewey, of the American Humanist Association, in the early 1940s. This society has served ever since as the bellwether of evolutionary humanism in America, never with a large membership, but always with a very influential membership. Its tenets correspond fully with what amounts to the state-established religion in our public schools today. It has also taken the lead in the drive against the creationist revival of recent years. In addition to Huxley and Dewey, some of the signers of the 1933 Humanist Manifesto, which eventually led to the A.H.A., were such notorious liberal humanists as Brock Chisholm, Margaret Sanger, Linus Pauling, H. J. Muller, Benjamin Spock, Erich Fromm, Buckminster Fuller, Hudson Hoagland, and Carl Rogers, along with many others of like belief.

Among the promotional literature of the A.H.A., circulated widely at the time of its founding and ever since, was the following definitive statement by Huxley:

> I use the word "humanist" to mean someone who believes that man is just as much a natural phenomenon as an animal or plant; that his body, mind, and soul were not supernaturally created but are products of evolution, and that he is not under the control or guidance of any supernatural being or beings, but has to rely on himself and his own powers.[2]

---

1. See his remarkable paper, "A New World Vision," written as his proposed framework for UNESCO, published later in The Humanist (Vol. XXXIX, March/April 1979), pp. 34–40.

2. Julian Huxley, as quoted in American Humanist Association promotional

Huxley and his fellow evolutionary humanists clearly regarded humanism as a religion. In fact, he even wrote an influential book on the subject entitled *Religion without Revelation*. The promotional brochure cited above confirmed this:

> Humanism is the belief that man shapes his own destiny. It is a constructive philosophy, a non-theistic religion, a way of life. . . . The American Humanist Association is a non-profit, tax-exempt organization, incorporated in the early 1940's in Illinois for educational and religious purposes.
>
> . . . Humanist counselors [can be called upon] to solemnize weddings, and conduct memorial services and to assist in individual value "counseling."[1]

Yet modern A.H.A. humanists hypocritically deny that humanism is a religion and want creationism banned from schools so that only their religion of evolutionism and atheism can be taught to young people!

Huxley accomplished many other things during his long life (1887–1975), including a number of valuable scientific contributions, though his greatest fame is as chief propagandist for evolutionism. Of special personal interest to me is the fact that he was the first Biology Department Chairman at Rice University, from its opening in 1912 until 1917, where as he said,

> I think I did something towards starting a tradition at Rice—a frame of mind.[2]

This he did indeed! I was a student at Rice (1935–1939) and later an instructor there (1942–1946), and the tradition of evolutionary humanism which he helped establish there was very strong. As an engineering student, I was not indoctrinated in this philosophy to the degree that other students were, in the "pure" sciences

brochure, distributed by Humanist Society, San Jose, California.

1. American Humanist Association brochure, distributed by Humanist Society of San Jose.

2. Michelle Gillespie, "Huxley at Rice," Rice University Sallyport, Sep. 1982, p. 7.

and humanities, but I did take many of these other courses[1] and thus became a theistic evolutionist myself, more by osmosis than by persuasion.

But to return to the Centennial Celebration and Huxley's convocation address, the most shocking thing about this was not his blatantly atheistic pronouncements (his beliefs were already well known), but the fact that none in that august assemblage raised any objection or presented a contrary point of view, in all the papers and panel discussions. Not even theistic evolutionism had any scientific defenders,[2] let alone creationism!

Evolutionism had, indeed, apparently become completely triumphant by this time. Creationism, except for isolated pockets of fundamentalists, seemed dead—most certainly among scientists! The immense and favorable publicity accorded to the Darwinian Centennial year, especially the great Darwin "worship service" at Chicago, where speaker after speaker rhapsodized about Darwin's contribution to the life of mankind, and exhorted each other and all their disciples on to further glories of evolutionary achievement, seemed to be the final nail in the coffin of creationism and even of meaningful Christian theism.

Another important outgrowth of the Darwinian Centennial propaganda was the establishment of the Biological Sciences Curriculum Study in January 1959. The BSCS was formed by the American Institute of Biological Scientists, representing 85,000 members, "as a means of contributing to the improvement of secondary school biological education."[3] They were convinced

---

1. Rice had such a strong "liberal arts" emphasis that even its engineering students had to take a large number of such courses. Consequently, I was able to make Phi Beta Kappa, the honorary liberal arts society, a privilege denied engineering students in almost all other universities.

2. There were two theologians, one Catholic and one Protestant, who gave papers advocating theistic evolution, but these were generally ignored and were published in the collection of miscellaneous papers, Volume 3, instead of the two volumes of scientific papers.

3. Bentley Glass and Arnold B. Grobman, Foreword, *Biological Science:An*

that "the major fault in the teaching of biology and other sciences in the secondary schools is that emphasis has been placed on authoritative content—facts, concepts, principles—instead of being placed on the investigative processes of science and the history of scientific ideas."[1]

That is, biological education should no longer deal mainly with the facts and principles, but with the social implications, of biology.

> We were also firmly convinced that in our new courses nothing should prevent a thorough, unbiased, and scientifically objective presentation of such supposedly controversial biological subjects as organic evolution, the nature of individual and racial differences, sex and reproduction in the human species, or the problems of population growth and control.[2]

Soon after its formation, the BSCS received a $7,000,000 grant from the National Science Foundation to develop a new series of biology textbooks which would achieve these goals. The minds of young people must be thoroughly programed toward evolution and all its implications, and the textbooks then in use were not doing this well enough.

> To help remedy this situation the National Science Foundation set up a program called the Biological Sciences Curriculum Study (BSCS) and gave it $7 million to create modern biology courses for the public schools. Three textbooks were developed, each emphasizing a different aspect of current biological research: molecular biology, cell biology, and ecology. All three reflected the fact that modern biological research is based on evolutionary assumptions, which were described as "the warp and woof of modern biology!"[3]

Inquiry into Life (New York: Harcourt, Brace, and World, Inc., 1963), p. xv. This book is the so-called BSCS "Yellow Version."

1. *Ibid.*, p. xvi.

2. *Ibid.* By "objective" is meant the avoidance of any mention of the creation alternative!

3. Dorothy Nelkin, "The Science-Textbook Controversies," *Scientific Ameri-*

As might be expected, the subsequent impact of these widely used textbooks on the minds of the young people of the present generation has been profound. A similar textbook project was undertaken shortly afterward in the social sciences. This project was entitled *Man: A Course of Study* (MACOS), and was also given $7 million by NSF.[1] If anything, it was even more saturated with evolutionary humanism and morally objectionable interpretations than the BSCS Series.

But, as it turned out, creationism was not dead, after all, and would shortly surface again—stronger than ever. Dr. Ronald Numbers, Professor of the History of Medicine and the History of Science at the University of Wisconsin called it "Creationism Underground" and analyzed the situation as follows:

> During the heady days of the 1920's, when their activities made front-page headlines, creationists dreamed of converting the world; a decade later, rejected and forgotten by the establishment, they turned their energies inward and began creating an institutional base of their own. Deprived of the popular press and unable to publish their views in organs controlled by orthodox scientists, they determined to organize their own societies and edit their own journals.[2]

During the three-plus decades between the Scopes trial and the Darwinian Centennial, the Lord raised up a number of scientists who would lay the foundations for a truly significant creationist revival in the 1960s and 1970s. The academic establishment was little aware of them, and even the fundamentalists and evangelicals took little note of them, but they were nevertheless plowing the ground and sowing good seed. A number of these men and their contributions will be discussed in the next chapter.

---

can, 234, Apr. 1976, p. 33.

1. *Ibid.* Nelkin is Associate Professor of Science, Technology, and Society at Cornell.

2. Ronald L. Numbers, "Creationism in 20th-Century America," *Science*, 218, 5 Nov. 1982, p. 541.

Chapter III

Voices in the Wilderness

During the period between the Scopes trial and the Darwinian Centennial, especially the last three decades of that period, there was very little public awareness of creationism. As noted in the last chapter, evolution was no longer questioned in the public schools or colleges, and even most of the fundamentalist schools and churches ignored the question, concentrating on "personal Christianity" and assuming that the geological ages could be handled simply by the gap theory.

However, there were a few creationist writers of significance, even in this barren period. It is the purpose of this chapter to survey the careers and writings of these men, who helped bridge the gap between the creationist revival preceding the Scopes trial and the modern creationist movement.

Price and the Seventh-Day Adventists

The most important creationist writer of the first half-century, at least in my judgment, was a remarkable man by the name of George McCready Price (1970–1962).[1] Many Christians today would take strong exception to this evaluation, both because of his six-day creationist, flood geology position and his religious denomination (Seventh-Day Adventist), which many "main-line" denominations, as well as inter-denominationalists, regard as an

---

1. His real name was George Edward Price. He later took the middle name "McCready" in honor of his mother, whose maiden name was Susan McCready.

eccentric cult.

As a Baptist, I obviously disagree with Adventist eschatology, as well as Adventist concepts of revelation and soteriology; but I have learned to have sincere respect for their integrity, intelligence, scholarship, and strong commitment to the inerrancy of Scripture and many of the basic doctrines of Christianity. At the very least, they are closer to the truth than the "liberals" among the "mainline" denominations. Although I never met George McCready Price, his tremendous breadth of knowledge in science and Scripture, his careful logic, and his beautiful writing style made a profound impression on me when I first began studying these great themes, back in the early 1940s.

I first encountered his name in one of Harry Rimmer's books (see the discussion of Rimmer later in this chapter) and thereupon looked up his book *The New Geology* in the library at Rice Institute, where I was teaching at the time. This was in early 1943, and it was a life-changing experience for me. I eventually acquired and read most of his other books as well.

Even though I never met Professor Price personally, I did engage in fruitful correspondence with him over a period of some 15 years before his death. He once sent me a photograph of himself and his wife Amelia (taken when he was 83 years old). He and his wife lived together and loved each other dearly for 67 years, until her death in 1954.

His friend and coworker for 40 years, Professor Harold W. Clark (1891–1983), who also lived a long and fruitful life, authoring many fine books on scientific creationism, was chosen to write Price's biography after his death, and I would certainly recommend it as a fascinating volume to read.[1] Clark lists a total of 25 books written by Professor Price, the first published in 1902, the last in 1955. He not only wrote many books on flood geology, but also a

---

1. Harold W. Clark, *Crusader for Creation* (Mountain View, CA: Pacific Press Publ. Assoc., 1966), 102 pp.

number of books on general apologetics and even a commentary on the book of Daniel. He published a 510-page textbook on general science, but by far his most ambitious project was his geology textbook, the 726-page *New Geology*, first published in 1923. In addition to these works, he produced a seemingly endless stream of articles, published not only in his denominational journals, but also in such widely read Christian magazines as *Sunday School Times, Moody Monthly, Bibliotheca Sacra, Princeton Theology Review*, and many others outside Adventist circles. He was even able to get a few articles published in such scientific establishment journals as *The Catholic World, PanAmerican Geologist,* and *Scientific American,* and that was no mean feat for a creationist writer! In 1925, he received the Victoria Institute's prize for the best paper published in its *Proceedings* that year. His literary output was prodigious and had a tremendous impact, both before and after the Scopes trial. In one of his letters to me near the end of his life, he wrote that it had been a special goal of his to produce as many books and articles as he possibly could, realizing that no one would read all of them, but that each one would reach some that had not seen the others, and also that on such subjects as these most people would need to read several presentations before the message could be adequately understood and appropriated.

Amazingly enough, Professor Price was almost entirely a self-taught man. He did get a B.A. from Loma Linda College in 1912, although he had already been teaching there in such subjects as Latin, Greek, chemistry, and physics, as well as general refresher courses in all fields for students in premedicine and prenursing. During his career he taught a wide range of subjects at various Adventist schools, but his main field soon came to be geology, as he had come to realize this was the critical discipline for refuting evolution and restoring faith in the Bible.

His limited formal training, naturally enough, provided an easy focus for the ridicule of his critics (including, unfortunately, a considerable contingent of compromising evangelicals), but it was probably this very fact which enabled him to spend time on only that which was really significant and to evaluate what he read as a truly independent thinker, constrained only by Scripture rather than the evolutionist party line of the schools and textbooks. He was a voracious reader, with the ability to analyze and retain what he read, as well as a clear and original thinker. He was certainly far better educated, in the true sense, than 90% of the Ph.D.'s and Th.D.'s cranked out by the assembly lines of the educational establishment. Furthermore, his reading included not only the sciences, but the classics, philosophy, and much of the great literature of past and present, and this was reflected in his skillful writing style. Nevertheless, after the Scopes trial, Price's writings, along with those of the other creationists of the period, began to wane in influence. Even his epochal work *The New Geology* soon went out of print. Though he wrote many books, the readership of the later books especially was quite limited.

However, in his own denomination, at least, interest in creationism has been strong ever since, and liberals have never been able to gain much of a foothold. Several of his students have gone on to make significant contributions of their own. These have included Harold Clark, already mentioned, Frank Marsh, Ernest Booth, Clifford Burdick, and others.

Clark took a course in geology from Price at Pacific Union College in 1920. Though his own professional field was biology, he did write two significant books on flood geology. *The New Diluvialism* was published in 1946, and *Fossils, Flood, and Fire* in 1968. In addition, he has written several other good books, beginning with *Back to Creationism* in about 1930. His *New Diluvialism* took issue with Price on the question of the relative significance of ecological zonation in the stratigraphic sequences of the geological column, and the two carried on something of a feud for a number of years over that subject, Price contending that Clark gave entirely too much credence to the supposed order of the fossils.

Figure 5. Adventist Creationist Scientists

In addition to George McCready Price, the Seventh-Day Adventists have contributed many key scientists to the creationist cause. Two of the most important were geologist Clifford Burdick (left) and biologist Harold Clark (right).

Frank Lewis Marsh (1899–1992), unlike Price and Clark, did obtain a *bona fide* Ph.D. from the University of Nebraska, in biology. He also taught at many Adventist schools and wrote a number of excellent creationist books, beginning with *Fundamental Biology,* published in 1941. Both Clark and Marsh held professorships in biology at various Adventist colleges. Marsh was the first Seventh Day Adventist ever to earn a Ph. D. in biology.

Dr. Ernest S. Booth, who was Head of the Biology Department at the Adventists' Walla Walla College, in Washington, wrote an excellent biology textbook, *Biology - The Story of Life* (1950), written entirely in a creationist framework. He also edited for many years an Adventist field biology periodical called *The Naturalist.*

Another student of Price's, Clifford Burdick, took graduate work in geology from the University of Wisconsin and spent a long and productive career as a consulting geologist, never wavering from the principles of flood geology taught him by Price. He wrote many important creation-oriented research papers, including one giving the first real critique of radiometric dating I had ever seen, back in 1945. This paper convinced me that I no longer had to dabble with the gap theory or some other means of allowing a great age for the earth. My first book was at the presses by then, allowing this possibility, and it was too late to change it, but none of my later books included this un-Biblical possibility. Burdick's paper was original and very incisive and convincing. He also was the first creationist to make a serious investigation and report on the famous footprints of man and dinosaur at the Paluxy River in Texas. He contributed important research studies on the invalidity of many so-called "overthrusts," as well as the discovery of "young" fossil pollen in the "old" rocks near the bottom of the Grand Canyon.

Several other Adventist creationists published papers in *The Naturalist* and other Adventist publications, as noted in the following chapter. Although the influence of most of them was largely limited to their own denomination, some (especially Price) have contributed quite significantly to the foundations of the modern creationist revival.

The Lutheran Testimony

Although no single individual stands out in the manner of George McCready Price, a number of highly significant books were published by Lutheran writers during the period we are considering. Just as Adventists to some degree have remained solidly creationist because their main teacher/founder, Ellen G. White, taught literal creationism, so do those Lutherans who truly respect the teachings of Martin Luther try to hold this position. Although Luther never claimed to have "the spirit of prophecy," as did Mrs. White, he was indeed a tremendous Biblical scholar and exegete, and he taught unequivocally that the creation was completed in six literal days.

Reverend Byron Nelson was a Lutheran pastor in Wisconsin who had received degrees in both science and theology. He took two years of postgraduate study in science and philosophy at Wisconsin and Rutgers, then later his Th.M. from Princeton Seminary. He was thus well qualified to enter the creation/evolution discussions of the 1920s and 1930s. He was very much impressed with Professor Price's books, having enough background in geology to understand and appreciate his case, and believing strongly enough in the Bible not to tamper with its plain meaning simply in order to accommodate the geologic-age system. His own research then led to an outstanding book on creationist geology entitled *The Deluge Story in Stone*, published in 1931. In this remarkable book, he traced the history of the flood theory of geology, showing that Price's position was not simply a minor aberration, but was essentially the same as that held by the founding fathers of geology. In addition, he discussed and analyzed many of the flood traditions held by the various nations and tribes of the world and published photographs of many of the out-of-order formations pointed out by Price. The book was published by the Augsburg Publishing House, associated with Nelson's denomination, the Norwegian Lutheran Synod.

Many years later, when Augsburg had become much more liberal in its orientation, another Lutheran-oriented company, Bethany Fellowship, brought out a new edition of *Deluge Story in Stone*, and Pastor Nelson gave me the privilege of writing the Foreword for it. When he died a few years later, Mrs. Nelson entrusted to me and ICR most of his letters and papers dealing with the Religion and Science Association, which is discussed in the next chapter. Pastor Nelson also wrote two other fine books, *After Its Kind* (1932) and *Before Abraham* (1948), on creationist biology and anthropology, respectively. In the latter, he argues strongly for an ice age after the Noahic Deluge (taking issue with Price on this point) and for long gaps in the genealogies of Genesis 5 and 11.

Concordia Theological Seminary, in St. Louis, is the key edu-

cational institution of the Missouri Synod of Lutherans, German
in background and with a strongly conservative tradition. Their
scholarly faculty, at least during this period, was solidly creationist
and Biblical, including such consecrated scholars as J. T. Mueller,
Theodore Engelder (author of *Scripture Cannot Be Broken*), and
William Arndt (author of *Bible Difficulties* and other works). The
most significant creationist works from this faculty, however, came
from Theodore Graebner and Alfred Rehwinkel.

Graebner was undoubtedly the chief spokesman for creationism
in this period among the Missouri Lutherans. He published a small
but pungent book called *Essays on Evolution* (1925) and then a
much larger work *God and the Cosmos* (1943).

Much later (though still well before the Darwin Centennial),
Alfred Rehwinkel, whose previous books had dealt with entirely
different subjects, published *The Flood* (1951), a 372-page book
following Price's flood geology approach.

Other Missouri Lutheran writers, also contributed to the creationist literature of the period. Theodore Handrich, a high school
teacher in Minnesota, wrote two useful books, *Everyday Science
for the Christian* (1947) and *Creation—Facts, Theories, and Faith*
(1953). Two very significant books from this denomination were
Genes, Genesis, and Evolution (1955), by John Klotz, and *Darwin,
Evolution, and Creation* (1959) edited by Dr. Paul Zimmerman.
The Zimmerman book included chapters by Wilbert Rusch, Raymond Surburg, and Klotz (who holds doctorates in both biology
and theology).

Not too many years later, I had the pleasant experience of joining
Dr. Klotz, Dr. Zimmerman, and Professor Rusch (as well as Burdick and Marsh) on the founding board of the Creation Research
Society. These men are all highly qualified scholars. Zimmerman's
field is chemistry, Rusch has studied in both biology and geology,
and Surburg is a seminary professor. I met Theodore Handrich on
several occasions, the first when he visited my home in Minneapolis in about 1948. Dr. Mueller once wrote a very encouraging

letter of commendation to me concerning my first book. I never had contact with the other men in this group (Graebner, Rehwinkel, etc.), but their books were excellent contributions to the creationist cause and of great interest and help to me in particular.

Two other Lutheran creationists that deserve mention are Leander S. Keyser and Herbert C. Leupold, both of them theologians and seminary professors. Keyser was very active in the modernist controversy of the 1920s, serving as a professor in the Hamma Divinity School of Wittenberg College in Ohio. He supported George McCready Price in his attacks on evolutionary geology and wrote a number of important books on apologetics, including a creationist polemic, *The Problem of Origins* (1926). Twenty years later, H. C. Leupold wrote one of the finest commentaries on Genesis ever published, his two-volume, 1220-page *Exposition of Genesis* (1949). Leupold, Professor of Old Testament at the Capital University Seminary in Columbus, Ohio, rigorously adhered to literal six-day creationism, the worldwide flood, and deluge geology as the only legitimate interpretation of the Hebrew text of Genesis.

Catholics and Creationism

There has been a continuing controversy between creationists and theistic evolutionists in the Roman Catholic denomination, just as in the various Protestant denominations. This controversy has, to some extent, been further abetted by the seemingly ambiguous Encyclical Letter of Pope Pius XII entitled *Humani Generis*, issued in August 1950.

Catholic evolutionists point to Paragraph 36 of the encyclical in support of their belief:

> For these reasons the Teaching Authority of the Church does not forbid that, in conformity with the present state of human sciences and sacred theology, research and discussions, on the part of men experienced in both fields, take place with regard

> to the doctrine of evolution, in as far as it inquires into the origin
> of the human body as coming from preexistent and living matter
> . . . for the Catholic faith obliges us to hold that souls are
> immediately created by God.

This statement plainly enough indicates that the theory of evolution is at least an open question, for Catholics to believe if they so choose, provided only they believe in the special creation of human souls. On the other hand, Catholic creationists point to the concluding sentence of this paragraph:

> Some however rashly transgress this liberty of discussion,
> when they act as if the origin of the human body from preexist-
> ing and living matter were already completely certain and
> proved by the facts which have been discovered up to now and
> by reasoning on those facts, and as if there were nothing in the
> sources of divine revelation which demands the greatest mod-
> eration and caution in this question.

Also the next paragraph, Paragraph 37, requires that Catholics believe that Adam was the first man and the father of all other men.

Humani Generis, of course, was not published until a quarter of a century after the Scopes trial. Whatever may have been the papal intent, the results have favored evolution, because evolutionism and liberalism have made tremendous gains among Catholics since that time. The extreme evolutionist priest, Teilhard de Chardin (1881-1955), whose writings were officially branded as heretical by the Church during his lifetime and even afterward, has by now somehow been largely (if not officially) rehabilitated, and his evolutionary gospel is today enthusiastically followed by multitudes of Catholics.

In the decades just prior to the encyclical, however, there were a number of excellent anti-evolutionist books by Catholic writers. I have already referred to the book *God or Gorilla*, by Alfred Watterson McCann, published first in about 1922. This book, with its devastating critique of the various fossils of the supposed ape/human intermediates that were being promoted at the time, was one of the first anti-evolution books I encountered, and it made a terrific impression on me at the time (the fall of 1942). Although McCann declined an invitation by Bryan to serve as a Scopes trial witness for the creationists, his book did contribute significantly to the creationist revival of the period.

A friend of McCann's was the British lawyer, Arnold Lunn. Although he was willing to become an evolutionist if the evidence so indicated, he always maintained—both in several books that he wrote and in a number of formal debates with evolutionists—that the scientific evidence made evolution untenable.

The most scholarly and influential of the Catholic writers of the time was George Barry O'Toole. O'Toole was a priest, but also a skilled biologist, Professor of Animal Zoology at Seton Hall College. He also served in China for a while and wrote a number of excellent articles against evolution in Catholic journals. His greatest contribution, however, was the thorough and very scholarly work entitled *The Case Against Evolution*, published by Macmillan in 1926, right after the Scopes trial.

Though the above were the best known of the writing Catholic creationists, there were many others. An extensive review of the impact of evolution on Catholic thought (actually a Ph.D. dissertation) by a Catholic nun written in 1934, included the following summary:

> Catholic writing on the subject has been from the beginning, and still is, enormous. Much has been said on evolutionism by men of every conceivable shade of opinion. Catholic writing on the subject can be said to be particularly abundant. In fact the evolution theory has been one of the most frequently discussed topics among Catholics since the time of its earliest whisperings. . . . Then, too, one must probably conclude that, as a whole, Catholic opinion leads away rather than toward evolutionism, i.e., judged on the basis of majority opinion.[1]

1. Sister Mary Frederick (Eggleston), *Religion and Evolution since 1859*. Ph.D. Diss., Notre Dame Univ. 1934. (Chicago: Loyola Univ. Press, 1935), p. 169.

Figure 6.   Byron Nelson and Harry Rimmer

Among the outstanding creationist writers of the period 1925–1950 were two scientist/theologians, both of whom had studied and practiced both in science and in the Christian ministry. Byron Nelson was a Lutheran, Harry Rimmer a Presbyterian. Rimmer was also a gifted evangelist and Bible conference speaker.

A Catholic scholar, Patrick J. O'Connell, S.J., has more recently written many articles and books, opposing evolution, the most important being *Science of Today and the Problems of Genesis*, published in 1963. O'Connell particularly was opposed to Teilhard de Chardin, accusing him not only of heresy but of dishonesty. He gave evidence to suggest not only that Teilhard was involved in the famous Piltdown Man hoax, but also that he fabricated some of the data upon which the later (now missing) Peking Man was based.

The Remarkable Dr. Rimmer

The most widely known creationist of this period was probably Dr. Harry Rimmer (1890–1952), a Presbyterian pastor and evangelist who also became something of a self-made scientist.

Although not as well known as Price or Bryan at the time of the Scopes trial (Bryan apparently did not even ask his help or advice), his books and lectures during the thirties and forties made him world famous, undoubtedly the most influential of the "fundamentalist" creationists before the Darwin Centennial.

Rimmer's formal education was very limited and heterogeneous (a year each at Hahneman College of Homeopathic Medicine, San Francisco Bible College, Whittier College, and the Bible Institute of Los Angeles); he was eventually awarded two honorary doctorates, a D.Sc. by Wheaton College and an Ll.D. by John Brown University. Like Price, however, he was an extensive reader. He also was a capable laboratory technician and built his own laboratory, so he did become quite knowledgeable in all the sciences pertaining to the question of origins.

He was an evangelist at heart and was a great public speaker, whether bringing a straight Gospel sermon, a Bible exposition, or a scientific lecture, using a variety of appealing illustrations and much humor in his messages. His audiences were often in the thousands. He was also a great personal soul-winner. Even his scientific books and lectures always had as their goal the winning of lost people to Christ. I had the privilege of belonging to the business and professional Christian group that brought him to Houston in 1943 for a week of meetings at the First Baptist Church there, and it was indeed an unforgettable week for me. I had already read most of his books by then, and it was delightful to hear him speak so effectively on these topics that had so recently become a great concern of mine.

Although he did not author as many books as George McCready Price, Harry Rimmer was quite a prolific writer, and his books were more popular and widely read than those of Price. Rimmer wrote books on prophecy, general apologetics, Bible archaeology, and other subjects, as well as on creationism. Probably the two best known creationist works were *Modern Science and the Genesis Record* (1940) and *The Theory of Evolution and the Facts of*

Science (1941). At a time when I was still wrestling with the advantages of theistic evolution in my own mind, the latter book did as much as anyone thing to convince me once and for all that evolution was false. Even though the book had some obvious scientific weaknesses and (as with all Rimmer's books) was un-necessarily laced with humorous sarcasm aimed at the evolutionists or others with whom he disagreed, the book did have more than enough solid, factual evidence and logic to settle the question for me. Rimmer also wrote two books dealing with other scientific difficulties in the Bible, *The Harmony of Science and Scripture* (1936) and *Lot's Wife and the Science of Physics* (1947). In addition, he issued many pamphlets and booklets on various relevant topics, through his Research Science Bureau, as he called it.

At the time I first encountered Rimmer's books, the whole subject of Biblical Christianity was new and exciting to me. This was right after coming back to teach at Rice Institute (now Rice University) in the fall of 1942. Trying to have an effective witness for Christ among the students (who, during World War II were mostly science and engineering students, sent there for special training by the U.S. Navy to prepare them as officers), I really needed this kind of information.

Naturally, I also thought it would be a wonderful thing if the Rice students and faculty could also hear him speak. Accordingly, I somehow got up the nerve to go ask the university president, Dr. Edgar O. Lovett, to set up such a meeting on the campus. Quoting a statement on one of Dr. Rimmer's book jackets, I assured Dr. Lovett that Rimmer was "the nation's top authority in Christian apologetics" and it would be an honor to Rice if he would speak on our campus. Before coming to Rice, however, Dr. Lovett had been Professor of Astronomy at Princeton University, and he was at least nominally familiar with the Seminary there and the great apologists on the seminary faculty (Machen, Allis, Wilson, *et al.*), so he was justifiably skeptical and reached over to check Rimmer's biography in *Who's Who in America*. Rimmer was in the book, all right, but his qualifications did not impress Dr. Lovett at all, and he declined my request. In the process, he did grill me rather intensively on such matters as creation, miracles, and the like, being especially concerned about the Bible's astronomical miracles (e.g., the long day of Joshua). He was quite knowledgeable about the Bible, even though his views were quite liberal and he was a theistic evolutionist. I have often wondered what he thought of that presumptuous young instructor and the naive answers he gave to those tough questions. He was quite a gracious gentleman, however, and patient.

In any case, although Dr. Rimmer was not allowed to speak to the whole campus, I did have him speak to our Rice Christian Fellowship group, with about 60 students present, a much smaller audience than that to which he was normally accustomed. I was happy with the turnout, because it had been an uphill battle to get such a group going on such a campus in the first place. As always, Dr. Rimmer brought an excellent message, but unfortunately he was unable to stay after the meeting. I had been eagerly looking forward to getting to know him personally, hoping to secure his guidance for what I hoped might become a future testimony in the university world somewhat like his own. No doubt he was tired from a heavy schedule, but I was disappointed. At any rate, I did have this one brief contact with the man widely recognized by fundamentalists as "the greatest Christian apologist of his generation."

Many years later, after the Institute for Creation Research was going well, Dr. Rimmer's wife sent me a copy of the biography she had recently written about her husband.[1] Dr. Rimmer had died of cancer in 1952, at the relatively young age of 62, but reading

---

1. Mignon Brandon Rimmer, *Fire Inside* (Berne, IN: Publishers Printing House, 1968), 362 pp. See also a biographical sketch by his daughter, Kathryn Rimmer Braswell, "Harry Rimmer, Defender of the Faith," Sunday School Times, 95, 28 Mar. 1953, pp. 263–264.

her account of his life is a great blessing, for few men have lived such a full and rewarding life as he. He was a great Bible teacher, flaming evangelist, fearsome debater,[1] persuasive writer, tireless worker, and—to those who knew him well—a kind, unselfish, loving person. Modern-day neo-evangelical critics who like to carp at his "Rimmerisms" are mere pygmies in comparison to such a giant.

From the perspective of the modern creationist movement, however, there was one serious weakness in Rimmer's approach (as with so many other creationists of the time). That is, while he was strongly opposed to evolutionism of any variety, he at the same time compromised on the vital issue of the age of the earth and flood geology. That was one question I *did* manage to ask him on that day long ago when he spoke to my Rice Christian Fellowship, and he also indicated this in his books.

Although he had great respect for the work of George McCready Price, agreeing that he had shown that uniformitarianism and geological dating were all wrong, and that the fossil beds had been formed catastrophically, he still believed that the earth was very old and that the Noahic Flood was only a regional flood. He was a proponent of the gap theory, with its pre-Adamic ruin corollary. He did believe in the six literal days of creation, even participating in (and, as usual, winning) two friendly debates on that topic with his good friend, Dr. W. B. Riley (who advocated the day/age theory). For some reason, he and many others—past and present—have been blind to the overwhelming Biblical and scientific problems associated with the great-age concept. Even Price allowed for the great age of the earth's core, as well as of the stars, while still insisting on a literal six-day creation, with all the fossils formed after the fall and curse. There seems (to me, at least) to be

---

1. Dr. Rimmer debated many leading evolutionists of his day, always before great crowds and always clearly winning each debate. Reading these accounts in Mrs. Rimmer's biography makes it obvious that present-day debates are amazingly similar to those of his time.

overwhelming scientific evidence—and absolutely conclusive Biblical evidence—that the entire universe was made in the six literal days of creation week.

That You Might Believe

At the time of Dr. Rimmer's visit to Rice, I was working on the manuscript for my first book. In trying to witness effectively to students on the campus, I had felt the need for a small book on practical Christian evidences—one that would include the scientific evidences for creation and the flood, as well as the general evidences for the Bible, Christ, and the gospel, all presented in an evangelistic context. I had been devouring many Christian books, on many subjects, but had not found one like that. I liked to write anyway and had once had ambitions to be a journalist, so decided to try to write one myself. The book had only one immediate purpose, that of trying to win students to Christ, so I didn't realize I was contracting an "occupational disease" that would stay with me throughout life!

Many people have asked me how a professional engineer such as myself ever got interested in writing books about evolution and creation, so maybe a brief biographical testimony might be in order at this point. I was content to be a theistic evolutionist and Sunday-morning Christian during my college days, but this began to change soon after graduation from Rice. As a junior engineer with the International Boundary and Water Commission in El Paso, with my fiancee back home in Houston, I began once again to read the Bible and think seriously about my responsibility to Christ. I had more or less ignored these matters since a few years after my conversion (which had also come about mainly through reading the Bible) and baptism as an eight-year-old boy in Corpus Christi. After my wife, Mary Louise, and I were married, we joined a sound Bible-preaching church and began trying to build a solid Christian home. We accepted jobs as teachers of junior-age Sunday School classes, and in 1942 I joined the Gideons. The latter fellowship especially encouraged me really to believe and see the saving power of the Word of God through personal witnessing for Christ.

It was also at about this time that Irwin Moon came to El Paso with his very impressive "Sermons from Science." It was not so much his visual electrical displays that impressed me, however, but a sermon dealing with fossils as caused by the flood and with the implications of the vapor canopy theory. I had never heard anything like this before, and suddenly I realized that it was really possible not only to defend the Bible against its scientific critics, but actually to use it as a reservoir of new scientific discovery.

Soon after this I was called back to Rice to teach. I had graduated "with distinction" in 1939 (the only type of special honor available to Rice graduates with high scholastic records at graduation). Also I had earned membership in the three honor societies, Phi Beta Kappa (humanities), Sigma Xi (science), and Tau Beta Pi (engineering). Consequently, even though I only had a B.S. degree plus three year's experience in hydraulic engineering on the Rio Grande, Rice officials thought I was qualified to teach undergraduates and appointed me as a full-time Instructor in Civil Engineering. In their defense, those were the war years, and good engineering teachers were in short supply; furthermore, universities then did not place nearly as much emphasis on Ph.D. degrees (especially in engineering) as they do now. I even had an invitation during those years to teach at Stanford, which I declined.

At the time of my call to Rice, I had already been approved for an Ensign's commission in the Navy Seabees. Unknown to me, however, Rice had arranged with the Navy to release me so that I could teach, since most of the male students at this time were in the Navy V–12 and ROTC programs, and Navy officials believed I would be more useful to the war effort this way. They were undoubtedly right; I would have made a very poor military man and probably would have flunked boot camp! In retrospect, this was all the Lord's doing. I had never entertained the remotest idea

Figure 7.   The Author at Rice

As an engineering student at Rice University (extreme right in top photo), the writer was a theistic evolutionist. Photo at lower left was taken on graduation day in 1939, with Mary Louise Beach, who became Mrs. Henry Morris in 1940. As an engineering teacher at Rice he soon became a strict creationist. The photo at lower right was taken at age 28, for jacket of *That You Might Believe*, written during this period.

of being a teacher, but this call to Rice was the beginning of a life-long career in education.

After arriving at Rice, I quickly felt the burden of reaching these students for Christ. They were all destined for active duty in the war immediately on graduation and, in the El Paso Gideons, I had been actively involved in witnessing to the servicemen at the army camps there, giving them Gideon Testaments and trying to lead them to Christ. Actually, quite a number of these Rice students (including my own brother, who took a night course in surveying which I taught) were killed in the later years of the war.

As mentioned before, I soon realized my need of answers in the science and apologetics areas and began to read everything I could find that seemed relevant. I read many books promoting evolution, as well as books attacking the Bible, in order to make as honest an evaluation of these key subjects as I could. On the creationist side, I found Rimmer's books, Price's *New Geology*, and some of the others mentioned previously, and these were very helpful. However, very few of these were written by real scientists with graduate degrees from recognized universities, and this was a matter of real concern to me. Furthermore, practically all of even the creationist books seemed to accept the geologic-age system, and it seemed clear even then that the gap theory and day/age theory—not even to mention the local flood theory—involved a very strange and forced type of Biblical exegesis which one would never use elsewhere in the Bible.

Finally, to try to settle this question in my own mind, I resolved to embark on a verse-by-verse search through all the Bible, listing and categorizing every passage that bore on creation, the flood, science, nature, and other relevant topics. By this time, my earlier doubts about the Bible itself had been settled. There was no doubt that it really was the very Word of God to man, inspired and inerrant throughout. I no longer believed there was any substance whatever to evolution, having become convinced of this fact almost as much by the evolutionist literature I had read as by the creationist books. The standards of evidence supporting evolution seemed ridiculously trivial compared to the evidence on which engineers have to base their systems, and also compared to the tremendous evidences for the divine origin of the Bible (fulfilled prophecy, the resurrection of Christ, etc.).

But there was still the problem of the age of the earth and the geological column. If this could be settled anywhere, it would have to be in Scripture (prehistorical events, by very definition, are beyond reach of the scientific method, as such, a fact which many evolutionists find hard to comprehend). It seemed impossible that God would have left such an important matter as this, with such profound ramifications in so many areas of life and study, unsettled in His Word. The very fact that this problem even today is still the main bone of contention in the modern creation/evolution conflict points up its importance. Surely God has the answer in His Word!

And that, of course, is exactly what my verse-by-verse study confirmed! The Bible could hardly be more explicit on this point. Everything was created and made in the six natural days of the creation week, several thousand years ago. There may be some uncertainty in the precise date, and different Bible scholars (all following the same premises) have arrived at different dates, but there is no legitimate way the Bible can be made to yield anywhere near an age of a million years ago, say, for the date of creation. Neither the gap theory, nor the day/age theory, nor the allegorical theory, nor the revelation-day theory, nor any other theory that tries to accommodate the evolutionary ages of geology will satisfy the straightforward teaching of the Bible on this vital subject.[1] Neither, for that matter, will any of them accommodate the scientific data.

This book, however, is not the place to argue these points, as I

---

1. This same study, in greater depth, has recently been made again by me, and the results published in *Biblical Creationism* (Grand Rapids: Baker Book House, 1993), 276 pp. There can be no legitimate doubt that the Bible clearly teaches a recent six-day creation of all things, as well as the world-destroying flood in the days of Noah.

have already discussed them in detail in various other books. It is enough to mention that this conviction henceforth became the basic premise of my own creationist studies and has continued so ever since, after once it was settled in my own mind that this—and this alone—was the firm teaching of Scripture. Furthermore, this has been the basis of the strength of the modern creationist movement, and uncertainty on this point has been the real reason why earlier creationist defenses (including that of Bryan at the Scopes trial) have fallen by the wayside. But more of this later.

At the time when I came to this conclusion, my book was already in the process of publication, and although it did include the evidence for flood geology and a very brief outline of evidences for a young earth, it also allowed the possibility of the "gap theory" as a means of accommodating a great age for the earth. I soon regretted this, of course, and rejected the gap theory and all other such accommodationist views in my later books.

Since the primary purpose of the book was evangelistic, I entitled it *That You Might Believe* (taken, of course, from John 20:31). It was not easy to get it published. I was an unknown author with only a B.S. degree, and it would be a risk for any publisher. I offered it first to Zondervan, since I knew Pat Zondervan personally through the Gideons. However, after a long delay, they turned it down. (Pat told me, many years later, that they had often regretted that decision.) I then offered it to Stacey Woods, head of the Inter-Varsity Christian Fellowship, since I also knew him personally. Our Rice Christian Fellowship had affiliated in 1945 with Inter-Varsity, thus becoming one of the first IVCF chapters in the United States. We had seen many real conversions among the students (at least 50 during my last year there, out of a student body of only 1200, including many of the student leaders), even though Rice had a highly liberal and intellectual reputation. All of this, of course, had been accomplished without any compromise on strict creationism or full Biblical inerrancy, perspicuity, and authority.

Stacey liked the book (as well as the fruitful results that had been demonstrated among the students with a no-compromise approach), but IVCF was not yet into book publishing in this country, so he got Clyde Dennis, founder and president of the Good News tract publishing company, to undertake it. Good News was just in the process of setting up a book publishing division, Good Books, Inc., and I believe my book was the first (possibly the second) book which they published.

However, they would only do it if I would agree to underwrite the first 500 copies. I was quite unable to do this myself, but a good Gideon friend, W. S. Mosher, president of the Mosher Steel Co., agreed to lend me the money, so the contract was signed.

That You Might Believe was finally published in the early spring of 1946. The war was over and things were changing. I knew I would be leaving at the end of that school year to start graduate studies. I had been working on the manuscript since early 1943 and teaching the materials in it all that time, so many students were looking forward to it. Mr. Mosher would not accept repayment, telling me simply to give away the 500 copies. I gave copies to all the IVCF and BSU students and offered copies to all the students in my engineering classes, and to anyone else who would come to my office and request one. (I had been making a similar offer of Gideon Testaments for several years, so the students were not too surprised.) I also gave copies to many—probably most—of the Rice faculty. I had witnessed to many of these men, without much response, and had never found anyone else on the faculty who was a Bible-believing Christian, let alone a creationist. The same was true with almost all secular faculties at the time. The number of Bible-believing Christian faculty members discovered either by Inter-Varsity or the Baptist Student Unions around the country was almost nil.

The response to my book offer was tremendous. A constant stream of students came to request copies, and a number of conversions followed, both before and after I left Rice. Even several faculty members wrote letters of appreciation, telling how the book had helped them. Mr. Mosher was very pleased. I have continued to receive many letters through all these years telling how this first book of mine has changed lives.

The credit must go to the Lord, of course. Only 156 pages long, by an unknown, uncredentialed author, published as a first venture by a small religious company, the book certainly was not very promising. Amateurish in many ways, it presumed to go against the all-but-universal opinion of the scientific and educational establishments. So far as I know, it was the first book (at least since the Scopes trial, if not since Darwin) published by a member of the science faculty of a secular university which was presumptuous enough to advocate flood geology and a recent creation, as well as absolute Biblical authority and inerrancy.

With all its faults, the Lord wonderfully blessed it. It received good reviews in various Christian periodicals and seemed to fill a need that had existed for many years. One result that would bear special fruit was at Princeton University, where it was read in February 1947 by a promising young student named John Whitcomb. He had accepted Christ as a freshman at the university in 1943, and now, after military service in Europe, was one of the student leaders (under Donald B. Fullerton) of the Princeton Evangelical Fellowship. Dr. Richard Seume had been pastor of my church in Houston and had reviewed the manuscript of *That You Might Believe* before it was published. He had moved to a church in Paterson, New Jersey, about the same time I moved to Minneapolis, and he had arranged to give copies (from Mr. Mosher's stock) to the Christian students there, including John Whitcomb. Dr. Seume specifically mentioned John's name and his great interest in the book, in writing to me about it afterward, and I tried to answer certain questions John had raised. John and I would eventually meet six years later, at Grace Seminary in Indiana and then, soon afterward, would come to collaborate in writing *The Genesis Flood*.

Eventually, the publishers suggested that I expand and update the book for a new edition. I worked on the revisions while I was simultaneously working on my doctoral dissertation at the University of Minnesota, and then it was published just after I had completed this work and moved to Louisiana, as Professor and Head of the Civil Engineering Department at Southwestern Louisiana Institute (now the University of Southwestern Louisiana). By this time Moody Press had bought the book from Good Books, Inc. Since it had a new publisher and was 25% longer than before, Ken Taylor (who was Director of Moody Press at the time, but who later founded the Tyndale Publishing House) persuaded me to change the name to *The Bible and Modern Science*. It was published in 1951.

The book was still primarily evangelistic in thrust, and God continued to use it as a soul-winning ministry. The first words in the Preface were as follows:

> The purpose of this book, very frankly and without apology, is to win people to a genuine faith in Jesus Christ as the eternal Son of God and their personal Savior, and to assist in strengthening the faith of those who have already received Him in this light. It is especially addressed to young people who are finding biblical Christianity under serious attack in many quarters in these days, nowhere more so than in the classes and textbooks of most of our colleges and universities, and even in the public schools.[1]

That same paragraph, though originally written almost 50 years ago, could still apply to every book I have written since, even those which are strictly scientific in content. The need is at least as great as then, even though we have seen the Lord raise up a great number of creationist scientists and other scholarly professionals since that time.

Sometime later, the Moody people decided the book would have

---

1. Henry M. Morris, *The Bible and Modern Science* (Chicago: Moody Press, 1951), p. 3.

even a wider ministry if it were placed in their Colportage Library of inexpensive paperbacks. However, this required a significant reduction in size, so much had to be eliminated. I also revised and updated it again, and this edition was published in 1956, just after I had moved to Southern Illinois University. There, once again, I had a great time giving away copies to all students who would request them. I could afford to do this myself now, in view of the very low cost of the books in the Colportage Library.

About a dozen years later, I again revised and updated the book. Altogether, it went through at least 35 printings. Then, Moody asked me again to update it, and it was completely rewritten and issued under the new title *Science and the Bible,* in a larger and more attractive format, in 1986.[1] This new edition has already gone through twelve printings (as of 1993). All in all this book, under its three different titles, has been the most widely used of all my books, with God's blessings abundantly manifest.

The book was even reissued in 1978 for a few years by the Good News Publishers under the original title, *That you Might Believe*, with Moody's approval, of course.[2] This time I used the enlarged cloth edition of 1951 as the starting point. My old pastor, Dick Seume (later Chaplain at Dallas Seminary, and now with the Lord) wrote the Foreword for this edition.

Other American Creationists of the Period

In addition to those already discussed (Price, Rimmer, etc.) there were a number of other men writing and speaking on creationism during this "creation underground" period between 1925 and 1960. One who played a significant part in my own life was Dr. Arthur I. Brown who, like the others mentioned in this section, is best

---

1. *Science and the Bible* (Chicago: Moody Press, 1986), 154 pp.

2. Henry M. Morris, *That You Might Believe* (Westchester, IL: Good News Publishers, 1978), 188 pp.

described as a "fundamentalist." I have discussed the Seventh-Day Adventists, Lutherans, and Catholics separately, since these groups don't fit the fundamentalist category very well. The Baptists, Presbyterians, Brethren, non-denominationalists, and various other groups, particularly the conservative evangelicals in each body, have tended more or less to work together, at least in the creation/evolution and fundamentalist/modernist controversies. Dr. Harry Rimmer, Dr. William B. Riley, Dr. W. H. Griffith Thomas, Dr. R. A. Torrey, and other such men have already been mentioned as leaders in this group. More competent as a scientist than any of these, however, was Arthur I. Brown.

Dr. Brown was an M.D. and for many years was a practicing physician in Vancouver, B.C., until he felt the Lord calling him into a full-time Bible Conference ministry. He was a wonderful teacher of the Word, and I had the privilege of hearing him speak several times at the Powderhorn Park Baptist Church in Minneapolis, just after we had moved from Houston in order for me to teach and do graduate work at the University of Minnesota. This was in the fall of 1946. We were looking for a church, and his meetings introduced us to the Powderhorn Church, which we joined soon afterward. Dr. Brown's messages were a great blessing right at that time to me, especially one on the sufferings of Christ, but they were also a blessing to multitudes all over the United States and Canada.

But it was his writings that were of still greater impact. He wrote a series of anti-evolution booklets that were well-documented and most effective, plus several fine books, including *Footprints of God* (1943), *Miracles of Science* (1945), and *God's Masterpiece—Man's Body* (1946). In addition, he wrote at least three excellent, well documented books on prophecy and the signs of the times, plus many articles and tracts.

After I met him and began to correspond with him, it turned out that he believed the gap theory, although this subject did not come up in his books. He was not a geologist, of course, so did not understand the basis of the geological-age system very well. Like Rimmer, he thought the evidence was stronger than it really is. I believe if he had lived a little longer, he would have come to understand this better. He died in a tragic automobile accident in November 1947.

When I first met him in Minneapolis, I had an unforgettable interview with him one night at his downtown hotel. He had already been using and widely recommending my book *That You Might Believe,* so he seemed quite willing to talk with me. I had just come to the University to try to get an M.S. and a Ph.D. degree, knowing that I would need these if I were to stay in teaching, which I thought was the Lord's will. However, Dr. Brown had been preaching on the imminent return of Christ, and the last chapter of my own book had dealt with that subject. The atomic bomb had just been released on an unprepared world, and it really looked like the end was near. Consequently, I really wondered if I should spend who-knew-how-many-years in acquiring further secular education, when the Lord might well return momentarily. Wouldn't it be better to devote all the few remaining months or years to winning people to Christ, possibly even going to some closed field as a nonprofessional missionary? I really expected Dr. Brown to advise me to leave engineering, as he had medicine, and get at the more urgent task of snatching souls, as brands, from the burning!

Instead, he fervently advised me to stay with my graduate studies! My testimony and influence would be greatly increased and more productive in the long run thereby, and we had no way of knowing when the Lord would return. The greatest need of the Christian world today, he assured me, was not more preachers or missionaries or lay witnesses, but dedicated Bible-believing scientists who were willing to undertake the hard training and study needed to bring science, with all its tremendous influence over the minds of men and women everywhere, back to God.

This was good advice, and I set about to follow it. Over the years, there have been many promising young Christian students who have come to me with essentially the same question, and I have given them the same answer (subject, of course, to the proviso, "unless the Lord clearly leads otherwise"). I still believe in the closely imminent return of Christ and have kept the plaque "Perhaps Today" on my office wall for fifty years, but we should nevertheless live and plan and work on the assumption that He still may not return for many years.

I still feel the sense of loss I felt when I received a letter from Mrs. Brown late in 1947 telling me of his tragic death. He had become a true friend and counselor. I still have the well-marked book he loaned me, Douglas Dewar's *Difficulties of the Evolution Theory*. Mrs. Brown insisted I keep it, to remember him by. But I would never have forgotten him regardless. He was perhaps the most godly, gracious Christian gentleman I ever met, as well as one of the finest Bible teachers and creationist scientists. The Lord used him at a critical time in my own life, and I look forward to renewing our friendship when the Lord *does* come!

Another man well worth mentioning is Carl Theodore Schwarze, for many years Professor of Civil Engineering at New York University. When I read his book *The Harmony of Science and the Bible* (1942), I was teaching civil engineering at Rice, so naturally I felt a real kinship to him. He was obviously a fine scientist and also a fundamentalist. I wrote him a long letter of appreciation and testimony, but did not receive a reply. He also wrote a number of other books, including *The Marvels of Earth's Canopies*. He believed in a worldwide flood, brought on by the collapse of an ice canopy, but also in an ancient earth and in the gap theory.

After his retirement, he lived in Lafayette, Louisiana, for several years, trying to witness to the Catholics there and to establish a church. He did win a number and started a Plymouth Brethren assembly. When I came to Lafayette in 1951, he was no longer there—in fact, had gone to be with the Lord—but I did meet many people who had known him, and they spoke highly of him. These included Rev. and Mrs. E. H. Gillespie (daughter of Dr. Griffith Thomas, previously mentioned), who were continuing some of his work.

Another fundamentalist creationist was L. Allen Higley, Ph.D., best known probably as the author of *Science and Truth,* an extensive defense and exposition of the gap theory and then the work of the six literal creation days. Higley was Chairman of the Science Division at Wheaton College during the 1930s, and also president of the Religion and Science Association during its brief existence in the mid-thirties. By all accounts, he also was a very gracious Christian gentleman.

Another important creationist was apparently of an altogether different temperament. This was Dudley Joseph Whitney (1884–1964). Whitney had a B.S. degree in Agricultural Chemistry from the University of California (Berkeley) in 1907 and was editor of various agricultural journals over a long period of time. Through his own personal study, Whitney also became very knowledgeable in geology and firmly committed to flood geology, following Price in almost every particular. Whitney was a deacon in a nondenominational charismatic church. He spent most of his life at his farm at Exeter, California, in the foothills of the Sierra Nevadas, while simultaneously writing for both agricultural journals and Christian periodicals.

Whitney, at least judging from his letters, was irascible and highly impatient with anyone who disagreed with him about almost anything. Nevertheless, he was an incisive thinker and made many highly valuable contributions to scientific creationism and flood geology. I never met him personally, nor did I ever know anyone who had, but we did carry on a rather voluminous correspondence for about fifteen years, until his death in the mid-sixties. He and I were in full agreement on most matters, but he did take strong exception to my advocating the canopy theory and a post-Flood glacial period (both being positions which I still favor but have always considered to be open questions).

Whitney had always maintained a firm Biblical and creationist faith and was a real "fighting fundamentalist," if there ever were such a thing. Even though subject to strong evolutionary indoctrination in his biology classes at Berkeley, he still considered evolutionism to be the rankest nonsense. It was not until he read one of George McCready Price's books, however, that he decided the "geological ages" also were nonsense. This was in about the mid-twenties, and for over 35 years after that he held the highest disdain for "ages geology," pouring forth a stream of articles and letters with multitudinous evidences for a young earth and world-wide flood. He was perpetually agitated—justifiably so—that none of his many critics would ever attempt to answer his scientific arguments. The following is a typical example of his rhetoric, directed in this instance against the members of the American Scientific Affiliation:

> As to my being uncharitable for condemning Christians for promoting unscriptural doctrine, I need only quote from Isaiah 58:1 "Cry aloud, spare not, and shew my people their sins." I obey that charge. It is absurd to try to combine piety and theological orthodoxy with disbelief in Genesis.[1]

Whitney wrote a whole stream of articles in such creationist publications as *The Bible Champion, Christian Faith and Life, Prophetic Monthly,* and others. However, he was also one of the few creationists in modern times who was able to get solidly scientific, frankly creationist, articles in established journals. In 1935, he published an article defending a young earth in the prestigious *Annual Report of the Committee on Geologic Time,* the paper having been invited by Dr. Alfred C. Lane, the eminent geologist who was chairman of the committee. He also had several excellent articles published in The *Pan-American Geologist,* as did George McCready Price. However, this open policy on the part of

---

1. D. J. Whitney, *The Creationist*, No. 8 (Malveme, NY: Christian Evidence League, Aug. 1952), p. 1.

the Editor of that journal proved very costly. Most of the subscribers to The *Pan-American Geologist* were, of course, orthodox evolutionary geologists, and the publication of these articles produced such a prejudicial reaction that the journal finally had to close down. Or at least that was what Dr. George Thiel, Head of the University of Minnesota Department of Geology, told our class in "Sedimentation" when I was taking my graduate work there.

Whitney was a very original and astute thinker. He was especially gifted at discerning evidences of a young earth and solar system in a wide range of geological, geochemical, and geophysical processes. Many of the evidences of recent creation that have been cited by me and other modern writers were originally suggested by Whitney.

So far as I can find, he only published two books, *The Case for Creation* (1946), and *The Face of the Deep* (1955). The second he had to finance himself and neither was read very widely.

I used to tell him that he might convince more people if he were more gentle and kind in his approach. I said that these evangelicals who compromised with "ages geology" were sincere Christians and would believe the truth if only they could be lovingly shown that Scripture and true science teach recent literal creation and deluge geology. However, more years and experience have shown me that he was right after all. Regardless of the fact that the Bible teaches it, these men will believe in recent creation if and when the scientific establishment accepts it, and not before, so that they won't have to take an unpopular stand against their "peers."

There were many other American creationists who stood strong against evolution in this period, and it would not be practicable to mention all of them, even if I knew about all of them. A pastor, Rev. William A. Williams, wrote a unique book, *Evolution Scientifically Disproved* (1928). This was the first book, so far as I know, to apply probability calculations against random evolutionary processes, and also to use population growth statistics as an argument for the very recent origin of the human race.

B. H. Shadduck, Ph.D., applied a remarkable talent in a widely used series of humorous cartoon booklets against evolution (*The Toadstool Among the Tombs, Puddle to Paradise*, etc.). Clarence H. Benson, especially known as a Christian educator, was also an active anti-evolutionist, with two well-known books, *Immensity* (1937) and *The Earth - The Theater of the Universe* (1938).

A gifted young scholar, Dan Gilbert, wrote several dynamic antimodernist books with strong implications of conspiracy, all well documented. The most important from my point of view was *Evolution, The Root of All Isms* (1942). Gilbert later died tragically, shot in a domestic scandal, amidst unproven charges that he was framed for assassination.

Dr. William J. Tinkle, with a Ph.D. in biology from Ohio State, wrote a textbook, *Fundamentals of Zoology* (1939) with a creationist framework. He later became active in the American Scientific Affiliation, and eventually was one of the founding members of the Creation Research Society.

A Presbyterian missionary scholar supported strict creationism and flood geology in a prestigious book on Christian evidences. His name was Floyd E. Hamilton and his book was *The Basis of Evolutionary Faith* (1946). Another Presbyterian missionary statesman, Samuel M. Zwemer, wrote many books on Muslim missions, as well as Christian evidences. He was also a Princeton Theological Seminary professor, in which capacity he wrote a creationist masterpiece which should have devastated all evolutionary concepts of religion, entitled *The Origin of Religion* (1945).

The above is not a complete listing, of course, but is at least representative and does include the most significant writers of the period. It is obvious that the modern creation movement has many roots and is not an overnight phenomenon. The road between the Scopes trial and the Darwinian Centennial may have seemed to be leading through a wilderness of evolutionary humanism, but there were still many voices of protest crying in the wilderness.

In Other Lands

In England, the land of Darwin, the Lord also had witnesses, even though there was never a revival of creationism like that in America before the Scopes trial. Much of the creationist testimony centered in the activities and publications of the Victoria Institute and the Evolution Protest Movement. The former has already been discussed and the latter will be introduced in a later chapter. A few of the key personnel will be mentioned in this section.

Sir John Ambrose Fleming has already been recognized, not only as one of the century's foremost scientists, but also as a strong creationist, one-time president of the Victoria Institute, as well as founder and president of the Evolution Protest Movement. His book *Evolution or Creation*? (1935) is considered a classic.

The most prolific creationist writer in England was probably Douglas Dewar (1875–1957). He was a Cambridge science graduate, later studied law, then spent many years in the civil service in India. He became an authoritative ornithologist, writing over 22 books on Indian birds and Indian history. He was an evolutionist until he was about 55 years old, when his intensive study of ornithology convinced him that evolution could not be true. His most important creationist books were *Man: A Special Creation* (1926), *Difficulties in the Evolution Theory* (1931), *More Difficulties in the Evolution Theory* (1938), and *The Transformist Illusion* (1957). Although he was a devastating critic of evolution, he felt he could not accept flood geology and advocated a form of the gap theory. He entered into lengthy correspondence on this point with Whitney, but always remained unconvinced that the Biblical flood could account for most of the geological strata.

He was a close associate of Col. L. Merson Davies, Ph.D., a creationist geologist of considerable training and experience in geology. He was a catastrophist, attempting to explain part of the geological column by the supposed pre-Adamic cataclysm and part by the Flood, influencing Dewar in this regard. He is the only geologist about whom I have ever heard or read who gave any credence to the gap theory, and his exegesis, both Biblical and scientific, was extremely forced. He and Dewar once engaged J. B. S. Haldane, the eminent geneticist, in a written debate (published as *Is Evolution A Myth?* in 1956). He also wrote *The Bible and Modern Science* (1943).

Another important British writer was Dr. A. Rendle-Short, Professor of Surgery at the University of Bristol. An advocate of the day/age theory, Dr. Rendle-Short nevertheless wrote effectively against evolution and for the Bible in such books as *Modern Discovery and the Bible* (1942), *The Bible and Modern Medicine* (1953), and *Wonderfully Made* (1951).

Robert E. D. Clark, a British Ph.D. physical chemist, has written a number of excellent books over a long span of years. He was one of the first Christians to write effectively about the entropy principle (which he called "the Law of Morpholysis") as a powerful argument against evolution. This was in a 1943 Victoria Institute paper, later amplified in his book *Darwin—Before and after* (1948).[1] Clark has also written a number of other fine books, but he also—like almost all British writers since Lyell—still assumes that the evolutionists' geological age system is inviolable.

Just about the only Britisher who insisted on recent creation and flood geology was Major E. C. Wren, who wrote at least two small but incisive books on this theme—*Four Worlds* (1946) and *The Case for Creation* (1949). His writing style was marked by pungency and impatience with compromises on these issues, much

---

1. Various writers have either credited me (or accused me, depending on viewpoint) of being the first to espouse this argument. In my 1946 book, I made the brief statement that: "As might be shown by numerous illustrations, the universal law of nature, unaided by man, seems to be stability or degeneration rather than evolution" (p. 48). A more extended discussion was given in my 1951 book (pp. 69–71), following Clark. However, I first encountered the idea in various books by Inge, Jeans, and Eddington, who wrote long before either Clark or me. It is my understanding that Lord Kelvin and others also wrote on this topic in the nineteenth century.

like that of D. J. Whitney in America.

In countries other than Britain, the Indian biologist, Professor H. Enoch, was noteworthy. He served many years as Professor of Zoology in Madras University, was very active in student evangelistic work in the Indian schools, and published his fine work *Evolution or Creation*? in 1966, as well as many earlier articles. My associate, Dr. Duane Gish, on a speaking tour through India in 1983, had the privilege of meeting Dr. Enoch, retired and quite elderly then. He died a few years later.

A Swedish writer of great importance was Dr. D. N. Heribert-Nilsson, Professor of Botany at Lund University and Director of the Swedish Botanical Institute. His 1300-page *Synthetische Artbildung* (1954) was one of the most devastating indictments of evolution ever written. An English summary of the book was published by the Canadian branch of the Evolution Protest Movement in 1973. Strangely enough, Dr. Heribert-Nilsson still professed belief in some mysterious form of quantum theistic evolution, even though his book utterly demolished any scientific evidence for evolution.

Mention should be made of Dr. John Howitt, a hospital psychiatrist and superintendent in Canada, who wrote a small booklet entitled *Evolution: Science Falsely So Called*. The booklet was well documented and frequently updated; it has gone through over 20 editions, with more than a quarter-million copies distributed. For many years, because of the danger of professional reprisals, it was published anonymously. It had a strong influence in making Dr. Duane Gish such an ardent advocate of creationism.

In Germany, there was Dr. Albert Fleischmann, Professor of Zoology and Comparative Anatomy at Erlangen University, who wrote *Die Descendenz Theorie* in 1933, a strong creationist work. Louis Vialleton, Professor of Zoology at the Medical Faculty in Montpellier, wrote *Illusion Transformists* (1929), and another French scientist, geologist Paul Lemoine wrote in 1939 (in the French encyclopedia) that "evolution is a kind of dogma which the priests no longer believe, but which they maintain for their people."

In Italy there were, among others, D. Carazzi, Professor of Zoology at the University of Padua, and Guilio Fano, Director of the Institute of Osteology and General Physiology at the University of Rome. In South Africa there were entomologist Desmond P. Murray and Dr. Duyvene De Wit, Professor of Zoology at the University of the Orange Free State.

This is only a sampling, of course. There is no question that the great majority of scientists in each country during this period (as in all other periods since Darwin) were evolutionists. Nevertheless, God "left not Himself without witness" (Acts 14:17). This is a divine principle for every time and place.

Chapter IV

Creationist Associations Before the Centennial

For most of the first half of the twentieth century, at least in America, creationists made no particular efforts to organize into a coherent movement. The modernist-fundamentalist controversy occupied the center of attention in the Christian world, and the evolution-creation question was only one somewhat peripheral aspect of this greater issue in the minds of most Christians of the time. Most of the leading creationist writers and speakers were primarily preachers or evangelists, and few seemed to understand the truly foundational nature of creationism in respect to Biblical Christianity on the one hand, or of evolutionism in respect to humanism and all forms of anti-Christianity on the other hand. Such organizations as were formed (and there were multitudes of them—missions, schools, societies, publications, etc., as well as churches and denominations) were built around certain key doctrines, such as the inspiration of the Bible, the deity of Christ, and the substitutionary atonement; but seldom was any creationist tenet explicitly stated in their doctrinal creeds. This tacit neglect of creationism became even more pervasive after the embarrassment of the Scopes trial. More and more of even the fundamentalist leaders were either ignoring or compromising with evolution.

So far as I have been able to find, the first attempt to develop an explicitly creationist organization was made by Dr. Harry Rimmer, who established what he called the Research Science Bureau in 1921. Through his meetings, he solicited and obtained a fair number of memberships for this organization, but the Bureau consisted essentially of just Rimmer himself and a small laboratory which he had set up in his home. The organization apparently held no meetings and had no other officers, but it did publish and distribute a succession of booklets on various Bible/science topics, all written by Dr. Rimmer.

The Religion and Science Association

The first real creationist organization in this country was evidently the Religion and Science Association, organized in the summer of 1935 primarily through the efforts of Dudley Joseph Whitney, encouraged and assisted by George McCready Price and Byron Nelson. The stated purpose of the organization, according to its published constitution, was as follows:

> The purpose of this association shall be to investigate various problems of science in their relation to religious belief, particularly their relations to the Holy Scriptures, and to make public the findings of such investigations.

A statement of the philosophy of the Religion and Science Association was also incorporated into its constitution, as follows:

> The officers and members assert their disagreement with the principle of evolution which governs so much of the thinking of modern scientists, this principle being that nature must be interpreted solely in terms of commonplace or "natural" processes, through the alleged action of matter upon matter in accordance with the so-called "properties" of matter. In opposition to this naturalistic philosophy, the officers and members affirm their conviction that the various phenomena of nature are only the objectified ways in which the God of nature conducts the affairs of His universe; that He is not hampered by any so-called "laws" of nature or "properties" of matter; and that He has often made matter act in ways that transcend what we call the natural processes. They affirm their belief that definite acts of fiat creation were used in the origin and the ordering of this earth and its inhabitants, and also in the rest of the universe. They also affirm that the Bible account of the origin and history

of the earth and of mankind is correct and should be believed.

The three chief organizers (Whitney, Price, Nelson) fully intended the association to be committed to six-day creation and flood geology, explicitly repudiating both the gap theory and the day-age theory. However, they made the mistake of recruiting Dr. L. Allen Higley, Chairman of the Department of Chemistry and Geology at Wheaton College, as one of the founding directors and then, at Price's suggestion, making him their first President. Nelson became Vice-President and Whitney, Secretary-Treasurer. Because of his previous visibility as a controversial creationist, Price thought it best that he himself serve only as a director.

There is some indication from the early correspondence[1] that Higley was selected by Price primarily because of the prestige his name might bring to the organization. Creationist scientists with *bona fide* academic credentials were few and far between at that time, and Higley did have a Ph.D., as well as a prestigious position at what many evangelicals thought was the nation's leading Christian college. Furthermore, they did not realize the intensity of his commitment to the gap theory, thinking that they would be able fairly easily to convince him of the fallacies of the geological age system once the Association began to function. Higley was a firm creationist and believed in a worldwide Flood, but he persisted in believing that the Flood had left no geological evidences. All the geological strata and fossil beds, he insisted, had been formed by the supposed pre-Adamic judgment on a previous world which had been controlled by Satan for a billion years or so.

The Association was to have two other directors. After being turned down by two outstanding Presbyterian theologians, J. Gresham Machen, formerly at Princeton Seminary and later at Westminster Seminary, and J. D. Eggleston, President of

---

1. Mrs. Byron Nelson donated her husband's Association correspondence to ICR after his death in 1970. Copies of most of the correspondence between the various directors had been sent to all of them, so this contained a fairly comprehensive file of the relevant data on the Association.

Hampden-Sydney College in Virginia (both men expressed agreement with the organization, but were too busy), they finally settled on Dr. Theodore Graebner, Professor of Philosophy and New Testament at Concordia Lutheran Seminary in St. Louis, and Harold W. Clark, M.A., Professor of Biology at the Seventh-Day Adventist Pacific Union College in California. Price at this time was Professor of Geology at the Adventists' Walla Walla College in Washington, Nelson was a Lutheran pastor in Oconomowoc, Wisconsin, and Whitney was busy writing, as well as editing his agricultural journal in California. This was hardly a prestigious group, scientifically speaking, but all had written influential books or articles on creationism and were well known to the active creationists of the day.

A few other articulate creationists became active members of the Association, including Dr. Leander S. Keyser, Professor of Systematic Theology at Wittenberg College in Ohio; John Leedy, Professor of Botany at Wheaton College; Rev. Clarence Benson, of Moody Bible Institute; and Dr. Hawley Taylor, Chairman of Physics and Mathematics at Wheaton College.

The organization's constitution provided for two categories of membership. Active members were those who either (1) held a position in some recognized institution of learning; or (2) had special training in natural science; or (3) had made a special study of some scientific problem which had a direct bearing on religious faith. Anyone could be an associate member by paying a one-dollar fee. Both grades of members, of course, were expected to subscribe to the constitution.

Despite the Association's good purpose and easy membership requirements, it never acquired many members, never published the journal that was planned, and only held one of its proposed annual conventions. The latter was held in Moody Church in Chicago on March 27 and 28, 1936, and included papers by each of the six directors, plus papers by Benson, Keyser, Leedy, and Taylor. In addition, there were papers or addresses by Dr. Glenn

Cole, Professor of Social and Political Science at Wheaton College, Dr. W. H. Haas, Professor of Geography and Geology at Northwestern University, Dr. W. Bell Dawson, Professor of Geology at McGill University, and Dr. Harry Rimmer. Attendance at the meeting was excellent.

The program was evidently mostly set up by Dr. Higley, since the three founders would never have approved of several of the speakers. Bell Dawson, like his father, the famous J. William Dawson, was an advocate of the day-age theory. Dr. Haas had apparently been invited simply to present the orthodox geological position on the geological ages, placing them in a theistic evolutionary context (so far as I can find, the papers of the convention were never published, although an unsuccessful attempt was made by some of the directors to get the Moody Bible Institute Colportage Library to publish them in book form). Whitney was quite unimpressed with Dr. Rimmer, to say the least, using highly uncomplimentary language about Rimmer in his letters to Nelson and others. What the opinion of the other leaders of the Association may have been about Rimmer I do not know, but, in any case, he was never even considered as a possible director of the Association, in spite of the fact that he was easily the best-known creationist of the day.

Rimmer, like Higley, was a strong proponent of the gap theory, which all the other directors of the Religion and Science Association considered to be utter foolishness, both Biblically and scientifically. Whitney, Price, Clark, and Nelson all believed in flood geology, of course. Graebner felt he could not accept flood geology, but he was also firmly committed to literal six-day creationism, just as Martin Luther had been, so he also rejected both the day-age theory and the gap theory. He used the standard geological nomenclature, but without the age connotations, taking the position that the true causes of the geologic strata would have to be determined through future research.

One result of the convention was that at least seven members of the Wheaton College faculty joined the Association. This was probably a mixed blessing, as far as the founders were concerned, for few, if any, of the Wheaton people were willing to accept flood geology. Higley's book *Science and Truth,* published several years later, was surely one of the strongest expositions of the gap theory ever published, and Rimmer, one of its ablest popular defenders, was awarded an honorary doctorate by Wheaton.

At the same time, the president of Wheaton College during this period was Dr. J. Oliver Boswell, Jr., one of the most ardent and capable defenders of the day-age theory of that or any other generation. Thus the Wheaton faculty, whether using the gap theory or the day-age theory, has been committed to the geological-age system for over 55 years, and it has had profound influence on the entire Christian community, first through the Religion and Science Association, and later through the American Scientific Affiliation, in persuading thousands of evangelicals to follow down this fatal path of compromise with evolutionism.

In any case, this convention was apparently the only public activity ever sponsored by the Association, although its founders had great hopes and plans for it at one time. Before another year had rolled around, the Association had disintegrated and died.

The membership after a year (by September 1936) had only grown to 56,[1] of which 31 were active members and 25 were associate members. An attempt was made to determine the numbers who believed in strict creationism (with flood geology), the day-age theory, and the gap theory. Not many questionnaires were returned, but the sample received indicated a more or less even division between the three views.

These divisions began to be more and more abrasive among the officers. Quite an extensive and increasingly heated correspondence developed between President Higley, defending the gap theory, and the others—especially Price and Whitney—who real-

---

1.   Letter from Secretary D. J. Whitney to the Directors, Sep. 26, 1936.

ized that any compromise with the geological ages was a dangerous concession to evolution, and that the gap theory, in particular, was theological confusion as well. Another conflict also developed, of somewhat lesser proportions, between Nelson and Whitney, Nelson arguing for the special creation of each species and Whitney insisting that the created "kinds" of Genesis were significantly broader than the species.

Furthermore, the various directors began to lose interest in working in the organization at all, desiring to have someone else elected to their respective positions. Price (as well as Higley) was 65 years old, complaining of health and fatigue; Whitney thought that the job of secretary should be held by someone in the east or midwest; and Nelson wanted to resign so he could take a more active part in the liberal/conservative battle in his own denomination. By this time, Whitney had begun to argue that Higley should be voted out as president in favor of Price, because of Higley's gap theory commitment, but Price disagreed.

By March of 1937, the organization seemed to be falling apart. Whether there was ever any formal decision to disband is not clear. In any case, Whitney and Price, whose concerns and energies had gotten the organization started and going in the first place, finally decided it was never going to accomplish anything with such sharp differences of opinion on basic issues, and they would do better devoting their remaining years to more productive pursuits. Without these two leaders pushing it, the others were not that concerned anyway, and the Association finally died.

The abortive history of the Religion and Science Association at least provided a significant lesson or two for the future. The most obvious was that compromise for expediency's sake does not work. Without Higley, Dawson, the Wheaton men, and others who wanted to compromise with the geological-age system, the founders feared the Association would be too weak and would not survive. As it turned out, it did not survive precisely because these compromisers *were* in it, and soon came to dominate it. Another weakness, of course, was the scarcity of qualified creationist scientists. This was not the fault of the Association, however. Such people apparently did not even exist in any significant numbers in those days. The Religion and Science Association was a noble and needed pioneering venture, and the seeds which were sown would eventually bear fruit.

The Creation-Deluge Society

George McCready Price, Dudley Joseph Whitney, and Harold Clark may have given up on the Religion and Science Association, but they still felt the need for an organization with the same purpose, yet more firmly committed to strict creationism and the worldwide, geologically significant flood of Noah. Therefore, they soon set about organizing another society which would meet these specifications.

In this they were helped by the enthusiastic support of Captain Benjamin Franklin Allen, a retired army officer and a relatively late recruit to the predecessor Association. Allen (like Price and Clark) was a strong Seventh-Day Adventist and had been profoundly influenced by Price's books. He also had considerable legal training and was a skillful logician and persuasive writer. After starting in civil engineering, he finished with an A.B. and then with the Ll.B. from the University of Arkansas. He worked in the office of the Arkansas Secretary of State for several years. He was a confirmed bachelor, about 45 years old at that time, and in his army experience had done much geological field work.

He had been vigorously promoting flood geology among the Adventists for several years, with considerable success. In 1938, Price also retired from full-time teaching and moved to Pomona, California. This was adjacent to Loma Linda, where the Adventists now have a fine university (Loma Linda University, with excellent graduate and undergraduate science programs, many of which teach creationism), which includes an excellent medical school.

The predecessor of this medical school was known as the College of Medical Evangelists, then located in Los Angeles, and many fine medical researchers, medical missionaries, and practicing physicians received their training there. Soon after moving to Pomona, Price was invited to give a ten-week series of lectures on creationism and flood geology at the College of Medical Evangelists. Many of the medical men and other southern California scientists who attended the lectures became highly interested in flood geology as a result. These, in addition to the people recruited by the intensive promotional activities of Ben F. Allen, provided the nucleus for the new society, organized just about a year after the demise of the Religion and Science Association, in late 1938. Ben Allen was named President of the Society, and later became Executive Secretary, which position he held until its demise in 1945.

The society had various official and unofficial names during its seven-year existence, ending in late 1945. Popularly known as the Creation-Deluge Society, or even just the Deluge Society, it was more formally organized as the Society for the Study of Deluge Geology and Related Sciences. Beginning in January 1943, its name was changed to the Society for the Study of Creation, the Deluge, and Related Sciences. Although the Society's leaders objected, it is not surprising that such an unwieldy title was abbreviated to the Deluge Society by most people. It was not officially incorporated until December 1944, and then it was under the name "The Natural History Research Group, A Society for the Study of Creation, the Deluge, and Related Sciences."

The most enduring work of the Society was its *Bulletin of Deluge Geology and Related Sciences,* published at various intervals from 1941 through 1944 (20 *Bulletins* were published altogether). Ben Allen was Managing Editor, as well as Secretary of the Society. George McCready Price and Cyril B. Courville, M.D. (who also served several years as president), comprised the Editorial Board. Courville was replaced on the Editorial Board by

Dr. Dell D. Haughey beginning in January 1943.

The first issue of the Bulletin (June 1941), in a Foreword by the Editorial Staff, said the Society was organized in 1938

> . . . under the encouragement and stimulation of Professor George McCready Price. The Society is nondenominational and has for its only essential thesis, the literal interpretation of the book of Genesis and other Scriptures relating thereto. If the Deluge did occur, it is believed that the scientific facts now available, or easily discoverable, will abundantly prove it.

> This Bulletin is published by the Society to provide for the use of resident and distant members and other interested individuals, worthwhile source material which has been presented before the organization. In this way it is hoped to accumulate material which will be useful to Christian workers and Bible students. This publication must, of necessity, be small at first. It has no endowment and therefore its continued existence depends upon the support of those interested in its message. As the number of members and subscribers increases, the BULLE-TIN will be correspondingly enlarged. The support of believers everywhere is therefore earnestly solicited.

The Society was thus firmly committed to the literal interpretation of Genesis. Although not explicitly mentioned in this Statement of Purpose, the commitment of the Society to Deluge Geology was evident in its very name.

Before the Society began to publish its *Bulletins,* its activities consisted of occasional meetings in the Los Angeles area, supplemented by various field trips and studies, Ben Allen being active in promoting both. Although the Society was intended to be inter-denominational, the majority of its members were Seventh-Day Adventists. So far as I can tell, all the 37 papers published in the *Bulletin* were written by Adventists, except two by Dudley J. Whitney, one by Dr. Will Tinkle, and two reprints of nineteenth century articles by the Duke of Argyll.

This in no way is meant as a rebuke to the Adventists for such domination of a supposedly inter-denominational Society. It is rather a rebuke to the conservatives and "fundamentalists" in the other denominations, who were either so unconcerned with these basic scientific issues or so enamored with their schemes of evolutionary compromise that they had nothing significant to contribute.

There were many outstanding papers in these *Bulletins,* all still very valuable and informative. Little if any specifically Adventist doctrine appears in them. It is a sad commentary on the state of the orthodox denominations—as well as the supposedly "fundamental" inter-denominational organizations—of the time, that the vital Biblical doctrines of genuine creationism and Noachian catastrophism had to be upheld almost exclusively during the quarter-century after the Scopes trial embarrassment by a denominational group which most of them considered to be a cult.

The Creation-Deluge Society was immensely more successful in recruiting members than the Religion and Science Association had been. By 1943 it had almost 500 members and in June of 1945,[1] just before the unfortunate takeover of the Society by an "old-earth" minority and its rapid dissolution thereafter, it had more than 600 members.

This growth was certainly not achieved through using a broad and innocuous doctrinal requirement. Voting members were accepted only on the following basis:

> Realizing that our success depends upon unity of faith and viewpoint, only those who believe in the literal six-day Creation as taught in the Bible, the Creator not being indebted to preexisting matter, that no geologic ages have elapsed since that event, and that the Deluge should be investigated as the possible cause of the major geological changes, shall be eligible for membership.[2]

---

1. *News Letter,* Creation-Deluge Society, 16 Jun. 1945.

2. *News Letter,* Creation-Deluge Society, 16 Jun. 1945.News Letter, Creation-Deluge Society, 20 Jan. 1945. The *News Letter* was issued bimonthly until 1944, monthly thereafter.

Figure 8.   Walter Lammerts at Chief Mountain

Dr. Lammerts was one of the early members of both the Creation-Deluge Society and the American Scientific Affiliation, eventually becoming first president of the Creation Research Society. He made on-the-spot studies of the so-called Lewis "Overthrust" during the late 1950's, finding what seemed to be strong stratigraphic evidence that the sequence of formations was a normal sedimentary succession, rather than the inverted order implied by the nominal geological ages assigned to them by evolutionary geologists.

In addition, there was a $2 annual membership fee, but this was the same as the subscription price for those who wanted the *Bulletins* without joining the Society.

The Society also established various grades of research memberships, based on amounts contributed for research. The Society's leaders, especially Ben Allen, laid great stress on creation-oriented research, and the research fund was used to fund a number of projects. An impressive list of speakers addressed the meetings of the Society and wrote for the *Bulletin*. Most were Seventh-Day Adventists, but there were others, as well. One of these was Dr. Walter Lammerts, who many years later would become the first president of the Creation Research Society. At that time, he was

Assistant Professor of Ornamental Horticulture at UCLA and, though not an actual member of the Society, was active on a research project of special interest to the Society, studying the nature and limits of variation and speciation in plants, and also in speaking at its meetings. Lammerts was a Missouri-Synod Lutheran, very active in his own church circles.

I myself joined the Creation-Deluge Society in June 1943, after learning about it in a footnote in *Genesis Vindicated,* one of George McCready Price's later books, written after his retirement and published in 1941. I struck up a correspondence then with Ben Allen which was most stimulating, and which continued for over seven years. I never met Allen personally, but he was evidently an immensely capable and highly motivated man, truly born again and with a strong faith in Christ and the Word of God. Naturally, I disagreed with him on the matter of Seventh-Day Adventism, but otherwise we quickly developed a real sense of agreement and camaraderie. I was only 25 years old and just getting into creationism, still in my first year as an instructor at Rice Institute, while Ben Allen was at least in his fifties, but we seemed able to give each other mutual appreciation and encouragement.

Two of the most widely publicized creationist research projects, both of them still continuing, were largely initiated by Allen's enthusiasm. I received a letter from him dated December 2, 1943, asking whether I could help on a project checking out and documenting a reported occurrence of giant human footprints with dinosaur footprints in a Cretaceous limestone formation in central Texas, near the small town of Glen Rose. He rightly considered this discovery to be a potential bombshell and was organizing the project on a hush-hush basis. These footprints had been studied by scientists from the American Museum of Natural History, but the human tracks had been ignored, at least publicly. An Adventist minister from Tucson, E. E. Beddoe, had later made casts of some of these tracks, and they seemed to be authentic human tracks, so the Society, under Allen's encouragement, undertook to do some serious excavation and documentation at the site. Geologist Clifford Burdick was later assigned to it, after he became active in the Society in mid-1944, and he soon began what would become essentially a life-long series of explorations and studies of these and other footprints and similar anomalous fossils—fossils that were out of their assigned evolutionary place in the geologic column.

As much as I wanted to at the time, it was not possible for me to participate directly in the project, since those were the war years and I was fully occupied in teaching in the Navy's engineering training programs at Rice. However, Burdick and others worked on it as much as opportunity permitted and did locate a number of what seemed to be *bona fide* human footprints, in addition to numerous dinosaur footprints. Before the project could really be firmly documented, however, the Society collapsed.

The second project referred to above was the search for Noah's Ark. Although there had been earlier explorations on Mount Ararat, these had all been forgotten until Allen began to promote the project as a means of conclusively demonstrating the validity of flood geology. Actually I had recently seen a tract in which a Russian aviator's reported sighting of the Ark, at the time of the first World War, had been mentioned, and had written Allen to ask if he knew anything about it. He had, indeed, since the tract was merely a highly fictionalized account based on evidence which Allen had given the author of this widely circulated tract. There was at least a kernel of truth in the story, although the details had been grossly popularized. Allen got the author of the tract to admit his fabrications and to retract his story.

Like the footprint project, Allen felt the Ararat project should be kept confidential until the actual discovery and documentation of the Ark could be established. First of all, sufficient funds would have to be raised to outfit an adequate expedition. This was impracticable until after the war, so he was only trying to lay the groundwork at the time we first corresponded about it. His foundational efforts would eventually bear fruit in the various expeditions which were established on this foundation some twenty years later, after Allen's death.

Although the southern California members of the Society normally met at monthly or bimonthly intervals, with many interesting papers and speakers, its most ambitious effort was a Symposium meeting held in November 1943. Seventeen papers were presented, on a wide range of topics, many of which were later published in the Society's *Bulletin of Deluge Geology and Related Sciences.* In addition, seven assigned public addresses were given.

Since these were the years of World War II *(the Bulletin of Deluge Geology* began publication in 1941, and the Society disbanded late in 1945), travel was difficult, and I was very busy with teaching and had no vacations of consequence. Consequently, I was never able to attend any of these meetings personally. I did profit tremendously from the Bulletins and Newsletters, as well as from my running dialogue, via correspondence, with Ben Allen. I was unaware that there was increasing internal dissension in the Society during 1944, since none of this was evident from its publications.

All of the Newsletters published in 1943 and after (I have not been able to find any written earlier), with one exception, were written by Ben Allen and frequently contained valuable technical information, as well as news of Society activities. The Newsletter dated March 18, 1944, was written by B. Clemson Marsh, M.D. (who was President[1] at that time) and George McCready Price. However, there was nothing in their remarks hinting of dissension.

Nevertheless, although 1944 seemed to be a very productive year, there was an increasingly restive minority among certain California Adventist members who were lukewarm to deluge geology and, especially, to recent creation. They felt that more

---

1. The only Society presidents ever mentioned as such, in any of the materials accessible to me, were Allen, Courville, and Marsh. In any event, it was Allen who was the effective leader and sparkplug of the Society.

emphasis should be placed on biology and less on geology, since they were increasingly convinced that radioactive dating had proven the earth to be two billion years old (this was the evolutionists' firmly settled "age of the earth" back in 1945!).

In fact, in 1937 a number of Adventist science teachers had had a meeting at which they decided they would have to accept the "old earth" view of the evolutionists. Allen did not learn of this until after the Society had disbanded, although he was always curious as to why so few of them took an active part in the Society. A number of them did join, however, including also a number of medical doctors who had been trained under them and shared their views, without letting their doubts be known openly.

As is usual in such sub-rosa activities, their opposition to the Society's basic premise was first expressed in other complaints. Not enough attention was being paid to biological evidences of design; the Bulletins were not being published rapidly enough; the Society's name was cumbersome and embarrassing in the academic world; more effort should be directed to reaching laymen who didn't understand geology and other technical material; the Secretary might be misusing funds, and thereby causing delays in publication schedules; more effort should be concentrated on highly technical material commanding the attention and respect of the most advanced evolutionary scientists; the governing board should be self-perpetuating instead of elected by the membership, with all officers selected from a group of highly credentialed "Fellows," etc.

The underlying reason for all these complaints, however, at least judging from future developments, was academic embarrassment at the strong position of the Society (especially its Executive Secretary) on the vital issues of recent creation and the cataclysmic deluge. Accordingly, plans were secretly being made to oust Ben Allen and to change the entire nature of the Society.

In spite of what had seemed to be adequate safeguards against any such thing happening, it did happen. In his final Newsletter, announcing the forthcoming annual election of officers, Allen wrote:

> This may be the last news letter by the present writer, in view of the annual election of officers at this meeting. Beware of disruptive action. Some 10 years ago I saw that *somebody* "had to jump off and swim out" in order to get these labors started as *an organized movement.* (Everyone else, and especially the more competent scientific workers, either are not organizers or have their noses to grindstones, or are in treadmills.) I have gone through some hardships, *but have been happier than ever before.* A band of more than 600 loyal and sacrificing people has been gathered together, many of them of first rate ability in this field. . . . I have done for the Society only what had to be done, and what no one else could be found to do. Please forgive the mistakes, most of which have been mistakes of zeal.[1]

What he had feared indeed came to pass. The meeting was packed with members who had been instructed how to vote in accordance with the plans of the takeover clique. A new set of officers was elected, and Ben Allen was voted out.

The new Board soon decided to abolish the original Society, without even asking the consent of the membership, and to constitute itself as a new and different organization. The money in the research and publications funds (approximately $1800—a fairly large amount by 1945 standards) was turned over to the new Secretary, Molleurus Couperus, M.D., along with all other properties of the Society, in the name of the new organization.

The new name was completely innocuous, the Society for the Study of Natural Science. That would hardly embarrass anybody! Neither would its doctrinal standards, which omitted "all references to the Bible, to the Deluge, to Creation, to Evolution, to religion, and to any of the real purposes of the original body."[2]

---

1. Ben F. Allen, *Creation-Deluge Society News Letter,* 16 Jun. 1945, p. 4. This was not only Allen's last newsletter; it was the Society's last publication.

2. Ben F. Allen, *The Original Society Illegally Supplanted and All Scriptural*

According to Ben Allen, "the whole 'revolution' was apparently developed by two men, and not more than 6 or 7 were actively and purposely involved in it."[1] The membership never voted on it at all, though a questionnaire was later circulated to them. The latter was confusing and the results never were tallied. Allen wrote:

> The status of membership in the original Society, has been abolished, all except an empty phrase. But almost all of the original members even yet do not know what has happened. The Board *constituted itself the Society, is self-elected,* and *elects its officers from itself.* [2]

All of this would seem to have been quite illegal and possibly could have been overturned in a lawsuit. However, presumably because of Biblical cautions on such matters, no one wished to go to court over it, and the takeover was successfully consummated.

Aftershocks of the Deluge Society Breakup

The new "Society for the Study of Natural Science," ostensibly interdenominational like its predecessor, soon became strictly Seventh-Day Adventist in practice. It had its roots in the revolt of Adventist science instructors against the doctrine of recent creation which had long been held by that denomination, and these younger intellectuals apparently wanted to use the revised organization as an instrument to undermine this doctrine in the denomination itself.

They were precluded from using the day-age theory or the gap theory, in their exegesis of Genesis, by the writings of their revered teacher, Mrs. Ellen G. White, whom Adventists believe to have been guided infallibly in her writings by the Spirit of Prophecy. They thought, however, that they could stretch her teachings to allow for the two billion years required by radiometric dating in

---

Standards Abandoned. Paper privately circulated by author late in 1946, p. 1.

1. *Ibid.*, p. 2.
2. *Ibid.*

the supposed gap between the first two verses of Genesis. They could not place the geological ages with their fossils in this gap however, as the other fundamentalists were doing, since Mrs. White had rightly stressed that no death had occurred in the world prior to Adam's sin. Consequently, they assumed that the earth had remained dormant in the "chaotic" state of Genesis 1:2 for all those two billion years. Thus all the Precambrian rocks, which they assumed to have no fossils, were attributed to this "primary creation," with the rest of the stellar universe two billion years ago, with Genesis 1:3–31 then describing the "secondary creation" of the six days, which were still taken as six literal days six thousand or so years ago.

After all this had happened, Ben Allen, realizing that this position was being pushed because of geochronological intimidation and then justified by distorting the teachings of Scripture (as well as those of Mrs. White), got two of his own colleagues to prepare definitive papers on these two subjects.

Clifford Burdick, who studied in geology at Wisconsin University, plus many years of experience in mining geology, therefore (with Allen's assistance) prepared a 21-page single-spaced mimeographed paper entitled "Recent Trends in Methods of Measuring Geologic Time," sharply critiquing radiometric and other methods of geologic dating, which was then circulated to about 50 key reviewers for comment and correction. Similarly, Dr. John L. Huenergardt, with a Ph.D. in Philosophy from Indiana University, wrote on "The Scriptural Integrity of Creation Week," showing clearly that recent six-literal-day creation is the plain and unmistakable teaching of Scripture.

These two key papers were later distributed to the Adventist science teachers and resulted in many of them returning to strict creationism.[1] The new Society also later incorporated them into

---

1. Ben F. Allen, letter to the writer, Feb. 18, 1950.

its own new publication,[1] both papers having been revised and updated by then, with Burdick's paper in the first volume, Huenergardt's in the second.

The new Board (with Molleurus Couperus, M.D., as Executive Secretary) decided to change the title of the *Bulletin of Deluge Geology* to *The Forum,* with the words "For the Correlation of Science and the Bible" as a subheading appearing in small print on the title page, but not on the cover. Volume I was published in 1946, nothing in 1947, Volume II in 1948. Nothing at all had been published in 1945, and *The Forum* ceased publication altogether after 1948.

All the papers in both volumes dealt with this controversy over whether the earth was old or young. In addition to the papers by Burdick and Huenergardt, papers defending the young earth were written by Harold Clark, Dudley J. Whitney, and another by Burdick. Advocating an old earth were three papers by J. Lowell Butler, two by Molieurus Couperus, and (surprisingly) one by George McCready Price. There was a sprinkling of quotations from Ellen G. White plus a number of brief "Letters-to-the-editor" in Volume II. All of the writers except Whitney were Seventh-Day Adventists, and Whitney's article was essentially a letter discussing Volume I. The book was clearly an Adventist document, intended essentially to convince Adventists that the age of the earth was still an open question, both Biblically and scientifically. None of the writers, however, advocated the gap theory or day-age theory. Also, all of them, even those favoring a young earth, assumed that the universe itself was very old, with stars and planets and probably living creatures existing at various times and places throughout the universe. This notion had been sanctioned by Mrs. White, the Adventist prophetess, and so was taken as fact by all

---

1. Clifford L. Burdick, "The Radioactive Time Theory and Recent Trends in Methods of Measuring Geologic Time," *The Forum,* Vol. I (1946), pp. 39-58; J. P. Huenergardt, "The Integrity of Creation Week," *The Forum,* Vol. II (1948), pp. 71-105.

the *Forum* writers.

I wrote a letter to the *Forum* editors, critiquing this latter idea along with the old earth idea. My letter was ignored by the editors, but Ben F. Allen later made copies and circulated it.

Since I am not in the Seventh-Day Adventist denomination, I know little about its internal divisions.[1] However, this same divergence of opinion still exists and apparently has broadened into a more widespread liberal/conservative type of division that also involves the law/grace question and even the question of Mrs. White's prophetic authority and integrity.

But that is another subject, not germane to this book. In any event, the Society for the Study of Natural Science died out, with its *Forum,* shortly after Volume II was published. It was serving no purpose—the controversy it sought to discuss had already been well discussed to no avail for over a hundred years. The tragedy was that this handful of compromisers was able to destroy so quickly a sound creationist testimony that could have made a tremendous impact for truth in the scientific and educational worlds of the post-war generation. Again, however, some good seed had been sown.

To provide an outlet for their research and writing, a number of the Adventist flood geologists (e.g., Allen, Clark, Frank Marsh, Burdick) began to publish in *The Naturalist,* the quarterly magazine of the Associated Nature Clubs, directed by Dr. Ernest Booth. These were nature study clubs sponsored by various local Adventist churches. Although most of the articles in *The Naturalist* were simply studies of various birds, plants, and other nature items, it did include one or more strong creationist articles in many of its issues. This small journal was published from 1942 through 1967 but was in perpetual financial straits and finally could survive no longer.

---

1. Geoffrey J. Paxton, *The Shaking of Adventism* (Wilmington, DE: Zenith Publishers, Inc., 1977).

In the meantime, Benjamin Allen, no longer involved in the Deluge Society, was able to devote more attention to his Noah's Ark project. He formed another organization, the Sacred History Research Expedition, with himself as President, and Clifford Burdick as Vice President. Another officer, until he had to drop out for health reasons, was well-known Christian archaeologist J. O. Kinnaman. Allen also enlisted the active support of H. M. S. Richards, the nationally known Adventist radio evangelist.

He was especially active in promoting this project from 1948 to 1950 or later, trying particularly to obtain financial backing for a systematic archaeological/geological exploration of Mount Ararat. He was never able to consummate the project, however.

Allen had quietly been accumulating evidence concerning the Ark from many sources for many years. A number of the reported sightings that have now been rather widely publicized were first researched by him. My son, John, who is currently in charge of our own ICR Ararat Project, has reviewed some of Allen's background studies in his own book.[1]

Many of the Ararat investigators of more recent years have also been Seventh-Day Adventists (e.g., George Vandeman, Ralph Crawford, Eryl Cummings, as well as Clifford Burdick, who was first a member of the Allen team, then later with Crawford, Cummings, and others). How much of their own knowledge and enthusiasm for the project may have originally come from Ben Allen, knowingly or unknowingly, I can only surmise. In any case, in this as in many other significant creationist activities, Allen was a genuine pioneer.

I lost touch with him after 1950. He was still reasonably young, probably late fifties or early sixties, but it is my understanding that he died fairly young, before seeing the fruition of most of his dedicated labors and incisive insights. In my last letter to him

---

1. John D. Morris and Tim LaHaye, *The Ark on Ararat* (Nashville: Thomas Nelson, Inc., 1976), pp. 74-83, 107.

(March 9, 1950), I mentioned that I would probably be going to Afghanistan soon, officially as an engineering teacher (I was to get my Ph.D. in December of that year, from the University of Minnesota), unofficially as a missionary to that closed Moslem country. I suggested the possibility of meeting him in nearby Armenia to join his Ararat expedition, if and when. As it turned out, neither of us ever made it, either to Afghanistan or Ararat.

The American Scientific Affiliation

Unlike the other organizations we have discussed so far, the American Scientific Affiliation, first formed in 1941, is still active. However, it is no longer active as a *creationist* organization, with its leaders and most of its members having long since capitulated to theistic evolution.

This was not the vision of its two founders, who were both associated with Moody Bible Institute, a school which had been firmly committed to creationism ever since it was founded in 1879 by D. L. Moody, the famous nineteenth century evangelist. The American Scientific Affiliation (ASA) originally was envisioned and encouraged by Irwin A. Moon, who became widely known for his "Sermons from Science" during World War II, which were sponsored by Moody Bible Institute, and by the president of Moody, Dr. Will H. Houghton.

Dr. Houghton's predecessor, Dr. James M. Gray, had been an active leader of the fundamentalists during their battles with the modernists in the period before and after the Scopes trial. Although he still tended to lean toward the gap theory, he was on good terms with George McCready Price and the other strict creationists of the time. He encouraged Price and the others as they were planning to form the Religion and Science Association, but he died just as it was getting under way. The one public convention of the Association was held in Moody Church in March 1936. It attracted good crowds and considerable publicity. How much Dr. Houghton himself may have been involved is not clear, but he must have been impressed with the importance and evangelistic potential of such a body of scientists who could be firmly committed to the Word of God and the Biblical doctrine of creation.

Soon afterward, Moody began to sponsor Irwin Moon's highly successful "Sermons from Science." These were greatly used by the Lord, both in citywide evangelistic campaigns and in military camps during the War. It was one of his meetings, held in El Paso early in 1942, that made a profound impression on me and first got me interested in the correlation of science and Scripture. I was especially fascinated and impressed by one of his sermons dealing with flood geology and the canopy theory, my first encounter with the scientific implications of the Biblical Deluge.

It was at another of his meetings, held in Salem, Oregon, in November 1940, that Moon had contacted Mr. F. Alton Everest, who was then teaching electrical engineering at Oregon State College, in order to discuss the need for another organization of evangelical scientists. The Religion and Science Association had foundered three years previously, and the Creation-Deluge Society, formed in 1938, was not broad enough to include "progressive creationists" and "gap creationists." Furthermore, it was dominated by Seventh-Day Adventists, an onus which had kept many "evangelicals" from joining it.

Moon put Everest in touch with several other creationist scientists interested in such a society, and then Everest undertook the selection of a name and preparation of a constitution. Moon and Houghton also worked hard in planning the society and then, in 1941, Houghton sent a letter to all the known prospective members, inviting them to an organizational meeting in Chicago scheduled for September 2-5, 1941. Travel expenses were to be paid by Henry P. Crowell, one of Moody's Board members.

According to Everest's account,[1] there were five men who came. In addition to Everest, the others were as follows:

Peter W. Stoner, Professor of Mathematics and Astronomy at Pasadena City College in California. Stoner was later author of a book,[2] advocating the day-age theory.

Dr. John P. Van Haitsma, Professor of Organic Science at Calvin College, a small liberal arts school of the Christian Reformed denomination in Grand Rapids. Van Haitsma had sponsored the Nature and Scripture Study Club, which functioned in Grand Rapids from 1935 to 1942.

Dr. Russell D. Sturgis, Professor of Chemistry at Ursinus College in Pennsylvania.

Dr. Irving A. Cowperthwaite, Plant Engineer for the Thompson Wire Company in Massachusetts.

All of these men were creationists, but none were strict recent creationists like those in the Creation-Deluge Society.

There were several others who were actively involved in the formation of the ASA almost from the first. One of these was Dr. Will Tinkle, who later was to become the first Secretary of the Creation Research Society. Another was Dr. Walter Lammerts, who held a more prestigious position than any of the others, being on the agricultural faculty at UCLA at the time (Lammerts later became first president of the CRS). However, he was also actively involved in the Creation-Deluge Society and was firmly convinced of the validity of recent creationism and flood geology. He tried to convince the other founders that they should write into the ASA constitution a commitment to these Biblical truths, predicting that the Society would eventually either collapse (as the Religion and Science Association had done) or else—even worse—would soon

1. F. Alton Everest, "The American Scientific Affiliation-The First Decade," *Journal of the American Scientific Affiliation*, 3, Sep. 1951, p. 37.

2. Peter W. Stoner, *From Science to Souls* (Chicago: Moody Press, 1944). This book was issued in a later edition (1952) under the title *Science Speaks*.

become dominated by theistic evolutionism, ultimately becoming simply another liberal ecumenical society.[1] However, the five original founders, led by Peter Stoner and his adamant commitment to the day-age theory, refused to adopt any such strict creationist frame of reference, even though all of them were, at that time, definitely creationists and fully intended for the ASA to provide scientific leadership for the evangelical world in its opposition to evolution.

Dr. Lammerts' prophecy eventually proved true, unfortunately. Over and over again, this same drift has occurred, from strict creationism to progressive creationism (or gap creationism) to theistic evolutionism to religious liberalism, and, finally, either to outright humanism or extinction. The road of compromise eventually leads to a precipice. While the ASA has thus far remained true to evangelicalism in some ways, it has long since ceased to be an influence for any form of creationism.

Nor did it take very long for the Affiliation to begin this drift, as we shall see. Everest was elected President and Cowperthwaite Secretary-Treasurer, the two constituting with Stoner, Sturgis, and Van Haitsma, the first Executive Council. Each member of the Council was to serve a five-year term, with one Council member to be elected each year. Dr. Marion D. Barnes, a research chemist in Arkansas, replaced Van Haitsma in 1942; Dr. Edwin Y. Monsma, a biology professor at Calvin College replaced Cowperthwaite in 1943; Dr. Russell L. Mixter, Head of the Wheaton College Science Department, replaced Sturgis in 1944; Dr. Allan A. MacRae, President of Faith Seminary replaced Stoner in 1945; Everest was reelected to a new five-year term in 1946; Dr. Roger J. Voskuyl, Dean of Wheaton College, replaced Barnes in 1947; Dr. Laurence Kulp, Assistant Professor of Geology at Columbia University, replaced Monsma in 1948; Mixter was re-elected in 1949; Dr. H. Harold Hartzler, mathematics professor at Goshen College, re-

---

1. Letter from Dr. Lammerts, n.d.

placed MacRae in 1950; Dr. Brian P. Sutherland, a mining engineer in British Columbia, replaced Everest in 1951; and Delbert N. Eggenberger, a Chicago research chemist, replaced Voskuyl in 1952.

The Executive Council was to elect one of its members President each year, and Alton Everest remained in this capacity until 1950, when Dr. Mixter was named President. Dr. Hartzler became President in 1954, continuing until 1960, when he was appointed as ASA's first Executive Secretary, initially on a part-time basis.

Of all the above men, only Monsma was clearly a believer in recent creation and a cataclysmic deluge. Others were nominally uncommitted to any specific view, while some (e.g., Everest, Stoner, Mixter, Eggenberger, and especially Dr. Kulp) were quite hostile to such views.

When the society was first organized in 1941, the rather innocuous name of "American Scientific Affiliation" was adopted. However, it did have a fairly good statement of faith required for membership. This statement was changed at various times. One of the early forms, possibly the first, was as follows:

> I believe the whole Bible as originally given to be the inspired word of God, the only unerring guide of faith and conduct. Since God is the Author of this Book, as well as the Creator and Sustainer of the physical world about us, I believe there can be no discrepancies when both are properly interpreted. Accordingly, trusting in the Lord Jesus Christ, the Son of God, my Saviour, for strength, I pledge myself as a member of this organization to the furtherance of its task.[1]

The Objectives of the ASA were stated as follows:

(1) To integrate and organize the efforts of many individuals desiring to correlate the facts of science and the Holy Scriptures.

(2) To promote and encourage the study of the relationship

---

1. Article II, ASA Constitution as of 1951.

between the facts of science and the Holy Scriptures.

(3) To promote the dissemination of the results of such studies.[1]

Although nothing specific was spelled out about either creation or evolution in these statements, there was at least an implication of Biblical inerrancy and the harmony of true science with Scripture. Even this relatively innocuous statement of faith soon proved onerous to many of its members, however, and a presumed stumblingblock to academic colleagues. Consequently, there were frequent movements to get things changed, usually in the direction of less rigorous membership requirements.

Initially there was only one class of membership. A new constitution was adopted around 1950, allowing for the grade of Fellow, with the Council to be elected only by the Fellows. Members had to agree to only a very brief doctrinal statement, Fellows to a much lengthier statement (which, however, did not require rejection of evolution).

A third constitution[2] was adopted in 1959, specifying four grades of membership: Honorary Fellow, Fellow, Member, and Associate. Voting rights were given to both Members and Fellows, and a single brief doctrinal statement was adopted for all, as follows:

> The Holy Scriptures are the inspired Word of God, the only unerring guide of faith and conduct. Jesus Christ is the Son of God and through His atonement is the one and only Mediator between God and man.

Members were required to have an undergraduate degree in one of the natural or social sciences, Fellows a doctoral degree.

---

1. Article I, ASA Constitution as of 1951.

2. See I. A. Cowperthwaite "Twenty Years with the American Scientific Affiliation," *Journal of the American Scientific Affiliation,* 13, Dec. 1961, pp. 98–102; for a survey of the changes taking place during its second decade. Cowperthwaite, one of the five founders, was chairman of a Historical Committee, which also included Barnes (first editor of the *Journal),* Everest, Mixter, and Hartzler (the first three presidents).

Some time later (about 1974), a third sentence was added to the doctrinal statement as follows:

> God is the Creator of the physical universe. Certain laws are discernible in the manner in which God upholds the universe. The scientific approach is capable of giving reliable information about the natural world.

This latter addition seems to have been made in response to the growth of the modern creation movement, but is actually innocuous, since by this time, the ASA had repeatedly stressed in its Journal that evolution was simply God's method of creation.

The ASA was founded just before Pearl Harbor, and wartime travel restrictions prevented any conventions until 1946. An annual convention has been held every summer since that time. During the war, Everest himself, however, did travel extensively throughout the United States in connection with his wartime work, and so was able to make many contacts. By the end of the war, the organization had a membership of about 50.

The main activity otherwise during this time was the assignment and preparation of papers for a symposium volume in which different specialists would deal with their individual scientific disciplines as they related to Scripture. This was finally published in 1948.[1] Several chapters in this book were excellent documents, including one by Walter Lammerts and Will Tinkle. However, the articles on astronomy, geology, and anthropology all accepted the standard evolutionary chronology of cosmic history, earth history, and human history, respectively.

It was at this time (1948) that I first learned about the organization and joined it. The Creation-Deluge Society and even its usurping organization had recently collapsed, and the ASA sounded quite promising to me at first. I was then at the University of Minnesota, doing full-time teaching and researching in hydrau-

---

1. American Scientific Affiliation, *Modern Science and Christian Faith* (Wheaton, IL: Van Kampen Press, 1948), 289 pp.

Figure 9. Hydraulics at the University of Minnesota

The writer's graduate studies were taken with a major in hydraulics, primarily because of the key role of the Noahic flood in the creation/evolution issue. The photograph shows some of the equipment used for his dissertation, at the large St. Anthony Falls Hydraulic Laboratory at the University of Minnesota, perhaps the finest facility of this type in the nation at that time.

lic engineering at the University's St. Anthony Falls Hydraulic Laboratory, while simultaneously doing graduate work in this field, majoring in hydraulics (the study of water and its effects in nature) and minoring in geology and mathematics. I had embarked on these studies primarily because of their importance in the study of the Deluge, and so wanted to maintain contacts with other scientists who were also Bible-believing Christians. The American Scientific Affiliation seemed to be the only thing then available directed to that end.

However, soon after joining it, I must have become the Affiliation's chief gadfly. My book *That You Might Believe* was having an increasing influence, and when I *read Modern Science and Christian Faith,* I immediately sent a rather extensive critique to President Everest objecting to its uniformitarian emphasis, and referring to my treatment of flood geology as the type of approach ASA should adopt.

This began a rather long and mostly friendly debate between Everest and the other ASA officers, on the one hand, and myself on the other hand. Our correspondence was kept on a courteous and friendly level, but our positions were poles apart, with neither able to budge the other.

I pointed out that the ASA Symposium had completely ignored the flood geology position, whereas many very competent Christian scientists (as in the Creation-Deluge Society) had argued with some cogency that it was a better geological model than uniformitarianism, as well as the *only* valid Biblical model. Thus it should at least be recognized and refuted, if possible, not simply ignored.

The ASA also produced that same year another symposium, this one on the age of the earth. Every paper (except one by Walter Lammerts) advocated an old earth. One, by Dr. Bernard Ramm, argued Biblically for the day-age theory. The others were mainly concerned with radioactive dating. This symposium was only distributed in mimeograph form to the membership, which was still less than 100.

My complaint and exhortation may have contributed to an assignment to Dr. J. Laurence Kulp to prepare what would amount to an ASA position paper on deluge geology.[1] Kulp was a Wheaton graduate who had gone on to get his Ph.D. in geology at Columbia University. He eventually became, for a while, one of the nation's top authorities in geochronometry and radiometric dating. He served for a term on the ASA Executive Council, but eventually dropped out of the organization, not because it had become liberal, but because it was too conservative for him! His paper was, of course, a vicious attack on flood geology and its proponents. Naturally, I wrote a rebuttal to it, trying to answer his various arguments, but *the Journal* editors never would publish it.

---

1. J. Laurence Kulp, "Flood Geology," *A.S.A. Journal.*

Before Kulp's article was published, however, Alton Everest actually paid a visit to my home in Minneapolis, both to get acquainted and also hoping to dissuade me from my position. He was accompanied by Bernard Ramm, who was then a young theologian on the faculty at Bethel Seminary in St. Paul. Ramm was considered by Everest and other ASA leaders to be one of the most promising young intellectuals in the Christian world, and he soon would become one of the most influential voices of neo-evangelicalism.

Ramm and Everest were unsuccessful in their mission, of course, but neither was I successful in persuading them of the validity of strict creationism, though I did try!

Kulp's diatribe against flood geology seemed to intimidate just about all remaining open commitment to recent creationism among the ASA members. Since the *Journal* would not publish my rebuttal, and no other defenders of this position seemed to be speaking out in ASA, I sent copies of Kulp's paper to Ben F. Allen and Dudley J. Whitney, suggesting they might like to respond in some way.

Allen was concerned, but too busy with other projects to do anything immediately. Whitney, on the other hand, responded with a long series of papers, which he entitled *The Creationist.*[1] He published these at his own expense and sent them to all the ASA members, over a period of some three years, during 1950–1953. These were cogent, well-reasoned papers, but their effect may have been minimized by the biting sarcasm and sharp condemnations which punctuated his writing. In any event, he elicited many editorial and other responses from ASA leaders. How many readers he won to strict creationism is not known, but he had no more success than I did in stopping the drift of the ASA into full-fledged theistic evolutionism.

---

1. Another journal of the same name was published by the Christian Evidence League, of Maverne, New York, for several years beginning in 1963, featuring articles by Whitney, Price, and others.

All of this time I was trying hard to be supportive of the ASA. Except for its diluted creationism, its journals did have many good articles on other Bible-science topics. I encouraged many to join, including two men who later became leaders in the organization. One of these, Walter Hearn, had been in my home Bible class when he was a student and I was an instructor at Rice during the early years of the War. Later, after he had received his Ph.D. in biochemistry at the University of Illinois and was on the faculty at Yale, he wrote that "we have the fondest memories of you, and have often thanked God for your strong influence on our lives and the lives of many of our dearest friends."[1]

I appreciated this testimony very much at the time, since Walter had been one of the finest and most promising students I had ever known. He was a strong Bible-believing Christian creationist as a student, and I felt he could make a great contribution some day. I encouraged him to join the ASA. He and his wife June, whom I had also known when they were students at Rice, both joined and became active. He soon was on the Council and was elected Secretary-Treasurer. Later he served many years as Editor of the ASA Newsletter.

The tragedy, however, was that he had become a total evolutionist, remaining so to this day, so far as I know. In fact, he was one of the leaders most instrumental in leading the Affiliation from a dominantly progressive creationist position to a dominantly theistic evolutionist position.

Another was Dr. Charles Hatfield, who was my closest friend on the Minnesota faculty, active with me in the Inter-Varsity Christian Fellowship chapter there. His field was Mathematics and I also encouraged him into the ASA. He was a creationist then and, in fact, reviewed the manuscript for *The Bible and Modern Science* for me. He didn't actually join the ASA until I had left Minnesota, but then he also soon became a leader. Years later, when he had

---

1. Letter from Walter Hearn to writer, Sep. 15, 1951.

become ASA President and I was President of the Creation Research Society, he wanted to do something to bring about a union or closer fellowship between the two organizations. By this time, however, "Chuck" also was a thorough going theistic evolutionist and so was his organization, and it was impossible. "Can two walk together, except they be agreed?" (Amos 3:3).

While I was at Minnesota, teaching assignments and graduate studies, combined with a limited income, had kept my ASA gadfly role limited to that of critical correspondence. Finally, however, in 1953 (after finishing my Ph.D. and moving to Louisiana in 1951), I was able to attend one of the ASA Conventions.

I prepared a paper entitled "Biblical Evidence for a Recent Creation and Universal Deluge" to present at the meeting, hoping this would be the opportunity finally to reverse the trend toward evolution in the ASA. Since all members professed to believe the Bible, I thought, if they could only be led to see that the Bible really taught these two basic doctrines (as I had discovered by myself a decade earlier), then surely they would choose to believe the Bible instead of modern scientism.

I was too naive, of course. Possibly my experiences during the last thirty years have changed me from naive to cynical, but it does seem now that there are multitudes of evangelical "intellectuals"—especially professional people, including theologians—whose view of the inerrancy and perspicuity of Scripture completely changes its perspective when they come to the first eleven chapters of Genesis. Modern scientism seems to dictate the hermeneutics, not the Scriptures themselves.

This was the reaction to my convention paper. There was intense interest and much discussion, both during the meeting and afterward. No one even attempted to answer or refute the Biblical arguments, which is what the paper was all about, but there were all kinds of equivocations to the effect that scientific evidence precludes belief in literal creation and flood geology, and that there have been many good people who believe Scripture can be adapted to whatever scientists dictate on these matters. There was a similar reaction later when the paper was published, not in the ASA Journal (which wouldn't accept it), but in *His,* the official publication of the Inter-Varsity Christian Fellowship.

Over the years since, I have been invited several times to speak to local sections of ASA, always on essentially this same subject. And always the reaction has been the same. The standard response to the overwhelming Biblical evidence for a recent creation and worldwide deluge is: "But there are good people who interpret the Bible to fit the evolutionary geological ages, and we can't afford to disagree with the scientists."

This drift toward total evolution continued. Although ASA leaders frequently protested to conservative critics that the ASA was open to the entire spectrum of beliefs on creation, the fact is that its meetings and journals only rarely included a paper advocating true creationism, and even these never advocated recent creationism or deluge geology. My 1953 paper was all but unique in all of ASA's 40-year history, and even it wasn't published in the Journal.

The complete capitulation of the ASA to evolutionism was signalled by the publication of a symposium volume on evolution[1] in 1959, in honor of the one hundredth anniversary of Darwin's *Origin of Species.* Although a few of the articles in this symposium allowed for the possibility of progressive creation, none of them (except the final chapter by theologian Carl Henry) offered any arguments of consequence against evolution itself, and several (e.g., the chapter on the origin of the universe, by George Schweitzer, and the chapter on the origin of life, by Walter Hearn) were totally evolutionist in treatment. Even Dr. Henry's chapter equivocated on whether evolution was true, and he seemed quite willing to accept it if the evidence were to become stronger.

This was, of course, the year of the Darwinian Centennial Con-

---

1. Russell L. Mixter, *Evolution and Christian Thought Today* (Grand Rapids: Wm. B. Eerdmans Pub. Co., 1959), 224 pp.

vocation, and it was accompanied by a veritable flood of books and articles eulogizing Darwin and promoting evolution. Thus, when even the one organization that professed to be the scientific voice of evangelicalism went along with the evolutionary propaganda, the evolutionists could indeed claim—as they did repeatedly—that evolution had completely triumphed, even among the fundamentalists.

The initial revival of creationism that was taking place in the late 1960s and early 1970s, however, forced the leaders of ASA to counter the growing reaction against Christian evolutionists. Accordingly, the last Journal issue of 1971[1] was devoted to the creation-evolution issue, with the theme being set by the lead editorial, "We believe in creation." However, the argument, made by the editor, Dr. Richard H. Bube,[2] was simply that evolution was God's method of creation.

This is a rather common defense offered by Christian intellectuals today, but it was also a common dodge employed by compromising Christians of earlier generations. "Certainly, we are creationists!" "The Bible tells us the *fact* of creation; the scientists must determine the *how.*" "We believe in creation *and* evolution," the ASA would say, through its spokesman, Dr. Bube.

By such semantic manipulation, one can define "black" as white" or "up" as "down." Creationists are well aware that many people believe in theistic evolution, but that is a form of *evolution,* not *creation.*

Another volley was fired in 1978, when the ASA published a special volume[3] consisting of collected papers from previous is-

---

1. R. H. Bube, ed., *Creation and/or Evolution: A Symposium, in Journal of the American Scientific Affiliation,* 23, Dec. 1971, pp. 121-160. For an analysis of the ASA reaction to *The Genesis Flood,* see John Whitcomb, *The World That Perished* (Grand Rapids: Baker Book House, Rev. Ed., 1988), pp. 107-139.

2. Dr. Bube became the *Journal's* editor in 1969. He later became Chairman of the Department of Materials Science and Engineering at Stanford University.

sues of the journal, all promoting either theistic evolution or an emasculated progressive creationism (except for one paper in a creation/evolution debate, with the conclusion implied that the evolutionist side had won).

As a creationist organization (as originally planned by Irwin Moon and Will Houghton), the American Scientific Affiliation has proven not only to be a sad failure, but even a strong opponent to the creationist cause. Because of the prestige of its scientists, and their professed commitment to Scripture, the ASA has led many Christian schools, colleges, and even seminaries into a similar compromise position. It even infected the school that originally sponsored it, Moody Bible Institute, through the Moody Institute of Science. The MIS was established about 1947, with Irwin Moon as Director, with the intention of gaining a wider audience for his successful "Sermons in Science" by putting similar materials on film. These Moody science films were, indeed, excellent and had a great ministry for many years.

However, Alton Everest, who was also ASA president for its first decade, was appointed Associate Director of the Moody Institute of Science. Furthermore, the Moody films were supposed to be released only if "approved" by the ASA. This effectively precluded any of them from taking a strong stand on creation, and consequently none of them even dealt with the issue at all. Several advocated a great age for the universe and the earth. The films gave strong evidences of design in nature and effectively presented Christ as savior, so the Lord used them, but they were not creationist films.

As time went on, more and more of the creationist scientists dropped out of ASA, especially after the Creation Research Society was formed. Some of us continued on for a long time. I still hoped against hope, for a while, that it someday could be reclaimed, and

3. David L. Willis, ed., *Origins and Change: Selected Readings from the Journal of the American Scientific Affiliation,* (Elgin, IL: American Scientific Affiliation, 1978), 76 pp.

was even made a Fellow of the Affiliation in 1961,[1] just before publication of our book *The Genesis Flood*. The reaction of ASA to that book was so vehemently negative that I am sure I never would have made it after 1961!

Eventually, the Journal articles became not only pro-evolutionary but also more and more centered on the social sciences rather than the natural sciences. Even after I had finally abandoned all hope that the ASA could ever be reclaimed for creationism, I still felt it worthwhile to continue my membership, simply in order to get the Journals and to keep up with what they were doing. Finally, with the large majority of articles focused on social and psychological issues, however, there seemed no longer any point even in this. The rest of the ICR staff and most of the CRS Board members had long since dropped out. In 1980, after 32 years of ASA membership, I also left. The American Scientific Affiliation, unlike the Religion and Science Association and the Creation-Deluge Society, has not passed out of existence, but it *has* ceased to exist as a creationist organization.

---

1. Fellows were elected as such by the other Fellows and were supposed to hold the Doctorate or its equivalent in a natural or social science, be actively engaged in science, and be active in ASA. I was first considered for this honor sometime before 1955, but until 1961 was repeatedly rejected, because of my deluge geology beliefs. Many Fellows with much less significant professional credentials than mine were elected before I was. Two men of similar belief, Dr. John Klotz and Dr. Frank Marsh, were elected the same year, along with 12 others who did *not* share our beliefs.

Chapter V

The Genesis Flood

The year 1959—the Darwinian Centennial Year—seemed to mark the zenith of evolution's ascendancy. All of the books and seminars eulogizing Darwin and evolutionary thought, climaxed by the great Centennial Convocation in Chicago, proclaimed creationism finally to be dead and buried, with evolutionism reigning unchallenged in the realm of human thought. Even the American Scientific Affiliation, the one organization presuming to speak for Bible-believing Christians in the field of science, had capitulated to theistic evolutionism and almost all Christian colleges and seminaries were going along with these Christian intellectuals. The few that still rejected theistic evolution were either teaching progressive creationism or ignoring the issue via the gap theory.

Yet, in that same year, the initial draft was finished on a book which the Lord would graciously use to catalyze a significant revival of creationism—this time largely among scientists rather than theologians. This book was entitled *The Genesis Flood.*

Please note that I used the term "catalyze," rather than "produce," in evaluating the impact of *The Genesis Flood* on the modern creationist revival. Although there were still a number of scientific creationists around, and much sound work had already been done in this field, creationists were generally disorganized and discouraged by this time. The Lord used the book, and the contacts that were made in getting these men to review the manuscript, to bring them together in an informal fellowship of correspondence which would eventually culminate in the Creation Research Society (See Chapter VI). It served as a kind of rallying point, providing a comprehensive exposition of strict creationism which was well documented and scholarly in its format, yet firmly committed to Biblical inerrancy and authority in its theology.

Dr. Ronald Numbers, Professor of the History of Science at the University of Wisconsin (Madison) called it "the most impressive contribution to strict creationism"[1] in almost forty years. In a book written 18 years later and devoted entirely to an attack on *The Genesis Flood,* geologist Davis Young acknowledged that it had "brought about a stunning renaissance of flood geology."[2] Perhaps these two evaluations—typical of numerous others written by men opposing our book and its influence—constitute an adequate reason to devote a chapter to it in this historical review.

Background of the Book and Its Writing

Dr. John C. Whitcomb, Jr., was for many years Professor of Theology and Old Testament and Director of Doctoral Studies at Grace Theological Seminary, one of the nation's leading evangelical seminaries. For ten years he served as Editor of the *Grace Theological Journal.* He is not only an outstanding scholar, but a gracious Christian gentleman and, in my judgment (shared by hosts of others) just about the finest Bible teacher one could ever hear.

When I first heard of him, however, he was an undergraduate at Princeton University, active in a group of evangelical students on the campus, each of whom had received a complimentary copy of my first book, *That You Might Believe,* as mentioned in Chapter III. That was in 1947. He graduated in 1948 with a B.A. in History, and then went on to Grace Seminary. After receiving his Master of Divinity Degree a few years later, he was given a post on the faculty, teaching Old Testament Studies.

I first met him personally in 1953, at the September meeting of the American Scientific Affiliation. This was the convention at

---

1. Ronald L. Numbers, "Creationism in 20th Century America," *Science,* 218, 5 Nov. 1982, p. 542.

2. Davis A. Young, *Creation and the Flood* (Grand Rapids: Baker Book House, 1977), p. 7.

which I presented my paper "Biblical Evidence for a Recent Creation and Universal Deluge," as discussed in Chapter IV. He was one of the few people at the meeting who responded favorably to the paper.

This began a long corresponding friendship which ultimately culminated in our co-authoring *The Genesis Flood.* In the first of these letters, written on September 20, 1953, he set the tone for our future fellowship and collaboration:

> I greatly appreciated your paper on "Recent Creation and Universal Deluge" which you read at the A.S.A. convention. I feel that your conclusions are scripturally valid, and therefore *must* be sustained by a fair examination of geologic evidence in time to come. My only regret is that so few trained Christian men of science are willing to let God's Word have the final say on these questions. . . . May God richly bless you in your ministry for His glory.

John Whitcomb began teaching the strict creationist position in his classes and found an excellent response from his students. Previously the Grace faculty, including its distinguished president, Dr. Alva J. McClain, had been teaching the gap theory, but Whitcomb was able to help many of them to see the scriptural validity of recent creation. In the meantime he was also working toward his Doctor of Theology degree.

Soon he decided, with faculty approval, to do his doctoral dissertation on the subject of the worldwide flood and its effects. He told me of this decision in a letter dated September 16, 1955, after a lapse of almost two years in our correspondence. I had previously written that I had been working on such a book myself for several years, so he wrote to ask for any suggestions or references I might have.

This manuscript of mine had been gradually growing since sometime in 1947, soon after I had gone to Minneapolis from Houston in order to work on my own Ph.D. at the University of Minnesota. I had chosen to major in hydraulics, with a minor in geology, primarily because of my conviction that this was the best combination with which to develop a sound system of deluge geology, and that this, in turn, had to be the key in a genuinely Biblical doctrine of creationism.

Accordingly, I set about working toward this goal as soon as possible after arriving at the University. The University had an outstanding library, including a separately housed geological library, and I used it at every opportunity. I began working on what I hoped would eventually become a definitive volume on recent creation and Biblical geology.

Among other things, I joined the American Geophysical Union and subscribed to the Annual Reports of the Committee on Geologic Time. Although I wasn't eligible yet for membership in the Geological Society of America, I did begin to read its bulletins at the library regularly, as well as many other scientific journals which had any potentially significant articles related to origins and earth history. I also joined the American Association for Advancement of Science and the American Meteorological Society and was already a member of Sigma Xi, the honorary scientific society (having been elected to membership several years earlier as a result of my hydrological studies on the Rio Grande). I began then the practice of clipping or copying significant articles, a practice which has proven extremely helpful over the years.

The writing of my proposed book, however, progressed very slowly. I had a full teaching and research load at the University (there were no government fellowships for graduate students in those days!), which required at least 40 hours of work each week, in addition to taking six hours of my own graduate courses each quarter. I also taught a Bible class at church each week, besides serving as deacon and leader of the church weekly soul-winning program, not to mention being a husband and father (three of our children were born in Minneapolis, and we already had two when we moved there). During much of the time, we were also preparing to go to Afghanistan, where I had tentatively accepted the job of organizing the civil engineering department in the proposed new Afghan Institute of Technology.

Consequently, the writing of my book had to take lowest priority and proceeded very slowly. By 1950, when I was finishing my doctoral dissertation, I had written first drafts of three chapters, totaling about 225 typed pages. I was calling the book *The Creation and Destruction of the World.* I had let Alton Everest (the ASA president) read it after he and Bernard Ramm visited me, on the occasion described in the preceding chapter, but he returned it merely with the comment that he was not qualified to evaluate its arguments. It seemed to me that although he didn't agree with it, he couldn't refute it, so preferred to ignore it.

After I finished work on my Ph.D., I accepted a position in Louisiana as Head of the Civil Engineering Department at the University of Southwestern Louisiana, which then was called Southwestern Louisiana Institute. This was in the summer of 1951. The position in Afghanistan had fallen through at the last minute, and although I had received more lucrative offers from three other state universities, the department chairmanship of SLI offered quite a challenge and (after much prayer) I felt the Lord would have me accept it.

I had hoped, now that my graduate studies were completed, to get back to the book, but once again a multitude of activities delayed it. Again I was a deacon, teacher, and visitation director at our new church, as well as busy with Gideon activities all over the state. At the school I was busy reorganizing and developing my department, trying to get it accredited—a goal which was finally accomplished in 1955.

The Minnesota library had been much superior to the one at SLI, which only had undergraduate degree programs at the time, so it was often difficult to get adequate information and documentation on the various problems I was trying to research. Nevertheless, by the time John Whitcomb asked to see the manuscript, I had been able to get one additional chapter done on the book, for a total of

300 pages. That, however, was as far as I ever got on my intended book.

I sent the manuscript to Dr. Whitcomb and he was greatly impressed, making copies of much of its documentation for his own use. He also encouraged me to continue working on it, not publishing it until I had really finished dealing with all important topics related to the creation/evolution and uniformity/catastrophism issues.

He continued his own work on his doctoral dissertation, finally receiving his Th.D. in 1957. This was the same year in which we moved again, first to Carbondale, Illinois, where I served only seven months as Professor of Applied Science, at Southern Illinois University, then on to Virginia. When the Illinois legislature voted against our proposed new engineering school there (I had gone there to plan and help organize an engineering school with the understanding that I would then become Dean of Engineering), I resigned and took a position at Virginia Tech (officially called the Virginia Polytechnic Institute and State University) as Professor of Hydraulic Engineering and Head of the Civil Engineering Department.

That was in the fall of 1957, and it was soon after that when we decided to collaborate on *The Genesis Flood.* Dr. Whitcomb had finished his dissertation in the spring of 1957 and had already had it tentatively accepted for publication by Moody Press, the publishing arm of the Moody Bible Institute. During the time I was in Carbondale, he had asked me to review the scientific chapters, since the Moody editor felt it would be desirable to have a scientist do this. With all the rush of moving from Illinois to Virginia, however, I was unable to finish reading it until October of that year.

While the earlier chapters of the manuscript, dealing with the Biblical and historical aspects of the Flood were excellent, it was obvious that the later chapters, dealing with its geological effects, were essentially merely a survey of George McCready Price's arguments. This was all right as far as it went, but Price himself had failed to make much of an impact with these same arguments 30 years previously, so I suggested that a new approach was needed, with better and more recent documentation. Dr. Whitcomb completely agreed, and so did the Moody editor, but he felt he was not able to do this himself.

The upshot of our further correspondence was a decision to collaborate as co-authors, with me contributing what I thought might be a couple of 50-page chapters, one critiquing geological uniformitarianism, the other outlining a Biblical framework for the data of historical geology.

Three More Years of Research and Writing

Since I was very busy with my new responsibilities at VPI, I did not actually agree to undertake the job until December 1957, just before Christmas. I thought I could finish my two chapters in about a year, and Dr. Whitcomb agreed to wait. By this time, however, it had been eight years since I had written those chapters in my own manuscript which might have been relevant to the new book, so they were already largely out-of-date, and I practically had to begin all over again.

As I got into the task, it turned out to be much more involved than I had thought. What I had originally estimated would be 100 pages eventually turned out to be 349 pages, in addition to Dr. Whitcomb's 151 pages. There would also be 28 pages of indexes. Fortunately, in those days I was not doing much traveling, so I was able to spend many hours in the VPI library—a library that was not the equal of that at Minnesota, but far superior to the one at Southwestern Louisiana, and quite adequate for my needs. In the meantime, Dr. Whitcomb continued to work on his own chapters, updating and expanding them significantly.

Even though we worked on distinctly separate portions of the book (he wrote the first four chapters and two appendices, I wrote

Figure 10. Civil Engineering and Virginia Tech

The Virginia Polytechnic Institute and State University, where the writer spent 13 years (1957-70) as Professor of Hydraulic Engineering and Chairman of the Civil Engineering Department (third largest in the nation at the time), was long known popularly as V.P.I. but is now better known as Virginia Tech. Photo at left shows the outstanding departmental faculty developed during that period, almost all of whom held doctorates in engineering. The photo of the writer was taken while at Virginia Tech, to be used on the jacket of *The Genesis Flood*.

the introduction and the last three chapters), each of us continually reviewed the other's contributions, and each made a number of contributions to the other's sections so that the joint authorship format was genuine.

Not only did the size of the book grow far beyond its intended original size, but so did the time required for its completion. This, of course, was mostly my fault, since most of Dr. Whitcomb's section was already finished before I even started on it. From the time I first started working on it (December 1957), it was almost three years (November 1960) before work on it was complete, including the indexes. The first printed copies were finally received in March 1961.

Of course, my civil engineering department also needed a great deal of attention. It was one of the largest in the nation, eventually growing to the third largest while I was there. It had been badly torn apart by internal strife just before I came, so there was a lot of healing and reorganizing to do. (This situation was almost an exact duplicate of what I had encountered at Southwestern Louisiana when I arrived there in 1951.)

Furthermore, although the undergraduate enrollment was large, the graduate and research programs were quite small, so I set about to upgrade these. I worked hard and the Lord blessed. We got approval for a Ph.D. program, only the second such civil engineering doctoral program in the southeastern states, and began a steady improvement of the staff, both in quantity and quality. When I arrived in 1957, there were seven professors in the department, only three of whom (including myself) had Ph.D. degrees. By the time I left in 1970, there were 20 professors, only three of whom did *not* have Ph.D.'s. By then we had about 600 undergraduate students and 60 graduate students. Of the latter, at least 50 had jobs as teaching or research assistants or held graduate fellowships of one kind or another. The sponsored research program had grown to be the second largest of any department in the university and the largest in engineering. Morale in the department was exceptionally high, with at least a third of the faculty evangelical Christians and all of them at least in sympathy with Biblical Christianity and with my beliefs, even though I never attempted to make this a factor in faculty selection.

I was particularly concerned to strengthen the hydraulics component of the program, since that was my specialty and there was nothing there in this field when I came. I started teaching a new senior course in hydraulic engineering, then kept adding graduate-level courses in various subjects in this field until we finally had thriving M.S. and Ph.D. programs in hydraulics and water resources. There were no textbooks available for these courses, so I began writing notes to give the students. These were all finally combined into one volume, which has become a standard textbook,[1] still widely used in many colleges and universities around the world.[2]

After *The Genesis Flood* was finally published and began to make an impact around the country, the leaders of the evolution-ary/humanistic establishments on the campus tried on at least two occasions to get me removed from my position, since I was con-sidered an embarrassment to the university (or so I was told by a high-level administrator there). However, the Lord had enabled our department to prosper so much that these attempts all failed.

During those years when I was writing my hydraulic engineer-ing textbook, we were also planning and then implementing a new civil engineering building and doctoral program, in addition to the regular routines of teaching and administration. There were many other pressures, too. By then we had six children, three of whom were in their teens, so we organized and sponsored a Youth-for-Christ club for the community. I was actively teaching a large college Sunday School class and working with the Inter-Varsity Christian Fellowship chapters and the Gideon camps in the area.

Nevertheless, even with all these other demands on time, the Lord marvelously led in the necessary research and writing of the book. Time and again, after encountering a difficult geological (or other) problem, I would pray about it, and then a reasonable solution would somehow quickly come to mind or hand, and the manuscript gradually took shape. I had to add another lengthy chapter on the problems of Biblical geology and all three of my chapters went through two complete rewrites before I got them

---

1. Henry M. Morris, *Applied Hydraulics in Engineering* (New York; Ronald Press, 1963), 455 pp.; Henry M. Morris and James M. Wiggert, *Applied Hydraulics in Engineering,* rev. and enl. (New York: John Wiley & Sons, Publ., 1972), 629 pp.

2. Although the book is currently (1993) over 30 years old, there is no compa-rable book available otherwise, so it is still being widely used. Altogether at least 100 colleges and universities have used this as a textbook at one time or another.

into final form. The same was true of Whitcomb's chapters.

When the book began to get so large and to deal with so many different fields, we realized we should have it reviewed by as many competent specialists as possible. Once we began to send it out for review, it seemed like there was no end to it. When it was finally done, our "Acknowledgments" section had to include the names of 21 scientists (10 of whom would later assist in founding the Creation Research Society), 9 theologians, and 2 grammarians, who had reviewed and critiqued part or all of the manuscript. By this time, we felt most of the bugs had been eliminated, and the reviewers were all at least supportive, and usually enthusiastic, about it.

In the meantime, we began to have second thoughts about the publisher. The Moody Press editors had originally seemed enthusiastic about the book (they had published my *Bible and Modern Science,* of course), but then gradually they seemed to become more and more doubtful. First they began to urge us to keep it down within 300 pages, but this would mean omitting a great deal of what we thought would be valuable material. Secondly, they let it be known they didn't agree with our "literal-day" view of the Genesis creation week, though how they thought we could harmonize the day/age theory with flood geology was never discussed. Then, they indicated that the main reason they were willing to publish the book was to be "fair." Since the American Scientific Affiliation and Moody Institute of Science people had received such wide promotion of their progressive-creation and local-flood views, the "other side deserved a hearing." Finally, they began to hint that publication schedules and priorities might cause a significant delay in getting the book in print.

One of the reviewers had been Rev. Rousas J. Rushdoony, an Orthodox Presbyterian Church pastor in California. He was quite enthusiastic about the book and wanted us to get it published in its entirety as soon as possible. He was a friend of Charles Craig, owner of a small, non-profit publishing concern called the Presby-

Figure 11. Publishers and Authors of The Genesis Flood.

At left above is Charles Hays Craig, whose Presbyterian and Reformed Publishing Co. published *The Genesis Flood*. The right photo shows the two authors, Dr. John C. Whitcomb and Dr. Henry M. Morris, in 1984, a quarter-century after they collaborated on the writing of the book.

terian and Reformed Publishing Co., in Philadelphia.

This company specialized in small printings of scholarly theological works, especially those in the strict Calvinist tradition. Some of their authors were Oswald T. Allis, B. B. Warfield, Cornelius Van Til, and, later, Rushdoony himself.

Rushdoony (who since has become widely recognized as one of the nation's outstanding educational philosophers) urged us to have *The Genesis Flood* published by Mr. Craig, through Presbyterian and Reformed. Craig also was enthusiastic. Consequently, after considerable study and prayer, we finally decided (in February 1960) to go this route instead of through Moody.

We have never regretted this decision; it was certainly, in retrospect, the Lord's leading. Charles Craig was notoriously chaotic in office management and other mundane affairs, but he did a splendid job of publishing books. Even though he did not cultivate book stores and did only minimal advertising, he did manage to get his books to the attention of libraries and key pastors and educators.

As soon as the decision was made, he proceeded to do everything he could to get the book out in as good a form as possible as soon as possible. We were still working on it, of course, revising and correcting and indexing, and he did everything he could to help us.

Craig himself had majored in geology at Princeton as an undergraduate, then taught chemistry and physical geology for five years at Lawrence School. He got an M.A. at Columbia University and was then in educational administration for several years until he decided (in about 1953) to devote full time to the non-profit publishing company founded by his father. He had accepted flood geology as a young man and was a firmly committed Christian.

He thus took a special interest in our book, even though he had never before published a scientific book. His own background was among the Presbyterians, and all his authors heretofore had been strong Calvinists. Both Dr. Whitcomb (Grace Brethren) and I (Baptist) seemed a little out of place among these Reformed and Presbyterian writers, but we all shared an absolute commitment to Biblical inerrancy and authority. In eschatology, all the P & R authors were either amillennial or postmillennial, whereas both John Whitcomb and I were (and are) "pretribulation" premillennialists, but we nevertheless had much in common with Craig and got along very well with him.

The book was promoted both before and after publication primarily by a four-page flier containing numerous recommendations of the book by scientists and others, which was mailed to a select list compiled by the three of us. One of those fliers was sent to each member of the American Scientific Affiliation, as well as to Craig's own mailing list of libraries, etc. This proved very effective and many orders began coming in even before the book was published.

I had only met Charles Craig personally one time, when the three of us got together at Winona Lake (Whitcomb's home) in July of 1960. We accomplished quite a bit at the meeting, since the manuscript revising and editing was reaching a crucial stage at that time. John Whitcomb and I had gotten together one time before this, in Pittsburgh the previous summer. I had to be in Pittsburgh for an engineering convention, and he was on his way back to Winona Lake from a speaking engagement. We had two days of wonderful fellowship and fruitful discussions on the manuscript. Other than these two occasions, all the collaboration needed for writing and publishing the book was accomplished by correspondence.

At the Winona Lake meeting, our families were also able to meet each other and this was a blessing. John Whitcomb's first wife, Edisene, and their three children (their fourth child was born a month later), were there, along with my wife, Mary Louise, and five of our six children (our oldest son, Henry, was in the army at this time). Mr. Craig was there with his little son Bryce. Bryce, now has taken over his father's business and is doing a fine job of it.[1] All the other children are grown now too, of course, and all are active Christian men or women, so we all have much more for which to be thankful than just the way He led in the writing of *The Genesis Flood*.

But in any case, that was the way it was. In a real sense, its writing began about 1947, when I began working on the manuscript for my never-to-be-published *Creation and Destruction of the World*. John Whitcomb began writing on his doctoral dissertation in 1955, but had been thinking about it and collecting materials for several years before that. Finally the book was published, early in 1961. But its publication merely marked a new chapter in the story, as the Lord has been graciously using its testimony ever since.

---

1. Charles Craig went to be with the Lord in 1983.

Reception of the Book by Evangelicals

Whatever may have been the impact of *The Genesis Flood* upon the Christian and non-Christian communities as a whole, it certainly changed the lives of its authors. Never again would there be the time available for the intensive library research that had preceded its publication. This is the reason also why we have never managed to revise and update the book for a new edition, despite many good intentions to do so at various times during the intervening years.

John Whitcomb had already begun to be in demand as a speaker, even before the book was published, especially among the churches of his own Grace Brethren denomination. He is remarkably eloquent and winsome in his messages, combining clear Biblical expository insight with a warm good humor which disarms even the most apathetic or hostile audience. His seminary students almost always will testify he is one of the best teachers they ever had, and I personally would testify that I enjoy and appreciate his messages as much as any to which I have ever listened. With the book's publication, the demand for his services quickly multiplied. For many years, his speaking schedule has been filled years in advance, and he has to turn down far more invitations than he can accept.

As far as I was concerned, I did speak occasionally in other cities, but even these were usually close by. Most of my outside speaking was for the Gideons rather than creationism.

There were a few occasions, however, resulting from my previous books and occasional journal articles. One of the most significant of these—even resulting in a number of converts—had been a series of messages to Harvard and MIT students in Boston. Another had been at William and Mary College in Williamsburg, and another at the University of Virginia.

When *The Genesis Flood* was published, however, speaking invitations began to come in abundance, and I tried to accept most of them. One of the first and most important such occasions was at a dinner meeting of the Houston Geological Society in Texas, in 1962. This is the world's largest local geological association, and there were about 500 geologists present. I spoke on the theme "Biblical Catastrophism and Geology," and the message certainly brought me and the book quickly to the attention of the geological profession. The reaction was, as one might expect, explosive! The chairman was quite insulting and quickly terminated the meeting after my talk, without even allowing time for discussion (however, he did call later and apologize, after being chastised by a number of members for his rudeness).

The Society normally published all such banquet papers in its regular journal, but decided not to publish mine. Accordingly, it was later published as a special booklet under the above title by Mr. Craig's Presbyterian and Reformed Publishing Company, in which form it had for many years a fruitful ministry (including the winning of Dr. Tom Barnes—about whom more later—to the creationist cause).

The invitation to speak at such an unlikely place had been arranged by some geologists in the St. Thomas Episcopal Church in Houston, whose pastor, Rev. T. Robert Ingram, had developed a strong Bible centered ministry in his church and was reaching many important people in Houston. He himself had become enthusiastic about *The Genesis Flood* and had invited me to bring a Bible-science conference to his church and school. This unique pastor, school, and church, have since that time, sponsored many important conferences and publications in the field of sound Christian education.

Shortly after this, I was asked to speak at the annual meeting of the Reformed Fellowship in Grand Rapids. This is an organization of concerned pastors and laymen in the Christian Reformed Church. The messages brought to this fine group were later published by them in 1963, through the Baker Book House of Grand Rapids, under the title *The Twilight of Evolution*. This book also has had a long and fruitful ministry and, like *The Genesis Flood,* is still in print.

While I was in Grand Rapids for this meeting, I was also invited to speak to the Calvin College and Seminary chapel and to its faculty. These institutions were schools of the Christian Reformed Church, and it was soon clear why a conservative organization had been needed in the church. The faculty, in particular, seemed quite displeased with my book. Most of them were obviously theistic evolutionists. As a result, I later submitted a report to the officers of the Reformed Fellowship about all this, and they conducted a sort of investigation about it, but it did not result in any significant action. The Calvin College faculty has ever since been hostile to me and to the creationist movement. The current(1993) science faculty, especially Davis Young, Howard Van Till and Clarence Menninga, have published a series of widely read books and articles sharply critical of creationism in general and of my writings in particular. A denominational investigation of the Calvin College and Calvin Seminary faculties, centered particularly on these three men, resulted in a whitewash, so it seems that these schools (despite resistance from many pastors and laymen in the Christian Reformed denomination) are rather permanently committed to theistic evolution(or "process creation" as some of them like to call it).

Another important invitation was to speak to the Lutheran Free Theological Conference in Minneapolis, early in 1963. Those messages were published verbatim by that organization (consisting of conservatives from various Lutheran groups) in booklet form, but never as a formal book.

Still another interesting opportunity about that time was a telephone invitation by Bill Bright, whose Campus Crusade for Christ organization was just then beginning to have a national outreach, to serve as the CCC-sponsored speaker at the University of Miami's Religious Emphasis Week. The Crusade representative in Miami was Jon Braun, who would later leave to form a parachurch organization of his own. I stayed in Jon's house and shared a room with Jon Buell, who was then a Crusade trainee and would, many years later, become one of the founders of Probe Ministries.

Other early invitations were to The King's College in New York state, Wisconsin Lutheran Seminary, and to John Whitcomb's own Grace College and Seminary in Indiana. One thing I especially remember about these early speaking assignments is that I traveled to and from most of them by train. I had never been on an airplane until after we moved to Virginia and was very reluctant to start (after all, my younger brother had been killed in an airplane crash in Burma in World War II, though this was not my only reason). Whenever it was close enough, of course, I went by automobile, and there were many such trips.

Finally, it became impracticable to continue this sort of thing. I did have to work at Virginia Tech, too! Consequently, I reluctantly began flying to my speaking engagements. Now it seems like I have spent almost half my time, over the past thirty years, in airplanes or air terminals. But I have never learned to like it!

In addition to more and more speaking engagements, I began to receive many invitations to write articles for Christian magazines. I had a whole series of articles published in *Bibliotheca Sacra,* the Dallas Seminary journal, and in numerous other publications. Finally, a collection of these was published under the name *Studies in the Bible and Science,* first in syllabus form by John Whitcomb at Grace Seminary, later (in 1966) as a regular book by Presbyterian and Reformed.

The book *Evolution and the Modern Christian* (Presbyterian and Reformed, 1967) was first prepared as a series of studies for a young people's summer camping program. An earlier invitation from Baptist Publications to write a series of Sunday School lessons on Genesis 1–11, was published in 1965 under the name *Science, Scripture, and Salvation.* After being used by many churches over many years, these quarterlies were updated and issued in book form in 1977, under the title *The Beginning of the*

World.

And so it went. Dr. Whitcomb also was speaking far and wide, more often and more widely than I was, and people were both reading and hearing the theme of *The Genesis Flood* in many places, both likely and unlikely. Many different denominations were being affected, as well as many interdenominational groups, and even many groups on secular campuses. Furthermore, our book had stirred up new interest in the few earlier creationist books, especially among the Lutherans and Seventh-Day Adventists, and some of *their* authors also began to be involved in more wide-ranging speaking activities than heretofore. Most of these had, of course, reviewed the manuscript for *The Genesis Flood* prior to its publication.

Thus was the modern creationist revival beginning to get under way. An extremely important development in 1963, just two years after the book was published, was the formation of the Creation Research Society. However, this story needs a chapter of its own and will be deferred for Chapter VI. The Bible-Science Association was formed that same year, but this also will be discussed later.

However, while on the subjects of speech-making and bookwriting, let me go on and describe a few other later effects of this sort, as far as my own activities are concerned. While I do not have convenient access to the speaking and writing calendars of John Whitcomb and the other men for this period, I would assume that my activities, and the types of places reached, would be typical for these others as well. Thus, the impact of my witness, whatever it may have been, could be multiplied many fold, since many others were doing the same kinds of things.

For example, over the next several years, I was invited to hold a lecture series at such significant Christian colleges and seminaries as Tennessee Temple, Bob Jones University, Los Angeles Baptist College, LeTourneau College, and Biola College (all of these, in fact, also offered me positions on their faculties). Others included Bryan College (the school erected in memory of William

Jennings Bryan and the Scopes trial), Columbia Bible College, Washington Bible College, Atlanta Christian College, Houghton College, Central Wesleyan College, Eastern Mennonite College, Cincinnati Baptist College, Grace Bible Institute, Cedarville College, Appalachian Bible College, John Brown University, Ozark Bible College, Cincinnati Bible Seminary, Trinity College, Piedmont Bible College, and various others. All of these were the direct result of *The Genesis Flood*, and many of the students in these audiences later became pastors or teachers who were strong advocates of creationism.

But undoubtedly the most significant such invitation was the honor of the W. H. Griffith Thomas Lectureship at Dallas Theological Seminary in 1967. Dallas is the largest evangelical seminary, as well as the most influential, in the nation, and the Griffith Thomas Lectureship is one of the most respected awards in the Christian world. Although not all Dallas faculty members subscribed then (nor do they now) to the strict creationism of *The Genesis Flood*, it was a singular achievement for it to be recognized this way. Until the time of its publications, most of its faculty (including its founders) had advocated the gap theory, with some committed to the day-age theory, but most of them by this time had accepted the strict creationism of *The Genesis Flood*.

Our book had made quite an impact there, and the lectures were extremely well received by the 400 students, as well as the faculty, with an exceptional standing ovation at their termination. The title of the series was "Biblical Cosmology and Modern Science." The four main lectures were published as a series of four articles in *Bibliotheca Sacra* and then later combined with several other articles I had written for other journals for publication in a book by that name. Dr. Charles Ryrie, one of the most distinguished members of the Dallas faculty, wrote the Foreword and later served for several years as one of the two theologian members (along with John Whitcomb) of our ICR Technical Advisory Board. The book was published by Craig Press, a newly established subsidiary of

Presbyterian and Reformed, since its chapter on "Biblical Eschatology and Modern Science" advocated premillennialism. Like *The Genesis Flood*, Moody Press had first approached me about publishing it, but when they wanted me to make various compromising changes in it, I went back to Craig.

In addition to the schools, there were, of course, numerous speaking engagements at churches of many denominations, pastors' conferences, summer Bible conferences, youth conventions, Christian teachers' conventions, and various other meetings. These even included a fair number of scientific meetings and other secular gatherings. My trips ranged from Washington to Florida, from California to Massachusetts (never yet to Maine!), and Texas to Minnesota. All of this was before 1970, while I was still in Virginia, trying to keep up with all the needs and challenges of my job and other responsibilities. In retrospect, it seems impossible, but the Lord was gracious and kept all of that going well, too. Life was indeed different, however, than it was before *The Genesis Flood*.

Response by Evolutionists

Not all of the reactions to *The Genesis Flood* were so favorable, of course, either in terms of my personal activities or in terms of the Christian and non-Christian publics at large. The reaction of the Houston Geological Society president and the Calvin College faculty were quite typical for the secular intellectual and Christian neoevangelical realms, respectively. These two groups had embraced evolutionism, and it was obvious that *The Genesis Flood* would raise penetrating questions about the validity of evolutionism, questions aimed at the real heart of its supposed evidence, the geologic-age system. Consequently, it was not surprising that these would strike back vigorously, particularly when the book began to make a serious impact.

As far as my personal life was concerned, there were immediate repercussions. As soon as the book was out, I gave a copy to the pastor of our church, and his reaction was quite negative. This was the last straw in our relationship with the church. He was a Southern Baptist liberal, and the lay leadership of the church (mostly VPI faculty) was also quite liberal, but there was no better church in the community, and we had stayed there for four years because I was teaching the college class and my wife a junior class. Many of the students were eagerly awaiting the book, and I had hoped that the pastor also could be won through the evidence given in the book, once it was published. However, he refused even to read it, with the curt remark that "all the scientists couldn't be wrong." Furthermore, the Sunday School officials decided not to let me teach the college class any longer. Since there was really no other suitable church, we decided (with one other family and a number of the Inter-Varsity students) to start an independent Baptist Church.

The new church was eventually incorporated as the College Baptist Church and soon joined the Independent Fundamental Churches of America. Although we never fought the other churches, nor tried to proselytize their members, they all bitterly opposed us and our strongly creationist Bible-centered teaching and evangelistic ministries. The church never became large, but did maintain a strong witness for many years. A great many students and a number of faculty were won to the Lord, and many others were able to grow spiritually during the time they were there in Blacksburg because of the church. In 1983, it merged with another group to become the Harvest Baptist Church.

Naturally, the church required a great deal of my own time and attention. I not only taught its college/adult class, served as deacon and trustee, but also had to do much of the preaching and visitation, until we grew enough to afford a pastor. Several of my later books grew, at least in some measure, out of messages originally prepared for presentation in the church. Furthermore, many of its new members were out-of-town arrivals who first came because they had read *The Genesis Flood* before they moved there.

The book also had a profound effect on my campus relations. I gave one of the first copies to my immediate superior, the Dean of the College of Engineering, and told him that it might cause repercussions in the academic community. However, he enjoyed the book and was always very supportive, as long as he lived.

However, he died soon afterward, and it was a different story with the new dean. He had been preceded into office by a new president and vice-president—all within a two-year period, as well as by various other new administrators. As is typical, this new administration had great ambitions, and sweeping changes were made in the whole university structure. By this time, my civil engineering department had grown considerably in both size and reputation, in comparison to most other departments, and this was somehow considered unseemly. The president was a physicist, the vice-president a chemist, and the dean an electrical engineer, and they wanted to push the more "sophisticated" areas of science and engineering, as well as the humanities and social sciences. Accordingly, whereas the former administration had been highly supportive and appreciative of our departmental contribution to the university, the new administration seemed to resent it and began to resist any further development. On one occasion, the new dean even tried to force through a drastic reorganization which would have eliminated the civil engineering department (as well as certain other "traditional" departments) altogether, but he encountered so much resistance from the faculty, students, and alumni that he had to withdraw his plan. In the meantime, my department continued to grow in quantity and quality in spite of them.

Naturally enough, the growing visibility of *The Genesis Flood,* as well as national news media attention on our Creation Research Society and on my own creationist lectures around the country, tended to aggravate this situation. I had given the new dean a copy of the book as soon as he arrived on campus, so that he would know the situation firsthand. He read it and was impressed with the research and analysis that had gone into it, but let me know in plain terms that he disagreed with and disapproved of it. Furthermore, the new vice-president would not allow me any longer to list it or any of my other creationist books and articles on my official resume. Fortunately, I still had more "professional" articles to list than most other faculty members, as well as a widely used textbook (I had also given copies of my hydraulic engineering textbook to the president and the dean).

The dean was fairly knowledgeable in the field of geology, since his father was well known in this field, as geology department chairman at an important western university. He had also asked his father to read the book; he again got the response that the research was impressive but the book totally unacceptable in its conclusions. Neither offered any refutation of any specific item, however.

It was also during this period (1963–64) that the local faculty—presumably the geology and biology faculties in particular—began to complain about me to the dean and president, maintaining that my book and my lecturing were making both them and the university in general look bad in the academic community. They wanted me removed from the faculty altogether, if possible, but at least from my department chairmanship. However, it was apparent that they had no legitimate excuse for such action, since my department was clearly one of the best in the university, with faculty and student morale high, so they were in a difficult position. I am convinced (though, of course, with no proof) that the subsequent difficulties I began having with the administration were essentially part of an attempt on their part to get me to leave or else to gradually break down the department.

In 1963, the student geological society asked me to speak to their members on the theme of our book. Their faculty had been commenting on it in their classes, and they wanted to hear me firsthand. The result was a rather heated three-hour session, with some 300 or more present. The geology and biology faculties were out *en masse,* along with many other professors. They had hoped to make me look bad, but it worked the other way. Many of the students, and a number of faculty members, were profoundly impressed, not only with the lecture but with my responses to the faculty questions and criticisms. Even several of the geology professors were at least partially won over, and some became good friends.

Nevertheless, the behind-the-scenes sniping grew worse. By 1968, it was obvious that, regardless of my record in the department, the administration was determined that I should go—one way or another. By that time, I had served as department chairman longer than any others in the entire university, except for two men who were scheduled for retirement shortly. Furthermore, partly because of all this opposition, and partly because of my need for more time for writing and speaking on creationism, I began to wonder whether the Lord was actually leading me to resign, either to go elsewhere or at least to relinquish the administrative headaches.

As mentioned earlier, at various times during this period I was offered positions at five different Christian colleges, mainly as a result of the ministry of *The Genesis Flood*. One of these, Bob Jones University, actually awarded me an honorary LL.D. degree in 1966. I seriously considered going to Bob Jones, and also to Los Angeles Baptist College, in 1967, but finally decided these were not in the Lord's will at the time. Also, a number of engineering schools approached me about changing positions, two of which I considered seriously enough to take interview trips. One of these would have been as Director of the Alabama Water Resources Center, located at Auburn University. The people at Auburn assured me that my creationist views would not be a hindrance, but the Alabama state geologist was on the selection committee and he decided to take the job himself. The other was at the University of New Mexico, as Civil Engineering Department Head, and they said the same thing, but then my own dean warned them of the possible academic backlash, so I withdrew my name from consideration before they could pursue it further.

In the meantime, with the situation deteriorating at VPI, I finally offered to resign my position as department head if they would give me a sabbatical at full pay for an entire academic year, during which time I proposed to revise and enlarge my hydraulic engineering textbook. Afterward, I offered to continue simply as a tenured full professor in the department. The university had never awarded a sabbatical with such generous provisions before, but this request was quickly approved.

This arrangement was clearly of the Lord. During the sabbatical year (1969–70), 1 did get my hydraulic engineering book ready for its new edition, and it still (as of 1993) is being used). It was also during that year that Auburn University again approached me, this time with the very tempting offer of a special endowed chair in civil engineering, with freedom to teach whatever courses I wanted, and also freedom to teach creationism as desired.

At about the same time, LeTourneau College offered me a position as dean of its engineering school. Since LeTourneau was just about the only Biblical Christian college in the nation with an engineering program, this also was very tempting. However, this school, like others, felt that a special center for creation studies such as I had suggested, would be too expensive and controversial, so I reluctantly turned it down.

However, it was also during this year that the events took place which would finally culminate in the establishment of Christian Heritage College and the Institute for Creation Research (see Chapter VII). Although the impact of *The Genesis Flood* had generated strong waves of opposition, both in my church life and my academic life, the Lord had worked it all out for good, as He had promised (Romans 8:28).

When the dean announced my resignation, my entire faculty petitioned him to persuade me to reconsider, but he said my decision was final. They conducted a search for a new chairman, finally appointing the man whom I had first recommended, a fine Christian creationist who was already in our department. He continued in the position for 13 years (one more than I had) until another new administration finally forced him out.

The foregoing account has to do, of course, only with the effect of the publication of *The Genesis Flood* upon my own personal life. As far as Dr. Whitcomb was concerned, his life also was significantly affected, but with the important difference that his own school (Grace Theological Seminary) was wonderfully supportive of his testimony. The Grace faculty and administration became convinced and committed advocates of recent creationism and flood geology, and they were already committed to full Biblical inerrancy and authority. Furthermore, his administration not only allowed, but encouraged him to speak in other places, and he has had a tremendously wide-ranging speaking ministry over the years since the book's publication.

He later wrote two "sequels" to *The Genesis Flood*. These were entitled *The Early Earth* (1972) and *The World That Perished* (1973), *as well as two books on creationist astronomy, The Origin of the Solar System* (1963) and *The Moon* (1978, co-authored with Dr. Donald DeYoung, Professor of Physics at Grace College). In addition, he has written a number of books on Old Testament studies and prepared several widely-used charts on Biblical chronology, as well as numerous articles for Christian journals and encyclopedias.

New editions of *The Early Earth* and *The World That Perished* were published in 1987. However, eventually a new administration at Grace Seminary forced him out early in 1989, just a few months before retirement. He had become too vocal in opposing certain liberal trends developing in the seminary in recent years. His speaking and missionary ministries continued, however, as effectively as ever. In late 1992, he was elected President of the Conservative Grace Brethren churches, resulting from a split in the Grace Brethren denomination over these trends.

On the other side of the coin, the reaction to *The Genesis Flood* in the neo-evangelical orbit was, as we had anticipated, quite negative. After all, the book had been written primarily to call Christians back from the dangerous path into which they were being led by the American Scientific Affiliation and the neo-evangelical theologians. Much of Dr. Whitcomb's discussion in his first part of the book, in fact, had been a point-by-point refutation of Bernard Ramm's arguments for a local flood and progressive creationism in a book[1] which had become almost an official textbook for neo-evangelicalism.

Although by far the majority of the published reviews of *The Genesis Flood* were very favorable, some of the most prestigious Christian journals published highly critical reviews. These were, by and large, the neo-evangelical journals, of course. William Sanford LaSor, Fuller Seminary professor, wrote a real diatribe in *Eternity,* as did Donald Boardman, Professor of Geology at Wheaton College in *Christianity Today.* Arthur Kuschke, Librarian at Westminster Seminary, wrote a very negative review in *The Westminster Theological Journal.* There were other critical reviews, of course, but most reviews were very complimentary, more than we had dared to hope for.

The American Scientific Affiliation itself, however, was strangely silent. It almost seemed they wanted to ignore the book altogether. It had gone through several printings, and scores of reviews had been published, before the ASA finally took official notice of the book, in its March 1964 issue, more than three years after its publication. This time, they published two reviews, both extremely critical, of course. Then, five years later, in September 1969, it reprinted a very critical and lengthy analysis of the book which had first been published in Holland by a Dutch geologist, R. Van de Fliert. Drs. Boardman and Tanner, two ASA geologists, published supporting negative critiques of our book in the same

---

1. Bernard Ramm, *The Christian View of Science and Scripture* (Grand Rapids: Eerdmans Pub. Co., 1954). Ramm was especially revered by the American Scientific Affiliation, which made him an Honorary Fellow, even though he was not a scientist.

issue. The revealing thing about *this* review was that its theological perspective was not even neo-evangelical, but blatantly neo-ortho-dox!

The editor, Dr. Bube, did allow me to write a reply to this attack, in the March 1970 issue, but was careful to surround it with other letters which were highly critical of *The Genesis Flood.* But at least, nine years later (and long after the Creation Research Society had become a strong competitor), the ASA was finally taking serious notice of the book.

By 1968, the book had been reviewed so widely and caused such a stir in the evangelical world that a Dallas Seminary student, formerly a meteorologist trained at MIT, actually wrote his Master of Theology thesis on a review and analysis of all the reviews and analyses of *The Genesis Flood.*[1]

The most interesting conclusion of his thesis was that not one of the critical reviews had dealt with the most important emphasis of the book—namely, that the Bible could not be harmonized with either the local flood theory or the tranquil flood theory. Granted that the Bible was indeed the inerrant Word of God (as all evangelicals at least professed to believe), our book had shown that a worldwide cataclysmic deluge must be accepted as real history. This implies, of course, that the geologic data have been badly misinterpreted, making them teach long evolutionary geological ages without any allowance for a global flood. If the flood really did occur, as the Bible clearly teaches, then it necessarily follows that many or most of the geologic formations must have been caused by the flood. We had tried to show how the geologic data could be interpreted this way, but we repeatedly stressed that our geological conclusions were tentative, subject to modification through further research, provided only that the basic Bible teach-

---

1. Charles Clough, *A Calm Appraisal of THE GENESIS FLOOD*, Th.M. Thesis, Dallas Theological Seminary, 1968, 196 pp. See also his summaries of this study in *Journal of Christian Reconstruction*, Vol. 1, 1974, pp. 35-48; and *Creation Research Society Quarterly*, Vol. 6. September 1969, pp. 81-84.

ing of a global cataclysm not be changed.

A number of similar theses have since been written at other schools.It was significant that *not one critical review* attempted to refute our exposition of this plain Biblical teaching. However, they all insisted that the flood must be local anyhow, strictly on the basis of the geological data, attacking one or another of our geological interpretations. This situation constituted strong evidence of the hypocrisy of their professed allegiance to Scripture, or so at least it seemed to us.

As far as the secular, scientific, and educational establishments were concerned, the book was largely ignored, at least until the strong anti-creationist reaction of the 1980s. There were occasional flurries of interest, such as the 1962 meeting of the Houston Geological Society, described earlier, but these were exceptions. Also, many individual scientists were being won to creationism, and even to the Lord, as multitudes of later testimonies have confirmed. But officially it was generally ignored.

This did not surprise nor disappoint us, of course. The book was written specifically for Christians, not for the world in general. Its basic premise was that the Bible was God's infallible Word, and its goal was to call those who believed this basic truth back to true creationism. It demonstrated—we thought conclusively—that the Bible taught a recent creation and world-destroying deluge. That being the case, all the facts of geology and the other sciences must, if understood correctly, confirm the historical factuality of these two great events. We then tried to show from a detailed study of the scientific data that this really was the case, but that these data had somehow been distorted to conform to the humanistic notions of evolutionism and uniformitarianism.

We urged Christians to recognize this and to come back to true Biblical creationism—and multitudes did. What really surprised us—and caused us great rejoicing—was the fact that many others actually were converted from skepticism and unbelief to true faith in Christ and His great salvation, at least partially through *The

Genesis Flood. The book was not written as an evangelistic tool at all, but God has graciously and abundantly used it to that end, for which we are very grateful.

Chapter VI

The Creation Research Society

Undoubtedly the most significant of the various creationist associations that have been formed, at least in this country, is the Creation Research Society. The Religion and Science Association survived only two years and the Creation-Deluge Society only six. The American Scientific Affiliation is still active, but it only survived as a *creationist* organization for a very few years, being largely oriented toward theistic evolutionism throughout most of its history. However, the Creation Research Society, organized in 1963, is still strongly creationist and very active as of this writing (1993), over 30 years after it started.

I am confident that the reason for this stability of belief and witness is the fact that, unlike its predecessors, it was founded upon a specific doctrinal commitment which included the literal historicity of the Genesis accounts of special creation of all things in six days and the worldwide cataclysmic Noahic deluge. Furthermore, unlike the original ASA statement of faith, it was constitutionally guarded so as to preclude change. Although there have been some people accepted as members who did not believe these doctrines very strongly, as well as many outsiders who tried to get them changed, the Society still maintains a strong and uncompromising witness for recent creation and flood geology.

Influence of THE GENESIS FLOOD

There were many people, events, and circumstances that contributed to the formation of the Society, but the catalyst that seemed to bring them together, in God's providence, was the writing and publication of *The Genesis Flood*. Even before it was published, several of the scientists who read it in manuscript form had begun to think in terms of the need for such an organization. Some of these had been fairly active in the American Scientific Affiliation, but it had become obvious by this time that the evolutionists were thoroughly in control, with true creationism being increasingly pushed out. The Flood manuscript led them to renewed confidence that the neo-evangelical compromises were both unscriptural and unnecessary, so that some sort of new association and journal outlet was essential for the further study and establishment of a truly Biblical system of creationism and earth history.

The key man among these scientists was Dr. Walter Lammerts, with Dr. Will Tinkle also playing a significant role. Lammerts had been active in the old Deluge Society, and his beliefs were fully in line with those of that Society. He and Tinkle had been early members of ASA also, and had published papers in its journal. The two were friends and had discussed between themselves the need for a new society. Eventually they were destined to become the two main officers of the CRS when it was finally organized.

Of course, I also (and who knows how many others!) felt strongly this need, but had few contacts, and was already so busy with other vital matters that there seemed no feasible way of going about it. The few ASA people I knew were certainly not prospects, although Tinkle and Lammerts did know a few who were.

The need for such a society had actually been proposed in correspondence between Lammerts, Whitcomb, and myself five years earlier, in 1957 and 1958. This was while *The Genesis Flood* was being written, and John Whitcomb had written Dr. Lammerts to get help on a couple of technical questions, the growth of the olive tree after the Flood, and the preservation of land vegetation through the Flood. This inquiry soon led to a most fruitful relationship and sequence of developments.

As noted earlier, Lammerts had been involved to some extent

with the old Deluge Society, though never actually a member, and was one of the earliest members of the American Scientific Affiliation. He had written a critique of radioactive dating[1] in the first publication of ASA, a collection of mimeographed papers on the theme of the age of the earth, most of which accepted the standard old-age view. He and Will Tinkle had co-authored an excellent article on creationist genetics in ASA's first book.[2] However, by that time ASA had become so dominated by theistic-evolutionist and progressive-creationist thinking that Lammerts had almost lost interest in it. It was difficult for him, heavily involved in horticultural research on the west coast, to get to most of the ASA meetings, and Tinkle was almost alone in standing for true creationism among the ASA leaders.

However, Dr. Lammerts' interest and concern were partially rekindled[3] when he read a book by a Lutheran theologian in his own Missouri Synod, a book on flood geology,[4] following fairly closely the approach of George McCready Price and his followers. This soon led to his making at least two trips to the Glacier National Park for the purpose of investigating the contact plane at the famous Lewis Overthrust in Montana and Alberta. This is one of the most famous out-of-order geologic regions, with vast areas of Precambrian limestones overlying Cretaceous shales, and Price had frequently referred to this so-called "thrust fault" as an argument against the validity of the standard geologic time scale.

Lammerts returned firmly convinced that Price was right and the "overthrust" was no overthrust at all, but a normal sedimentary

1. W. E. Lammerts, Chapter VI in A *Symposium on the Age of the Earth* (American Scientific Affiliation, 1948), 4 pp.

2. W. E. Lammerts and W. Tinkle, "Biology and Creation," Chapter IV in *Modern Science and Christian Faith*, by Members of the American Scientific Affiliation (Wheaton, Illinois: Van Kampen Press, 1948), pp. 58-97.

3. W. E. Lammerts, Personal communication, November 16, 1983.

4. Alfred M. Rehwinkel, *The Flood (St.* Louis: Concordia Publishing House, 1951), 372 pp.

sequence. He later sent me a set of slides he had made of the contact plane, some of which we then published in *The Genesis Flood,* with his permission. His trips to the Lewis Overthrust had been made in the summers of 1956 and 1957, just before our correspondence began with him.

In a letter to John Whitcomb, dated November 27, 1957, he had indicated his disappointment with ASA and his hope that an informal creationist association could be formed someday. Dr. Whitcomb suggested I write to him, which I did in a letter dated December 22, 1957, making the following comments:

> I am especially pleased with your suggestion that we consider the formation of a new society to study these problems. The Creation Deluge Society was always too localized, both geographically and denominationally, to do much good, and the American Scientific Affiliation of course is very substantially committed to orthodox geology and other positions that seem to compromise a full-orbed doctrine of Biblical inspiration. Nevertheless, I am sure there is a very substantial number of evangelical scientists, who hold essentially the same convictions we do about these matters, and who could be actively interested in such a new association. Perhaps a first step might be to select a tentative name (such as Association of Evangelical Scientists, or some such) and statement of belief, and then to send out letters inquiring as to possible interest, to men that we know are qualified and might be interested.

Lammerts replied quite positively to everything I had said, including even the suggested name. However, he indicated he could not undertake the work of organizing it himself, since he lacked the necessary energy and didn't have any names to contact. He encouraged me to proceed with it, however, and said he would be an active member. Whitcomb also was interested and favorable, but lacked the necessary time and contacts.

I made a few contacts and found some interest, but I was heavily involved with research and writing on the book at this time, as well as all my regular responsibilities at the school. Consequently, we

**Figure 12.
Walter Lammerts**
The chief founder of
the Creation Research
Society was Dr. Walter
Lammerts. He served
as the Society's first
President and Journal
Editor, leaving an in-
delible stamp on the
Society. Dr. Lammerts
has long been an out-
standing horticultural
geneticist, winning a
number of prizes in the
breeding of new varie-
ties of roses, camellias,
and other plants.

all more or less decided that the society would have to wait until
the book was completed. Hopefully, the book itself would help
generate interest, and there would be more time to work on it then.

As it turned out, the manuscript itself served this purpose rather
well. It was reviewed prior to publication by 19 scientists, 8 of
whom would later become members of the so-called "Team of
Ten," which Lammerts and Tinkle organized in 1962, and 10 of
whom would eventually serve on the 18-member founding Board
of the Creation Research Society. Of the other eight initial Board
members, at least four were contacted as a specific result of *The
Genesis Flood* soon after it was published. It seems clear that the
Lord used the book as a catalyst, stirring up latent interest and
convictions among those scientists who read it either before or just

after it was published, until finally there were enough to serve as the necessary nucleus.

Lammerts may have discussed the need in the interim with others besides Whitcomb and me, but unfortunately he left all his earlier correspondence in Livermore when he retired in 1961. By then, Lammerts and I started to correspond further about such a society right after he read the published book, in May 1961. Will Tinkle had also become so disillusioned with the ASA that he had written several other creationists, asking whether they would be interested in participating with him in an informal creationist committee within the ASA. Interest gradually became crystallized, and in 1962 a ten-man committee began to take concrete form. Lammerts had become quite active by this time and was taking the lead in these contacts and in formulating plans. However, the ten men who were originally invited included three who soon dropped out (Edward Kessel, Philip Livdahl, and Molleurus Couperus). The other four (besides Lammerts, Tinkle, and myself) were Frank Marsh, Laird Harris, Edwin Monsma, and Duane Gish. The three who dropped out had not read our manuscript, and Couperus had been directly involved in the break-up of the Creation-Deluge Society. The three who replaced them on the team of ten later were John Grebe, Wilbert Rusch, and John Klotz.

When Dr. Tinkle first wrote me about it, on November 28, 1961, he suggested an informal committee within ASA, with a rather weak statement of faith. I replied, on December 25, 1961, stressing that we needed an entirely new society, with a very strong statement of faith. Tinkle, who was somewhat of a leader in the ASA, didn't want to go that far, fearing that a split and subsequent fighting between the two organizations might destroy them both. He thought his proposed committee, by helping each other, might be able to reform the ASA from within. I replied (March 13, 1962) that we could work in both organizations, and there was no need for fighting, but that we would never really accomplish anything trying to work only within the ASA; it was too permeated with evolutionism ever to be reclaimed, especially with all its Executive Council members of that persuasion.

Lammerts agreed with me, but we all decided that we could start with the committee. Then, as the Lord led, this could be expanded sooner or later into a new society.

In recounting the events leading up to the Society, Dr. Lammerts wrote the following summary of his experiences:

> My own interest in the evolution question waned considerably after I left the University of California, Los Angeles, in 1945. . . . I had little time for consideration of any evolution versus creation argumentation in the period from 1945 until 1960. Then Henry Morris asked me to read a manuscript he was writing called *The Genesis Flood.* In this manuscript, he argued most persuasively for the historicity and actuality of a worldwide flood. . . . As a result of this proof-reading, my interest again was aroused concerning the various problems involved in this whole concept. I was still a member of the American Scientific Affiliation, but it was clear that there was no hope of reclaiming this organization. . . .[1]

In the Introduction to the first publication of the Creation Research Society after it was formed, he also had made this comment.

> We then set up a Creation Research Committee, or "team of ten" as Tinkle called it, for mutual exchange of ideas. By this time Henry M. Morris and John C. Whitcomb published their now famous book, *The Genesis Flood.* The many facts so well presented by them here reestablished Biblical catastrophism as an intellectually sound alternative explanation of geological and geographical facts. The two concepts of creation and catastrophism are so closely interwoven that our Creation Research Committee decided to start a Creation Research Society.[2]

1. Walter E. Lammerts, "The Creationist Movement in the United States: A Personal Account," *Journal of Christian Reconstruction* (Vol. 1, Summer 1974), pp. 56-57.

2. Walter E. Lammerts, "Introduction," *Creation Research Society Annual,* Vol. 1, No. 1, 1964, p. 1.

Meteorologist/theologian Charles Clough, who had done his Th.M. thesis at Dallas Theological Seminary on the subject of the impact *of The Genesis Flood,* had this evaluation:

> *The Genesis Flood* has led to the formation of a new community of strict six-day creationists. Several organizations form the concentration points [Clough mentioned particularly the Creation Research Society in this connection] for pooling ideas, dissemination of information, and publishing of papers. This separation will in the long run prove to be *The Genesis Flood's* most important contribution. The foreboding of LaSor quoted above has come true; and it is a blessing, not a cursing.[1]

The reference in the above quotation is to an early highly critical review of the book published in *Eternity* magazine by Dr. William S. LaSor, a Fuller Seminary professor who had expressed the fear that the book might divide the evangelical community into two camps, one committed to strict creationism, the other allowing an accommodationist position. The Creation Research Society was the first fulfillment of that prediction.

The Team of Ten

The ten creationist scientists with whom Dr. Lammerts and Dr. Tinkle started corresponding in 1961 have been referred to as the "Team of Ten." The original idea was simply to have these scientists exchange ideas, and perhaps papers, among themselves, trying to develop further evidence for a comprehensive scientific model of creationism and catastrophism, but this was never really implemented. It quickly became evident that enough interest and concern about creationism had been generated to warrant an entirely new society. Recalling this initial group, Dr. Lammerts said:

> Increasingly dissatisfied with the theistic evolutionary view-

---

1. Charles A. Clough, "Biblical Presuppositions and Historical Geology: A Case Study," *Journal of Christian Reconstruction,* Vol. 1, Summer 1974, pp. 47-48.

point of the ASA, I had begun to correspond with a "Team of Ten," who were dedicated creationists. These were Henry M. Morris, William J. Tinkle, Frank Marsh, John J. Grebe, John W. Klotz, Wilbert H. Rusch, Duane T. Gish, R. Laird Harris, and Edwin Monsma.[1]

All of these names have been mentioned previously but, in view of their strategic importance in the beginnings of the modern creationist revival, it may be worthwhile to give a brief summary of their professional background, just for the record.[2]

Walter E. Lammerts is a graduate of the University of California at Berkeley, majoring in entomology (B.S., 1927) as an undergraduate and receiving his Ph.D. there in genetics in 1930. He worked in rose and peach breeding at the Armstrong Nurseries in Ontario, California (1935-1940), then served from 1940 to 1945 as Assistant Professor of Ornamental Horticulture at UCLA. From 1945 to 1964, he did horticultural research, first for Descanso Gardens in Los Angeles and then in Livermore, California, for Germains Seed Company. He then "retired" in 1964, actually going into private business and research, on his own ranch near Watsonville, California. He has won many honors and prizes for his work, especially in rose breeding, as well as in camellias and other plants.

William J. Tinkle had a Ph.D. in zoology from Ohio State University. He served as chairman of the Biology Department at two Christian colleges in Indiana, Anderson College and Taylor University. He wrote a Christian biology textbook, *Fundamentals of Zoology*, while he was at Taylor. He was long active in the ASA and had even written a creationist biology book which they had

---

1. Walter E. Lammerts, "Early Steps in Formation of Creation Research Society," *Creation Research Society Quarterly,* Vol. 12, March 1976, p. 213.

2. Several more extensive biographies of the early leaders in the Creation Research Society can be found in various issues of the *Creation Research Society Quarterly,* as follows: William J. Tinkle, June 1967, p. 3; Walter E. Lammerts, June 1970, pp. 3, 4; John J. Grebe, June 1971, pp. 3, 4; Thomas G. Barnes, June 1972, pp. 3, 4; Frank L. Marsh, June 1976, pp. 3, 4; Wilbert H. Rusch, June 1981, p. 3.

once promised to publish under ASA sponsorship, finally resigning his membership when they reneged on that commitment. Later he authored three other creationist books. Dr. Tinkle died in 1981.

Wilbert H. Rusch, Sr. had a B.S. degree in science from Illinois Institute of Technology and an M.S. in biology from the University of Michigan, as well as an honorary LL.D. from Concordia Seminary. He had spent almost 35 years teaching science, almost all of the time in various Lutheran colleges. He authored one creationist book and chapters in seven creationist symposium volumes. He served several years as academic dean and also as acting president at Concordia College in Michigan.

John W. Klotz is both a scientist and theologian, with an M.Div. degree from Concordia Seminary and a Ph.D. in biology from the University of Pittsburgh. He authored an outstanding book, *Genes, Genesis, and Evolution,* in 1955, as well as several other books later. He served 15 years (1959-1974) as head of the science department at Concordia Senior College in Fort Wayne, and has since been academic dean and, then, director of graduate studies at Concordia Seminary in St. Louis. Both Klotz and Rusch eventually retired.

Duane T. Gish has a B.S. in chemistry from UCLA and a Ph.D. in biochemistry from the University of California at Berkeley, in 1953. He spent 18 years in biochemical and biomedical research, at Cornell University, at U.C. Berkeley, and then mostly at the Upjohn Company in Kalamazoo. It was while at the latter position that he joined the ASA, soon finding that his creationist views were in the minority there. Since 1971, he has been my own close associate at the Institute for Creation Research.

Frank Marsh had an M.S. in zoology from Northwestern University and a Ph.D. in botany from the University of Nebraska. He spent over 40 years as a professor of biology in various Seventh Day Adventist colleges. As a follower of George McCready Price, he had written (and continued to write) a number of excellent books on creationist biology. He was the first scientist appointed to the Adventists' Geoscience Research Institute. In addition, he published numerous articles in secular scientific journals. He died in 1992.

R. Laird Harris is, like John Klotz, both scientist and theologian. His undergraduate degree was in chemistry, but his Ph.D. in Old Testament Studies. He spent most of his career as Professor of Old Testament at Covenant Theological Seminary in St. Louis, specializing also in archaeology and apologetics. However, although strongly opposed to evolution, he remained committed to the geologic-age system and the day-age theory, and so only remained in the Society about a year after its statement of belief was formulated.

Edwin Y. Monsma, with a Ph.D. in biology, was for many years Professor and Chairman of the Department of Biology at Calvin College in Grand Rapids, the main liberal arts college of the Christian Reformed denomination. He was one of the earlier members of the ASA, and one of the few who defended strict creationism. However, for health reasons, he also was forced to drop out of the Society within its first year, and died soon afterwards.

John Grebe was Director of Nuclear and Basic Research at the Dow Chemical Company in Midland, Michigan, retiring in 1965 after 41 years of distinguished service there. He had the B.S., M.S., and D.Sc. degrees (the last in 1935) from Case Institute of Technology, as well as an honorary LL.D. degree from Hillsdale College. During World War II, he was Chief Scientist to the Army Chemical Corps at Edgewood Arsenal, Baltimore. He has received numerous honors and patents. Dr. Grebe died in 1985.

All of the nine men listed above (I was the tenth) had reviewed the manuscript of *The Genesis Flood* prior to its publication, except for Dr. Gish and Dr. Grebe. All had been very favorable to the book, except for Dr. Harris, who had been impressed but not convinced. Dr. Grebe had read it and written me about it soon after its publication, enthusiastically concurring with it and offering to help the cause in any way he could. As a result, I had written Dr. Lammerts about him, suggesting that we place him on the new committee. Dr. Grebe was actually in the same denomination as Lammerts, Rusch, and Klotz (Missouri Synod Lutheran), and he entered heartily into the committee's plans.

Dr. Gish was at that time entirely unfamiliar with flood geology and he did not read *The Genesis Flood* until some years later. However, he was an ardent and articulate creationist, as well as a Baptist fundamentalist, and he entered enthusiastically into the developing organization.

Early in 1963, Dr. Lammerts and Dr. Tinkle decided to go ahead and organize their team of ten on a somewhat more formal basis, assuming the offices of chairman and secretary, respectively, of what they decided to call the Creation Research Committee. Letterheads were printed up with the names and positions of the ten members listed on it. Tentative plans were made to expand the Committee into a full-fledged Society as soon as the members could get together and work out organizational plans. At the top of the Committee's letterhead, Dr. Lammerts had printed the text of Exodus 20:11, as the Committee's *Haec Credimus:* "For in six days, the Lord made heaven and earth, the sea, and all that in them is, and rested the seventh day."

The opportunity for a meeting of the Committee came propitiously at a scheduled joint meeting of the American Scientific Affiliation and the Evangelical Theological Society, to be held on the campus of Asbury College in Wilmore, Kentucky, on June 19-21, 1963. The main theme of the meeting was to be the creation/evolution issue, which had come to the fore in evangelicalism again as a result of *The Genesis Flood.* Dr. Tinkle, still active in ASA, was on the program committee, and so invited several members of the Creation Research Committee, including myself, to present papers at the meeting. What the outcome might be was to be decided after the meeting.

Several members of the Committee—Lammerts, Tinkle, Harris,

Klotz, Marsh, Rusch, Grebe, and myself—planned to go to the ASA/ETS meeting and, while there, to have a sort of creationist caucus. I had also written Harold Slusher about it, and he was planning to come. If the general reaction of the entire group turned out to be negative, as anticipated, then the Creation Research Committee would plan to proceed with the organization of a Creation Research Society, independent of the ASA.

Dr. Grebe, who had only joined the Committee in January, offered to host the group for a follow-up meeting at his own home in Midland, Michigan, where they would all drive the next day after the ASA/ETS meeting, and where they could all continue long enough to get everything ironed out and the new Society under way. Everyone except Gish and Monsma said they could attend the Asbury meeting, and even Gish and Monsma (who both lived in Michigan) indicated they could probably get to the after-meeting in Midland.

Also, three new prospects—John Moore and David Warriner at Michigan State and Karl Linsenmann, a long-time friend of Dr. Grebe's in Midland—planned to attend the after-meeting at Dr. Grebe's home. These plans were all fairly well firmed up by April.

However, right at this time my own schedule suddenly changed, so that I was unable to go either to Asbury or Midland as planned. I was awarded a grant by the National Science Foundation as a participant in a four-week Conference on Water Resources, to be held at New Mexico State University in Las Cruces.

This was both a prestigious honor and also a valuable learning and witnessing opportunity, so I felt I had to accept it. Furthermore, it could provide a wonderful vacation for my family. Las Cruces is only 44 miles from El Paso, so Mary Louise and I were also looking forward to revisiting our old home for the first time since we had left it 21 years before.

However, the Water Resources Conference did occupy the month of June, and the ASA/ETS meeting was on June 19-21, so I had to be absent from the founding meeting of the Creation

Research Society, much to my chagrin. Otherwise, the meeting and organization proceeded as planned. Frank Marsh read my paper at the ASA/ETS meeting, a paper entitled "The Spirit of Compromise." Will Tinkle later told me that he and others had thought I would be proposing some sort of workable compromise with the ASA evolutionists. Instead, of course, I merely reviewed the various compromise theories (day-age theory, gap theory, etc.) showing that none were either Biblically or scientifically viable. I also showed that one compromise leads to another, with the evolutionary establishment satisfied only with full atheism. The paper urged the ASA theistic evolutionists and progressive creationists to return to a sound Biblical creationism. The paper, not surprisingly, proved "controversial," the neo-evangelical journal *Christianity Today* reporting in its news account of the meeting that the "anti-intellectual," Henry Morris, had given a "disturbing" paper there!

The committee met at Asbury and hammered out a preliminary statement of faith and constitution, with Dr. Marsh and Dr. Klotz doing most of the composition. Afterward they continued on to Midland, where they were joined by Gish, Moore, Warriner, and Linsenmann. Monsma was not able to come, and Tinkle and Harris, who had been at Asbury, were not able to continue on to Midland.

In any case, the Society was organized, and tentative plans were made to publish the first issue of its proposed quarterly journal within a year. Dr. Lammerts was named President, as well as Publications Editor, Dr. Tinkle was elected Secretary, and Dr. Rusch, Treasurer. Dues were set at $5.00 per year and membership, in addition to an acceptance of the statement of faith, was limited to scientists having an M.S. (or equivalent in experience), Ph.D., D.Sc., Ed.D., o r. M.D. degree.

In the meantime, I was having a good time in El Paso, where I was able to recruit three important new members—Thomas Barnes, Harold Slusher, and Willis Webb—for this initial steering committee of the Society. In addition to participating in the Water

Resources Conference, I had eight significant speaking engagements in the Las Cruces/El Paso area while I was there. The most important of these was to a group of about 35 scientists connected either with the White Sands missile research installation or with Texas Western University (now the University of Texas at El Paso). Dr. Barnes had arranged this meeting, Willis Webb chaired it, and the entire group received it very well. Dr. Barnes, as mentioned earlier, had become an enthusiastic creationist as a result of reading the paper which I had given a year previously to the Houston Geological Society, and he in turn had recruited Willis Webb. Harold Slusher, who had reviewed the manuscript of *The Genesis Flood* and had, in effect recruited his colleague Tom Barnes, was out of El Paso for the summer. However, I had met and talked with him in Knoxville, where he was spending the summer, while our family was driving out from Virginia to El Paso. He was anxious to work with the new Society. Also, after leaving El Paso, we drove out to Tucson, where I talked with Clifford Burdick about joining the Society.

On his way from Michigan back to California, Dr. Lammerts came to see me in El Paso to report on the meeting and to get my input. He spent several days with us, talking also with Barnes and Webb.

Thus, to the original "Team of Ten," a number of others were added to what Lammerts now chose to call the "Steering Committee" of the Society. These were Moore, Warriner, Linsenmann, Burdick, Barnes, Slusher, and Webb. Also, a colleague of Wilbert Rusch's, Paul Zimmerman, was added as well. This made a total of 18. The Steering Committee soon came to be called the Board of Directors, with each member serving a three-year term, eligible for reelection to an unlimited number of terms. With a total of 18, this meant that 6 were to be elected each year, each group of 6 serving staggered three-year terms. The Board is essentially self perpetuating, since it selects the nominees each year, and almost routinely nominates the outgoing directors for reelection.

This may seem undemocratic, but the purpose was to prevent any future takeover by evolutionists, as had happened in the ASA. Actually the Board has frequently nominated a number of other candidates in addition to the existing Board members, thus giving the voting members of the Society at least some choice. Also, there is a constitutional provision by which members can have another person nominated through getting 25 names on a petition. Finally, the voting members do actually elect the six Board Members each year, by mail ballot. "Sustaining members" (those who agree to the statement of faith, but who do not have a master's or doctor's degree in science) are not eligible to vote, although they are able to publish papers in the Society's *Quarterly.*

Since biographies were given earlier for the original ten members of the team, it is appropriate here to give brief resumes for the additional eight members of the original Board of Directors. These follow below.

Thomas G. Barnes was Professor of Physics at the University of Texas at El Paso (formerly Texas School of Mines and later Texas Western University), as well as Director of its Schellenger Research Laboratories. With an M.S. from Brown University and honorary D.Sc. from Hardin-Simmons University, Dr. Barnes had 43 years of distinguished research and teaching service in El Paso. After becoming Emeritus Professor at UTEP, he served two years as the first Dean of the ICR Graduate School. He is author of a widely accepted textbook on electricity and magnetism, as well as many monographs and technical papers, and two books critical of modern pyhsics.

Clifford L. Burdick had a B.S. and later an honorary D.Sc. from Milton College, as well as additional study in geology at the University of Wisconsin. He completed all work for the Ph.D. in geology, including his dissertation, at the University of Arizona, but was rejected for the degree because of his creationist writings. As a student of George McCready Price, he was one of the first flood geologists of recent times and had a long career as a consulting economic and mining geologist. He had been a member of the old Creation/Deluge Society and had been a reviewer of *The Genesis Flood* manuscript.

Karl M. Linsenmann was a medical doctor and a personal friend of Dr. Grebe's for about half a century. He joined the original committee mainly because of this friendship, but was a faithful and active member of the Board for almost ten years, until illness forced him to resign. Dr. Linsenmann died soon afterwards.

John N. Moore was Associate Professor, later full Professor, of Natural Science at Michigan State University. He had an A.B. from Denison University, M.S. (biology) and Ed.D. (science education) from Michigan State. He taught evolution in his classes for many years; later, after his conversion to creationism, he taught both evolution and creation, on a two-model basis, to all his classes until his retirement in 1982. He became the first Managing Editor of the *CRS Quarterly*, retaining that office almost 20 years.

Harold S. Slusher has a B.A. from the University of Tennessee, M.S. (geophysics) from the University of Oklahoma, and Ph.D. from Columbia Pacific. He has been Assistant Professor of Physics at the University of Texas at El Paso continuously since 1957. Despite a good teaching and research record, he was repeatedly refused promotion because of his outspoken creationism.

David A. Warriner was a colleague of Dr. John Moore at Michigan State and had been instrumental in leading Dr. Moore to Christ and creationism, having himself been strongly influenced by *The Genesis Flood.* He had a Ph.D. and also a theological degree (Dallas Seminary). He was a strong political conservative and resigned from the Board a year later.

Willis L. Webb had only a B.S. degree, but a long record of outstanding research experience. At the time, he was Chief Scientist in the Environmental Sciences Department at the White Sands Electronics Research and Development Activity of the U.S. Army. His field of specialty was meteorology. He also remained on the Board only a year.

Paul A. Zimmerman is another man with both scientific and theological training. He has the M.Div. degree from Concordia Seminary (St. Louis) and the Ph.D. in chemistry from the University of Illinois. He has been a teacher and administrator at various Lutheran schools since 1944, including service as president of Concordia College (River Forest, Illinois). He resigned from the Board in 1969 because of administrative responsibilities, but was elected again in 1980.

These were the 18 men whom the Lord used to start the Creation Research Society. Although only a few held prestigious scientific positions, all had excellent scientific training and experience. Most importantly, all were firmly committed to an inerrant Bible and strict creationism, as well as believing in Christ as Lord and Savior.

The Early Years

Dr. Lammerts served as president of the Society for its first four years and as editor of its *Quarterly* for its first five years, and he left an indelible mark, being chiefly responsible not only for organizing the Society, but also for setting its course and delineating its character. With the failed examples of previous societies in mind, especially that of the American Scientific Affiliation, he insisted on certain guidelines right from the start. He is a large, forthright, outspoken man, with firm opinions on just about everything, and can be quite intimidating, so everyone went along with him at that first meeting. As someone said: "He may be in error sometimes, but he is never in doubt!"

Fortunately, the subsequent history of the Society has shown that he was right about at least most of these basic decisions. Whether anything would have come out differently if I had been present at that first meeting will never be known, of course, but it did seem that the Lord providentially kept me from being there. Consequently, Lammerts, with some input from Rusch, Tinkle, Marsh, and Klotz especially, did set out the course of the Society right at the start which it has followed ever since.

The most important decision was to set forth a firmly creationist statement of faith to which all members must subscribe and which could never be changed. This statement has four sections, dealing respectively with the following topics: (1) inerrancy of Scripture and the simple historicity of the Genesis record of creation; (2) special creation of the various "kinds" of organisms in the Genesis creation week, with subsequent variation only within the kinds; (3) the global extent and effects of the Genesis Flood; (4) the historicity of the Fall of Adam and Eve, the need of the Savior, and salvation only through accepting Christ as Lord and Savior.

The full statement is reproduced in Appendix B. The following statement of purpose was also adopted and is still in effect: "Members of the Creation Research Society, which include research scientists representing various fields of successful scientific accomplishment, are committed to full belief in the Biblical record of creation and early history, and thus to a concept of dynamic special creation (as opposed to evolution), both of the universe and the earth with its complexity of living forms."

It was also written into the first constitution that the statement of faith could not be changed. At this writing (1993), the Society has continued for over 30 years as a strong creationist organization, which in itself is a clear testimony to the wisdom of this initial action.

Right from the start, certain other attributes were established and later reaffirmed by Board action from time to time. These included the following: (1) the Society would always be strictly a membership organization, with all its work carried on voluntarily and without any paid staff; (2) the Society would always be strictly independent, not affiliating in any way with other organizations; (3) the Society would be strictly a research-and-publications society, not holding conventions, seminars, or other meetings; (4) the Society would be strictly non-political, never seeking to promote creationism through legislation, litigation, or other political means;

and (5) the Society would not publish any kind of membership directory, so that an individual scientist's affiliation with the Society could remain confidential if he so chose.

The membership of the Society began to grow immediately, and more rapidly than anyone had anticipated. By the end of 1963, there were well over 50 voting members (scientists with post-graduate degrees) and by the end of Lammerts' four-year term as president, over 200. Furthermore, right from the beginning, the number of non voting members and subscribers has always been about 2 1/2 to 3 times the number of voting members. By the end of the first four years, in 1967, the total number of members and subscribers had grown to more than 800.

Despite all good intentions, it proved impossible to have another meeting of the full Board until March of 1965. Since that time, the Board has met once each year, in April. In the interim between June of 1963 and March of 1965, Society business was carried on by correspondence and, to some degree, decisions were made simply by the three officers. Dr. Lammerts, with his Editorial Board (Klotz, Tinkle, Barnes, and myself, together with botanist George Howe and geophysicist Donald Acrey) and with much help from both John Moore and John Whitcomb, did manage to get the journal published each quarter, beginning with the 1964 "Annual," in May 1964. This *Creation Research Society Quarterly* soon became recognized as the main journal for disseminating creationist research and review studies and has continued to maintain high standards ever since.

As noted before, there were four members of the original Board who were replaced in the first two years. These were Laird Harris, Edwin Monsma, David Warriner, and Willis Webb. Their replacements were George Howe, Richard Korthals, Bolton Davidheiser, and Douglas Dean. Brief resumes of these men are given below.

George Howe, who was destined soon to become one of the main leaders of the Society, was a graduate of Wheaton College who had gone on to receive the M.S. and Ph.D. degrees from Ohio

State University, in the field of botany. Initially, as a Wheaton graduate, he had been somewhat skeptical of the flood geology and young earth concepts, but a reading of *The Genesis Flood,* as well as association with other CRS members, convinced him of their validity. He was Chairman of Natural Sciences for several years at Westmont College, in Santa Barbara (replacing Dr. Davidheiser, who had moved to Biola), but eventually became frustrated with its neo-evangelicalism (as had Davidheiser). In 1968, he became Chairman of the Science Division at the Los Angeles Baptist College (now Masters College), where he has had a fine ministry ever since.

Richard Korthals, a colonel in the Air Force, had a B. S. and

Figure 13. Biology Textbook Editors

One of the first major projects of the CRS was the preparation of a creationist high school biology textbook. Serving as co-editors for this project were two members of the Board of Directors, Dr. John N. Moore, at Michigan State University, and Dr. Harold Slusher, at the University of Texas at El Paso.

M.S. from the Air Force Institute of Technology in the field of astronautical engineering. He was a full professor at the Air Force Academy until 1964, after which he taught at two Lutheran colleges, serving also as Dean of Students at Concordia Teachers College from 1974 to 1978, when he retired.

Bolton Davidheiser received his Ph.D. in zoology from Johns Hopkins University when he was still an unbeliever. Later he became a Christian and a creationist and has had a strong and uncompromising testimony for many years. He was Head of the Science Division at Westmont College and later at Biola College, resigning in each instance when the institution became too liberal to correspond to his own convictions. He is author of several excellent creationist books, the best known being his *Evolution and the Christian Faith.*

Douglas Dean was for many years Professor of Biology at Pepperdine University, a Church of Christ school in Los Angeles. He has been one of the leaders for creationism in his own denomination. Both Dr. Dean and Dr. Davidheiser only stayed on the CRS Board for two years, however, finding it too difficult to attend the annual meetings. Nevertheless, both of them did make significant contributions to the CRS biology textbook, which was in preparation for some four years beginning in 1965. Dr. Dean died in 1992.

The decision to prepare a high school textbook in biology, oriented about creation instead of evolution, was one of the most important actions taken by the Society during its early years. Many requests had come from Christian school leaders for such a book, but no Christian biologist or publisher had been willing to undertake this project before, because of the tremendous amount of work and financial risk entailed.

However, it was just at this time that Mel and Norma Gabler, of Longview, Texas, began their ministry of critiquing public school textbooks. They had filed complaints with the Texas State Board of Education about the pervasive evolutionary teaching in the textbooks being used in Texas, especially the recently published

BSCS series. They had been supported in their testimony by Dr. Barnes, Dr. Grebe, and others. However, when the Education Board challenged them to suggest alternatives, they found there were none available (the Seventh-Day Adventist book by Dr. Booth was not suitable for public schools). Consequently, they also began to urge the CRS to undertake such a project.

Accordingly, at the March 1965 Board meeting, it was decided to undertake this project. Dr. Lammerts appointed Dr. Tom Barnes as Chairman of the Textbook Committee. As a physicist, he would not write any of it, but he was willing to undertake the task of selecting and directing those who would.

He went to work on this right away and found many who were both willing and capable writers. Among those who participated were such Board members as Davidheiser, Dean, Gish, Howe, Klotz, Lammerts, Marsh, Moore, Rusch, Tinkle, Slusher, and Zimmerman. In addition, there were others not on the Board who took part, including: Dr. Russell Artist, Professor of Biology at David Lipscomb College in Nashville; Dr. R. Clyde McCone, Professor of Cultural Anthropology at Long Beach State College in California; Rita Rhodes Ward, high school biology teacher in El Paso, and others. Although many made significant contributions, major portions of the work were accomplished by Dr. Tinkle and Mrs. Ward. Dr. Tinkle was retired and also had published his earlier textbook, *Fundamentals of Zoology,* while Mrs. Ward was in the same city as Dr. Barnes and had much experience teaching high school biology.

The committee never got together as a whole, so that all the writing, checking, editing, and coordinating had to be done by correspondence. It was a monumental task and took five years to accomplish. Eventually, however, it was published in 1971, a beautiful and effective volume. The final editing was done by two coeditors appointed by Dr. Barnes and approved by the Board, John Moore and Harold Slusher.

It was noted above that Dr. Davidheiser and Dr. Dean only

remained on the Board a short time. Their replacements were Emmett Williams and Larry Butler, both of whom had been significantly influenced for creationism by *The Genesis Flood* and were suggested by me for the Board. Both would later serve terms both as Research Committee Chairman and Vice President. Brief resumes of these men are given below.

Emmett L. Williams had a B.S. and M.S. from Virginia Tech in metallurgical engineering and a Ph.D. from Clemson University in 1966. While serving as an assistant professor at VPI, he was a strong political conservative, though not a Christian. He visited my Sunday School class while I was teaching a series of studies on "Christ and Communism," and as a result I had the privilege of helping to lead him to Christ. After he completed his Ph.D., I recommended him for a position at Bob Jones University, and he served as Professor of Physics there for 13 years, returning to a position in private industry in 1979. He is author or co-author of three important science textbooks for Christian schools published by the Bob Jones University Press, as well as editor of the CRS Monograph *Thermodynamics and the Development of Order.* He served as Editor of the *Creation Research Society Quarterly* from 1983 to 1990.

Larry Butler received the Ph. D., in biochemistry, from UCLA in 1964. He did post-doctoral work at both UCLA and the University of Arizona. While studying at UCLA he also served several years on the science faculty at the Los Angeles Baptist College. In 1966 he went to Purdue University, where he has been ever since. For a number of years he has been full Professor of Biochemistry at Purdue.

Because of my experiences with the Creation-Deluge Society and the American Scientific Affiliation, as well as all of our contacts, studies, and feedback in connection with *The Genesis Flood,* both John Whitcomb and I had hoped that the new Society would take a clear and firm stand on the recent literal six-day creation of all things, as well as flood geology. We were disappointed when these were not spelled out more clearly in the statement of faith adopted at Midland. Nevertheless, the statement as adopted at least *implied* these truths and was a tremendous improvement over anything previously used by any similar organization.

I did try, at the first Board meeting I attended, in March 1965, to get the Board to amend the statement to include these items. Dr. Lammerts fully concurred in this, as did a number of others, but there were several who still had reservations. Apparently only Laird Harris (who was not present) was strongly committed to the day-age theory and the geological age system, but there were several who were still somewhat unsettled about the issue, particularly about flood geology. Also, several felt that putting this in the doctrinal statement would unnecessarily keep other strong creationists, who were open to these doctrines but still not sure about them, from joining the Society. Finally, it was noted that the constitution adopted at Midland (as previously mentioned, I was not present) included a provision that no change could ever be made in the statement as adopted there.

All of these arguments had merit, of course, but I was still very sensitive to the dangers of leaving these vital issues open to future accommodationist "interpretations." Finally, the Board did go on record with an understanding (one that would remain unwritten, however) that no publication of the Society, including articles published in the *Quarterly,* would ever advocate the "old-earth," geological-ages position. Of course, this unwritten understanding will probably maintain this doctrinal integrity just as long as the Society president and *Quarterly* editor agree with it. So far, this has been the case (as of 1993).

By 1967, Walter Lammerts had reached the age of 63 and, even though he was semi-retired, he felt that having both jobs (president and editor) was too much. Consequently, he asked me to take over as president if he would serve at least one more year as editor.

Naturally, I was reluctant to do this, in view of my very heavy other responsibilities. However, of the two jobs, that of editor was much more time-consuming than that of president. Also, I was quite concerned that the Society should continue to be committed to recent creation and flood geology and was fearful that this might not be the case if some other possible candidates should become president, so I finally agreed.

Consequently, at the Board meeting on April 8, 1967, Dr. Lammerts declined renomination, and I was elected president. George Howe was elected vice-president and Dick Korthals corresponding secretary. Will Tinkle and Bill Rusch were reelected, as secretary and treasurer/membership secretary, respectively. George Howe also agreed to work with Walter Lammerts as assistant editor of the *Quarterly,* with the goal of eventually taking over as editor. Although Dr. Lammerts was no longer president, he continued to exercise strong influence in the Society for many years,; but this meeting can be considered as the terminal point of the first stage of the Society's history.

The On-Going Work of the Society

By the end of Dr. Lammerts' four-year tenure as president, the Society and its characteristics had become well established. The voting membership had grown to 200, the total membership over 800 (including subscribers).

Although many developments and changes were yet to come, there is no need to discuss these in as much detail as for the formative years of the Society. The major chronological segments can be related to the tenures of the respective presidents and editors, which have been as follows:

President	Editor
1963-67 Walter E. Lammerts	1963-68 Walter E. Lammerts
1967-73 Henry M. Morris	1968-73 George F. Howe
1973-77 Thomas G. Barnes	1973-83 Harold L. Armstrong
1977-83 George F. Howe	1984-88 Emmett L. Williams
1983-88 Wilbert H. Rusch	1989- Donald DeYoung
1988- Wayne Frair	

The most significant measure of the influence of the Society is probably its voting membership, since these members are all scientists with post-graduate degrees in science ("science" here includes the applied sciences such as engineering and medicine, but not social science). These numbers (some of the figures for the early years are approximations) as of the dates of the annual Board meetings are as follows:

1963 - 10	1973 - 412	1983 - 597
1964 - 100	1974 - 514	1984 - 608
1965 - 135	1975 - 506	1985 - 575
1966 - 170	1976 - 451	1986 - 550
1967 - 200	1977 - 532	1987 - 600
1968 - 256	1978 - 595	1988 - 641
1969 - 277	1979 - 657	1989 - 625
1970 - 318	1980 - 660	1990 - 635
1971 - 341	1981 - 693	1991 - 673
1972 - 391	1984 - 608	1992 - 672

Generally speaking, the number of other members and subscribers have averaged about three times the number of voting members. Although these statistics may not be overwhelming, they are quite comparable in total to those for the American Scientific Affiliation. Although the categories and qualifications for the two organizations[1] are not parallel, it is reasonably certain that the number of natural scientists with post-graduate degrees in science is significantly greater in the CRS than in the ASA. There are many other scientific societies also with fewer members than CRS. Furthermore, there are undoubtedly many times more creationist scientists eligible for voting membership in the Society than are

---

1. Membership in ASA is open to anyone with a Bachelor's degree in either science or philosophy, where "science" includes "social science." The grade of Fellow requires a doctorate in "science" or "philosophy" but there are no more than 200 Fellows in the Affiliation.

actually members. All of which is simply to say that the creationist revival in science today is reaching significant proportions.

As far as my own tenure as president of the Society is concerned, the voting membership more than doubled, and the caliber of the *Quarterly* under George Howe's editorship attained high standards of excellence. One of the most significant events was the publication in 1971 of the long-awaited biology textbook, *Biology: A Search for Order in Complexity,* published by Zondervan Publishing House in Grand Rapids.

A fascinating footnote to this publication event, however, was the difficulty of finding a publisher. Our original intention was to have it published by one of the standard high school textbook publishers. We felt the book would be profitable, even if only the Christian schools used it. We also knew the book was at least the equal in quality of treatment and caliber of authorship to others on the market, so there seemed a reasonable possibility that at least some public school districts would adopt it.

We were naive, to put it mildly. In spite of the fact that most students and parents (and even teachers) would have found the book more than satisfactory, the evolutionary *establishment* in science and education was too powerful for it even to be considered. Dr. Barnes approached the 15 leading high school textbook publishers, told them all about the manuscript, and was expecting them all to compete for the contract to publish it.

But not one of them would even look at the manuscript! They said (no doubt remembering the infamous "Velikovsky affair" of the early fifties) that all of their textbooks would be boycotted if they would dare to publish a creationist book. Consequently, Dr. Barnes and I finally turned to a Christian publishing house. This type of book, of course, was a new type of project for Zondervan, but the editorial staff entered into it willingly and did a fine job. Then, almost immediately after the book was published, John Moore was appointed to work on a revised edition, as well as teachers' manuals and a student laboratory manual.

Two other books were published about this same time, two anthologies of articles published in the *Quarterly* during its first five years. The two books were edited by Walter Lammerts and were entitled *Why Not Creation?* and *Scientific Studies in Special Creation.*

I arranged for Charles Craig, who had published *The Genesis Flood* through his Presbyterian and Reformed Publishing Co., to publish these also. He did a good job on them and they enjoyed at least a reasonable sale. Five years later, a third anthology was published, *Speak to the Earth,* under the editorship of George Howe, who had edited the *Quarterly* during its second five years. Bill Rusch offered to get a team of Lutheran teachers to work on a junior high biology textbook. This project was approved but never completed, and was finally abandoned.

We lost the services of one Board member about this same time, one of the original ten, Dr. Frank Marsh. For the first few years, the Board held its annual meeting on Sunday instead of Saturday, out of deference to the convictions of Dr. Marsh who, as a strong Seventh-Day Adventist, felt he could not meet with us on his Sabbath, which was Saturday. This was very inconvenient for most of the Board members, however, so they finally voted (unanimously, except for Marsh, who was absent that year) to meet on Friday night and Saturday each year after that. Dr. Marsh took this rather personally, but the Board stressed that they still regarded him very highly as a person and as a scientist, and that the decision was not against him, but merely for the best interests of the Society as a whole. Later, an Annual was dedicated to him, and he was elected a Fellow of the Society. The other Adventist on the Board, Clifford Burdick, did not object to meeting on Saturday and continued on the Board until 1986. As it has turned out, Adventist scientists on the whole have played very little part in the work of CRS, although a good number of them have continued to make significant contributions to creationist science in their own research and writing. This is in contrast to their dominant influence in the old Creation-Deluge Society.

Paul Zimmerman also resigned about this time, because of his heavy administrative responsibilities as president of Concordia College in Ann Arbor, the location of all the annual Board meetings. Replacing Marsh and Zimmerman were two important new members of the Board, Wayne Frair and Harold Armstrong, whose resumes follow.

Harold Armstrong, unlike most Board members, did not have a Ph.D., but was a man of unusually wide reading and knowledge, especially in his field of physics. He had an M.Sc. degree from Queen's University in Ontario in 1951 and had been on the physics faculty there almost ever since. He became editor of the *CRS Quarterly* in 1973 and served in that capacity eleven years, more than twice as long as either of his two predecessors, Walter Lammerts and George Howe. However, he died soon after that.

Wayne Frair is one of the few leading CRS members who is still also a member of the ASA, in which he has been active for over 40 years. He has a Ph.D. in serology from Rutgers and has been on the science faculty at The King's College (a small college on the Hudson River just north of New York City) since 1955. He became Secretary of the Society in 1973, when Will Tinkle resigned, and served in that capacity until he became president in 1988.

While I was president, the ASA—especially through its Executive Secretary, Dr. Harold Hartzler—made several overtures to me and to John Whitcomb (perhaps also to others) to try to have some kind of joint meeting between CRS and ASA, with the goal of somehow uniting the two societies. Also, Dr. Charles Hatfield, who had been my old-time friend and colleague at the University of Minnesota (and whom I had originally recruited for the ASA), was elected ASA president in 1970, and he also wrote me with a similar purpose, thinking that our contemporaneous presidencies might be a propitious time to get the two groups together again. However, it was still quite obvious, both from their discussions and from the increasingly liberal articles in the *ASA Journal,* that any such dialogue or potential merger would be one-sided and would have the effect of submerging our testimony for true creationism in a quicksand of pseudocreationist evolutionism. Consequently, the Board more than once voted against any such rapprochement, stressing that individual members of CRS were free to attend and speak at ASA meetings if they wished, but that CRS as an organization would never hold meetings of any sort. Furthermore, our purpose had never been to fight ASA but simply to provide a medium of research and publication in strict Biblical creationism and catastrophism, which ASA had never provided.

There had also been similar proposals from time to time to enter into some kind of relationship with the Bible-Science Association or with other organizations. All such proposals were rejected.

In 1970, right in the middle of my six-year term as CRS president, I decided (after much study and prayer, finally becoming convinced that this was God's leading) to move to California, with the goal of helping to found a truly creationist liberal arts college and creation studies center. This development is discussed in Chapter VII. The Society had, at its recent Board meeting, decided against undertaking any new textbook projects, opting to concentrate solely on research and its *Quarterly.* However, I was still convinced that there was an urgent need for an actual scientist-staffed institution, which could not only do research but also writing, publishing, speaking, and other things to try to win the scientific and educational worlds back to Christ and creationism.

I was confident that this would in no way compete with, but rather supplement and assist, the ministry of CRS. Several Board members were also quite positive about it and even agreed to serve on our Technical Advisory Board (Barnes, Butler, and Moore). Two others (Gish and Slusher) actually joined our staff soon after we began. However, a number of others were rather negative about it, fearing that this would compete with CRS. Some even resented the fact that I had left a fairly prestigious secular position, thus possibly forfeiting my previous influence in the academic and scientific worlds.

Consequently, although I was reelected president in 1971 and 1972, it was obvious that some still felt there was an apparent conflict of interest involved. Being heavily occupied with the burdens of my new organizations, I would have been happy to be relieved of the CRS office if I could be confident that the new president would not lead the Society into a softer position on the vital issue of recent creation.

The ideal solution was Tom Barnes. He held the most prestigious secular position of any Board member, had done a splendid job as chairman of the textbook committee, and was adamant as far as the young earth and flood geology were concerned. I talked with him at length, and he reluctantly agreed to take over the job of president. Consequently, at the 1973 meeting, the rest of the Board agreed and Dr. Tom Barnes was elected president of the Society, serving for the next four years. Portions of my letter, written to the Board right after the meeting, may be of some historical and philosophical interest.

> As outgoing president of the Society, I want to express my personal thanks to each one of you for your work for CRS the past six years. I also want to urge you to give our new president, Tom Barnes, full support in every way. I believe he is the one man God has prepared for this job, at this most important stage in CRS history.
>
> As you know, the cause of creationism, as well as witnessing for the Lord Jesus Christ in general, has been a major part of my life for over thirty years. . . . The Lord has been wonderful in directing, protecting, and providing through all these years.
>
> It is especially thrilling to see what He has done through the Creation Research Society the past ten years. . . . The next decade, I am convinced, will see even greater things accomplished, . . . *as long as we remain sound in doctrine and motive.*
>
> We must, by all means, continue to resist all efforts to dilute

our commitment to a recent literal creation and a worldwide flood, as required by sound Biblical exegesis. Uncertainty on these points at ASA's inception (as Walter has told us) was the direct cause of that organization's rapid drift into theistic evolution and the social gospel. A worldwide flood, of course, implies flood geology—the concept of a "tranquil" global deluge is both Biblically and scientifically absurd. . . . This must be the primary focus of our research and publications activities if we are ever to make a permanent impact on science and to accomplish the task God has given us to do for His people.[1]

One of the main accomplishments of the Society during Dr. Barnes' term as president was the publication of the improved second edition of the biology textbook, edited by Dr. Moore, together with the lab and teachers' manuals.[2] These also had a good sale in Christian schools, but made little headway in the public schools, although several states had placed it on their "Approved" list. Then, in a highly publicized case, litigated by the Indiana Civil Liberties Union, the Indiana Supreme Court in April 1977 banned the book from the state-approved list of textbooks. Other states seemed to take their cue from this action and have refused any longer to consider the book.

As a result, the Zondervan Company decided to quit publishing the book once the second edition copies on hand were sold. Since, according to the Indiana decision, the book was too religious, the Board decided that a new edition should be prepared, with a format more suitable for public school use, a true "two-model" approach. Since Zondervan did not want to undertake it, however, a new publisher needed to be found and a new revision committee appointed. The Creation-Life Publishers, which had by this time published a number of the books being produced by our new Institute for Creation Research, offered to take over the book. We volunteered the ICR staff to undertake the actual work of revision.

---

1. Excerpts from my letter to CRS Board members dated May 11, 1973.
2. Published by Zondervan in 1974.

This offer was made as a gesture of good will, offering our help to the Society in what seemed to be a time of need. However, several on the Board were still fearful of ICR "competition," and interpreted this offer as a "take-over" attempt. Instead, therefore, Bill Rusch offered again to organize a committee of Lutheran teachers to do the revision, and a contract was signed with Mott Media to do the publishing. Progress was very slow, however, and the project was eventually abandoned.

Another publishing decision, in 1977, was to produce a series of technical monographs (ICR had published a number of such monographs), as well as reprints of "classical" books on creationism. The latter project was later cancelled, but several monographs have been produced, the first being *Thermodynamics and the Development of Order,* edited by Emmett Williams and published in 1981. Several other books have been published and C.R.S. Books has become a successful division of the Society, with Emmett Williams as managing editor.

George Howe, of Los Angeles Baptist College, was elected president in 1978. Perhaps the main decision during his five-year tenure was taken in 1981, when it was decided that CRS would establish an actual research station and conduct on-site research. While the Society had accumulated a modest research fund (largely from textbook royalties) and had sponsored a succession of research projects over the years, it had often proven difficult to get reports from the grantees which were publishable in the quarterlies.

A subsequent fund-raising drive enabled the Society to purchase several acres of native grassland at Chino Valley in Arizona. Under the leadership of John Meyer, plans have been developed and zoning approval granted for a future museum and nature center there, scheduled for completion in 1993. Meyer was appointed as full-time director early in 1993.

During Dr. Barnes' term as president, two new Board members were elected, Dr. John Meyer and George Mullinger. They replaced John Grebe and Karl Linsenmann, both of whom resigned in 1975

Figure 14. Presidents of the Society

Following Dr. Walter Lammerts and Dr. Morris, there have been four later presidents of the Society, as follows: Dr. Thomas G. Barnes, of the University of Texas at El Paso, followed by Dr. George Howe at Master's College (then Los Angeles Baptist College). Shown below are Professor Wilbert Rusch of Concordia College in Ann Arbor and (currently) Dr. Wayne Frair of The King's College in New York.

for age and health reasons. Dr. Butler resigned in 1976, for personal reasons, and his place was later taken by Dr. David Boylan.

George Howe's term as president began in 1977. Board changes thereafter have included the resignations of Walter Lammerts in 1978 and Will Tinkle in 1979. These two "founding fathers" of the Society did continue to attend Board meetings, however, as time and health permitted. Dr. Tinkle died in 1981.

I myself finally decided to resign from the Board in 1982, having missed three meetings in a row because of the pressure of other administrative and speaking responsibilities. By this time I was not contributing much time to Society activities; however, I was (and still am) on the Editorial Board and was on the Research Committee until that year. The following year, Dr. Barnes also resigned, to devote full time to his own research. At this meeting, Dr. Barnes and I were elected Fellows. Rusch had been made a Fellow several years previously.

The newer members were then, respectively, E. Norbert Smith, Paul Zimmerman (returned to the Board after an absence of several years), and Glen Wolfrom.

Resumes of these more recent Board members are given below. Zimmerman's vita was given earlier.

David R. Boylan received a B.S. in chemical engineering from the University of Kansas in 1943 and the Ph.D. from Iowa State University in 1952. He was Dean of the College of Engineering at Iowa State for many years. He is author of a book in his own scientific field plus many technical articles.

John R. Meyer has a Ph.D. in zoology from the University of Iowa. He spent four years each on the faculties of the Colorado University and Louisville University Medical Schools. He then was on the science faculty for a while at Los Angeles Baptist College and, since 1982, at the Baptist Bible College in Clark's Summit, Pennsylvania. In 1992 he resigned to become full-time director of the Society's research center in Arizona.

George Mulfinger had an A.B. in chemistry and M.S. in physics from Syracuse University. He had been Professor of Physical Sciences at Bob Jones University since 1965. He had co authored two science textbooks for Christian Schools. He died after faithful service for many years.

E. Norbert Smith received his Ph.D. from Texas Tech in 1975 and has served on the faculties at Fort Hays (Kansas) State College, Rochester Institute of Technology, and Northeastern Oklahoma State University, finally being denied tenure at the latter because of anticreationist prejudice, in spite of an excellent record of scientific research and publication in his field.

Glen W. Wolfrom has a Ph.D. in animal science from the University of Missouri in 1976. He is currently working in industry in the field of animal nutrition. He was co-founder and former president of the Missouri Association for Creation.

Later changes in the Board have included: the 1984 election of Dr. David A. Kauffmann, of the University of Florida to replace Dr. Barnes; Dr. Don De Young, Professor of Physics at Grace College in Indiana, in 1985 to replace Harold Armstrong, who had served ten years as Editor of the *Quarterly* and who had recently died; the resignations of Harold Slusher in 1985, Clifford Burdick in 1986, John Moore in 1986; Richard Korthals in 1988, and Norbert Smith in 1989; the death of George Mulfinger in 1987; the election of Eugene Chaffin, Vice President and Professor of Physics at Bluefield College, and David J. Rodabaugh, formerly Professor of Mathematics at the University of Missouri and now with the Lockheed Co. in California, in 1988; The current Board (as of 1993) thus has only 15 members instead of the original 18, the Directors having voted in 1985 to allow for a Board membership of any number from 12 to 18. When Rusch resigned, Dr. Lane Lester, Head of the Center for Creation Studies at Liberty University and Dr. Russell Humphreys, physicist at the Sandia Labs in Albuquerque, were elected in 1991. Geologist Robert Gentet was added in 1992, and Rusch resigned.

The Creation Research Society has now been in existence for

over 30 years and has had a strong and consistent testimony for true Biblical creationism and catastrophism all that time. Wilbert Rusch was elected president in 1983, with George Howe again serving as vice-president. Wayne Frair was elected president in 1988, with Howe continuing as vice president.

John Klotz and Duane Gish are the only members of the original "eighteen-man Board of Directors" who are still on the Board. Other than these two "old-timers," the current CRS Board members have all been elected at various times after the Society was started. However, the doctrinal position, goals, and activities have remained unchanged, and God has blessed and used the Society in a remarkable way.

A number of faithful men who served on the Board at one time or another, are now with the Lord in heaven. These include: John Grebe, at whose home the original meeting was held; Harold Armstrong, who served as *Quarterly* editor for ten years; Edwin

Figure 15. Arizona Research Center of the Society

Architect's drawing of the new C.R.S. Research Center, near the Grand Canyon, scheduled for completion in 1993.

Y. Monsma, who was never on the Board, but was on the original "Team of Ten"; Will Tinkle, one of the chief organizers and who also served many years as Secretary; Karl Linsenmann, one of the original Board members; Douglas Dean, who served briefly on the Board in an early year, and George Mulfinger; who was in the Board for eleven years and who edited the Society's monograph on astronomy.

Chapter VII

Other Early Creationist Associations and Organizations

In addition to the Creation Research Society, there are today a great number of other creationist societies, organizations, and publications, most of them both arising from and contributing to the modern creationist revival. There are far too many of these for me to discuss them all individually in this book. Each one has had an interesting history of its own which would be well worth telling if time and space made it feasible. Even though the individual histories are not included, however, I have tried to list the names and addresses of all of these in Appendix C, in so far as I know them. If any have been overlooked, I apologize to those concerned. These organizations have been at least partially listed in a number of previous compilations, and I have used all of these (as well as our own files) in an attempt to get as complete and up-to-date a record as possible. Readers who are interested in the history and work of particular organizations can then write them directly for information.

In this chapter, I do want to discuss briefly the backgrounds and activities of some of the older and more influential of these organizations and associations. The two which have been *most* active and influential are discussed in separate chapters—the Creation Research Society in Chapter VI and the Institute for Creation Research in Chapter VIII. But there are also several others which have played key roles and which, therefore, need to be reviewed individually in some detail.

Evolution Protest Movement

The most venerable of the creationist societies is centered in England. The *Evolution Protest Movement* was organized in London in 1932 (more than 40 years before the Creation Research Society, in the year when I was just entering high school) and has been continuously functioning ever since. The name was changed to the *Creation Science Movement* in 1980.

There is one older society in England, of course, and it also is still in existence—namely, the *Victoria Institute*. As discussed in Chapter II, this society was organized in 1865, in the immediate wake of the publication of Darwin's *Origin of Species*. Although it was never a specifically creationist, or anti-evolutionist, association, its journals for many years did carry articles of real value for creationism. George McCready Price had two of his papers published in the *Victoria Institute Transactions*, one of them even winning its prize for that year (1925). However, like the American Scientific Affiliation, the Victoria Institute has now long since ceased to be even a partially creationist organization. Its meetings and publications for many years have been dominated by theistic evolutionism. The same is true of the Research Scientists Section of the Universities and Colleges Christian Fellowship (formerly the Inter-Varsity Fellowship, which was the parent organization of the Inter-Varsity Christian Fellowship in this country).

The need for a truly creationist organization was first openly expressed by Captain Bernard Acworth. He wrote a series of articles on the scientific fallacies of evolution and its harmful effects on society, which were published in various secular and professional periodicals in the mid-twenties, and which formed the basis of his book, *This Bondage,* published in 1929.[1] Captain Acworth was a career naval officer as well as an amateur, but

---

1. Bernard Acworth, "The Origin and Start of the Movement," *Evolution Protest Movement Interim Newsletter,* May 1957, pp. 1-3.

highly competent, ornithologist. His book brought him to the attention of another creationist ornithologist, Douglas Dewar, who at the time was quite active in the Victoria Institute, having served many years as one of its vice-presidents.

There were a number of other active creationist members in the Victoria Institute membership and Acworth also became acquainted with these. He published another book in 1932, entitled *This Progress - The Theory of Evolution.* Shortly after that, he proposed to Dewar and his other creationist friends that a new society was needed specifically to combat evolutionism and its evil influences among the British people. Dewar agreed, but stressed that (although he himself was a strong Bible-believing Christian) the activities of the new organization should emphasize the scientific arguments, rather than the Biblical or philosophical arguments.

Accordingly, the first meeting of the EPM was held in 1932 in Captain Acworth's office on Essex Street in Strand, London, in a building that was later destroyed in the World War II bombings. Following the first meeting, a membership solicitation letter was sent out over the signatures of the seven members of what was first called the Advisory Committee, with Captain Acworth himself as Chairman. This Advisory Committee later became known as the Council and has ever since been in responsible charge of the organization's affairs. The Council has always been a self-perpetuating body, rather than one elected by EPM members. The organization had no specific constitution and no specific statement of faith required of the membership, but the movement has been kept free of later dilution through compromise by this self-perpetuating aspect of its leadership.

This original Council was composed of seven distinguished men,[1] including Acworth and Dewar, with the other five listed

---

1. C. E. A. Turner, *A Jubilee of Witness for Creation Against Evolution: CSM/EPM 1932-1982.* (Booklet issued by the Creation Science Movement, July 1982, 17 pp.), p. 3. Much of the information in this section has been

below:

Basil Atkinson, M.A., Ph.D. (Canterbury), the Under Librarian (and, as such, an important official) in the University of Cambridge.

James Knight, M.A., D.Sc., F.R.S.E., a distinguished scientist and vice-president of the Royal Philosophical Society.

Sir John Latta, Bart., a ship owner, listed in *Who's Who.*

Rev. Hugh Miller, Principal of the London School of Bible Studies.

Rev. Dinsdale Young, the Methodist minister of the Westminster Central Hall, also listed in *Who's Who.*

The solicitation letter sent out by this first Committee is a document which seems even more relevant today than when it was first issued over sixty years ago. It is reproduced as a matter of historical interest, but also as a modern challenge, in Appendix D.

The first president of the Evolution Protest Movement was Sir John Ambrose Fleming, whose credentials have already been outlined in Chapter III. He was the author of over 90 scientific papers in the field of electronics, receiving many honors and prizes, certainly one of the most distinguished scientists of the twentieth century. He wrote a number of creationist papers for the Victoria Institute and at least one important creationist book. He served as EPM president until 1941.

Sir Ambrose was succeeded in the presidency by another distinguished scholar, Sir Charles Marston, who served until his death in 1946. Sir Charles was an industrialist, as well as an archaeologist, leading a number of archaeological expeditions and writing a number of books on Biblical archaeology, the best known being *The Bible is True,* published in 1934.

When Sir Charles died, Dewar himself accepted the presidency, continuing in that office until he died in 1957. He was undoubtedly the most active of all the members of the EPM in those early years,

---

based on the account in this booklet.

writing over 20 of its pamphlets and representing it vigorously to both the scientific community and the general public. More of his outstanding contributions to the creationist cause have been reviewed in Chapter III.

When Dewar died, Captain Acworth consented to become president, though reluctantly, since he did not consider himself to be a scientist. He had been Chairman of the Council up until that time. He had retired from active duty in the Navy some years previously, leaving London for a home on Hayling Island, Hants. Many of the earliest meetings of the Council had been held in his London office, with many of the later meetings at his home on the island. This first epoch of EPM history ended with the death of Captain Acworth in 1963.

The last surviving member of this original Council was Dr. Basil Atkinson, the Under Librarian at Cambridge. He was a fine scholar and Bible expositor, authoring a number of widely used books. Near the end of his life, he sent me an autographed copy of his commentary on Genesis, expressing appreciation for my own writings and for the work of the Creation Research Society. We shared an enjoyable correspondence friendship for a few years until he died. The Evolution Protest Movement did not publish much during its first several years and until the end of World War II, with the exception of a few pamphlets. Beginning about 1946, however, it put out a stream of pamphlets on many evolutionary topics, incisively and effectively criticizing the theory, especially on scientific grounds. Some of these, unfortunately, are not dated and, since they were not issued as a regular journal or in any other regular fashion, it is now difficult to refer to them effectively. However, many are still very valuable papers, especially those by Dewar, Acworth, Merson Davies, W. E. Filmer, D. S. Milne, and others. Altogether, by the time of its jubilee year, a total of 232 pamphlets had been issued,[1] in addition to newsletters. Members

---

1. C. E. A. Turner, *op. cit.,* p. 14.

of the Society (especially Dewar and Davies) often participated in creation/evolution debates and other meetings. Occasional protests, well-documented and vigorously argued, were presented to such establishment organizations as the British Museum and the British Broadcasting Corporation. Nevertheless, such protests were generally ignored, and British schools and other institutions, like those in the United States, came more and more to be utterly dominated by evolution. The EPM also published a number of books, one of the best being *Fossil Man,* by Frank Cousins, one of its more recent Council members.

Although the scientist membership in EPM was never large, it did boast a number of highly qualified men. The first four presidents (Fleming, Marston, Dewar, Acworth) were outstanding men, and this has been true of the succeeding presidents as well. A year or so before Captain Acworth died, following a long illness, he became President Emeritus and was followed by Sir Cecil P. G. Wakeley, who was Professor of Surgery at the University of London and Past President of the Royal College of Surgeons. He was also President of the Bible League. Dr. Wakeley served as EPM president longer than any of his predecessors, from 1962 until his death in 1979.

The current president (as of 1992) is Dr. Verna Wright, who holds the Chair of Rheumatology in the University of Leeds. An active witnessing Christian, Dr. Wright was a gracious host to ICR's Dr. Duane Gish for a portion of his British lecture tour in 1979.

To a degree, the two Council chairmen have been more active in regular leadership responsibilities than the presidents. Captain Acworth served in this role until 1957, when Dr. C. E. A. Turner assumed the position. Chairman Turner has M.Sc. and Ph.D. degrees, with honors in chemistry and research in science education. He was chairman until recently, shortly before his death, which means that only two men had held this strategic position in the first half-century-plus of the society's existence. The current chairman (as of 1992) is David Rosevear, FRSC, who has a Ph. D. in Chemistry.

The position of Secretary has been, in some respects, most important of all. The first man to hold this position was the founder's nephew, 0. R. Acworth, who directly assisted his uncle for the first three years.

Douglas Dewar assumed the position in 1935, continuing until he became president in 1946. The new Secretary then was W. E. Filmer, who continued until 1955. Like Dewar, Filmer was the author of many excellent EPM pamphlets.

The most prolific writer of pamphlets, however, was the next Secretary, A. G. Tilney, who held this position until 1976, when ill health forced his retirement. He died shortly thereafter, at the age of 85. Tilney wrote over 100 of the pamphlets and booklets published by the movement. Many of these, however, unlike most of the others published by EPM, tended to stress the Biblical and philosophical aspects of evolutionism, instead of dealing only with scientific matters. Tilney was simultaneously Secretary of the Prophecy Investigation Society and wrote numerous pamphlets for this organization as well.

Professionally, Mr. Tilney was not a scientist, but a linguist and specialist in modern languages. He had received a B.A. with honors from the University of London, but his doctoral dissertation was never accepted, apparently because of its strong creationist overtones. He was a schoolmaster and pastor in Hayling Island, Hants. This was the location of Captain Acworth's retirement home, and he worked closely with Tilney on EPM business there for many years, apparently having recruited him into membership there.

When our book, *The Genesis Flood,* came out in 1961, Tilney made it the subject of one of the EPM pamphlets, giving it a most favorable review and recommendation. Soon afterward, he invited me, with the Council's approval, to be one of the EPM vice presidents, and I have been shown on their official roster ever since. This is strictly an honorary position, however, as I have never been asked to participate in any EPM business or meetings. Tilney also devoted a pamphlet, with a glowing recommendation, to my commentary, *The Genesis Record*, when it was published in 1976.

Along with other Americans, I had the opportunity of meeting Mr. Tilney personally when he visited this country in 1972. When he died late in 1976, Mr. Alan Radcliffe-Smith, a research botanist in London, was appointed as Secretary. There have been several who have briefly held the office in recent years. Current Secretary (as of 1993) is Mrs. J. C. Rosevear.

The position of vice-president, as noted above, is essentially an honorary position, those holding the position presumably being capable of lending moral support to the EPM work by virtue of their positions or reputations. Current men in this position include Sir Cyril Black, Dr. D. B. Gower, Dr. A. E. Wilder-Smith, and myself.

There have been, and are now, many other distinguished members and leaders of the Evolution Protest Movement, but we cannot list them all. By far the majority of members, however, have not been scientists, but simply interested and concerned Christians. The total membership as of 1993 has recently climbed to about 1500.

The influence of the Evolution Protest Movement has not been limited to Great Britain. There have been active branches at one time or another in New Zealand, Australia, South Africa. Canada, and the United States. The Canadian branch, led by W. Dennis Burrowes, distributed publications in Canada and U.S.A. up to the end of 1988.

Interestingly (and contrary to the usual trend), although the Evolution Protest Movement has always been strictly creationist, its position on the young earth and flood geology has tended to become more conservative with the passing of time. Its first chief spokesman, Douglas Dewar, tended to accept the geological ages at face value, placing them in the context of the day-age theory. Then, A. G. Tilney, the prolific pamphleteer, favored the gap theory, although—after *The Genesis Flood* came out—he more and more attributed the fossiliferous geologic column to the Flood. In recent years, evidently following the lead of the creationist revival in the United States, the young earth/flood geology position is now held by all officers and members of the Council of the Society in the (now) Creation Science Movement in England as well. There has been a significant upsurge in the society in recent years, after a long period of decline. With its new name, a regular semi-annual journal *(Creation,* started in 1971), and a more positive approach, both the quantity and quality of its membership seems to be growing. Its recent publications have been excellent and very helpful, so, in my judgment at least, the Creation Science Movement has an excellent future, as well as (under the EPM name) a venerable and honorable past.

Bible-Science Association

Except for the Creation Research Society, the Bible-Science Association is the oldest creationist membership society still active in this country. It has had a great effect, especially among pastors and Christian laymen, in popularizing and promoting the same creationist position advocated among scientists by the Creation Research Society, as well as set forth in our book *The Genesis Flood.*

The Founder and Director of the Bible-Science Association (BSA) was an energetic Lutheran minister, Rev. Walter Lang. Because of this background, the BSA has always been more actively involved with, and supported by, Lutheran churches than any other group, although it is officially inter-denominational. Its present newsletter editor, Rev. Paul Bartz, and many of its active officers and speakers, are also Lutherans, and the speaking schedules of these leaders have served more Lutheran churches than all

Figure 16.
Founders of the Bible Science Association
Lutheran Pastor Walter Lang founded the Bible Science Association in 1963 and served as its director and inspirational leader for over 20 years. His wife, Valeria, did most of the editing of the Association's Newsletter during that time. The photo was taken in 1984.

others combined. Nevertheless, its impact, as well as its formal structure, has been trans-denominational right from the beginning.

Walter Lang received his ministerial training in Concordia Seminary (St. Louis), the leading educational institution of the Missouri Lutheran Synod, graduating in 1937. He then served various Lutheran congregations in St. Louis, Houston, Denver, and Caldwell (Idaho) until 1966.[1] As a pastor, often involved in interracial work, and as a Bible-believing conservative, he became increasingly concerned about the liberal trends that were beginning to affect his own traditionally conservative synod, as they already had done in so many other Christian denominations. He had especially been disturbed by the evolutionary philosophy which was infiltrating his own seminary, as well as Valparaiso College, the Missouri Lutheran school his son was attending. Becoming more

---

1. Walter Lang, "Twenty Years of the Bible-Science Newsletter" *(Bible-Science Newsletter,* Vol. 21, Sept. 1983), pp. 1, 2, 10. Some of the information in this section is derived from this article.

and more active in this battle within his church, Lang got in contact with Rev. Herman Otten, a recent Concordia graduate who had started a new periodical, *The Lutheran News* (later changed to *Christian News*), dedicated to opposing liberalism in the denomination.

Both Otten and Lang realized that the real root of the problem was evolution, and Lang began to promote such creationist literature as was available at the time. When *The Genesis Flood* was published in 1961, both considered it very significant. Lang has written:

> What really sparked the modern Creationist movement was the publication in 1961 of the book titled The Genesis Flood. . . . Creation Research Society members have done outstanding research and publishing. In our opinion the catalyst which brought all these scientists together was publication of The Genesis Flood.[1]

Otten also promoted the book through his newspaper and has continued to promote the modern creation movement ever since. Many people have credited him and his paper with being the most important single influence in helping the conservatives regain control of the denomination and its seminaries from the liberals several years later—a remarkable turn-around hitherto unique in the long sad history of denominational apostasy. Since the conflict in the Missouri Synod largely centered around Genesis and the creation issue, the Lutheran leaders in the Creation Research Society (especially Klotz, Rusch, and Lammerts) also played key roles in the victory.

When the Creation Research Society was organized in the summer of 1963, Lammerts notified Otten, and Otten contacted Lang. Lang, in turn, decided that he would do something to let his fellow ministers, and others who were concerned, know what was hap-

---

1. Walter Lang, *Two Decades of Creationism.* This is an unpublished book manuscript on the history of the Bible-Science Association. Much of the data in this section has been derived from this manuscript also.

pening. Accordingly, in September 1963, he put together a small mimeographed newsletter consisting of two legal-sized sheets containing short articles about the Creation Research Society formation and the evolutionist drift of the American Scientific Affiliation. There was also a listing of the known creationist materials then available, featuring especially *The Genesis Flood.* This was the first issue of *The Bible-Science Newsletter,* mimeographed in Lang's church in Idaho, and sent out to a select list of his acquaintances and others he thought would be interested. Although we had not corresponded previously, so far as I can recall, he was kind enough to send me a copy and to request my cooperation in establishing some kind of interchange with other creationists.

In view of the fact that the Evolution Protest Movement had never published a regular journal and the fact that the first issue of the *CRS Quarterly* did not come out until the summer of 1964, the *Bible Science Newsletter* can rightly be regarded as the oldest extant periodical devoted primarily to creationism. Its original purpose, as stated in its first issue, was to foster "an exchange of ideas by those who are concerned with science developed from a framework in harmony with a conservative view of the Bible." This purpose has been focused more specifically on the following articles of faith, as carried on the masthead of later issues of the paper, right up to the present:

> Dedicated to: Special creation; Literal Bible interpretation; Divine design and purpose in nature; A Young Earth; A universal Noachian flood; Christ as God and Man—our Savior; Christ-centered scientific research.

This clear-cut position and purpose obviously is honoring to Christ and His Word, and God has blessed the Association accordingly.

The Newsletter rapidly caught on, and five months later began to be printed on offset equipment at a local potato-processing plant in Caldwell. By the spring of 1964, over 5000 copies were going out each month, and the operation had to be moved to a local printing firm. From its small beginning, it became a monthly magazine of about twenty 11 1/2" x 17" pages, with a wide variety of interesting and significant articles, along with numerous illustrations and special features. Because of financial difficulties, the newsletter in late 1991 had to be changed to a smaller, magazine-style format, with fewer issues per year.

The Bible-Science Association itself was organized in the summer of 1964, partially due to the suggestion of Paul Hackstedde (Lutheran) along with Jean Sumrall (Lutheran) and Nell Segraves (Baptist), all of whom were in southern California and had become concerned over evolutionist indoctrination in the schools attended by their children. Hackstedde was named president, and Lang, in cooperation with these and other interested people in southern California, began to plan a Los Angeles creation seminar. This would involve a roundrobin series with five churches and five scientists as speakers.

This seminar was notably successful, receiving nationwide newspaper attention and reaching, according to Lang's estimate, 15,000 people. Since the two main speakers were Walter Lammerts and Wilbert Rusch, the Creation Research Society probably received most of the publicity. As a result, Lang and the others, especially Mrs. Segraves, argued for a merger of the Society with the Bible-Science Association. Lammerts and Rusch demurred, however, sensing that such a union might be controlled by laymen, with the scientists merely serving as speakers and writers for various projects initiated and planned for them by the others. This, of course, was not at all the program envisioned by the founders and directors of the CRS. This same question continued to be raised, in various modified forms, by Lang, and especially by his southern California members, over the next several years, but each time the Society's Board reaffirmed that it could not affiliate in any way with any other organization, including BSA.

In addition to the seminars, which began to be held regularly in Los Angeles, as well as other places (Seattle, Little Rock, etc.), the

Bible-Science Association has developed a remarkable variety of supplementary activities, all intended to promote creationism in one way or another. This all reflects the remarkable energy and originality of Walter Lang, one of the most dedicated men one could ever encounter. A man of only average stature, he nevertheless has a powerful voice and dominates every conversation in which he is engaged. His output of work is prodigious. He is not what one would call a careful scholar, but he reads and writes voluminously. Seemingly indefatigable, he has criss-crossed the country time and again in an old automobile on back-breaking speaking and bookselling schedules and has traveled all over the world on all kinds of missions promoting creationism. Living sacrificially on a minimal income, for the sake of the ministries, he accomplished in 23 years an almost incredible amount of testimony for the truth of creation. To many, his approach has often seemed undiscerning, but he has compensated in quantity and sincerity for what may have seemed lacking sometimes in quality and consistency.

For details concerning the wide-ranging ministries of BSA, one should refer to the book previously cited.[1] Here, a mere listing and summary description of many of these activities will suffice to illustrate the outreach and influence of the Association. In addition to the monthly *Bible-Science Newsletter,* around which all else centers, the following facets of the ministry are notable.

1. *BSA Branches.* Unlike the Creation Research Society, the Association has encouraged and sponsored the development of local branches. Each of these is autonomous, conducting its own meetings and other functions, and several have actually split off to form separate creation organizations of their own (e.g., Canadian branch, Southern California branch, Wichita branch—each of which will be discussed separately). A total of perhaps 20 or more of these branches are currently active.

---

1. *Ibid.*

2. *Creation Conventions*. The Association has organized and sponsored national conventions of creationists in a number of cities, including Milwaukee, Seattle, Philadelphia, Atlanta, Anaheim, Wichita, Minneapolis, and Chicago. The first was at Milwaukee in 1972. Each of these has involved the presentation of special papers by many different creationist scientists and others, as well as banquets and public meetings.

3. *Publications*. In addition to the *Newsletter,* the Association has published a number of small books. These have included collections of papers given at various seminars and conventions, a book on the creationist interpretation of the Grand Canyon by geologist Clifford Burdick, and others. Devotional guides and children's science readers have been published in the past.

4. *Book Distribution*. In a ministry begun even before the first issue of the *Newsletter,* Pastor Lang and the Bible-Science Association started selling creationist books of all authors and publishers. Book tables at seminars, as well as a mail-order catalog, made available the most complete selection of creationist books in existence—all having first been reviewed and recommended as compatible with the BSA doctrinal position. The Association opened a very attractive bookstore in Minneapolis in 1989. However, because of financial problems, the bookstore had to close in late 1991.

5. *Geology Tours*. The Bible-Science Association has sponsored numerous tours to points of special geological interest, with a view toward interpreting these formations and phenomena in terms of flood geology. The tour groups have been small in number, but comprised of dedicated creationists who would use the information acquired in their own respective ministries. Such sites as the Grand Canyon, Yellowstone Park, the Canadian Rockies, Hawaiian volcanos, and others have been featured on these tours.

6. *Other Tours*. In addition to those tours of special geologic emphasis, the BSA has sponsored many international tours, covering such places as Switzerland, Scotland, Germany, Alaska,

Galapagos Islands, Peru, South Pacific, India, and others. On one such tour in 1971, to the Holy Land and then to Turkey to view Mount Ararat, my son (Dr. John Morris, who was then working as an engineer for the city of Los Angeles), was inspired to dedicate his life to the cause of creationism, including particularly the search for Noah's Ark, as well as Christian witness in general.

7. *Speaking Ministries.* Walter Lang has, for over 30 years, carried out a very demanding schedule of speaking engagements, not only in organized seminars and conferences, but also on a night-after-night basis, speaking in church after church as he has traveled on his various itineraries. This is also true more recently, though not quite as intensively, of his other colleagues in the Association. The members of the various branches also speak frequently in their own areas.

The above is not an exhaustive list of BSA activities, but is at least indicative. For a few years, Lang tried to carry it out concurrently with his pastoral duties at the Grace Lutheran Church in Idaho. In 1966, however, the work had become so heavy that, in faith, he felt the Lord was leading him to devote full time to it. Then, by 1978, he needed more help of a professional nature, including computerization of all the Association's, by-now-very-complex, operations.

At this point, the Lord providentially led William Overn, who was active in the Minneapolis branch, to offer to go to work with BSA, at least on a part-time basis. According to his own testimony, Overn had become a convinced inerrantist and creationist many years previously as a result of reading my first book, *That You Might Believe,* while he was an engineering student at the University of Minnesota. I was teaching there at the time and had picked him up one day in 1948 as he was hitchhiking to school, witnessing to him and then giving him a copy of the book. The Lord used it to change his life and 30 years later would direct him into a similar ministry. I did remember this occasion myself, when he told me about it many years later, and was thrilled and thankful to learn about its results.

In the meantime, he had enjoyed a long and productive career in engineering and computer science and was ideally equipped to computerize the operations and to establish the Association's activities on a more businesslike and soundly scientific basis. In 1978, Walter Lang and the entire organization moved from Idaho to Minneapolis, and Bill Overn became its Co-Director.

Walter Lang's wife, Valeria, has been another vitally important BSA worker, having served as typist and editor on the *Newsletter* (even much of the writing, paste-up, and mailing) from the time it started. My wife, two youngest daughters, and I had the privilege of staying in her home one night in 1969 while we were on a business trip to Utah. While there, we saw her efficient basement work room. Walter had arranged for me to speak in a church in Caldwell, even though he himself was off on a speaking tour of his own.

Mrs. Lang retired in 1981, after 18 years on the job, Rev. Paul Bartz took over then as Executive Editor of all BSA publications. He has continued in that capacity ever since. Walter Lang resigned in 1986, however, and Bill Overn in 1989. Current Director is Greg Hull, a philosopher and former pastor. The BSA has also been sponsoring "Creation Moments," a daily three-minute radio program heard on hundreds of stations.

Creation Science Association of Canada

Originally formed as the Bible-Science Association of Canada, this organization has been for many years an independent organization known as the Creation Science Association of Canada. Its first Executive Director was Dr. Earl Hallonquist of Vancouver, a very competent scientist and Bible student who had a productive career as an industrial chemist prior to his retirement to work full time promoting creationism. The Canadian Association also has active provincial divisions, the Creation Science Associations of

Figure 17. Dr. Hallonquist Debating in Canada

Dr. Earl Hallonquist, founder and director of the Creation Science Association of Canada. As a retired industrial chemist, Dr. Hallonquist (now deceased) was for many years a vigorous proponent of scientific creationism, then later an effective and popular creationist debater. Here he is shown at the University of British Columbia, where he debated Fred Edwords, a well-known evolutionary philosopher and leader in the American Humanist Association.

Alberta, Saskatchewan, Quebec , and Ontario, respectively. Since the Canadian work largely originated in the Vancouver area, mostly through the efforts of Dr. Hallonquist (this was around 1969), the national organization also functions as the division for the province of British Columbia.

The Canadian association has sponsored a number of cross Canada speaking tours by ICR scientists and others. Such men as Dr. Duane Gish, Dr. Richard Bliss, Dr. Harold Slusher, Dr. John Morris, Dr. Gary Parker, and myself have been on such tours, speaking usually to large crowds. On one occasion, in 1970, I spoke in both Victoria and Vancouver. On another (in the late fall of 1971), I traversed Canada with Dr. and Mrs. Hallonquist, speaking in numerous churches and universities from Edmonton to

Toronto, in the provinces of Alberta, Saskatchewan, Manitoba, and Ontario. From Toronto, I flew with Dick Holliday, one of the Toronto area pastors, to Los Angeles, where my wife joined us and we went on to Hawaii, for a speaking tour in the churches and colleges on Oahu, including especially the University of Hawaii. That was one tour to be remembered! I still recall with joy meeting a chaplain in Honolulu who turned out to be a young man that had been won to Christ through our Christian Fellowship group on the Rice University campus 25 years before.

Returning to the Canadian work, Dr. Hallonquist especially was (he died in 1985) very active, participating in important debates, writing and distributing an excellent booklet called *The Bankruptcy of Evolution,* and in various other ways. An outstanding slide set prepared by Luther Sunderland, a General Electric Company engineer in Schenectady, was promoted and distributed throughout Canada by the Association, also being sent to missionaries. Cassette commentaries have been produced for the program in the Spanish, French, and Indonesian languages.

One of the provincial associations, that in Alberta, produces a quarterly magazine, eight pages in size, called *Dialogue.* The Vancouver (British Columbia) group set up an effective display at the summer conference (1983) of the World Council of Churches, held in Vancouver. All the provincial associations are very active in speaking, promoting seminars and summer institutes, literature distribution, and various other ministries.

Most of these groups are still loosely affiliated with the Bible-Science Association. Another small Canadian group called North American Creation Movement, was located in Victoria, B.C. (1969-1988) under the direction of W.D. Burrowes, and was affiliated with the Creation Science Movement (previously Evolution Protest Movement) of England. For many years, this group distributed EPM/CSM publications in Canada and the USA, along with occasional newsletters.

Loma Linda and the
Geoscience Research Institute

An entirely different sort of creationist organization is the Geoscience Research Institute, which is sponsored and controlled entirely by the Seventh-Day Adventist denomination. In a sense, this organization is continuing in part the work of George McCready Price and the old Creation-Deluge Society.

It was originally established in 1958, with Dr. Frank Marsh as the first scientist appointed on its staff. Marsh had been an associate and disciple of Price and was also one of the founding members of the Creation Research Society. He had been one of the reviewers of the manuscript of *The Genesis Flood.* At that time he was on the faculty of the Adventists' Emmanuel Missionary College in Berrien Springs, Michigan. The name of this school had just been changed to Andrews University when Marsh was called to head the newly established Institute.

The purpose of the Geoscience Research Institute was, as the name implies, to do research in the problem areas of geology and biology relating to the question of origins and earth history. At the time Marsh was appointed, P. Edgar Hare, with a Ph. D. in chemistry, was also appointed. Two years later, a young Ph. D. in comparative anatomy from Harvard, Richard Ritland, was also appointed to the G.R.I. science staff. The three researchers were essentially of equal status, although Marsh was by far the senior scientist of the three. All were under the S.D.A. General Conference Counseling Committee, which acted as the Institute's "Director." The two younger men were, at best, old-earth creationists; as were at least two of the Counseling Committee. In 1964 at age 65, Marsh was rushed into retirement and dismissed from the Institute with Ritland then being made Director. Soon thereafter, however, a new Conference president who was a strict creationist undertook to restore the Institute to its original purpose, and Ritland resigned.

The Institute was eventually moved from Michigan to Loma Linda University in California, where it is now closely associated with the science graduate programs there. From 1970 to 1972, Dr. Ariel Roth, Head of the Biology Department at Loma Linda, and a former student of Harold Clark's, served also as Director of the Institute. He was succeeded by Dr. R. H. Brown, a physicist whose specialty has been radiometry and radiometric dating.

Dr. Brown, while committed to creationism and a worldwide flood (as required by fidelity to Ellen G. White's teachings), seems also to be committed to the general validity of radiometric dating, thus believing in an old earth and universe. This is essentially the position held by those Adventists who took over the Creation-Deluge Society back in 1945 and eventually caused its demise. They believe in what is called "primary time," the supposed billion years of existence of the primordial unstructured earth before God created the living world in six literal days. This position seems to most strict creationists to be inconsistent with both the plain statements of Scripture (e.g., Exodus 20:11) and also the facts of geology, whether or not it agrees with Mrs. White. There still appears to be a division of opinion among the Adventists on this point, just as there was in the days of the Creation-Deluge Society.

Nevertheless, the Institute is committed to flood geology and has been doing some excellent research in developing a comprehensive "flood model." Much of this research has been published, along with significant review articles on important topics in scientific creationism, in the Institute's semi-annual journal *Origins,* which was started in 1974. Dr. Roth has been the Editor of *Origins,* and again became Director of the Institute in 1982.

Loma Linda University is the only nominally creationist university (some of its faculty do not seem to take a clear stand on creation), so far as I know, which has Ph.D. programs in biology and geology. It has a high-quality staff of creationist scientists. One of them, paleontologist Harold Coffin, has written an excellent book, *Creation: Accident or Design?* Although many of us wish it would take a more clear-cut stand supporting the Biblical doctrine of recent creation, Loma Linda and its Geoscience Research Institute are certainly making a significant contribution to the cause of special creationism and flood geology.

Christian Heritage College

There are many Christian colleges, but there is one which I believe warrants special attention in any study on the history of creationism. Not only was Christian Heritage College closely related to the Institute for Creation Research, but also it was—so far as I know—the first college in modern times formed in order to provide a liberal arts education based specifically on strict Biblical creationism and full Biblical controls in all courses. As one of its three founders, as well as the planner of its first curricula and the author of its original statement of faith, this was my intent and motivation right from the start. I had spent most of the first half-century of my life in secular education, either as student or teacher. Almost 30 years of that time had also been spent in diligent study and teaching of the Scriptures, particularly in relation to the unbelieving intellectual world with which I was interacting daily. From both study and experience, it had become crystal clear to me that the foundation of false teaching in every discipline of study, and therefore of ungodly practice in all areas of life, was evolutionism. In every secular school, at all levels and permeating every curriculum, the false philosophy of evolution had been made the foundation upon which everything else was built. Evolutionism is always the underlying rationale for naturalism and humanism, which lead eventually to atheism and ultimately to Satanism.

Furthermore, this system had even permeated Christian schools to an alarming degree. Even though I was teaching all this time in secular universities, I had been given the opportunity of speaking to students and faculties at scores of Christian schools, as well as reading articles and engaging in correspondence from scores of others. The reaction of the Christian liberal arts college community to *The Genesis Flood* and to the Creation Research Society had been largely negative, even though their criticisms always seemed to ignore all the Biblical arguments and evidences for strict creationism. Many evangelical colleges were openly espousing theistic evolution or a diluted progressive creationism. Even those fundamentalist colleges which officially repudiated evolution were, perhaps unintentionally, compromising with it in many ways. Practically all Christian schools implicitly accepted the geologic-age system, which not only was explicitly contradicted by the Scriptures but also provided the basic framework and best evidence for evolution, and was, in actuality, itself based on evolution. These unnecessary concessions to the evolutionary framework were, in turn, leading to humanistic emphases in the humanities and social sciences, even in "solid" Christian schools.

One major problem, of course, was that secular textbooks were used almost everywhere, since no others were available. Another was that teachers had to get their own graduate training in secular graduate schools, since there were no Christian graduate programs anywhere, with a few minor exceptions such as in Bible or music. Another was the increasing pressure toward conformity imposed by the supposed need for secular accreditation of schools. It seemed more and more obvious that there was a great and urgent need in the Christian world for a truly Christian—that is, creationist and Biblical—educational system. That would mean, especially, a genuine Christian university, with majors not only in so-called religious vocations, but also in the sciences, humanities, and the various professions. Such a university should provide graduate training in all these fields, as well as carry out needed research. Its faculty members should also be writing the textbooks and carrying out extension programs throughout the country.

Every state in the United States has several such universities, but the Christian world has *none!* There are a few denominational universities which are nominally Christian (e.g., Southern Methodist, Notre Dame, Baylor) but all of these are saturated with evolutionism and Biblical skepticism. There were a few large evangelical or fundamentalist colleges which called themselves universities, but they were nowhere near being universities in the comprehensive sense defined above, and they also were beset with these pressures toward compromise and conformity. So far as I have been able to find, not one Christian college of consequence, at that time, considered creationism sufficiently important to have it spelled out in its statement of faith—at least not with sufficient precision to preclude its being interpreted in terms of long ages and/or theistic evolution. Certainly none specified creation of all things in six literal days or the universal cataclysmic Noahic flood, and thus all were relatively easily open to compromising opinions and interpretations.

But what, if anything, could be done about all this? A number of Christian leaders had expressed the great need for a true Christian university, but even these had not recognized that such a university, in order to be really effective and lasting, would have to be founded on strict and true creationism, not on some compromise with the evolutionism which dominates the present university world.

At any rate, I began to dream and pray about this need. I discussed it with the administrative leaders of various Christian colleges, and at least six such colleges offered me positions on their faculties. All of them believed in creation and agreed that it was important, but none seemed able to comprehend how important and vital it was. None were willing to establish a center for creation research on their campuses nor to restructure their programs within a creationist framework. In every case, I prayed and thought about these opportunities, but it did not seem the Lord was really leading in them. It began to be obvious that such a creationist university would have to start from scratch, not from an existing college.

In January of 1970, during my sabbatical year at Virginia Tech,

I was one of the speakers at the annual Torrey Memorial Bible Conference at Biola College, near Los Angeles. One of the other speakers was Dr. Tim LaHaye, pastor of the Scott Memorial Baptist Church in San Diego. Dr. LaHaye, now widely known as a best-selling writer, as well as a national leader in the battle against the humanistic moral influences subverting our nation, had just decided to try to start a Bible College in San Diego. He had read some of my books, attended several of my lectures at Biola, and then somehow felt led to ask me to consider coming to teach science in his proposed Bible college.

I was not interested in that, of course, but did go ahead and share with him and his associate, Art Peters, the dream of a Christian university founded on creationism.[1] A university could not be developed overnight, of course, but the way to begin would be a Christian liberal arts college with an associated creation research center. Their desire for a church-centered Bible college could also be met by including Bible and missions majors (also oriented around true creationism) in the liberal arts college.

After further discussion, much prayer, and two trips to San Diego, the decision was made to go ahead on this basis. Dr. LaHaye would be president, Dr. Peters executive vice-president, and I would be academic vice-president. I laid out the curriculum and wrote the statement of faith. Dr. LaHaye recruited the initial faculty (all of whom had to be part-time and therefore working in the San Diego area) and raised the financing. Dr. Peters set up the administrative structure and worked out the other logistics. The church congregation voted to sponsor the college, which I suggested be named Christian Heritage College, and it was decided to begin classes in September, only eight months after Dr. LaHaye and I had begun to discuss the possibilities.

The four initial degree programs offered were in the fields of

---

1. I have included my first letter to Dr. LaHaye, dated February 12, 1970, as Appendix E, as a matter of interest, since it expresses the same educational goals which I outlined above and which I still hold.

Figure 18. Tim and Beverly LaHaye

The three "co-founders" of Christian Heritage College in San Diego were Dr. Tim LaHaye, Dr. Art Peters, and the writer. Dr. LaHaye, now a well known Christian writer and leader, who was then pastor of the Scott Memorial Baptist Church, which sponsored the College, became the College's first president. His wife, Beverly, now Director of Concerned Women for America, was the College's first Registrar.

Bible, Education, Missions, and Liberal Arts. These were considered the most urgent needs, but other majors were added from year to year as resources allowed. The statement of faith was unique among Christian liberal arts colleges, so far as I know, since it included specific articles on literal special creation of all things, as well as the worldwide flood, and also explicitly rejected any form of evolution. See Appendix F.

Another important innovation was to incorporate a strong component of apologetics into all curricula. Each student was given six semester-hours of instruction in "Practical Christian Evidences" as a freshman, then six semester-hours in "Scientific Creationism" in the sophomore year. For several years I taught these courses myself and, since there were no appropriate textbooks available for them, I prepared class handouts which eventually grew into textbooks. These books have since become fairly widely used as text or reference books in other schools. For the first course, the notes became *Many Infallible Proofs* and *The Bible Has The Answer;* for the second, they became *Scientific Creationism* and *The Troubled Waters of Evolution.* Later on, we also used Dr. Gish's book *Evolution? The Fossils Say NO!* and Dr. Slusher's *Critique of Radiometric Dating.*

The entering class of the College was only a handful of students, but the enrollments grew steadily, eventually reaching almost 500 by 1978. The variety of degree programs also grew, to well over 20. Some of these were unique, including the only B.S. degree program in geophysics anywhere which was based on scientific Biblical creationism and catastrophism, under the leadership of Dr. Harold Slusher. The graduates of this program have all done well in graduate school, the oil industry, and elsewhere. Other unusual majors included missionary aviation, Christian home economics, and Biblical psychology, in addition to the more common majors (biology, history, education, etc.). All were developed within the framework of creationism and full Biblical controls.

Many have been the graduates of Christian Heritage who have later testified to the great value which the Bible-centered creationist approach in general, and the apologetics courses in particular, had in their Christian lives after graduation. Furthermore, this example, and the availability of suitable textbooks, has encouraged many other Christian schools—high schools, colleges, seminaries—to place more emphasis on apologetics and true creationism in their own curricula. Another book which was written specifically to expound the Biblical doctrine of education,[1] as implemented at Christian Heritage and as recommended for all schools of all levels, has been widely used as a text or reference

---

1. *Christian Education for the Real World,* by Henry M. Morris (Third edition, San Diego: Master Books, 1991) 285 pp. This edition is considerably enlarged from the first, published in 1977.

book in education courses at other Christian colleges.

Dr. LaHaye was president of the College until 1978. I then served as president for two years, then Art Peters for two years. Dr. Eddy Miller, who originally came as Dean in 1973, was president from 1982 to 1984. Dr. Earl Mills was made president in 1985 and served until 1988, when Dr. David Jeremiah (who had replaced Tim LaHaye as pastor of Scott Memorial Baptist Church) took over the presidency.

During the early years, it was easy enough to find science professors who were knowledgeable and committed creationists, and we also found a number of dedicated Bible-centered creationist teachers in the other fields, but some of those who came later had less understanding and conviction about the College's foundational doctrines and goals than I had hoped. Likewise, most of the students who came were young people of solid Christian character, who had come precisely because of the unique nature and teachings of Christian Heritage. But there were others, particularly as the College grew and became somewhat more socially acceptable, who felt the College should try to conform more to other schools. However, the most serious problems were generated by the desire to be accredited. The various regional accrediting agencies are supposed only to evaluate the quality of education offered by a school, not its philosophy or beliefs. Since accreditation does, indeed, offer many advantages to a school and its students, it was decided right from the beginning that we would try to attain accreditation, provided it was not necessary to compromise our doctrinal standards to do so. We did all we could to follow the recommendations of the accrediting commission (the Westerm Association of Schools and Colleges, "WASC") that related to legitimate academic matters (library, record-keeping, faculty, student services, etc.), and the quality of education was at least as good as for numerous accredited schools in the state. Nevertheless, time after time, the various examining teams objected in various ways to our creationist and Bible-controlled curricular philosophy, especially objecting to the open way in which this was spelled out in our catalogs and other literature. There were six accreditation visits by WASC teams to the campus by 1984, before accreditation was finally achieved (the "candidacy" status had been acquired at the second visit), plus several "consultative" visits by WASC officials, and it has repeatedly (though often deviously) been made clear that the Christian Heritage educational philosophy (all courses based on strict creationism, with no compromise with evolution, plus full Biblical inerrancy and authority in all subjects) was simply not acceptable. The College's close affiliation with the Institute for Creation Research was a particularly sensitive issue, especially with the growing national visibility of ICR and the increasing concern of the education establishment with stopping the creationist revival.

The fourth such accreditation visit, in connection with the application for the third—and presumably final—two-year period of "candidacy" status, occurred while I was serving both as president of the College and director of ICR. Not one member of the visitation team interviewed me at all, but they all made it plain in their report they had decided we were "indoctrinating," rather than educating, students and that this was unacceptable.

At this time the Institute for Creation Research (see next chapter) was still a division of the College, and it was finally agreed that it would be better for both organizations, under these circumstances, for the two to separate. Furthermore, this would make it possible for ICR to begin science graduate programs, which were urgently needed but would be precluded as long as the College was trying to achieve, and then maintain, accreditation with WASC.

Accordingly, I resigned as president of the College in 1980, and ICR "spun off" as a separate educational institution shortly thereafter, beginning its graduate programs in 1981. A contract was set up between the two institutions, allowing for much cooperation between them, but the administrations were completely separate thereafter.

This separation of ICR from Christian Heritage College naturally pleased WASC officials very much, but they still continued to exert pressure on the College for further compromise. As a result, the College eventually softened its statements of mission and educational philosophy. Even that was insufficient to satisfy certain WASC officials. They proceeded further to demand that the College change its Statement of Faith! In particular, certain key WASC officials verbally insisted that the reference to special creation in six natural days be removed, and also the reference that indicated evolution was completely false. This, of course, was the real heart of the matter, constituting the essential distinctive of Christian Heritage, assuring that evolution could never be interpreted as God's method of creation, as had been done in so many older Christian schools. However, the College has rejected the WASC demand to cut out the references to six-literal-day creationism from its Statement of Faith, although a number of other changes were made. In 1984, WASC finally granted full accreditation.

In spite of the various concessions which were made in order to get WASC accreditation, Christian Heritage College thus still has the clearest creationist Statement of Faith of any liberal arts college in existence, so far as I can determine. The same is true of its Bible-governed, creation-oriented, Scripturally integrated curriculum, and I trust its administration and faculty will continue to resist future pressures to make further concessions. However, the enrollments have declined, the science majors deleted, a distracting emphasis on intercollegiate athletics added, and the courses in Christian evidences and scientific creationism diluted, so the College is not what some of us had hoped it would be.

Many Christian educators have argued that secular accreditation could be achieved without compromising their belief in creation. However, none of their schools have ever taken this kind of stand, a stand which would absolutely preclude further compromise with evolution and the geologic-age system. Therefore, their assertion has never really been tested. It *was* tested at Christian Heritage College, however! And there it was clearly demonstrated that the evolutionary humanists who largely control our scientific and educational establishments will simply not tolerate an educational institution which repudiates their basic premise, if they can help it. Evolutionism has no place in true Christian education, and Biblical creationism is intolerable to the secular humanists who dominate our educational establishment. I earnestly hope that the administrations and faculties of other Christian colleges will realize this fact before it is too late and evolutionary humanism appropriates the same degree of control over Christian education which it already has over public education. A truly Christian creationist accrediting association would be the best answer to this need, and the Trans-National Association of Christian Schools (TRACS) was established in 1979 for this purpose. See Chapter IX, pages 322-326, for a discussion of this organization.

The Creation-Science Research Center

The Creation-Science Research Center as it now exists had a hybrid origin, when two different creationist organizations attempted to merge for a time, back in 1970. One group was formerly part of the Bible-Science Association, led by Nell Segraves and her son, Kelly. The other was the creation research division of Christian Heritage College, founded by me when Dr. LaHaye and I started the College, under the sponsorship of San Diego's Scott Memorial Baptist Church.

The Southern California branch of the Bible-Science Association was very active from the start, with its annual seminars in the Los Angeles area. Walter Lang had started a regular Bible-Science radio program but, as the BSA work grew, he got Kelly Segraves to help with it. Soon after that, Segraves and other Los Angeles BSA leaders formed a separate organization, Bible-Science Radio, and took over the radio work completely.

At the same time, Nell Segraves and Jean Sumrall, two members of this board, became active in trying to get California to incorporate creation into its textbooks and curricula. A real breakthrough seemed to come in 1969, when the State Board of Education voted to include creationism in its "Science Framework." This was accomplished mainly through the efforts of Board member Dr. John Ford, a Seventh-Day Adventist medical doctor in San Diego. However, there were also several other conservatives on the Board at the time, appointed by Governor Ronald Reagan. Oddly enough, the most effective testimony supporting creation teaching in the schools was given by Vernon Grose, a teacher in a vocational school near Los Angeles, who was a member of the American Scientific Affiliation and was inclined toward progressive creationism in his own thinking.

The Bible-Science Radio group decided, then, to form a corporation to be called Creation Science, Inc., with the purpose of getting creation-oriented textbooks prepared for use in California as soon as the State Board directive was implemented. However, they needed scientists to write the textbooks for them. An attempt to affiliate with the Creation Research Society for this purpose was rebuffed. When they learned of our plans in San Diego, Segraves persuaded me to let them merge with us.

I had also been concerned with the need for textbooks, of course, long before I heard about the California situation, and this had been one of my reasons for wanting to form a creation research center in connection with a Christian college somewhere. Dr. LaHaye had agreed that this would be appropriate for our proposed new college, and we were proceeding on that basis.

We agreed on the name Creation-Science Research Center for the combined organization. Segraves was named Assistant Director and his mother Librarian, with myself as Director. They and their board were all in the Los Angeles area, so they both moved to San Diego and were given offices in the church facilities where the College was set up initially. The board of directors of the Center consisted of the eight board members of the previous Creation Science, Inc., including both Nell Segraves and Kelly Segraves, plus Dr. and Mrs. LaHaye, Dr. Peters, and myself. The College, on the other hand, had its own Board of Trustees, all elected or appointed by the church.

During the next two years, I was largely occupied with college affairs, although I also did much traveling, speaking, and writing on behalf of the CSRC. The main project undertaken was to prepare what would become the *Science and Creation Series,* consisting of a set of supplementary books for public schools, a student and teacher book for each of the first eight grades, plus an over-all reference book. A team of writers, including both scientists and public school teachers, many of whom were members of the church, were recruited to write the various books of the series. Two former Biola College science faculty members, biologist Robert Koontz and chemist William Boardman, were hired to work with me on the reference book.[1] Dr. Jimmy Phelps, then Assistant Superintendent of Education for the Santee School District, near San Diego, and later Head of the Education Department at Christian Heritage College, served with me as Co-Editor of the *Series.*

However, in order to have these books considered for adoption in the California public schools, they had to be submitted in Sacramento in September of 1971, and this deadline was too close to do a satisfactory job on the entire series. We did get the reference handbook finished, but it was impossible to get the rest of the series done properly. I decided that it would be better not to submit them to the state at all that year (1971), since it was vitally important that the first creationist books submitted be of top quality, and especially since I had to be out of town most of that summer, speaking at Bible conferences and attending to other matters. However, in my absence Kelly Segraves and his mother decided

---

1. William Boardman, Robert Koontz, and Henry M. Morris. *Science and Creation: A Handbook for Teachers* (San Diego: Creation-Science Research Center, 1971), 98 pp.

to go ahead and push the books to completion regardless. The cost for the rush job was exorbitant and, although the books looked good superficially, they contained numerous errors and deficiencies.

About a year after we had started, I was pleasantly surprised by a letter from Dr. Duane Gish, my colleague on the Creation Research Society Board of Directors. He had been working for many years as a research biochemist with the Upjohn Pharmaceutical Company in Kalamazoo, Michigan, but said he felt the Lord was leading him to join our staff in California. Even though financing another staff salary seemed very questionable, I was anxious by this time to have a scientist colleague, particularly one of the caliber of Dr. Gish (Kelly Segraves had only a B.A. degree in Bible from Biola), so we decided to go ahead on faith, and he joined us that fall. He soon proved to be an excellent speaker, as well as knowledgeable in many areas of science.

Another major addition shortly after Dr. Gish came was Harold Slusher. He took a leave of absence from his job in the Physics Department at the University of Texas in El Paso. He came to start the geophysics major at Christian Heritage College (which we called Planetary Science, since it also included a significant component of astrophysics), and also to work for our research division. His first assignment was to do a critical analysis of radiometric dating, a study which eventually resulted in his monograph, *Critique of Radiometric Dating*.

However, it became more obvious all the time that the two groups in the CSRC had different interests and wanted to pursue different methods, even though we were in agreement doctrinally. Both desired to promote creationism, but we believed it should be done by educational and scientific means, whereas the group formerly known as Bible-Science Radio believed that political and promotional efforts would be more productive.

Finally the Board decided by an 8 to 4 vote (the eight former directors of Bible-Science Radio versus the four of us connectd with the College) in April 1972 that the CSRC should separate from the College. As a result, Gish, Slusher, myself, and practically all the rest of the staff (except Nell and Kelly Segraves) resigned from their positions with the Center. We all then reorganized, with the same structure and projects, under the name, Institute for Creation Research, as discussed in the next chapter.

The Creation-Science Research Center then moved to another location in San Diego and continued on under the leadership of Nell and Kelly Segraves, with the same board as in their original form under Bible-Science Radio.

One notable addition to their staff, made soon after the separation, and still continuing today, was that of Dr. Robert Kofahl. With a Ph.D. from California Institute of Technology, Dr. Kofahl is a competent scientist, although little of his career had been spent in scientific work. He had for many years been president of Highland College in Pasadena, a small school sponsored by the Bible Presbyterians, the denomination led by Carl McIntyre. Dr. Kofahl's services became available when his college closed down about this same time. He had already been working some with the Segraves in their Southern California BSA branch.

The CSRC produced two useful books, *The Creation Explanation* and *The Handy-Dandy Evolution Refuter* since the separation from Christian Heritage College. Most of their efforts were political, however, attempting (though with little success) to get the *Science and Creation Series* adopted in various states and supporting creation-oriented legislation wherever possible. Kelly Segraves also produced a series of brief television segments and published a number of popularized books under a company formed by him called Beta Books. Their best-known activity was a lawsuit filed in Sacramento designed to prevent California schools from teaching evolution dogmatically. Although the judge's ruling was partially favorable, it has not been enforced, and the new Science Framework pushed through in 1989-90 by Superintendent Bill Honig and his Berkeley-based associates requires evolution to be taught exclusively as scientific fact. The CSRC currently (1992) continues on a limited scale, with offices in Kelly Segraves' home. Nell Segraves has retired and moved away from San Diego.

Chapter VIII

The Institute for Creation Research

If one can judge by the fulminations of today's anti-creationists, the Institute for Creation Research is the main organization to blame for the modern revival of creationism. As previous chapters have shown, there have been many other people and organizations who were promoting creationism long before this organization was even in existence. However, the Institute for Creation Research (or ICR) has been the first one to have a full-time staff of creationist scientists actively dedicated to research, writing, and teaching in the field of scientific creationism, and it has, indeed, made a very significant worldwide impact for this cause. In fact, its influence has been far out of proportion to the small number of people on its staff and the minimal resources available to them. We are convinced that the only adequate commentary is Psalm 118:23: "This is the Lord's doing: it is marvelous in our eyes."

This chapter, therefore, will outline the origin and history of the Institute for Creation Research. A number of its projects and programs will be discussed, and the credentials and contributions of the various scientists associated with ICR will be summarized.

The Early Days of ICR

The Institute for Creation Research, as organized in April of 1972, was essentially a continuation of the organization which I had established in September 1970 as a division of Christian Heritage College. This had been the culmination of a long-cherished dream, the beginning of a creationist liberal arts college, with a special creation studies division, commissioned to do research, writing, and extension teaching on creationism. Those plans had been complicated by the temporary attachment and subsequent detachment of the Bible-Science Radio group from the organization, but the work continued essentially unchanged after the brief period of reorganization. This has all been discussed in the preceding chapter.

When Kelly Segraves and the Bible-Science Radio board (constituting a majority of the CSRC board) voted to separate from Christian Heritage College, they took with them essentially all the assets of the Creation Science Research Center, including its name, its copyrights, its inventory, and its mailing list. But we retained a most important asset—the small but dedicated staff the Lord had brought to us.

When these dedicated workers made the decision to resign from the CSRC and stay with the college research division, we had no assurance we could pay their salaries. I took an additional salary cut (I had already taken a sizable cut when I left Virginia Tech to come to Christian Heritage), and we all tried to cut expenses to the bone. We didn't ask anyone else on the staff to take a reduction, since their salaries were already quite low anyhow, but they were all stepping out on faith that they could be paid at all!

The day after the Board meeting at which the vote was taken to separate the CSRC from the College, I had to leave town for several days on a speaking engagement, so was not around while the CSRC people relocated. Immediately upon my return, however, I called everyone together for a time of study, prayer, and planning. I brought a brief devotional message based on Psalm 127:1, "Except the Lord build the house, they labor in vain that build it," and we had a beautiful time of prayer and rededication. There it was decided to continue as before, with the same goals, same staff (except for Segraves), same titles, same methods. We had to change the name, of course, and I decided on the name Institute for Creation Research. I wondered at first whether the other officers of the Creation Research Society (I was still president of the Society at the time) might object to the similarity in names, but a check with them indicated they would not.

Rather than forming a separate corporation, however, as had been the case with the CSRC, we decided simply to function—at least for the present—as a division of the College, even though all operations and finances would be kept quite distinct. Until such time as we could develop a regular flow of income, the College would lend us money from its own operations. This had to be done for several months, but the College itself was operating on a shoestring, so it was difficult. Many times, in answer to special prayer, money came in just in the nick of time to pay the salaries and other bills. I had ordered that my own salary be lowest in priority, and there indeed were several times of real testing, but inevitably the Lord supplied all needs in good time. We decided to set up our operations on a pay-as-you-go basis, and thus far the Lord has enabled us to operate this way, without borrowing from the bank or other outside sources. One exception, however, was the loan needed to pay for the new ICR building, occupied late in 1986, but in this case all payments were made in time, and the entire note was paid off long before its full contract term. Nor have we ever failed to pay any of our bills, in good time. The Lord has been faithful, and our creditors have always been very understanding and cooperative.

We not only had to select a new name for the organization, which was fairly easy, but also a name for a monthly report and periodical. I believe the Lord gave me the name *Acts & Facts* for this newsletter —at any rate, it seemed to come just "out of the blue" almost as soon as the question was raised. This has proven to be a unique and popular little paper, and the response to it has been tremendous. After the first several issues, we decided to incorporate in it each month a special insert designed to be of particular Biblical or scientific help to the reader, rather than only the various reports on ICR activities. Thus began the popular "Impact" series.

A new mailing list had to be developed for *Acts & Facts,* but it grew fairly rapidly, as it seemed to meet a real need. We have always followed the policy of sending *Acts & Facts* only to those who have specifically requested it. Furthermore, every two years or so, the list is updated, retaining those who either have specifically requested to remain on it or who have been donors to ICR. Thus, our regular mailing list (currently over 100,000) consists almost entirely of people genuinely interested in the ICR ministry.

Right from the start, the financial support for the work has come mostly from individuals (also a few churches) on the *Acts & Facts* mailing list. Each issue of the newsletter is sent out accompanied by a return envelope plus a cover letter. We have never employed professional fund-raising organizations, such as most other religious and charitable organizations do. I have always written the cover letter myself, and Dr. John Morris writes the "thank-you" letters to those who contribute. Furthermore, although my cover letter usually mentions the financial need, it always does so in an easy, low-key manner. We have never felt that emotional or high-pressure fund appeals were appropriate for the ICR ministries. Even though many other Christian organizations have used such methods with success (and, perhaps, the end in such cases may justify the means), we believe the Lord has honored the ICR approach. That is, we simply let those who are interested (that is, those on our mailing list) know the need, as well as what ICR is accomplishing through their support, then trust the Lord to supply the need, as He leads and enables, through these friends.

We have tried also to be careful stewards of all money received, trying to carry on all operations with an optimum combination of frugality and professionalism. For example, salaries, which constitute the largest single item of cost, are kept sufficiently high to support a respectable standard of living for the staff, but also always somewhat lower than comparable salaries for the same type of job (whether as a science professor or secretary or whatever), with the same qualifications, in the secular world. The latter criterion assures us that no one will join the ICR staff simply for the money involved—the motivation should be spiritual, not carnal.

Contributions through the *Acts & Facts* mailing list typically have provided about 70% of the necessary support. The rest has come from such items as honoraria, royalties, book sales, and tuitions. The staff agreed right from the start that all receipts from speaking honoraria and book sales at meetings would go to ICR. Some tuition income has been received from our summer institutes and, more recently, from the graduate school. As far as royalties are concerned, these are from books written by ICR scientists. The first such book, published immediately after ICR was organized, was my little book, *The Remarkable Birth of Planet Earth.* As the book had been written entirely on my own time (nights and week-ends), I was therefore entitled to donate the royalties and profits on it to ICR, which I chose to do. Later, however, we worked out an equitable royalty-sharing arrangement between ICR and its various authors. This allocation is based on the relative amount of ICR-paid time, as well as ICR facilities (secretarial, art, etc.) used in preparing a book to the personal time (nights, holidays, vacations) spent by the author. This seems to be an eminently fair arrangement, since it does provide an incentive for our scientists to spend more of their outside time and effort in writing books. This is important in view of the critical need to produce good creationist books, and in view of the difficulty of finding time for writing in the typical work-day of an ICR staff scientist.

The ICR Scientists

The ICR science staff in the beginning consisted only of Duane Gish, Harold Slusher, and myself. John Morris, my second son, also joined the staff in the summer of 1972 to lead our first Ararat expedition, returning after the summer to his job as an engineer with the City of Los Angeles. He then came to work for ICR and the College on a full-time basis in 1973. Like John, all of us worked

Figure 19.   The ICR Scientists

Top Row: Henry M. Morris, Duane T. Gish, John D. Morris,
Middle row: Kenneth Cumming. Larry Vardiman, Richard B. Bliss,
Bottom Row: Steven A. Austin, Gerald E. Aardsma, Ken Ham.

part-time for ICR, part-time for the College.

The same was true of our two main support staff members, Donald Rohrer and George Hillested. The former had come as Business Manager for the College in 1971; the latter came several months later as Development Director. Rohrer eventually became full-time ICR Business Manager, and Hillested eventually moved to Creation-Life Publishers as General Manager, after serving several years as the College's Vice-President for Business Affairs.

After several months, the Institute became self-supporting and has remained so ever since. In various times and ways, it has been able, over the years, to more than repay the College (and the Church) for the financial help received in those difficult months right at the start.

ICR continued to operate as a division of Christian Heritage College until 1980, when it finally became completely autonomous. During that eight-year period (1972–1980), it became increasingly independent, though always working compatibly within the over-all administrative framework of the College. ICR did not have its own Board during that period. Its reports, budgets, etc., always were more or less superficially reviewed and routinely passed by the College Trustees, who usually had more urgent College matters with which to deal at their meetings. Thus, ICR was functioning almost as a separate organization even while it was a division of the College.

Mention should be made at this point of the key personnel (in addition to Duane Gish and Harold Slusher) who joined the staff from time to time.

John Morris stayed two years, working as Field Scientist, not only on the Ararat project but also on several other field projects, especially the Paluxy River human/dinosaur footprint project. He took a leave of absence in 1975 to do graduate study at the University of Oklahoma in the field of geological engineering, being awarded an excellent Department of Energy fellowship for this purpose. He received his M.S. in 1977, and his Ph.D. in 1980.

He then served for four years as Assistant Professor of Geological Engineering at Oklahoma while also serving (part-time) as Associate Professor in Planetary Sciences in the ICR Graduate School. He returned to ICR full-time in 1984, and is currently (1993) Professor of Geology and Administrative Vice President.

Lane Lester served as Research Associate in Biology from 1973 to 1975 and has since that time been ICR's Southeastern Representative. He has a Ph.D. in Genetics from Purdue University and is currently Professor of Biology and Head of the Creation Museum at Liberty University. He serves as an ICR Summer Institute and seminar speaker from time to time.

Richard B. Bliss joined the ICR staff as its Director of Curriculum Development in 1976, after 23 years experience in public school science education, most recently as Director of Science Education for the Racine, Wisconsin, Unified School District. He has the M.S. in biology from the University of Wisconsin and the Ed. D. in science education from the University of Sarasota. He now is also Head of the Science Education Department in the ICR Graduate School.

Gary E. Parker came to ICR in 1977 and was Professor of Biology in its Graduate School, as well as one of its most popular lecturers and debaters. He has a B.S. degree from Wabash in biology and the M.S. and Ed.D. from Ball State University. He had taught previously at Eastern Baptist College and Dordt College. He was also Curator of the ICR Museum of Creation and Earth History. He currently holds a corresponding appointment at Clearwater Christian College in Florida.

Theodore W. Rybka joined the staff in 1978, as part-time Associate Professor of Physics. He has degrees from the University of British Columbia, University of Saskatchewan, and University of Oklahoma, receiving his Ph.D. from the latter in 1973. He was with ICR until 1984, when he accepted a position with General Dynamics.

Steven A. Austin served at various times as a part-time visiting scientist with ICR while concurrently doing graduate work, coming full-time as Associate Professor of Geology in 1979. He has the B.S. in geology from the University of Washington, the M.S. from San Jose State University, and the Ph.D. from Pennsylvania State University, specializing in the field of coal geology. He became Professor of Geology and Head of the Geology Department in the ICR Graduate School in 1985.

Kenneth B. Cumming received a B.S. from Tufts University and the M.S. and Ph.D. degrees from Harvard University, the latter majoring in ecology. After a distinguished career as a fisheries biologist with the federal government, plus serving on the faculties at Virginia Tech and the University of Wisconsin, he came to ICR in 1979. He has been Chairman of the Biology Department and is now (1993) Dean of the ICR Graduate School.

Donald B. De Young served one year (1978–1979) as Visiting Scientist while on sabbatical from Grace College, in Indiana, where he is Professor of Physics. Since that time he has been ICR's Midwestern Representative. He has a Ph.D. from Iowa State University.

Thomas G. Barnes served on ICR's Technical Advisory Board from the beginning, also coming as visiting scientist from time to time, and finally became the first Dean of the ICR Graduate School in 1981. Dr. Barnes had spent many years as Professor of Physics at the University of Texas at El Paso. His biography is also outlined in Chapter VI, as one of the first Directors of the Creation Research Society. He resigned in 1983 to devote full time to his own research in El Paso. Harold Slusher then became Dean, on Dr. Barnes' recommendation, continuing until 1985, when he also resigned to return to his full-time position at the University of Texas in El Paso.

David R. McQueen joined the ICR staff in 1982 part-time, then full-time in 1983, as Assistant Professor of Geology. He has geology degrees from Tennessee and Michigan and completed residence work for the Ph.D. at the University of Michigan, being denied admission to candidacy because of his creationism. He also worked several years as a geologist for the U.S. Geological Survey. He is currently (1993) on leave to work on a doctoral degree.

Larry Vardiman came as Associate Professor of Meteorology in the ICR Graduate School, coming in 1982. He has degrees from the University of Missouri and St. Louis University, plus the Ph.D. in Atmospheric Physics from Colorado State University. Dr. Vardiman was also Head of the Physical Sciences Department at Christian Heritage College. He also served two years there as Academic Dean, but then came full-time to ICR, where he is currently Professor and Head of the Physics Department and Assistant Dean.

Gerald Aardsma came to ICR as Assistant Professor of Physics in 1987. He has a Ph. D. in nuclear physics from the University of Toronto and is a specialist in radiocarbon technology.

Kenneth Ham came to ICR in 1986 from Australia, where he had been Founder and Director of the Creation Science Foundation. Although he does not teach in the Graduate School, he has become an exceptionally popular speaker on creationism, leading in the development of the Back-to-Genesis Seminars which have been very effective in recent years, usually reaching thousands in each community where they are held.

With the exception of Ham and Aardsma, all of the above men also have taught at Christian Heritage College. Each one is a fully qualified scientist and also a convinced, dedicated creationist. Each also is a born-again Christian, sound in doctrine and godly in his Christian life and walk. I believe each came in answer to prayer (both his and ours) and each was led here by the Lord. Each one is making and will no doubt continue to make a vital contribution to the cause of creationism. I am grateful to God for the men He has sent to work with us in ICR.

In addition to the men on our own staff, ICR has had a number of outstanding people on its Technical Advisory Board. Many of these have contributed effectively in reviewing book manuscripts, writing "Impact" articles, and in other ways. Two of the original members, Dr. Ken Cumming and Dr. Tom Barnes, later joined the staff. There have been other changes from time to time, but the following have been on the Advisory Board ever since we began in 1970:

1. Dr. Edward F. Blick, Professor of Petroleum Engineering at the University of Oklahoma
2. Dr. David R. Boylan, professor of Chemical Engineering and former Dean of Engineering at Iowa State University
3. Dr. Malcolm A. Cutchins, Professor of Aerospace Engineering at Auburn University
4. Dr. Donald D. Hamann, Professor of Food Technology at North Carolina State University
5. Dr. Joseph L. Henson, Chairman of the Science Division at Bob Jones University
6. Dr. John C. Whitcomb, Jr., Formerly Director of Doctoral Studies and Professor of Theology and Old Testament at Grace Theological Seminary

All of the above were personal friends of mine while I was still at Virginia Tech, and all are outstanding Christians and strong creationist scientists. Dr. Whitcomb, of course, is a theologian but, as co-author of *The Genesis Flood* and one of the finest and most active creationist speakers in the world, his presence on the Advisory Board is invaluable.

The others that have been added from time to time are as follows.

8. Dr. Galen Marshall, Assistant Professor of Internal Medicine at University of Texas, Houston
9. Dr. John R. Meyer, Director of the Arizona Research Center of the Creation Research Society
10. Dr. Robert N. Eckel, Associate Professor of Medicine at the University of Colorado Medical School
11. Dr. David N. Menton, Associate Professor of Biochemistry at Washington University (St. Louis)
12. Dr. John W. Oller, Professor of Linguistics at the University

of New Mexico

13. Dr. Carl Fliermans, a consulting microbial ecologist in Augusta, Georgia, and Visiting Professor in the University of Georgia Medical School

14. Dr. Ker A. Thompson, former Head of Geophysics Research for the U.S. Air Force and Professor of Geophysics at Baylor University

All of these also are fine scientists and strong Christians and creationists. From time to time, other scientists have spent various periods of time on their own at ICR, as (unpaid) visiting scientists, working on various teaching, research, or writing projects. Some have served as speakers at ICR summer institutes and seminars, and some have taught individual science or apologetics courses at Christian Heritage College. Present or former Board members of the Creation Research Society who have been involved in one of these various ways include Dr. Will Tinkle, Dr. Walter Lammerts, Dr. George Howe, Dr. John Klotz, Dr. John Moore, Dr. Bolton Davidheiser, and Dr. Wilbert Rusch.

Marlyn Clark, Professor of Theoretical and Applied Mechanics at the University of Illinois, wrote a fine research monograph on the fluid mechanics of blood while spending his sabbatical with us one year. Wendell Bird, not a scientist, but undoubtedly the nation's leading creationist attorney, now heading his own Christian legal firm in Atlanta, spent two years on the ICR staff, making many invaluable contributions to the work, especially to the establishment of ICR as an independent organization, including its graduate school.

Finally, a good number of other scientists are considered *Adjunct* or *Visiting* professors, either teaching from time to time in the ICR Graduate School, speaking in seminars, or otherwise directly involved in ICR. These include the following:

Dr. Dimitri Kouznetsov, Adjunct Professor of Biochemistry, a prominent Russian scientist, with three earned doctorates, and organizer of a creation scientists association in Moscow.

Dr. Richard Lumsden, Adjunct Professor of Biology, and former Dean of the Tulane University Graduate School.

Dr. Donald Chittick, Adjunct Professor of Chemistry.

Dr. Russell Humphreys, Adjunct Professor of Physics.

Dr. John Baumgardner Adjunct Professor of Geophysics.

Dr. Kurt Wise, Adjunct Associate Professor of Paleontology.

Dr. George Lindsay, Adjunct Associate Professor of Science Education.

Dr. T. V. Varughese, Adjunct Associate Professor of Mathematics.

Dr. Dennis Englin, Adjunct Associate Professor of Geophysics.

Dr. Andrew Snelling, Adjunct Professor of Geology.

Dr. Robert Franks, Adjunct Associate Professor of Biology.

Dr. Stephen Deckard, Adjunct Assistant Professor of Science Education.

Dr. Danny Faulkner, Adjunct Assistant Professor of Astrophysics.

Dr. Chris Osborne, Adjunct Assistant Professor of Biology.

All in all, there are, or have been, over 50 scientists directly associated with ICR in one way or another, practically all of whom have doctoral degrees from accredited universities, and all of whom are firmly convinced and committed creationists.

The Pen and the Sword

The Institute for Creation Research has, from the beginning, tried to stress education rather than legislation as the best means to restore creationism as the true understanding of origins and meanings in the world. Other organizations have filed lawsuits and tried to get bills passed about creationism, but we have always urged that persuasion is more effective in the long run than coercion.

On the premise that the pen is mightier than the sword, we developed our activities around a three-fold program of literature,

Figure 20. Teaching Ministries of ICR

Two of the many programs aimed especially toward the teaching of creation in the schools are illustrated here. Top photo shows Dr. Tom Barnes, the first Dean of ICR's Graduate School, lecturing at one of ICR's Summer Institutes on Scientific Creationism. The bottom photo features the team of teachers brought together one summer to prepare two-model student work books, under the direction of Dr. Richard Bliss (front row, center).

teaching, and research. Many other sincere creationists have felt this process was too slow and so have tried to hasten things through political means. We certainly have not actively opposed those who have gone this route and have even helped as consultants or witnesses when requested. We have appreciated their concern and sincerity and would certainly rather see them succeed than fail, but we have always argued that the better way is simply to teach the truth wherever the Lord opens the door.

Although all three types of activity—research, teaching, and literature—are vital in accomplishing this goal, it is probable that the widest and most lasting effects are achieved by the production and distribution of appropriate literature. The impact of Darwin's *Origin of Species* is a prime case in point. Accordingly, ICR has

Figure 21. ICR Books

This view shows a montage of some of the approximately 75 books produced at ICR since its beginnings.

placed top emphasis on its publications, and well over a million copies of its creationist books have been sold.

When we started ICR, there were already a number of books available—notably *The Genesis Flood* and my other early books, as well as the CRS biology textbook and anthologies. We promoted these as widely as possible, but also began preparing other key books. We set a rather ambitious goal—creationist books in every field at every grade level, including textbooks for both public and Christian schools. We knew this was needed, since practically all textbooks today are oriented exclusively around evolution. Such a goal was not feasible for any one organization such as ICR, of course, but we hoped that our influence would also encourage others to write such books, and, possibly, even the big secular publishers would begin encouraging their publication.

We tried first to get books written which seemed to be most urgently and widely needed. Some of these,[1, 2, 3] were textbooks prepared for the apologetics courses I had set up at Christian Heritage College. Others[4, 5, 6] were monographs dealing with key issues related to the over-all creatio/evolution conflict. All of these have, indeed, been widely used in stimulating the creationism revival.

---

1. *Many Infallible Proofs,* by Henry M. Morris (San Diego: Creation-Life Publishers, 1974), 381 pp.

2. *Scientific Creationism,* ed. by Henry M. Morris (San Diego: Creation-Life Publishers, 1974), 275 pp.

3. *The Troubled Waters of Evolution,* by Henry M. Morris (San Diego: Creation Life Publishers, 1975), 217 pp.

4. *Evolution? The Fossils Say NO!,* by Duane T. Gish (San Diego: Creation-Life Publishers, 1972; rev. ed., 1979), 198 pp.

5. *Speculations and Experiments Related to Theories on the Origin of Life: A Critique,* by Duane T. Gish (San Diego: Institute for Creation Research, 1972), 41 pp.

6. *Critique of Radiometric Dating,* by Harold S. Slusher (San Diego: Institute for Creation Research, 1973; rev. ed., 1981), 58 pp.

The book *Scientific Creationism* warrants special mention, since many people (especially the opponents of creationism) have come to regard it as a quasi-official textbook of the creation movement. In less than ten years, it went through a dozen printings. It was prepared in two editions—a general edition and a public school edition, the latter with a completely non-Biblical, non-religious treatment of all the relevant scientific data. Although I had written the basic text of the book, it was reviewed by all the scientists on our staff and advisory board, and many made significant additions and suggestions.

We tried at first to do the publishing and marketing of our books, but it soon became obvious this was impracticable. ICR did not have sufficient capital to set up a viable publishing and sales operation; also our attorney had cautioned us that this might jeopardize our tax-exempt status with the IRS. Consequently we made the decision, in 1974, to form a separate corporation, specifically to publish the books written by ICR and Christian Heritage staff members. Other Christian publishers, we knew, would have only marginal interest in promoting creationist books and could not be relied upon to keep them in print if they were not profitable financially.

Therefore, several of us, all on either the ICR, CHC, or Scott Memorial Church staff, pooled our personal resources to form a publishing company. The chief original stockholders were Dr. LaHaye and myself, the others being George Hillestad, John Morris, Art Peters, Don Rohrer, Williams Lyons (Professor of Missions at the College), and Arnold Ehlert (Librarian at the College). None of us had very much we could invest, and it was barely enough to get started, but start we did, and the company has been going ever since, under the name Creation Life Publishers. Two divisions of the company—Master Books and CLP Video—were later added.

The company, however, has never been able to operate profitably and has not yet been able to pay any dividends or interest to its investors. It was under-capitalized to start with, and, even though several new investors (not connected with the founding organizations) came in later, it has never really been enough to finance a consistent advertising and sales program. At best, of course, our books are specialized and do not have the broad appeal that the more "frothy" religious books have. Nevertheless, the company has at least provided an outlet through which many creationist books have been kept available and has thus provided a key service to the cause. It has also published a number of important creationist books by outside writers, such as the outstanding European scientist, Dr. A. E. Wilder-Smith, and the Australian Biblical archaeologist, Dr. Clifford Wilson.

Altogether, the ICR staff turned out a total of 75 or more creationist books[1] and monographs in the period from 1972 through 1992. In addition, there were many, many articles, tracts, and other special publications. The ICR staff scientists have also written at least 25 other books, plus numerous articles, in their own scientific fields. It is impracticable to discuss, or even to list, all of these publications in this volume,[2] but the net impact has been great.

The most visible piece of ICR literature, however, has undoubtedly been its monthly Acts & Facts newsletter, each containing

---

1. These have included many children's books (e.g., *The Amazing Story of Creation*, by Dr. Gish, *Noah's Ark and the Lost World*, by Dr. John Morris), many popular-level books (e.g., *The Lie-Evolution*, by Ken Ham), Bible Commentaries (e.g., *The Genesis Record*, by Henry Morris), School textbooks (e.g., *Good Science for Christian Schools*, by Richard Bliss), books on the history and impact of evolution (e.g., *The Long War against God*, by Henry Morris), and many others.

2. A listing of most of these has been compiled in an ICR booklet entitled *Publications of ICR Staff Scientists* (San Diego: Institute for Creation Research, 1983), 29 pp. A descriptive catalog of all ICR publications available through ICR is available free upon request to the Institute for Creation Research, P. O. Box 2667, El Cajon, CA 92021. A more complete catalog containing these publications plus other creationist books, films, and videotapes is available free upon request to Master Books, P. O. Box 983, El Cajon, CA 92020.

news items plus a distinctive "Impact" article. This periodical goes out, free of charge, not only to the 100,000 on the "active" mailing list, but thousands of copies are distributed at seminars, through churches, and in other ways. It has proven very popular, with its news accounts of debates and other activities, along with the interesting and useful Impact articles.

Because of the many requests from new readers for back copies, it was decided in 1974 to combine all the Impact articles for each two-year period, plus the more significant news articles for that period, into an anthology volume, issued bi-annually. These news items are grouped by categories into separate chapters (debates, international outreach, etc.). Also each volume contains an Introduction, summarizing the activities and significance of that two-year period relative to the ongoing creationist revival. These biennial anthologies thus provide a convenient running history of the creation movement in general, and in particular that of the ICR contribution to it. Five volumes were published[1, 2, 3, 4, 5] before the series was discontinued.

One special writing project of interest was what Dr. Richard Bliss called his Summer Writers' Workshop. Each summer for several years, he gathered a team of about 25 writers, mostly public school teachers, coming from many parts of the country, to work on a series of supplementary student books for different grade levels designed to introduce children to the origins question on a two-model basis.

---

1. *Creation: Acts, Facts, Impacts,* edited by Henry M. Morris, Duane T. Gish, and George Hillested (San Diego: Creation-Life Publishers, 1974), 188 pp.

2. *The Battle for Creation*, edited by Henry M. Morris and Duane T. Gish (San Diego: Creation-Life Publishers, 1976), 321 pp.

3. *Up with Creation,* edited by Duane T. Gish and Donald H. Rohrer (San Diego: Creation-Life Publishers, 1978), 341 pp.

4. *The Decade of Creation,* edited by Henry M. Morris and Donald H. Rohrer (San Diego: Creation-Life Publishers, 1980), 316 pp.

5. *Creation: The Cutting Edge,* edited by Henry M. Morris and Donald H. Rohrer (San Diego: Creation-Life Publishers, 1982), 240 pp.

Creation Research

As its very name implies, one of the important components of ICR's work ought to be research on the problems associated with origins and primeval earth history, especially in relation to the Biblical revelation concerning these matters. The problem, however, has always been lack of funds. Experimental research is costly, and creationist organizations do not have access to government largesse. Although all of ICR's scientists had performed significant research investigations prior to coming to ICR and had published their results in the standard professional journals, our detractors have repeatedly charged that creationists never do research of their own, but merely attack evolution. The difference, however, is that in our pre-ICR days, we could get significant research grants, and we also had available the large and well-equipped university laboratories, most of which had been largely developed by tax dollars. This, of course, had been my experience at Minnesota and Virginia Tech, Dr. Gish's experience at Berkeley, Dr. Cumming at Harvard and in his time at government labs, Dr. Austin's at Penn State, and so on.

With the very limited funds we *have* been able to obtain, we have indeed been able to accomplish some worthwhile creation-oriented research, but this lack of large research programs admittedly has been a weakness of the creation movement. The Creation Research Society and the Adventists' Geoscience Research Institute, along with a few undergraduate science departments in Christian colleges, have also been able to do some research, but all encountered the same problem—the evolutionary establishment which controls science, education, and government in this country is not about to supply funds or facilities or outlets for creationist research if they can help it. Neither is research a very popular area for Christian people and churches to support with *their* limited resources.

So we have done what we could, trying to concentrate our

research efforts wherever the potential impact in terms of Christian witness would be greatest in relation to expenditures. To a large extent, this criterion has led us to focus on geological field studies, especially on so-called overthrust formations and on anomalous fossils. If it can be shown, by studies at the thrust planes, that enough of these "thrust faults" are not really overthrusts but only normal sedimentary sequences, or if it can be shown that several supposed out-of-place fossils have not really been displaced at all but have been normally deposited with the encasing sediments, then the standard geologic age system would eventually have to be abandoned in favor of the creation/flood model of earth history.

Teams have therefore been sent to study overthrusts in Colorado, Nevada, and other places. Other teams have studied anomalous fossil sites in Utah, Oklahoma, and other places. In each case, the evidence seemed strongly to favor the creation/flood model, but was not sufficiently compelling by itself to settle the question, and so we did not publish the results at the time.

The most extensive studies of this sort were made in Texas, checking out the various sites where human footprints had been reported to be associated with dinosaur footprints in so-called Cretaceous strata, thus making man and dinosaur contemporaneous instead of separated by 70 million years, as evolutionists allege. John Morris made many trips to these areas over a 10-year period, especially along the Paluxy River near Glen Rose, Texas, making detailed measurements and photographs of all the known tracks and trails. Although he found that many of the claims were unconvincing, some did indeed seem to be strongly supportive of the creationist position. All of the evidence, pro and con, was finally written up in an excellent research monograph on the subject.[1]

These Paluxy footprints have been the object of many other

---

1. John D. Morris, *Tracking Those Incredible Dinosaurs and the People Who Knew Them* (San Diego: Creation-Life Publishers, 1980), 240 pp.

studies by other creationists, both before and after the ICR studies. More recently, they have become the object of an extensive debunking campaign by evolutionists, which at least confirms the critical significance of the project.

The most ambitious ICR research project has been its Ararat Project, sponsoring expeditions to Mount Ararat in Turkey search-

Figure 22. Ararat Project

One of the most fascinating of the many creationist research projects has been the continuing search for the remains of Noah's Ark, believed on the basis of many evidences still to be preserved high on Mount Ararat. Here are shown Dr. John Morris (left) and the ICR search team, high on the mountain in 1972.

ing for Noah's Ark and other ancient artifacts of the immediate post-Flood period. John Morris has been in charge of this project also, which has been active since 1972.

Only occasionally has the ICR Ararat team actually been able to acquire permits from the Turkish government to explore the mountain itself, once in 1972 and then in 1983, 1988 and 1989. A number of field studies were made near the mountain in other years. The Ark has not yet been located, either by ICR's team or by any others, although many evidences have been acquired pointing to its existence there.

The 1972 ICR expedition also encountered much excitement and danger, which Dr. Morris wrote up in a fascinating little volume,[1] based on his diary. The 1983 expedition likewise experienced a host of difficulties and, like the first, found a number of interesting archaeological sites, but still no sign of Noah's Ark. The team was finally able to get permits to use an airplane, in 1988 and 1989. One site looked very promising from a distance, but closer viewing from the plane indicated it was merely a cave.

Many other groups have tried to find Noah's Ark, especially since about 1965, all apparently following up on the preliminary evidences compiled by Ben F. Allen back in the 1940s. These evidences, as well as various reports tracked down by Eryl Cummings and others, do seem to indicate that Noah's Ark still survives somewhere on Mount Ararat.[2] At least the evidences are so numerous and so independent of each other as to indicate that *something* is there, demanding explanation. No doubt, if circumstances permit, creationists will continue the search for the Ark

---

1. John D. Morris, *Adventure on Ararat* (San Diego: Institute for Creation Research, 1973), 128 pp.

2. For probably the best compilation and analysis of all the evidence, see *The Ark on Ararat,* by John D. Morris and Tim F. LaHaye (Nashville: Thomas Nelson Publ., 1976), 275 pp. Another comprehensive treatment is: *Has Anybody Really Seen Noah's Ark?* by Violet Cummings (San Diego: Master Books, 1982), 389 pp.

either until it is found or until the mountain has been so completely explored as to prove it is not there.[1] Its documented discovery would prove beyond reasonable question that the Flood was global (Mount Ararat is 17,000 feet high!) and, therefore, that flood geology is basically sound. The potential impact thus seems to warrant the costs and risks involved.

However, because the latter are so great, ICR has treated this project differently from its other research projects. It has been financed exclusively by contributions designated specifically to that one project, not from the ICR general funds. Also, personnel on the exploration teams, even though covered by insurance, have signed waivers of any potential liability claims against ICR.

A number of very significant field studies have been conducted by Dr. Steve Austin and others on the remarkable geological phenomena produced by the 1980 explosion of Mount St. Helens. These have shown that such catastrophes may well be sufficient to explain most of the phenomena normally attributed by geologists to slow processes operating uniformly over long periods of time. Dr. Austin and colleagues have also carried out significant field research in the Grand Canyon and other geological sites. Dr. Austin has documented serious discrepancies in the supposed ancient dates of Grand Canyon formations.

Much ICR research has been either theoretical or library research. This type of research can be quite significant, however. Experimental data in most fields are already abundantly available in published form and so are accessible for reanalysis in terms of the creation model. An experimental measurement or an observed fact should be the same whether obtained by an evolutionist or a creationist. As published, such data have commonly been interpreted in an evolutionary framework, but creationists are convinced they can all be better understood in terms of creation-

---

1. Claims by some that the remains of the ark have been found in a location at some distance from Mount Ararat are dubious at best.

ism. Thus, there is an immense amount of experimental data already available, merely awaiting reanalysis and correlation with a theoretical structure based on creationism. This means that there is an essentially unlimited number of fruitful research studies already at hand that do not require further experimental measurements, but only a new theoretical framework.

Accordingly, all the ICR scientists are continually reviewing data published in their own fields which might be relevant to scientific Biblical creationism or catastrophism, and then reinterpreting them in that context. This library research is valuable and necessary. Also new analytical studies are regularly being devel-

Figure 23. Barnes and Rohrer

Two key ICR personnel, shown here in the El Paso Air Terminal, have been Dr. Thomas G. Barnes and Donald Rohrer. Dr. Barnes was the first Dean of ICR's Graduate School and Mr. Rohrer, a business administration graduate of Bob Jones University, has been the ICR Business Manager since 1971.

oped—for example, identification of processes which can be applied as geochronometers to support the Biblical doctrine of recent creation.

With the completion of a new ICR building in 1985, new laboratories became available—one each for biology, geology, physics and science education. A number of research projects, as well as instructional uses, are now being carried out in these labs.

The Gospel of Creation

The third major aspect of the ICR ministries (in addition to research and publication) has been education, but this has taken on many facets. Not only have formal courses been conducted, but also ICR speakers have traveled far and wide with the spoken word, adapted to many types of audiences and many varied circumstances. The overriding theme in all these lectures and messages, of course, has been the absolute truth and preeminent importance of the special creation of all things by God in the beginning. Sometimes the emphasis is solely on the scientific aspects of creationism, especially when lecturing on a university campus or in a public school classroom. The theme in church services, on the other hand, often will be centered around the *Biblical* record of creation and earth history. At Christian colleges, both approaches are important. The goal everywhere, of course, is to persuade people that evolution and humanism are false and harmful philosophies and that they need to recognize and honor God as Creator, Redeemer, and Lord of all things.

There is much resistance to this message, of course. The scientific community insists that creation is a purely religious concept, not scientific. The liberal and evangelical religious communities often insist that it is not even an important religious concept. Our message thus must often deal with both objections, demonstrating that creation is both critically important and truly scientific, meriting full commitment of both mind and heart.

The Lord Jesus Christ commanded His disciples to preach the Gospel to every creature (Mark 16:15), and it is this command we have sought to obey. However, the true Gospel ("good news") has been sadly misunderstood and is seldom preached in its fullness by most modern professing Christians. It involves far more than the "personal Christianity" so much emphasized today, something which merely helps a person feel good and have a positive outlook, following the advice and example of Jesus in order to have an abundant life.

The Gospel focuses especially on the person and work of the Lord Jesus Christ, the incarnate Creator (John 1: 1–3, 14) who died in our place for the sin of the world (John 1:29). This is stressed in the great definition passage of the Gospel (I Corinthians 15:1–4), which says the Gospel requires saving personal faith in the substitutionary death, physical burial, and bodily resurrection of Jesus Christ. But even that is not all. A comprehending faith in His death for our sins must be predicated on a personal realization that sin is real and has offended our Creator and separated us from God. An understanding faith in His bodily burial and resurrection requires an acknowledgment that only He has conquered death, and, therefore, that He is Lord of all, able and sure to restore the whole creation someday to its primeval perfection.

Thus, the Gospel is based on the good news that Christ Himself is the true Creator of all things and the good news that He, therefore, is King of Kings and Lord of Lords, sovereign of the universe, coming again someday to purge all evil and consummate all His purposes in creation. Without these vital components, the Gospel is without foundation and without purpose, and the tragedy is that most so-called evangelism today ignores them both. This is why the first mention of the Gospel in the New Testament (Matthew 4:23) stresses the coming kingdom and the last mention of the Gospel (Revelation 14:6, 7, where it is called the "everlasting gospel") stresses the primeval creation. This is also why the glorious description of the past, present, and future work of Christ in the first chapter of Colossians stresses that He first created all things (Colossians 1:16), now is sustaining (or "saving") all things (Colossians 1:17), and will eventually reconcile all things (Colossians 1:20), and that all of this wonderful news is the Gospel (Colossians 1:23). All of this content is implicit in every use of the word "Gospel" in the New Testament and in every reference to preaching it. Even the definitive passage in I Corinthians 15:1–4 goes on, in the same chapter, to emphasize the creation and fall (verses 20–22, 36–47) and the coming consummation (verses 23–28, 48–56).

The ICR speakers, therefore, have especially emphasized the foundation component of the Gospel, the Creation, since so few others seem to do this, but they have by no means neglected the rest of it. And even when circumstances prevent the full presentation of the Gospel, as in a creation/evolution debate on a university campus, the awakening of the conscience which occurs when a listener first realizes God has indeed created him will usually lead him to further investigation and, often, eventually to full conversion.

The geographical range has been almost unlimited. ICR scientists have held meetings in all 50 states (I myself have spoken in 45 different states—all except the Dakotas, Maine, Vermont, and Delaware), and many hundreds of different towns and cities (over 100 in California alone). Several messages or lectures are usually given at each locality, so that a significant impact is made on the school or church or community where we speak. ICR books are usually available for purchase at a book table, so this provides still further follow-up influence.

Nor has the witness been limited to this country. ICR scientists have spoken extensively in Canada, in almost every province. Dr. Duane Gish has made long itineraries into such nations as England, Scotland, Wales, Ireland, Sweden, Norway, Denmark, Germany, Holland, India, Arabia, Israel, Korea, Australia, New Zealand, Trinidad, Barbados, Jamaica, Russia, Japan, Thailand, Honduras, and South Africa. I have spoken in Hong Kong, Papua New Guinea, Mexico, and Greece, as well as England, Israel, Korea, New Zealand, and Australia. Dr. Bliss has lectured widely in New Zealand, Hong Kong, Tonga, El Salvador, the Philippines and England, Dr. Parker in Australia, England, and Scotland, Dr. Slusher in Australia and Holland, and Dr. John Morris in Turkey, Russia, Korea and Australia, and Dr. Vardiman in Bolivia.

Thus ICR scientists have held meetings in at least 30 nations. In addition to these countries where they have spoken, ICR books and literature have been translated into the languages of many other nations, and then widely used in those nations—including Japan, Taiwan, China, France, Spain, Italy, Russia, Yugoslavia, Romania, Brazil, and practically all of the Spanish-speaking countries of Latin America. Many other countries where English is spoken as a common second language (Sri Lanka [Ceylon], Singapore, various African countries, etc.) have also used significant numbers of ICR publications. Thus, the Institute has had a great impact on foreign missions as well as domestic evangelism.

The type of audience has also varied widely. The most challenging, of course, have been the university community and the scientific society. Lectures on scientific creationism only are usually given to such audiences, commonly followed by question-and-answer sessions. As might be anticipated, these occasionally become heated, although we always try diligently to speak objectively and reply graciously to questions, even when being insulted or ridiculed. People have often told us following such meetings that they were as much influenced by our attitude and behavior under fire as by the scientific evidence itself. In any case, and in almost every case, these campus and convention lectures have been effective, both in creating much more awareness and respect for creationism, and also in gaining actual converts to creationism, including numerous scientists and multitudes of students.

Occasionally even a faculty member is reached and won, though these seem the most difficult of all. College professors are so conditioned to intellectualism, to scientism, and to academic prestige and peer pressure as to be utterly unwilling to pay the price of becoming creationists. Nevertheless one can now find a nucleus of genuine creationists on almost every college and university faculty in the country. They tend to be quiet about it or, if vocal, usually persecuted for it, but they are there! Such a condition would have been unheard of 45 years ago, when I was almost alone as a creationist faculty member in the secular university world, so far as I could determine.

At the other end of the spectrum would be our meetings in Bible-believing churches. There our Bible-centered messages on creationism are usually received warmly, almost like a breath of fresh air or a release from bondage. These "fundamentalists" have wanted to believe the Bible, and tried to do so, but had been so intimidated by evolutionary pressures in the schools and news media, that they did not know where to turn. To find suddenly that the plain teachings of Scripture could be supported scientifically after all has been of great encouragement to them. The ministry of ICR to Christians has thus been one of its greatest contributions.

It has been my own privilege (despite lack of any formal training either in Bible or public speaking) to preach the Gospel of creation in some of the nation's greatest churches—Thomas Road Baptist (Lynchburg), Highland Park Baptist (Chattanooga), Coral Ridge Presbyterian (Ft. Lauderdale), First Baptist (Dallas), People's Church (Toronto), First Baptist (Van Nuys), Briarwood Presbyterian (Birmingham), First Baptist (Houston), St. Thomas Episcopal (Houston), First Baptist (Lubbock), People's Church (Fresno), Calvary Baptist (New York), Calvary Chapel (Costa Mesa), and many others, plus hundreds of smaller churches.

We have also spoken at a large percentage of the nation's Bible colleges, seminaries, and Christian liberal arts colleges, as well as many conventions of Christian teachers and pastors. Dr. Bliss, in particular, has conducted numerous "Workshops," designed to help public school teachers use the "Two-Model" approach in their classrooms, using evolution and creation objectively as alternative scientific models of origins. In recent years, he has also conducted numerous "Good Science" workshops, designed to help science teachers in Christian schools, as well as home-schooling Christian parents, to teach good science, illustrating the attributes of God, to children. For this purpose, he has prepared "Good Science Workbooks," along with necessary instructional tools.

Of special effectiveness have been the Summer Institutes on Scientific Creationism, which were five-day intensive courses requiring 30 hours of instruction and usually carrying two-semester hours of college credit to enrollees. Each summer several of these are held around the United States and Canada, usually sponsored by a Christian college which will offer the course credits. Students could also, if desired, get undergraduate credit for the courses through Christian Heritage College or graduate credit (by doing an additional research paper) through the ICR Graduate School.

The Summer Institute program was begun in 1972 at Evangel College in Springfield, Missouri. Each year beginning in 1972 an Institute has been offered at Christian Heritage College. Other schools which have sponsored them include Moody Bible Institute (Chicago-three times), Baptist Bible College (Pennsylvania-three times), Dallas Bible College/Dallas Seminary (twice), Grace College/Grace Seminary (Indiana-twice), Northwest College (Seattle-twice), Tennessee Temple University (twice), Evangel College (twice), Liberty Baptist College (twice), Philadelphia College of the Bible (twice), Old's College (Alberta-three times), Briercrest Bible Institute (twice), Piedmont Bible College (four times), Southeastern Bible College, Dallas Seminary, Cedarville College (Ohio-twice), Biola University (Los Angeles), Multnomah Bible Institute (Oregon), Concordia College (Michigan), Western Bible College (Denver), Northwestern College (Minneapolis-twice), Grand Rapids Baptist College, Washington Bible College,

Clearwater Christian College (twice), and various others.

Some of the leading conservative seminaries which have featured ICR speakers include Dallas Seminary, Grace Seminary, Concordia Lutheran (St. Louis), Reformed Presbyterian (Mississippi), Westminster Presbyterian (California), Northwest Baptist (Tacoma), Wisconsin Lutheran, Luther Rice Seminary, Grand Rapids Baptist, and many others.

Although no attempt has been made to keep precise records, it is estimated that ICR scientist speakers have reached audiences totaling well over two million people. They have brought lectures or messages in probably 1500 churches and in at least 700 colleges and universities, plus many other types of meetings and audiences, all in the period from 1970 to 1992. It is small wonder that evolutionists have been focusing their bitterest attacks on the Institute for Creation Research.

The above figures do not, of course, include those also reached through radio and television. Almost as soon as the ICR had been formed, in the spring of 1972, we were contacted by the local Christian radio station and invited to put on a weekly radio program. This station, KECR, in El Cajon, was a member of the Family Radio network, and the 15-minute programs—which we called "Science, Scripture, and Salvation"—were soon on all the stations of the network. Gradually other stations have been added until currently we are on almost 260 stations (in 40 states, plus several foreign countries). The program has been produced continuously for over twenty years. Transcripts of each broadcast were supplied to listeners free on request, and everyone has been different. No requests for money are made on the broadcast. Using translators, the program is now heard weekly in at least 525 different areas nationwide, not including the foreign outreach. Recently, a daily one-minute program, "Back to Genesis", has been broadcast on some 300 or more stations, plus 270 translators.

In addition, ICR speakers have appeared as guests on several hundred other radio and television programs around the country and in many other countries. Some of these have been nationwide telecasts, such as *Twenty-Twenty, CBS Evening News, Today Show, In Search Of, The 700 Club, Sunday Morning, Nova, Phil Donahue,* and various others. Often the emphasis has been negative, with the program attempting to put down the creationists, but even these have invariably generated many good effects, including many new requests to be on our mailing list. Many people have, by now, learned not to trust the liberal journalists who control our news media, particularly on issues that impact on the humanistic biases of these "opinion makers." The very fact that these media figures are usually against ICR almost automatically produces a pro-ICR reaction among many listeners.

With the arrival of Ken Ham in 1986, a remarkable series of "Back-to-Genesis" Seminars began. These have been held in numerous cities around the country, usually attracting thousands of paid registrants, and generating great enthusiasm for creationism in those who attend. These are week-end adult meetings, usually with two ICR speakers in addition to Ken Ham, preceded by a very large assembly of elementary children and high-schoolers. The interest in these, stimulated first by a pastors' breakfast with Ken Ham about a month ahead of time, followed by active support of their churches, has been phenomenal, especially the accompanying sales of ICR books.

I have not discussed any of these meetings in detail, though the personal-interest stories stemming from experiences and contacts made in them are numerous and thrilling. We have records and testimonies of many conversions and changed lives, though we never give "altar calls" or anything of that sort.

For that matter, we have never even solicited invitations to speak, nor tried to set up formal itineraries. We have simply gone where we were invited, as our time and abilities permitted. Even so, we have had to decline many invitations, because of conflicting schedules or other reasons. Usually (though not always) the sponsors have reimbursed travel expenses and also given an offering to ICR as partial reimbursement for the speaker's time and other overhead costs. The Lord's leading and blessing have been evident.

The Debate Arena

Of all the many types of meetings held by ICR speakers, the campus creation/evolution debates have probably received the greatest attention. This has proven a tremendous open door for the spread of creationism.

We were not the first ones to do this sort of thing, of course, although many people have that impression. Douglas Dewar, of the Evolution Protest Movement, participated in a number of very significant debates in England, back in the 1930s and 1940s. So did Harry Rimmer and others in this country.

Even in the more recent creation movement, three professors from Bob Jones University debated three evolutionists from Notre Dame University in a noteworthy confrontation in an Indiana church in 1969. The three Bob Jones creationists were Dr. Joseph Henson, biologist; Dr. Emmett Williams, chemist/physicist; and Dr. Stewart Custer, theologian. All accounts indicate that the creationists easily won the debate, at least as far as the church audience was concerned.

At a lecture at the University of California at Davis in the spring of 1972, Dr. Duane Gish became involved in a sort of extemporaneous debate with famed evolutionist G. Ledyard Stebbins and other UCD faculty members. The first formally structured ICR debate, however, was one between Dr. Robert Gentile, Professor of Geology at the University of Missouri at Kansas City and myself in October 1972. 1 was in Kansas City for other meetings and a student Christian organization asked me, since I would be in the area anyway, if I would be willing to debate on campus.

I rather reluctantly agreed, not having any idea what might be involved, since I had never taken a course in debate, or even in public speaking. Although I had been writing and speaking on

Figure 24. The Great Debates

Dr. Duane Gish, shown here in a typical debate (at table left of screen) frequently appears in creation/evolution debates before university audiences often numbering in the thousands.

creationism for many years, my knowledge of biology and other relevant sciences was distinctly limited, and I did not know what new evidences and arguments a supposed expert in evolution would be able to present in a debate.

My fears proved groundless. Dr. Gentile's case was extremely weak and largely irrelevant to the issue. He made only a very feeble attempt to answer my own arguments. I am sure he could have done better, but he evidently didn't take it seriously and was badly unprepared. In any case, it was a clear victory for creationism, according to the student newspaper, and the word began to spread.

Soon Dr. Gish and I were getting many other invitations to participate in similar debates on other university campuses. The story proved similar everywhere we went. Even the campus and community newspapers all seemed to agree that the creationists were winning the debates. To Dr. Gish and me, who, of necessity had to become thoroughly acquainted with the evolutionary literature and arguments, it seemed that our evolutionary opponents were, by and large, very poorly prepared. They were not even acquainted with current data in their own fields and completely unequipped to deal with our quantitative data and arguments for creation.

Most of the early debates involved only two men—either Dr. Gish or myself—versus an evolutionary spokesman at the university hosting the debate. Occasionally the two of us debated together against two evolutionists. The first of the four-man debates was at the University of Oklahoma in January, 1973. The two evolutionists were geologist David Kitts and biologist Hubert Frings, both outstanding scientists and well respected in their own fields. Over 1,000 students crowded into the 500-seat auditorium, filling the aisles and the stage and every available nook and cranny. Again, it was a clear victory for creationism, as far as the audience and newspapers were concerned.

I quickly learned that there was nothing much to fear from these encounters, at least not in the scientific evidence, but I have never learned to enjoy them. For a person who does not even like to socialize, and who intensely dislikes arguing, I somehow seem always to be involved in controversies! I would never in the world have sought involvement in debates, and I still try to avoid them if possible, but I have by now participated in at least four dozen of these debates.

Dr. Gish, on the other hand, is really in his element in a debate. He is gregarious, has a great store of knowledge, and a tremendous memory. He relishes these confrontations and indeed is a fearsome debater. He has participated by now in well over 250. Always supremely confident before they start, he is always equally confident afterward that he has won. Furthermore, even though his evolutionist opponents might occasionally disagree with this verdict, the audience almost always agrees, and that's what counts!

I believe most or all of my debates also—as well as those of more recent years involving Dr. Parker, Dr. Slusher, Dr. Bliss, Dr. Austin, Dr. John Morris, and others—have been victories for creationism, even though it is very seldom that an actual vote is taken. Sometimes, people question the value of these debates, even as I myself did before we started having them. After all, it is pointed out, no one ever really wins an argument, and debates tend to generate more heat than light. Isn't it better simply to give a straightforward creationist message instead of debating?

The answer to such questions is simply a matter of pragmatics. A typical campus lecture on creationism, if well advertised and promoted, may draw an audience of about 300. A debate on the same campus, with the same amount of promotion, will draw around 3,000! Multitudes will at least hear a case for creationism this way (even if not as complete a case) who would never have come to a straight lecture at all. Furthermore, we know from numerous subsequent testimonies that a profound spiritual impact is often made by such a debate, not infrequently leading someone eventually to genuine conversion to Christ. Even though debating is certainly not my preference, it has undoubtedly been of profound significance in furthering the modern creationist revival. Probably more than any other single factor, it has brought scientific creationism to the sharp attention of the scientific establishment.

The typical debate format is fascinating. Instead of the creationist using religious arguments against the scientific arguments of the evolutionist, it is often the other way around!

The proposition to be debated is simply the relative scientific merits of the creation and evolution models of origins—not the Biblical or sociological merits. Usually there will be an hour each for the first presentations, then about 45–50 minutes for the rebuttals, plus another 45 minutes or so for questions to both sides from the audience. The entire session lasts from three to four hours, yet the large audiences stay right there at least through all the rebuttals, and the interest level is very high, sometimes intense and emotional.

We are always careful to stick strictly to scientific arguments, especially using the fossil record to show that macro-evolution has not occurred in the past, the characteristics of mutation and natural selection to show that it is not occurring in the present, and the laws of thermodynamics to show that it could not occur at all. Also the principles of probability are used to show that complex functioning systems could never arise by chance.

The evolutionists, however, more often than not, do *not* stick to scientific arguments. They will attack the Bible, show that creationists have religious motivations, argue that one can be religious and still believe in evolution, contend that creationism is not scientific, or attack our personal character or credentials. They may talk about variations in fruit flies or the similar morphology of men and apes or the history of evolutionary thought.

But one thing they will *not* do is give any real scientific evidence for macro-evolution. This is because there isn't any real scientific evidence for macro-evolution!

This is why creationists almost always win the debates. We win, not because we are better debaters, but because creation is true, evolution is false, and real science confirms this. Evolutionists cannot show fossils of evolutionary intermediate forms which never existed, nor can they make the second law of thermodynamics generate higher complexity, nor can they demonstrate evolutionary changes which never occur. Variation within limits is horizontal change, not vertical; similarities argue for a common Designer more than for a common ancestor; mutations as observed are never beneficial; natural selection is a conservative principle, not a creative principle.

Altogether ICR scientists have participated in well over 300 of these creation/evolution debates since 1972. It is certainly not feasible to discuss all these here. However, Marvin Lubenow, who is both a pastor and scientist, has discussed and analyzed the taped records of most of them in a recent book[1] devoted just to that one subject.

An indication of the significance of the debates is derived from the locations where they have been held and the numbers in attendance. A few of the more prestigious universities whose campuses have been the site of an ICR creation/evolution debate include the University of California at Berkeley, Princeton University, University of Michigan, UCLA, University of Texas, University of Pennsylvania, Brown University, Iowa State University, Northwestern University, Purdue University, University of Wisconsin, University of California at Santa Barbara, University of North Carolina, Virginia Tech, University of Minnesota, Kansas University, University of Virginia, Ohio State University, Penn State, University of Washington, and Oregon University. Debates have been held in at least 40 states and 6 Canadian provinces, as well as England, Holland, Australia, New Zealand, Trinidad, and Barbados.

---

1. Marvin Lubenow, *"From Fish to Gish"* (San Diego: Creation-Life Publishers, 1983), 293 pp. Rev. Lubenow formerly pastor of the First Baptist Church of Fort Collins, Colorado, is now Professor of Bible at Christian Heritage College. He has both Th. M and M.S. degrees.

The attendance twice has hit 5,000 (University of Minnesota and Liberty Baptist College), and the average attendance has been well over 1,000 at each debate. Lubenow has calculated that, if radio, television, and newspaper debates are included, well over 6,000,000 people have seen, heard, or read one of these ICR debates.[1] Beginning in 1981, evolutionists became very concerned about the influence of the debates and began to develop a strategy to reverse the trend. This will be discussed in more detail in Chapter X.

Graduate Education in Creationist Science

The central division of the ICR ministries is the ICR Graduate School. My original goal (or "dream") had been a genuinely Christian and creationist university, the key component of which would have to be a graduate school, especially offering graduate training in the key sciences related to the study of origins and earth history. There were (and are) no other such schools in existence, so far as I know.[2] There are many religious and denominational graduate schools, of course (Notre Dame, Baylor, Southern Methodist, Abilene Christian, etc.), and many of these have strong science programs, but few believe in Biblical inerrancy, and none—so far as I know—are committed to strict creationism, without compromise.

Since all schools, Christian or otherwise, want their teachers to have graduate training (and accrediting agencies require it), this

---

1. *Ibid.*, p. 257.

2. One possible exception should be mentioned. The Seventh-Day Adventist school, Loma Linda University, does have a number of graduate programs in science. The problem is that, though these are creationist, they are not necessarily committed to *recent* creation. Also, their commitment to Ellen G. White's teachings as inspired prophecy is objectionable to most Christians, since this means that their authority is not *uniquely* centered in the inerrant Bible, the only Word of God.

means that science teachers have all received their advanced training in evolution-dominated universities. Almost inevitably, this has influenced them in some degree toward compromise. Furthermore, the social sciences and humanities have been more affected by evolutionary humanism than even the natural sciences, and these all justify their faith in evolution by the fact that they *think* evolution has been proven in the natural sciences.

There has thus been a great need for graduate education, especially in the key sciences, which would be sound academically, but would not compromise in any degree with evolutionism and humanism. This, in turn, required sound undergraduate programs of this type upon which to build, together with a sound creation research/extension/publication division to support it. Since no other Christian college could be found both willing and able to do this, we had to start our own, Christian Heritage College, as already mentioned in Chapter VII.

However, after ten years of struggle, being especially frustrated by the demands of the accrediting organization, the Western Association of Schools and Colleges (WASC), it began to seem that we would never be able to go on to establish a graduate school. In fact, WASC had specifically advised us not even to begin planning a graduate school if we wanted to achieve undergraduate accreditation. Furthermore, the WASC authorities were exerting pressures that were increasingly difficult to resist, urging the CHC administration and faculty to compromise the College's strict creationist and Biblical stand in order to gain the much-desired accreditation status. The WASC people were making it plain that they looked with strong disfavor on ICR's influence over the College.

Consequently, after much study and prayer, we decided that ICR should separate completely from the College, becoming a separate educational, research, and writing institution. We could then go ahead with the projected graduate school, without inhibiting the College's plans. At the same time, we could set up a contract with the College to continue the same type of practical cooperation we had always followed in the past. This also meant, of course, that I would resign as President of the College and henceforth devote full time to ICR.

After considerable evaluation and discussion, the separation was eventually approved by the College Trustees and then (unanimously) at a meeting of the entire corporation (same as the congregation of the sponsoring Church) early in 1981. With the invaluable assistance of creationist attorney Wendell Bird, who was on our regular staff during this period, a state charter was obtained, along with IRS recognition as a tax-exempt educational/charitable corporation. A complete constitution was drawn up, including a new doctrinal statement prepared by me which was even more extensive and explicit (with respect to strict creationism) than the one used by the College. Also, a detailed contract was drawn up with the College and a leasehold arrangement with the Church, granting ICR a long-term lease rent-free (except for utilities and maintenance) on that part of the Administration Building which had been paid for out of funds raised and contributed by ICR. The contract provided for sharing of facilities and staff by ICR and CHC, on an equitable cost-sharing basis. However, each organization was to be completely independent of the other, and the contract was to be renewed year by year on approval of both.

The new doctrinal statement is listed not only in the By-laws, but in the Educational Philosophy section of each year's Catalog of the ICR Graduate School (which is, of course, available free upon request to the ICR headquarters office). The doctrinal statement is divided into two segments: (1) "Tenets of Scientific Creationism"; (2) "Tenets of Biblical Creationism." It is stressed that each of these two sets of tenets is fully compatible with the other, but that it is possible to utilize each independently of the other if circumstances warrant (for example, in public schools in the one case and in churches in the other). This entire Educational Philosophy section of the Graduate School Catalog is reproduced herein as Appendix G.

Figure 25. The New ICR Museum

The ICR Museum of Creation and Earth History, newly enlarged in 1992, is seen by 2,000 or more visitors each month, especially including classes of school children. Shown here is the outside entrance, along with views of a few of the exhibits.

It was obvious that an institution with such an educational philosophy would have no chance of secular accreditation, even if it met all other requirements. Consequently, it was decided right from the start that the ICR Graduate School would not aim at WASC accreditation. The state of California Department of Education permitted unaccredited schools to operate under its Office of Private Post-Secondary Education (OPPE), either as an "Authorized" school or "Approved" school. The latter category is the more difficult to attain, requiring an institutional self-study and a site visit and review by a state-appointed committee of educators. It is quite similar, though not quite as rigorous, as a regular regional agency accreditation evaluation. More importantly, it did not consider a school's philosophy. ICR received its OPPE "Approved" rating in June 1981, on the first attempt and had maintained good standing with OPPE since that time.

A new Board of Trustees was set up, consisting of fifteen highly qualified and dedicated business and professional leaders, from various geographical regions and various Christian denominations, elected for staggered three-year terms. The Board is chaired by the ICR president and meets semi-annually, with its Executive Committee (composed of members from the San Diego area) meeting more often as needed. The Board is responsible for budget and salary approval, for major policies, and for major personnel decisions. Members can be reelected for one additional term, with the Board itself responsible for electing its members. All trustees, of course, as well as all staff members, must be fully committed to the ICR statement of faith.

We hope that ICR may eventually be able to offer M.S. and Ph.D. programs in all the major sciences. It was necessary to start small, however, so it was decided to begin with only four M.S. programs, in what were judged to be the most strategic fields for the future of the creation movement. These programs, with corresponding faculty members, were as follows:

Astro-Geophysics. Harold Slusher, Chairman
Other faculty: Barnes, H. Morris, J. Morris, Rybka, Vardiman
Biology. Kenneth Cumming, Chairman
Other faculty: Gish, Parker, Courtois
Geology. Harold Slusher, Chairman
Other faculty: Austin, McQueen
Science Education. Richard Bliss, Chairman
Other faculty: Lindsay, A. Morris, Edwards
Most of the above have been mentioned in a previous section.
Dr. Louis Courtois was Assistant Professor of Biology at Christian

Figure 26. ICR Headquarters Building

A New ICR building was built and occupied in late 1985 in Santee, California, a suburb of San Diego. Facilities include science research labs, library, museum, classrooms, offices and various service areas.

Heritage. George Lindsay and Andrew Morris were also on the Christian Heritage College staff but were also assisting Dr. Bliss in the Science Education Department. Dr. Lindsay is a biologist and specialist in audiovisual education. Andy Morris (who was my youngest son) was Director of Information Services for the College and Chairman of its Business Administration Department. He taught Statistics and Math for ICR and assisted in developing its computer operations. Dr. Seth Edwards was a geologist and specialist in science education on the faculty of the University of Texas (El Paso). Each of these men taught one or more courses in ICR's summer sessions.

Dr. Tom Barnes, who had just retired after a long and distinguished career as Professor of Physics at the University of Texas at El Paso, agreed to become the first Dean of the ICR Graduate School. Classes opened in the summer of 1981, and good enrollments were experienced right from the start, including many exceptionally fine students. Most of the activity thus far has been in the summer sessions, but more academic year courses will be added as full-time enrollments increase. The programs are now (1993) in their 13th year. There are currently about 50 students at one stage or another in their programs, with 35 having finished and many others almost through. Each student, of course, was required to do an M.S. thesis, as well as 6 credit-hours in scientific creationism, in addition to at least 24 hours of formal course work in the chosen field. Recently a non-thesis option was added.

There were a number of faculty changes during the Graduate School's first decade. Professors Barnes, Slusher, Rybka, Parker, Courtois, and Edwards resigned at various times. David McQueen and Andrew Morris went on leave to get their Ph. D. degrees. Andy Morris (my son) received his Ph. D. in Management Information Systems from Texas Tech University in 1987 and accepted a position as Assistant Professor at Florida State University. After only two years there, however, he developed an incurable lymphoma and went to be with the Lord in May 1989. He was a

Figure 27. Typical Back-to-Genesis Seminar

Back to Genesis seminars, featuring Ken Ham and other ICR speakers, are among the many extension speaking ministries of the ICR scientists. These seminars usually draw thousands of people in each city where they are held.

scientist of great promise, as well as a strong Christian and creationist, and is deeply missed for these reasons—not to mention the
loss of a beloved son.

The present faculty is very strong, however, both academically
and spiritually. Their names and credentials have been listed previously, and they are in every way comparable to the credentials
of faculties at secular graduate schools of similar size.

The facilities were greatly improved with the completion of a
new ICR building in late 1985, about six miles away from the
Christian Heritage campus, where ICR had been centered during
its first fifteen years. The programs as a whole continued to im-
prove—larger labs, more equipment, larger and better staff, larger
museum, more financial support, etc.

The "Back-to-Genesis" seminars initiated and organized by Ken
Ham when he joined the staff, have generated a great increase in
interest. Although lacking the academic qualifications of the other
ICR scientists, he has a remarkable ability to communicate the
scientific and Biblical arguments for creation on a popular level,
and audiences almost everywhere seem to respond enthusiastically
to his presentations. Attendance at seminars has multiplied, as well
as the dissemination of ICR's message through books.

With the rise of the modern home video interest, ICR has also
produced a large selection of video cassettes, featuring messages
by the various ICR speakers. Another relatively new program
involves annual field tours to the Grand Canyon, Mount St. Helens,
the Smithsonian Institution, and Australia, featuring one or more
ICR lecturer-guides, and these have proved extremely fruitful.

The new ICR Museum of Creation and Earth History was
opened in 1992 and drew over 25,000 visitors in its first year of
operation. Its exhibits are professionally crafted and its message
is clear and persuasive.

Many books have been produced—books for children, technical
monographs, books on scientific creationism, Bible commentaries
emphasizing creation, books on Christian evidences, and others.

Figure 28. ICR Field Tour to Grand Canyon

Lecture to tour party on rim of Grand Canyon. ICR sponsors annual tours to Grand Canyon and other locations of special significance to creation/flood studies.

In my opinion, sound creationist literature bears more fruit in the long run than anything else, and this should continue to be the key component of the ICR testimony.

The tremendous impact of ICR around the country, not surprisingly, soon began to generate a wave of angry reaction from the evolutionary establishment—especially in science, education and the news media. This came to focus especially on the ICR Graduate School. Its graduate programs in science had been approved by the California Department of Education from the beginning, and this fact gave ICR a measure of scientific prestige which evolutionists resented. The pressure they brought to bear on the Department eventually resulted in a protracted attempt to close the school. These efforts—thus far unsuccessful—are discussed more fully in Chapter X.

Chapter IX

Proliferation of Creationist Organizations

Previous chapters have discussed the older creationist societies and organizations, the ones that have laid the foundations upon which the modern creation revival has been built, especially the Creation Research Society and the Institute for Creation Research. Recent decades, as a result, have seen a remarkable proliferation of creationist activities of many kinds and many levels. Some of these newer organizations and their contributions will be surveyed in this chapter.

I recall how, in the very early years of the Creation Research Society, there were some of its Directors who rather strongly felt that all creationist efforts should be channeled through the Society, reacting specifically against the prospective development of the Bible Science Association as a rival creationist organization. I strongly argued against this attitude, stressing that there was far more work to be done than any one organization could possibly handle. The more the better, it seemed to me. If, perchance, all creationist testimony were controlled and orchestrated through one central directorate, then all the enemies of creationism would have to do to destroy creationism would be to undermine that one central control center. The proliferation and decentralization of the creation movement actually constitute its greatest strength, at the human level at least. There may be a certain amount of overlapping, perhaps some competition, and even disagreement among the different organizations, but this lack of unity in details and coordination is more than outweighed by agreement on essentials and ultimate goals, as well as the large number of people and wide range of activities that are thereby contributing to the cause.

In any case, my original hope of seeing a great multiplicity of creationist activities has certainly been abundantly fulfilled in recent years. There are now so many organizations that it is completely unrealistic to try to describe them all in this one book. There are probably many of which I am not even aware, but the names and address of those about which I know are listed in Appendix C, as a matter of record. The ones discussed in this chapter—all quite briefly—are those which seem to have the greatest potential for significant impact in the future. These are the organizations of national scope and interest, rather than state or local organizations. The latter are also important, but the scope of this book does not allow us to discuss all of them.

Trans-National Association of Christian Schools

At this writing (1993), the Trans-National Association of Christian Schools (TRACS) is still relatively small. However, it is greatly needed, and is growing steadily. The schools which are involved in TRACS at this time have a variety of individual motivations but, in my judgment, two of its goals are of overriding importance. One is the development of a consortium of Christian schools at all levels and in all fields which are firmly committed to literal creationism and flood geology, as well as full and unique Biblical inerrancy and authority in all fields. The other is that of providing an accrediting organization for such schools, one which can assure academic excellence without also undermining their Biblical and creationist educational philosophies.

I have already referred to the great need for a true Christian university system, firmly creationist and Biblical in all teachings and activities. If such an institution, or institutions, existed, they could provide the personnel training and over-all directional guidance for Christian schools at all levels. Since such a university does not now exist, and may be exceedingly difficult to develop, a more immediate means of achieving the same end could well be through a consortium of Christian schools, some specializing in certain areas and others in different fields, but with all maintaining comparable standards and with mutual transfer of credits and other ways of cooperation. An organization such as TRACS could work efficiently toward such a goal.

The need for a Christian, creationist accrediting organization is also very real and will become more critical as time goes on. Unfortunately most Christian schools don't yet see this need, and whether enough will see and act on it before it is too late remains to be seen. The secular regional accrediting associations are not, in principle, supposed to evaluate the particular beliefs or philosophies of their member schools, but only their academic caliber. However, the degree of correlation of principle with practice inevitably depends on the makeup of each particular site visitation committee and accrediting commission. There are many examples of real anti-Christian—and especially anti-creationist—bias in these secular agencies, regardless of their equivocating denials. With the existing pervasive domination of secular science and education by evolutionary humanism, it could hardly be otherwise. Our experiences at Christian Heritage College, discussed in Chapter VII, are illustrative.

There have been a number of abortive attempts in the past to start Christian college accrediting associations, but none have focused on the key issues of creationism and Biblical authority. The American Association of Bible Colleges has become a recognized accrediting agency for Bible colleges, but its schools still have achieved only limited acceptance among the secular colleges. It does not try to accredit Christian liberal arts colleges or graduate schools, leaving them to the untender mercies of the secular agencies, and even at that does not require its own member Bible colleges to adhere to creationism. The same is true of some Christian associations which accredit Christian elementary and secondary schools. While the great majority of Bible colleges and

Christian day schools are still creationist, there is nothing in the accreditation criteria which requires this or assures their constituents of this fact.

The accreditation awarded by TRACS on the other hand, would give assurance of both sound doctrine and sound academics, and no other agency does so at the college level, so far as I know, at least if sound doctrine is understood to include (as it ought to do) sound creationism. Thus there is a genuine need for TRACS, and the need is bound to become more urgent as time goes on.

The need was first discussed by Dr. Robert Witty, President of Luther Rice Seminary (Jacksonville, Florida), and my son, Dr. Henry M. Morris III, then Administrative Vice President at Christian Heritage College, during a visit by Dr. Witty to the CHC campus in 1978. This was followed by correspondence and finally an organizational meeting in 1979 at the Criswell Center for Biblical Studies in Dallas. Dr. Paige Patterson, President of the Criswell Center, was named TRACS president, and I was named vice-president. Dr. G. Edwin Miller, who was Academic Vice-President at Christian Heritage at the time (I was President) became Executive Secretary, agreeing to take charge of preparing accreditation standards for TRACS. It was Dr. Witty who suggested the name and acronym for the new organization.

Progress was slow, but it was essential that good standards be established and good materials be prepared. Dr. Patterson served as president for three years, then asked to be relieved (for several years he had been the leader in the successful fight of the conservatives and inerrantists to regain control of the Southern Baptist Convention from the liberal hierarchy that had dominated its affairs for many years, as well as heading a large and growing Bible college and graduate school at Criswell), so he and I interchanged positions.

Dr. Earl Mills, of Liberty University, served as (unpaid) Executive Director beginning in 1980, working with Dr. Miller to develop the accreditation standards, manuals and other materials for the organization. Eventually TRACS became strong enough to employ a full-time Executive Director, and Dr. J. Gordon Henry, former president of Northeastern Bible College, was appointed to that position in 1984. Dr. Henry had also served as Academic Dean at Liberty University during its early years.

TRACS accreditation involves four levels of membership: (1) Accredited Member; (2) Candidate Member; (3) Associate Member; (4) Correspondent Member. The criteria for the first two grades are those for the "Associate" grade plus essentially the same academic criteria expected for accreditation or candidacy by one of the standard regional associations. An Associate Member satisfies the TRACS "Basic Criteria" (doctrinal, philosophical, moral, and financial) but not necessarily the "General Criteria" required for candidacy or full accreditation. A Correspondent Member is an institution outside the United States that has submitted information relative to its adherence to the Basic Criteria. For more detailed information, one should consult the official TRACS literature.[1]

As of 1993, nine schools had received "Accredited" status with TRACS, with sixteen recognized as "Candidate" and 36 accepted as "Associate" Members. Over 260 schools had indicated strong interest in TRACS when it could become officially recognized as an approved accrediting association by the U.S. Department of Education. The latter was very difficult to achieve, however, in view of the (not unexpected) opposition of the existing accrediting agencies. Nevertheless, officials of the Education Department have thoroughly investigated the TRACS materials, site visits, commission and board meetings, and all other aspects of its structure and work, and acknowledged that it was functioning on a par with other accrediting organizations, meeting all criteria except the hurdle of acceptability to these organizations. Two direct appeals were made to the U.S. Secretary of Education,

---

1. For information, contact Dr. J. Gordon Henry, Executive Director, TRACS, 2114 Arrow Court, Murfreesburo, Tennessee, 37130.

asking that this one criterion be set aside as unreasonable and probably illegal. The last appeal was finally successful and TRACS was officially recognized in 1991 as the accrediting association for post-secondary institutions committed to creationism and to full Biblical integrity and authority in all fields. It remains to be seen how many Christian schools will choose to align themselves with TRACS and its distinctives.

Creation Social Science and Humanities Society

Another relatively new organization that is assuming increasing national significance is the Creation Social Science and Humanities Society (CSSHS), organized in 1977. It is patterned somewhat after the Creation Research Society, except that its focus is on the social sciences and humanities instead of the natural sciences, as in CRS.

This is a tremendously important emphasis, for evolutionary humanism today dominates the humanities and social sciences even more, if possible, than it does the natural sciences. Conversely, true creationism can be tremendously illuminating and effective if properly applied to these fields, and it is these which impinge most directly on human life.

The CSSHS was the outgrowth of prayerful discussions by Mrs. Ellen Myers, Mrs. E. Sue Paar, and Dr. Paul D. Ackerman, who were then three officers of the Mid-Kansas Branch of the Bible-Science Association, centered in Wichita. As strong Christians and creationists, whose training and interests were in the social sciences and humanities, they felt a strong need for an organized witness in these important areas. The result was their decision to organize and to send out membership invitations. They received IRS approval in December 1977. The statement of faith was taken almost verbatim from that of the Creation Research Society. An early newsletter effectively stated a primary goal of the new society to be as follows:

> We will endeavor to show that *the only true and sure* foundation of man's knowledge of himself (psychology)—of his relationship with other men (sociology)—of his communications and creativity (literature and fine arts)—of his institutions of social order (administration of justice, economics, political science)—of his activities and their descriptions (history)—is *the creation of man in God's image* as infallibly revealed in the Bible. All other attempts to account for man are vain and doomed to failure.

Dr. Paul D. Ackerman has served most capably as President of CSSHS ever since its beginning. He is Assistant Chairman of the Department of Psychology at the Wichita State University and has a Ph.D. in Social Psychology from the University of Kansas (1968). Vice-President was Mrs. E. Sue Paar, who has a B.S. in Applied Arts from Arizona State University (1961).

Mrs. Ellen Myers, a widow and the mother of seven children, is Secretary-Treasurer. Born in Germany, she endured Nazi persecution during World War II, coming to the United States in 1948. A writer and teacher, she is fluent in several languages and author of several books and numerous articles, currently working on her Ph.D.

The first *Creation Social Science and Humanities Quarterly* was published in the fall of 1978 and has been issued regularly since that time, containing a wealth of fascinating and useful articles on many topics. Ellen Myers and Paul Ackerman contribute many of the papers, but many other capable and scholarly writers have published in the *Quarterly*.

In his introductory editorial, Dr. Ackerman, who serves also as Editor of the *Quarterly*, eloquently expressed his hopes for their journal as follows:

> In closing I want to pray to our Lord that He will cause this journal to help believers to be more confident in the intellectual profundity of the faith and be better able to articulate an academically sound defense of the faith. By His grace may we help our Christian readers be able to more effectively communicate

the Gospel of Christ in love to this generation. We hope to publish articles that are firm but gentle, intellectually solid but easy to understand. God grant that it may be so.[1]

I believe this goal is being admirably accomplished. I have had the privilege of serving as a member of the Board of Reference of the Society, along with Dr. John C. Whitcomb, Dr. Duane T. Gish, and other well-known creationists. The work was started in prayer and has been Christ-honoring in every respect. Currently (1993), the Society has a total distribution (members plus subscribers) of its *Quarterly* of over 400.

Other Organizations of Nationwide Outreach

Many other creationist organizations have been formed in recent years, most of them local or state organizations. There are still a number of others, however, which are national in scope.

The creationist meetings on college and university campuses have been sponsored by various Christian student organizations. There is only one major student organization, however, whose specific ministry is that of promoting creationism among students. This is *Students for Origins Research,* headquartered in Santa Barbara, California.

A very active student creationist organization had been founded by several students on the campus of the University of California at Santa Barbara in 1976, one of their main projects being to sponsor a creation/evolution debate with Dr. Gish and myself debating two outstanding evolutionist scientists, geologist Preston Cloud and botanist Aharon Gibhor. This was one of the few debates where a vote was taken from the audience, and it was a clear victory for creationism. Dr. Cloud, in particular, took this defeat

1. Paul D. Ackerman, "Editorial," *Creation Social Science and Humanities Quarterly* (Vol. 1, No. 1, Fall 1978), p. 32. For information on membership in the Society or subscription to its *Quarterly*, write to CSSHS, 1429 N. Holyoke, Whichita, KS 67208.

Figure 29. Paluxy Project

One of the most famous creationist research projects has been the discovery and continuing analysis of the apparently contemporaneous footprints of man and dinosaur in the limestones of the Paluxy River in Texas. ICR's Dr. John Morris has made extensive field studies there, documented in a book by him, and the Films-for-Christ movie, "Footprints in Stone," has been seen by great numbers of people. Dr. Clifford Burdick, shown in bottom photo with Dr. Morris, was one of the first creationist geologists to document these footprints. Stanley Taylor, shown at upper right, founder of Films for Christ and producer of "Footprints in Stone" made many key discoveries in his research at the site. Although these original discoveries have been controversial, research is currently (as of 1993) continuing at the site by Carl Baugh and others in the hope that incontrovertible evidence will yet be found there.

quite bitterly and remained a vitriolic anti-creationist until his death some 15 years later.[1]

Three of the students most active at this time were Karen Jensen, Dennis Wagner, and Dave Johannsen. After graduation, Karen moved to ICR, where she worked on various projects, most importantly that of developing the initial plans for our Museum of Creation and Earth History. Later she went to Loma Linda University and eventually earned a Ph.D. in paleobiology. Dennis and Dave, on the other hand, stayed in Santa Barbara to establish a base for a nationwide organization of student creationist clubs. They were joined later by Art Battson and Kevin Wirth.

The venture has proven surprisingly successful. Clubs have been established on about a dozen campuses, and an excellent newspaper, *Origins Research,* is published semi-annually. In recent years, however, this organization has become somewhat equivocal on literal six-day creationism.

A promising creationist organization is the Alpha Omega Institute, co-directed by a dedicated husband-and-wife team, David and Mary Jo Nutting, both of whose strong educational backgrounds include M.S. degrees from the ICR Graduate School. This relatively small organization has conducted numerous seminars and other meetings, including meetings in Europe; conducts creation-oriented family camps and mountain adventures; and publishes a bi-monthly newsletter, *Think and Believe.*

An entirely different type of organization is *Films for Christ,* with its subsidiary, *Eden Films.* Founded in the early 1960s by Wheaton College graduate Stanley Taylor, its original ministry was to produce gospel motion picture films with a strong apologetics content. He soon became convinced of strict creationism through reading *The Genesis Flood* and had been especially intrigued with the photographs provided for that book by Dr. Clifford Burdick,

---

1. See especially his article "Scientific Creationism: A New Inquisition," The *Humanist* (Vol. XXXVII, January/February 1977), pp. 6–15.

showing footprints of both man and dinosaur in the Cretaceous limestones of the Paluxy River in Texas. Taylor finally decided to produce a documentary film on this theme, embarking on what would become a project of major proportions and impact. It involved several seasons of excavation, important new footprint discoveries, and finally an outstanding film, *Footprints in Stone,* released in 1971. Shown in hundreds of schools and churches, this documentary has convinced many people that dinosaurs and men actually lived at the same time, just as the Bible teaches. It has been seen by over 600,000 students in public school showings and by over one and a half million people around the world.

Since that time, Films for Christ has concentrated almost exclusively on creation-oriented films. *The World That Perished,* issued in 1975, is an excellent film on the worldwide Flood. After Stan Taylor's tragic death from cancer in 1976, his wife Marian and son Paul have continued the work, first with a documentary indicating that the legendary dragons of antiquity were actually dinosaurs (*The Great Dinosaur Mystery*), then by a 1983 award-winning series of six films entitled *Origins: How the World Came to Be.*

More recently, the Taylors withdrew the *Footprints in Stone* film from circulation, in deference to the questions that had been raised about the legitimacy of some of the human-like tracks featured in the film. Their other films, however, continue to be widely used. In particular, *The Genesis Solution*, featuring Ken Ham, has been extremely effective in promoting creationism among Christians in particular.

Among publishers, no other company has made a specialty of creationist books to the extent that *Creation-Life Publishers* (now Master Books) has done. This company has either published or co-published at least 100 books by ICR writers or other creationist scientists since it was formed in 1973. Although the company was established as a regular commercial corporation, it has actually lost money ever since it was formed, so that it should be considered as really a creationist ministry, kept operating just to be sure creationist books will be published.

Although many other publishers have published one or a few creationist books, the only ones that have published a significant number are the Baker Book House (Grand Rapids) and the Presbyterian and Reformed Publishing Co. (Phillipsburg, New Jersey).

Baker has published several of my major books, *The Genesis Record*, *The Biblical Basis of Modern Science* , *The Long War against God,* as well as others. They have also published a number of creationist books by other authors. Presbyterian and Reformed were the publishers of *The Genesis Flood*, of course, along with five other books of mine, as well as the CRS anthologies, books by Bolton Davidheiser, and others. In neither case, however, could creationism be said to be a primary interest of the company.

One new association specializing in books on apologetics, including some on creationism, is the *Apologetics Press, Inc.,* located in Montgomery, Alabama. Especially catering to the Churches of Christ, this organization is firmly committed to the strict creation, young earth, and global cataclysmic deluge positions, as well as an inerrant Bible and the deity of Christ. The Apologetics Press publishes a monthly journal, *Reason and Revelation,* as well as many valuable books and cassettes dealing with various aspects of Christian apologetics. Its two chief writers and speakers are Bert Thompson (Ph.D. from Texas A & M in food microbiology) and Wayne Jackson (M.A. in religion and hon. Litt.D. from Alabama Christian School of Religion).

Creation Conventions

With the modern increase in interest in creationism, a number of creation conventions have been held. As noted in Chapter VIII, the Bible-Science Association has been sponsoring such conventions for many years.

More recently, two significant gatherings of creationist scientists have been held in Pittsburgh, in 1986 and 1990, with the intention of repeating these quadrennially. Many technical papers were presented at each, covering many different scientific fields and aspects of scientific creationism. The papers were then issued in bound volumes of the *Proceedings of the International Conference on Creationism.*

A similar convention was held in the Minneapolis/St. Paul area in 1992, with the hope of making this also a quadrennial event. In this case, as with the Pittsburgh conferences, sponsorship is provided by the local creationist organization rather than by any national group. Both the Creation Research Society and the Institute for Creation Research have, from their beginnings, rejected the idea of conventions as a component part of their respective programs, but their individual members are free to participate if they so choose.

Quasi-Political Associations

One of the main concerns shared by most creationists is the fact that public school courses and textbooks have long been heavily biased in favor of evolution. This concern has been discussed to some degree in preceding chapters and has been one of the consistent themes in the modern creationist revival.

It is not surprising, therefore, that a number of creationist associations have been organized with the specific objective of securing a more balanced treatment of the critical and sensitive topic of origins in schools and other public institutions. Since such institutions are governmentally financed, controlled, and operated, many people believe that political methods would be required to attain such a goal.

I personally have always disagreed with this political approach, and so have most of my colleagues in the Creation Research Society and the Institute for Creation Research. We certainly favor the objective, of course, but not the use of political means (especially legislation and litigation) to achieve this goal. I have discussed the reasons for our reservations elsewhere[1] and need not repeat them here, since this is primarily a book of history. I can understand, however, why many earnest creationists do feel that mere persuasion on such matters will never work, and so should be replaced by coercion, if necessary.

For example, there is an organization called *Citizens for Fairness in Education,* founded in 1978 by Paul Ellwanger, its Executive Director. An active and concerned Roman Catholic layman, Ellwanger has been encouraging the passage of legislation to require a two-model approach in origins teaching in public schools, enlisting the aid of some very competent creationist attorneys in drafting model bills on the subject. A possible measure of the effectiveness of these efforts may be the fact that creationist bills have actually been introduced in almost half of the nation's state legislatures. At least some of these, including the law that occasioned the famous Arkansas creation trial of 1981, were largely based on one of Ellwanger's model bills.

Another organization was *Citizens against Federal Establishment of Evolutionary Dogma,* the purpose of which was to get a national creation law enacted, requiring equal federal funding of creationist research, museum exhibits, curriculum, and textbook development, or any other projects, as for evolutionist causes. The "National Coordinators" of CAFEED were Marshall and Sandra Hall, journalists who, soon after their conversion to creationism, wrote two strongly anti-evolutionist books entitled *The Truth: God or Evolution?* and *The Great Evolution Deception.* However, unlike Ellwanger and most creationists, the Halls did not endorse the two-model approach, but rather a complete national prohibition of evolutionary teaching.

The Creation Science Research Center has already been mentioned as being specially concerned with political actions related

---

1. Henry M. Morris, *King of Creation* (San Diego: Creation-Life Publishers, 1980), 239 pp.

to creation in the schools. This organization, directed by Nell Segraves and her son, Kelly, received national publicity in early 1981 through a lawsuit filed against the state of California on behalf of Kelly's three sons. The allegation was that the religious beliefs of the children were being harmed by the exclusive teaching of evolution to which they were being subjected in the public schools.

Although the media did their best to make a "Scopes Trial" circus out of this Sacramento trial, they were disappointed in that many of the expected scientist witnesses were not called, with the anticipated ridicule of creationism and fundamentalism which presumably would have resulted. Judge Irving H. Perluss, in an equivocating decision, ruled that the state's Science Framework already provided sufficient accommodation to the religious beliefs of creationist children, but that this needed to be communicated more effectively to teachers. In effect, it was ruled that evolution could be taught exclusively, as long as it was not taught in a context of dogmatic atheism.

Following this trial, Segraves formed another organization, called *the Creation Creed Committee,* in conjunction with Rev. Robert Grant and his *Christian Voice* organization in Pacific Grove, California. The purpose was supposed to be that of monitoring compliance with Judge Perluss' ruling by individual California teachers and also to raise money to file suits wherever non-compliance is encountered.

The most important of this group of organizations was the *Creation Science Legal Defense Fund,* formed primarily to finance and provide a good legal defense whenever a creationist law or teacher is attacked in the courts. The American Civil Liberties Union has undertaken a self-appointed mission to prevent the teaching of creationism in any public school (strange crusade for an organization purporting to protect "American civil liberties"!) and has intimidated school boards all across the nation with its threats of lawsuits.

The CSLDF was first formed to attempt to provide a defense against the ACLU in its lawsuit against the state of Arkansas and its creation/evolution two-model law, enacted in March 1981. One of Paul Ellwanger's model laws had been introduced in the Arkansas Senate by Senator James Holsted, largely at the behest of the Greater Little Rock Evangelical Fellowship, and sailed through both Senate and House with minimal discussion, being signed into law by Governor White on March 19, 1981. Two months later, on May 27, the ACLU filed its lawsuit challenging the constitutionality of the act, but the judge denied the motion of the CSLDF to intervene.

This trial, held December 7–17, did indeed provide the media circus which the humanists desired. The ACLU had a number of famous evolutionary scientists as its witnesses (William Mayer, Stephen Gould, Brent Dalrymple, etc.) and placed much emphasis on the "religious" character of creation. The ACLU attorneys were able also to show that the defense witnesses were religiously motivated in their creationism, and the media strongly played this theme. Presiding Judge William R. Overton rendered his decision on January 5, 1982, and it was essentially a polemic against creationists, fundamentalists, and the literal interpretation of Genesis, declaring the act unconstitutional.[1]

Most creationists (and many others) believe that Judge Overton's decision was inexcusably biased and filled with numerous factual errors. At the same time, many were also disappointed with the defense as organized and presented by the office of the Arkansas Attorney General. The Creation Science Legal Defense Fund, with its outstanding creationist attorneys, Wendell Bird and John Whitehead, offered its services as a friend-of-the-court, but these were declined. Bird felt that the defense as a whole was half-hearted and disorganized. The media accounts clearly gave this

---

1. For the complete text of Judge Overton's decision, see "Creationism in Schools: The Decision in McLean versus the Arkansas Board of Education," *Science* (Vol. 215, February 19, 1982), pp. 934–943.

impression, but there is no doubt that these news reports were highly selective and distorted just as anticipated.[1]

An interesting aspect of the Arkansas trial was the strong suspicion that the decision was based neither on the merits of the creation law as written nor the testimony of the witnesses. Although the act specifically prohibited teaching the Bible, Judge Overton repeatedly insisted that was its intent:

> It was simply and purely an effort to introduce the Biblical version of creation into the public school curricula.[2]

Also, despite much excellent testimony and argumentation from the state's scientist witnesses, Judge Overton largely ignored them, making only a patronizing reference to the evidence of Robert Gentry's polonium haloes as a "minor mystery" and a similar reference to Chandra Wickramasinghe's ideas about the origin of life in outer space.

On the other hand, he made repeated reference to me and ICR, even though we had nothing whatever to do with either the Arkansas law or the trial itself. We did not even know Arkansas was considering such a law until it was passed. At the trial, neither I nor any other ICR scientist was a witness (I would have declined even if asked), but we were somehow very much present in influence.

> The term "scientific creationism" first gained currency around 1965 following publication of *The Genesis Flood* in 1961 by Whitcomb and Morris. . . . Perhaps the leading crea-

---

1. For a complete account of the trial and a critical analysis of Judge Overton's conduct of the trial and the text of his decision, see the book *The Creator in the Courtroom*, by Norman Geisler (Milford, MI: Mott Media, 1982), 242 pp. Dr. Geisler, a professor at Dallas Theological Seminary, was one of the defense witnesses. Most of his testimony was very good but this was not reported by the press. Unfortunately, the ACLU attorneys got him to acknowledge his evaluations of UFOs as demonic in origin, and the press had great sport with this.

2. "Overton decision," *Science, loc cit.,* p. 937.

tionist organization is the Institute for Creation Research. . . .
The ICR, through the Creation-Life Publishing Company, is the
leading publisher of creation science material.[1]

Judge Overton cited my own writings no less than ten times and
Dr. Gish and Dr. Bliss three times each! All of this had nothing to
do with the Arkansas law, and it seems entirely arbitrary for it to
be dragged in prejudicially in this manner. Naturally all these
citations were from statements in our writings confirming that we
believed the Bible and in God as Creator.

The Creation Science Legal Defense Fund played even a more
significant role in relation to the Louisiana law than it did in
Arkansas. The Louisiana law, also based somewhat on Ellwanger's
model law, except that it was more independent of Biblically-ori-
ented connotations, was passed and signed into law by Governor
David Treen on July 21, 1981.[2] The ACLU immediately announced that they would file suit in Louisiana, as they had just
done in Arkansas. However, on the day before the ACLU filed suit,
the CSLDF filed a preemptive suit, asking for a declaratory judgment that the act was constitutional. This made the creationists the
plaintiffs rather than the defendants, as they had been in Arkansas.
This was in December of 1981.

The next two years were occupied with a variety of legal ma-
neuvers by the ACLU trying in effect to get the Louisiana law
thrown out without a trial on constitutionality taking place at all.
All of these proved unsuccessful,and the case began to move
through the courts in 1984, eventually reaching the Supreme Court.
The U.S. Court of Appeals had ruled against the law by a narrow
8–7 margin.

---

1. *Ibid.*, p. 935. ICR is referred to by name at least four other times in the
    decision, not including citations from ICR literature.

2. The original sponsor of the Louisiana legislation, Senator Bill Keith, has
    published an interesting book on the background and prospects of the law
    and the corresponding lawsuit. See his book *Creation vs. Evolution-Scopes
    II, the Great Debate* (Lambertviile, NJ: Huntington House, 1982), 193 pp.

This was undoubtedly the most important creation/evolution trial to date, more important even than the Scopes trial. Top constitutional attorneys Wendell Bird and John Whitehead were lead attorneys for the state, while the ACLU had a bevy of eminent attorneys to fight the law. They also had a host of the most influential evolutionists in the country available as witnesses.

Wendell Bird undoubtedly made the most extensive study of this subject of any attorney practicing today and was uniquely qualified to lead the case for the creationists. John Whitehead had also been singularly successful in defending Christian schools, churches, and individuals against secular discrimination and governmental usurpation of religious rights.

Nevertheless, the Supreme Court declared the Law unconstitutional after rather cursory review, on June 19, 1987. The vote was 7 to 2. The majority opinion was written (not surprisingly) by liberal Justice William Brennan, who had stated in effect that the Constitution itself must "evolve" in step with society's evolutionary "progress". Brennan wrote that "the preeminent purpose for the Louisiana legislature was clearly to advance the religious viewpoint that a supernatural being created humankind." Thus the Supreme Court, with Brennan its spokesman, has ruled now that belief in a supernatural God is merely a narrow "religious viewpoint."

The two dissenting justices were Chief Justice Rehnquist and Anton Scalia, who wrote the minority opinion. Justice Scalia, who alone seemed to have carefully studied Wendell Bird's powerful brief, acknowledged that creationism could indeed be taught with purely scientific content and also that evolution was far from proven scientific fact.

Even Justice Brennan, however, did not go so far as to preclude the teaching of the *scientific* evidences for creation and against evolution, if this is done voluntarily and without a "religious purpose." Unfortunately, most school boards and school principals have interpreted the Court's decision as banning *any* teaching on creation from science courses in public schools. Clarification on this point may await some future court decision.

International Creationism

There are many statewide or local creationist societies that I have not tried to discuss in this book. However, all those that I know about are listed in Appendix C.

In this section, I want to review a remarkable development in the modem creation revival that was not experienced in earlier creationist movements. Dr. Ronald Numbers, eminent historian of science at Wisconsin University, has noted this:

> It is still too early to assess the full impact of the creationist revival sparked by Morris and Whitcomb, but its influence, especially among evangelical Christians, seems to have been immense. . . . Unlike the anti-evolution crusade of the 1920's, which remained confined mainly to North America, the revival of the 1960's rapidly spread overseas as American creationists and their books circled the globe. . . . Creationism had become an international phenomenon.[1]

I think one reason for this phenomenon has been the devastating effect of evolutionary teaching and its fruits in all these nations. Missionaries often tell us or write to us that the greatest hindrance to the spread of the gospel on the mission fields where they serve is not the native religion but evolutionism. Furthermore, evolution is the supposed scientific basis of Marxism and communism, which have engulfed so much of the world. The most effective antidote to these poisons is true scientific Biblical creationism.

The venerable *Evolution Protest Movement* (now the *Creation Science Movement)* of England has already been discussed in some detail. Although this organization antedates even *The Genesis Flood* by a quarter of a century, the modern revival of creationism

---

1. Ronald L. Numbers, "Creationism in 20th-Century America," *Science* (Vol. 218, November 5, 1982), pp. 543, 544.

Figure 30. Spurgeon Tabernacle

The famous Metropolitan Tabernacle in London, once the pulpit of Charles Haddon Spurgeon, in 1973 was the locale of a creationist challenge by the writer to 2200 Baptist pastors and leaders from many nations. The members of the present-day local congregation at the Tabernacle, with their pastor, Peter Masters, are enthusiastic creationists. Entrance to the Tabernacle is shown at left. At right, the writer is shown in conversation following his message there.

did help revive a rapidly dwindling EPM.

> Largely as a result of stimulation from America, including the publication of a British edition of *The Genesis Flood* in 1969, membership in the British Evolution Protest Movement, founded in 1932, quadrupled, and two new creationist organizations sprang into existence; the appearance of one, the Newton Scientific Association, coincided with a visit by Morris to England in 1973.[1]

Another significant British creationist society was formed more recently, and is still somewhat ambiguous with respect to literal six-day creationism and flood geology. This is the *Biblical Creation Society,* headquartered in Glasgow, Scotland, with Dr. E. H. Andrews (Professor of Materials Science at the University of London) as its first President. Frankly emphasizing Biblical

---

1. *Ibid.*, p. 544.

authority and Biblical arguments, supplemented, of course, by scientific evidence and arguments, the BCS rapidly grew to a membership over 800 since its beginnings in 1978. The Society has sponsored the publication of several books and a small quarterly journal. More recently, however, this society has begun to equivocate on the Biblical doctrine of recent creation.There are also several local creationist or quasi-creationist societies in the United Kingdom. A very active creationist scientist, Dr. A. J. Monty White, has written several books and for a while published his own newsletter. He has given many lectures in England, Wales, and Scotland, and has even conducted four seminars in France. Other significant creationist ministries in Great Britain are listed in Appendix C.

Ken Ham, of ICR, has recently established (on his own) a branch of Australia's Creation Science Foundation in England, in addition to conducting a number of Back-to-Genesis Seminars under CSF Sponsorship. Another increasingly active British organization is the Creation Resources Trust, headquartered in Somerset, and led by Geoff Chapman. It publishes interesting "Factsheets," and books, in addition to running a lending library and a mail-order book service.

Probably the most active creationist movement in Europe, at least outside of England, is in Holland.[1] Organized only in 1974, *Stichting tot Bevordering van Bybelgetrouwe Wetenschap* ("Foundation for the Advancement of Studies Faithful to the Bible") has had an amazing impact in this small but strategic nation. In addition to holding a number of national conferences on the Bible and science, this foundation started a bimonthly magazine, *Bybel en Wetenschap* ("Bible and Science"), edited by Dr. William J. Ouweneel, subscriptions to which had climbed to over 2,000 within its first two years.

---

1. W. J. Ouweneel, "Creationism in the Netherlands," in *Decade of Creation*, H. M. Morris and D. H. Rohrer, eds. (San Diego: Creation-Life Publishers, 1981), pp. 23–30.

Dr. Ouweneel is probably the leading creationist scientist in the Netherlands. After leaving his job as a research biologist with the Royal Netherlands Academy of Science late in 1976, he has been spending full time in various creationist ministries, including the writing of at least half a dozen major books on creationist science, with wide influence in his country and elsewhere. It is estimated that well over a hundred Dutch scientists are now active creationists.

An associated organization is *Evangelische Omroep* ("Evangelical Broadcasting Company"), which has produced many notable creationist television programs. Included among these was a six-man creation/evolution debate in 1977, attended by a full house of 1,100, each of whom paid over $6.00 to come. The creationist debaters were Dr. Duane Gish and Dr. Harold Slusher of ICR, along with Dr. Donald Chittick, a chemist then at George Fox College in Oregon. Three Dutch scientists defended evolution, but clearly lost the debate to the three American creationists. This organization produced the six excellent creation films, featuring Dr. A. E. Wilder-Smith, which were later modified for American use into the popular "Origins" series by the Films for Christ company.

These groups were even able to establish a creationist college in that same year (1977), with an engineer, Dr. Cornelius Roos, as president, and with Dr. Ouweneel as Chairman of the Faculty. It may be significant that all of these remarkable developments were preceded by translation into the Dutch language of three American creationist books—in chronological order *The Twilight of Evolution* (Henry M. Morris), *The Flood* (Alfred M. Rehwinkel), and *After Its Kind* (Byron C. Nelson).

There are also now active creationist organizations or periodicals functioning in Germany, France, Spain, Sweden, Italy, Russia, Poland, Finland, Italy, Greece, Belgium, and possibly other countries. ICR speakers, especially Dr. Gish, have lectured in many European countries and one or more ICR books are now available

Figure 31.
Dr. A. E. Wilder-Smith
Probably Europe's leading creationist scientist is Dr. A. E.
Wilder-Smith. Author of many
creationist books and holder of
three earned doctorate degrees,
Dr. Wilder-Smith has lectured
extensively in Switzerland, Germany, England, the United States,
and other countries, making a
great impact for the truth of
Scripture and, especially, scientific creationism.

in almost every European language. In addition to Dr. Ouweneel,
a number of other European creationist scientists have had much
influence in these developments, especially Dr. A. E. Wilder-
Smith, of Switzerland. Dr. Wilder-Smith, holding three earned
doctorates, was evidently the creationist pioneer in continental
Europe, with his *book Man's Origin, Man's Destiny,* published in
German in 1969. He has spoken in numerous churches, universities, and military posts, and authored many other outstanding
books, many of which are available in both English and German.

Lecture tours in Western Europe by Dr. John Whitcomb, beginning in 1975, have been of great significance in promoting
creationism in several key countries. His meetings have included
numerous churches, schools, and seminaries in England, Wales,
France, Germany, Switzerland, Belgium, Holland, Spain, Italy,
Luxemburg, Scotland, and Sweden. Most important has been his
influence and encouragement to Bible-believing creationist pastors, seminary students, and missionaries in all these countries.

Creationist efforts in modern France were primarily stimulated
by visits by John Whitcomb and the translation of one of his books
into French. A number of American creationist books are now
available in French, including three from ICR scientists, thus far.
Successful creation seminars have been held in Lausanne, Mar-

seilles, Paris, and other cities.

In Spain, Santiago Escuain has been very active, translating a number of ICR books and conducting creation seminars. Mr. Dante Rosso, an American engineer greatly burdened for Spanish-speaking peoples, has translated several ICR books into Spanish, some of which (e.g., *The Genesis Flood)* have been published, with others still awaiting a publisher.

Small creationist works have been started in Switzerland, Denmark, Bulgaria, Greece, Ukraine, Portugal, and Romania.

A fine creation museum was operated for a time by Dr. J. Scheven in Germany. A group of German creationist scientists, including Dr. H. W. Beck and Dr. H. Schneider, publish an outstanding German language magazine, *Factum,* edited by Bruno Schwengeler. Two Italian university professors, Guiseppe Sermonti and Roberto Fondi, published an excellent book against Darwinism in 1982, which has already gone through four printings.

The Biblical Creation Society of Sweden was formed in 1979 and has grown to a membership of 400. It publishes a quarterly journal, holds an annual creation conference and conducts a biennial summer   course on creationism, in addition to numerous lectures in schools and churches.

One of the most remarkable developments was in the Soviet Union. My little book *The Scientific Case for Creation,* first published in 1977, had been translated into Russian by Eugene Grosman, of the Slavic Gospel Association, and published there in 1981. Grosman, once a Russian atheist, had been converted to Christ in Moscow, then later emigrated to America. He had a great burden for the Russian people, and believed the greatest need was to provide them scientific evidence to refute the atheism and evolutionism with which they had been indoctrinated in school all their lives.

The book was judiciously distributed by Grosman in Moscow and soon began to bear fruit, several years before *glasnost.* A number of important scientists were won, including Dr. Dmitri

Kouznetsov, who has since become a real leader of scientific Biblical Creationism in Russia. A brilliant scientist, with three earned doctorates (M.D., Ph.D., D.Sc.) and numerous honors, he has since lectured widely in America on both creationism and his own scientific field of molecular genetics. He is now also an adjunct professor in the ICR Graduate School, and ICR is sponsoring some of his creation-supporting scientific research in Russia. He and other eminent Russian scientists have formed a very active association of Russian scientific creationists (membership over 185, as of 1992). He and Eugene Grosman (who also translated two other ICR books into Russian as a part-time ICR staff member) arranged three successful lecture tours in 1990 in Moscow for Dr. Duane Gish and Dr. John Morris, respectively, which reached many key audiences in the universities and scientific organizations there. Several other ICR books are being translated into Russian sponsored by Dr. Kouznetsov's Moscow Creation Science Association, which has been identified in Russia as a branch of ICR. There is also an active creation group at St. Petersburg University and in Ukraine.

With the decline of communism in eastern Europe, there have come many request for ICR literature in Poland, Czechoslavakia, Romania, and other countries. A window of opportunity has opened in these nations for the true gospel, and Christian creationists must take advantage of it while they can.

Thus, although creationist efforts in Europe are still small, they do seem now to be well-grounded and rapidly growing.

On the other side of the world, in Asia and the South Pacific, a number of active creationist organizations have emerged in recent years. Undoubtedly the most active and influential are in Australia and South Korea.

There have been various creationist organizations in Australia and New Zealand in the past, especially during the earlier days of the Evolution Protest Movement, when there were active branches in both countries. These had dwindled almost to the vanishing point by 1970, however. Of the newer organizations established in these countries (and there have been two or more in each), the most active is the *Creation Science Foundation,* centered in Queensland. Another, the *Creation Science Association* of South Australia, founded by Dr. Carl Wieland and others, later merged with the Creation Science Foundation.

The latter organization, founded only in 1978, has grown to the point that it currently (1993) has 14 employees, several of whom are well-qualified scientists who conduct creation seminars in schools and churches throughout the country. The original director, Ken Ham, moved to the United States in 1986 to join the ICR team, where he has been greatly used by God, as noted earlier. He still maintains close ties with CSF, however, and has spent a portion of each summer working in Australia with the team there. Dr. Wieland became Managing director of CSF on a full-time basis when Ken Ham left and, in spite of many difficulties, has led the organization in an outstanding ministry in Australia, with some 25 active support groups. Several other key scientists work with CSF. Dr. Andrew Snelling, a Ph. D. geologist and excellent researcher, has been full-time with CSF since 1983. He has also become an adjunct professor at ICR. The Creation Science Foundation publishes an excellent *Technical Journal* twice a year, edited by Dr. Snelling. It also publishes the colorful and highly professional quarterly magazine *Creation ex Nihilo,* edited by Robert Doolan, and now widely read in the United States and other countries, as well as Australia. The CSF has recently formed branches in England and New Zealand.

Scientists in the CSF have published several intriguing discoveries and studies, and even a number of books in recent years. Another Australian creationist of note is Dr. Clifford Wilson, archaeologist, psycholinguist, and prolific writer. Dr. Wilson has made numerous lecture tours in this country, and several of his books have been published by Creation-Life Publishers.

Interest had been growing in both Australia and New Zealand

Figure 32. Creation Science Foundation, Australia

The headquarters building of Australia's dynamic Creation Science
Foundation in Brisbane.

ever since a six-week intensive lecture tour which I made through-out New Zealand in 1973, including one lecture in Brisbane, Australia, while enroute to New Guinea. Dr. Gish made a similar New Zealand tour in 1975, Dr. Bliss in 1981, and Dr. Gish again in 1983. Dr. Gish, Dr. Slusher, Dr. Parker, Dr. Wilder-Smith, Dr. John Morris, Dr. Kurt Wise, Dr. Russell Humphreys, and Dr. Steve Austin, have all had lecture tours in Australia under CSF sponsor-ship.

The Korea Association of Creation Research was first organized in a dinner meeting in Seoul in August 1980, with Dr. Gish and myself present for counsel and assistance. This followed our par-ticipation in a large creation seminar held in connection with meetings of the Worldwide Evangelization Crusade of August 12-15 that year in Seoul. There were about 20 scientists involved at the beginning, and the organization grew rapidly. Invitations were sent out, with an accompanying letter from me on ICR letterhead, to many Korean scientists to attend an Inauguration Assembly on January 31, 1981. The assembly, and especially the speech by Dr. Young Gil Kim, Associate Professor of Materials Science at the Korean Advanced Institute of Science, received wide press and radio coverage. Dr. Kim was installed as President of the Association.

By April of that year, the Association had about 60 scientist members (with M.S. or Ph.D. degrees in science) and 60 sustaining members. It has been very active in conducting seminars, work-shops, and conferences on creationism in universities, schools, and hundreds of churches throughout Korea, and has had a great impact on the nation. A number of ICR books are available in Korean and the Korean Association itself has now published several books, including a biology textbook which may be adopted for use in Korean public schools.

The Korea Association now (1993) numbers also a thousand active creation scientists in its membership, and they are making a great impact in Korea. They are currently planning a large and

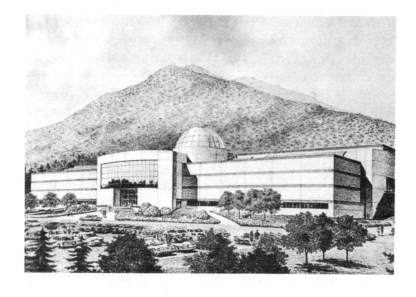

Figure 33. Creation Science Education Center in Korea

Architect's drawing of the large building planned by the Korea Association of Creation Research. Located 25 miles south of Seoul, it is
scheduled for 1994 opening.

beautiful Creation Research and Educational Center near Seoul.

A tenth-anniversary celebration was scheduled in Seoul in the summer of 1991 to commemorate a decade of outstanding Korean advance in nationwide creationist impact. Still under the leadership of Dr. Young Gil Kim, a large number of Korean scientists, as well as several guests from other countries (including Dr. Gish, Dr. Austin and Dr. John Morris from ICR) were invited to present papers at the convention. The Korean Association has even established branches in the United States in communities where significant numbers of Koreans dwell. Dr. John Morris also spoke at their 1993 convention.

The important nation of Japan has a small but effective creationist witness under the leadership of Dr. Masami Usami, with assistance from missionaries Carlton and Nathan Elkins. Dr. Usami is a highly respected Japanese medical doctor and professor, as well as an active soul-winning Christian. He and his son attended an ICR Summer Institute on Scientific Creationism at Christian Heritage College in 1977, in order to become better able to get the creationist message to Japan. He, along with many other Japanese Christian leaders and missionaries, are convinced this is a desperate need in intellectually and scientifically oriented modern Japan. Dr. Usami and several other Japanese leaders again attended an ICR Summer Institute in 1990, as well as the International Creation Conference in Pittsburgh.

Dr. Usami and his colleagues have, since 1978, been translating our ICR *Acts & Facts,* especially the "Impact" articles, into Japanese. Also they have translated and published my books *The Genesis Record, The Bible and Modern Science, and The Scientific Case for Creation,* as well as Dr. Parker's *From Evolution to Creation,* and *What is Creation Science?* co-authored by Dr. Parker and myself. They have established the Bible-Science Press of Tokyo for this purpose.

Other Japanese missionaries, especially John Schwab and the late Bud Chase, as well as Japanese pastors, especially Rev. Nobuji

Horikoshi, have also been very active in promoting creationism in Japan, the latter publishing an excellent book on creationism in 1983. Marvin Lubenow, author of the book *"From Fish to Gish,"* mentioned before in connection with the ICR debates, was invited by Japanese Christians to conduct an illustrated creationist lecture tour through Japan in 1980. His lectures and messages were very well received on many campuses and in many churches. Dr. Gish himself later made two very successful lecture tours in Japan.

Elsewhere in Asia, significant creationist organizations and ministries exist in Taiwan, India, Sri Lanka, Singapore, and Hong Kong, with significant literature and radio penetration into other nations, even Red China. In 1982, Dr. John Whitcomb's seminars in Manila twice attracted crowds of 3,300 people. He has also lectured in Taiwan, Singapore, Hongkong, Korea, and Japan.

The Creation Scientists' Forum of India was formed in June 1978, under the leadership of Professor H. Enoch, Dr. J. P. Azariah, and other Indian scientists. Its structure is patterned after that of the Creation Research Society and its activities after those of the Institute for Creation Research. Dr. Gish counselled with many of its leaders during his first six-week lecture tour through India in early 1983.

I have been particularly interested in the Hong Kong work since my lectures there in November 5-11, 1981. I spoke on a number of campuses and to strategic groups of educators and scientists. These meetings were sponsored by the *Schools for Christ Foundation* under the dynamic leadership of Dr. Paul Pang. The many Christian schools in this association are all dedicated to creationism and other aspects of true Christian education, as set forth in my book *Christian Education for the Real World,* which they had been using as a key guide book. With the current concern over the imminent return of Hong Kong to Chinese rule, many Hong Kong Christians are preparing to leave. However, Dr. Pang and his associates are committed to maintaining a center and witness for true Christian education, including especially creationism, there

Figure 34. Creationism in the Far East

Dr. Young Gil Kim is shown at upper left interpreting for the writer addressing a large gathering of students in Seoul. Shortly after this seminar, a very active society of Korean creationist scientists was formed, with Dr. Kim as president. Dr. Masami Usami, leader of Japanese creationists, is shown at lower left. Upper right photo shows a group of creationist educators in Hong Kong, while the photo at lower right shows the writer addressing a teachers' seminar organized by them.

after the takeover. They have recently formed an *Institute for Christian Education* to train teachers and serve as a center for Bible-oriented education in the future. They have also published a number of books and creationist student materials. In 1982, John Whitcomb also spent a week in Hong Kong, speaking to many college and seminary students and others. Dr. Richard Bliss has also lectured in Hong Kong, as well as in the Philippines.

Several opportunities have also been used to get the creation message into mainland China, and these are bearing fruit. The Chinese translation of Scientific Creationism has been judiciously distributed, and a 1993 Christian convention in Beijing, encouraged by the Chinese government will include at least one ICR speaker.

For some reason, our ICR ministry has had less contact with the Latin American nations than with those on more distant continents. However, Dr. John Whitcomb, Dr. Tom Barnes, Dr. Duane Gish, and I have lectured in Mexico, and Dr. Gish has lectured in various West Indies countries (Trinidad, Barbados, Guyana, and Puerto Rico). Dr. Bliss has held successful meetings in El Salvador and Dr. Gish in Honduras, Puerto Rico and the Caribbean.

There are small creationist societies (or centers) in Brazil, Argentina, Mexico, El Salvador, Dominican Republic, Puerto Rico, and possibly others. A number of our books have been translated into Spanish and Portuguese and are being used and distributed by missionaries and other Christians in the Latin American nations, so it is hoped this activity will soon increase. Some American scientists (e.g., Dr. Donald Chittick of Oregon, Tom Hendersen of Texas and Dr. John Meyer of Pennsylvania) have also conducted creation seminars at different locations in Latin America. In Peru, missionary Peter Hocking has conducted effective creation seminars, using ICR materials, in universities and other places. Dr. John Whitcomb has held creation seminars in Mexico (1967), Guatemala (1971), Argentina (1974, 1984), Brazil (1974, 1975, 1984, 1987), Ecuador (1984) and Haiti (1980). Dr. Larry Vardiman and Dr. Duane Gish have held meetings in Bolivia, and the Bolivian government is considering including creationism in its schools.

In North America, creationist activity in Canada has already been discussed at some length in previous chapters. We need only note here that creationists have been more active and productive in Canada than in probably any country except the United States, Australia and Korea. The various provincial Creation Science Associations (Alberta, Quebec, Saskatchewan, Ontario) are all loosely affiliated with the *Creation Science Association of Canada,* which is headquartered in Vancouver and serves also as the creationist association for British Columbia. As noted before, this was originally formed in 1967 as the Bible Science Association of Canada and was for several years affiliated with the Bible Science Association in the United States.

Each of these Canadian associations has its own interesting history, but I have not tried to include specific discussions of the state, provincial, or local associations in this country, so should not do so for Canada either. Various publishers, film companies, schools, and other institutions in Canada have been especially interested in creationism, and there also exist a number of local societies. One that warrants special recognition is the *International Christian Crusade,* a small organization located in Toronto, that has been functioning nearly 50 years. Its chief contribution has been the useful little handbook *Evolution,* written by Dr. John Howitt and issued through many editions since first published in the 1940s.

One interesting individual testimony coming out of Canada may be mentioned as indicative of the Lord's working in that great country. Christopher Chui was a scientist born and educated in Communist China, as an atheistic evolutionist. After migrating to Hong Kong to please his mother, several years later he became a Christian, but still believed in theistic evolution. While attending graduate school at the University of Toronto, he happened to hear my lecture on scientific creationism there in October 1974. He then became an ardent creationist and was instrumental finally in organizing the *Creation Science Association of Ontario,* which he served as president until moving to California a few years later. In California he founded and headed the *Creation Science Association of Orange County,* which is has been one of the most active local societies in this country. He has written a number of excellent creationist tracts and articles and has had a fine ministry.

One other great continent remains largely unreached, except through missionary use of creationist literature, and that is Africa. A small creationist group was formed in Nigeria in 1978 by a Christian geologist, David Afalyan, but he left shortly afterward for further study in this country. Dr. Mary Stanton, co-author of the ICR-sponsored textbook on world history, *Streams of Civilization,* has had much influence on the teaching materials in the schools of the Sudan and has incorporated a creationist approach into them. There have been significant local creationist outreaches through individual missionaries or pastors in Egypt, Kenya, and other countries. Dr. John Whitcomb has lectured on creationism in the Central African Republic, helping to establish a Biblical seminary there.

South Africa has long had much interest in creationism, but nothing much of an organized witness until the extensive lecture tours by Dr. Gish throughout that nation in 1983 and 1990. While he was there, a new creation association was formed under the leadership of biochemist J. C. Erasmus.

The Islamic nations have been difficult to reach, of course, in spite of the ostensibly creationist theology of the Koran. Nevertheless, there are significant creationist testimonies here and there in these countries, maintained by individuals who have been profoundly affected by the ICR literature reaching them. Such pockets exist especially in Turkey (where two ICR books have actually been translated and used there), Indonesia, Saudi Arabia (following lectures by Dr. Gish to the American community there), Morocco and Egypt.

A significant impact was made in Turkey by lectures there in

Istanbul by Dr. Gish and Dr. John Morris (already known there by virtue of his Ararat expeditions). The ICR scientists were invited by the Turkish government to lecture to an enthusiastic audience of 1500 Turkish students and professional men.

Finally, there is significant creationist interest in Israel, especially among Orthodox scientists following Dr. Gish's lectures at the university in Haifa. A Christian archaeologist who is also a graduate of Christian Heritage College, Gordon Franz, has also had an influence there. Interestingly, the ICR book *Scientific Creationism* is used as a textbook in a number of synagogue schools in this country, and many orthodox Jewish scientists have sent testimonies of endorsement for the ICR ministry.

Summary and Significance

It is obvious that this chapter has been able to take only a superficial look at the multitude of creation-oriented societies, organizations, and companies that have been established around the world in the past two decades (1971–1993). Many such organizations have not been discussed at all and even those that *have* been treated have been only lightly surveyed. In addition, I realize that the whole discussion is slanted somewhat toward those groups with which ICR scientists have had the greatest amount of contact.

Nevertheless, even the unequal treatment in this book makes it clear that the modern creation movement has reached unprecedented dimensions. As will be discussed in the next chapter, the anticreationist opposition has also become intensely strong and bitter but, whatever the final effect of this opposition will be, things will never go back the way they were before. The movement is far too widespread and varied, and there are too many people involved (including thousands of committed scientists), for the evolutionists ever to regain the obsequious submission of the public which they used to enjoy and abuse. The revelation of Scripture, the real facts of science, and all human experience refute evolution and support creation, and there are *multitudes* of people who *know* that today!

Furthermore, one should realize that there are hundreds of other organizations and institutions today that have incorporated strict creationism into their teachings (as a direct result of the impact of modern creationism), even though this is not their primary focus or ministry. Such organizations as the *Family Life Seminars* of Dr. Tim LaHaye, the *Education Research Analysis Service* of Mel and Norma Gabler, Jerry Falwell's *Old Time Gospel Hour,* the late Dr. Theodore Epp's *Back-to-the-Bible* organization, now headed by Dr. Woodrow Kroll,and scores of similar ministries are committed to literal creationism today. The same is true of multitudes of Christian schools and churches.

Even many organizations which do not specifically incorporate literal creationism into their tenets find that most of their member institutions are themselves committed to it in practice. This includes such large groups of Christian schools as the *Association of Christian Schools International,* headed by Dr. Paul Kienel, and the *American Association of Christian Schools,* founded by Dr. Al Janney.

Many Christian colleges also (Bob Jones University, Liberty University, Grace College, Cedarville College, Baptist Bible College, Masters College, Tennessee Temple University, Bryan College and others) are likewise committed now to strict creationism. The Transnational Association of Christian Schools already has over 60 post-secondary institutions affiliated with it, all committed to strict creationism. ICR has a list of over 150 post-secondary institutions (liberal arts colleges, Bible colleges and seminaries) that now take a stand on literal creationism. However, there is still a great deal of compromise on this vital issue among evangelical intellectuals, both theologians and scientists, as well as other professionals. This will be discussed briefly in the next chapter.

In this connection, there are a number of important Christian organizations which accept Biblical inerrancy and authority and which consider themselves to be creationist in doctrine (especially in their commitment to the special creation of the first man and woman), but which still refuse to accept the Biblical doctrine of *recent* creation, preferring instead to cling to the evolutionary doctrine of immense geological ages and to adopt the distorted exegesis of the day/age theory in Genesis.

Although many of these have made valuable contributions to Biblical Christianity and sometimes even to creationism, they are not really very sympathetic with the modern creation movement as discussed in this book, and so are not included within its purview. The same is even more true of Christian organizations which are comfortable with theistic evolution, such as the *Inter-Varsity Christian Fellowship, Youth for Christ,* and others, as well as most evangelical liberal arts colleges and publishing companies.

Regardless of all this, the creation movement is clearly here to stay. The final chapter will survey the current scene, especially the intensifying battle with evolutionary humanism and will also attempt to place it all in the perspective of future significance.

Chapter X

The Coming
Battle For Creation

In the preceding four chapters, the various organizations and individuals contributing most strategically to the modern creation movement have been reviewed, with an attempt to place them all in correct historical perspective. This is necessary for proper understanding of both present events and future prospects in the age long conflict between evolutionary humanism and theistic creationism.

Since this conflict is, indeed, intimately involved in the "conflict of the ages," as pointed out in the very first chapter, we should not be surprised to find it coming into climactic intensity as we approach the end of this present age. We have just shown that the creation movement is here to stay and, with great numbers of key young people becoming convinced creationists, it is certain to become stronger as time goes on, regardless of the outcome of current lawsuits and legislative actions. But the opposition inevitably will also become stronger and more bitter.

In this chapter, I want to review some of the more recent developments in the conflict, then attempt to anticipate what may happen in the near future, and finally try to place the entire creation movement—past, present, and future—in the context of its ultimate significance. The past is prologue, as they say, and it is inevitably true that one's concept of origins will determine his understanding of ultimate meanings and purposes.

Creation and Public Opinion

For a long time, the evolutionary establishment took little notice of the creationists. After the Scopes Trial (1925) and even more so after the deluge of propaganda accompanying the Darwinian Centennial Year (1959), the control of the schools and news media by the evolutionists seemed so secure that nothing could ever shake it. By 1970, however, the impact of the creation movement was at least making itself felt in the world of evangelical Christianity. Then, with the rapidly growing ministry of the Institute for Creation Research, especially with its wide-ranging and well-attended meetings and debates, as well as its many books and other literature, the decade of the seventies found creationism finally penetrating the consciousness and arousing the concern of the public at large—even the scientific and academic communities!

The national news media paid little attention to the creationists until the late seventies. The California textbook hearings, beginning in 1969 and continuing for several years, received some attention, as did the Tennessee creation law, passed in 1973 and declared un- constitutional in 1974. The various expeditions to Mount Ararat in the late sixties and early seventies did get considerable notice. After his 1972 expedition and the publication of his *Adventure on Ararat* book, John Morris appeared on many radio and television programs, most importantly the NBC *Today Show*, with an estimated viewing audience of 20 million. This was in April 1974. In addition to the Ararat project, he was able also to talk about the ICR work and the scientific case for creation in general. In September he appeared on the similar program in Canada, *Canada A.M.*

The first national science journal to give real attention to the creation movement was the *Biological Sciences Curriculum Study Newsletter,* edited by BSCS Director William V. Mayer. Its November 1972 issue was devoted almost entirely to an attack on the creation movement. After some little correspondence following this, Dr. Mayer rejected my challenge to debate him on the subject of the scientific evidence for creation versus evolution.[1]

We did begin to receive more and more *local* news coverage, in connection especially with our various debates and other meetings. The first really significant national article, however, was a front-page, center-column article in the *Wall Street Journal,* on June 15, 1979. It was unusually insightful and fair, for a newspaper article on creationism, most of which are badly distorted and misleading. The article particularly noted that "the creationists tend to win" the debates, and that they were "making progress." There were also reasonably fair articles in the September 1979 issue of *Bioscience, the Science Digest Special* for Winter 1979, the July 1979 issue of *Scientific American,* and the June 1, 1979, issue of *Science.*

In 1976, the Hollywood film company Sun Classics, Inc., issued its hit movie *In Search of Noah's Ark,* which was seen by millions of people. This included several segments featuring John Morris and other ICR scientists, including myself, and in general presented creationism and the Bible in a favorable light. The same was true of the television documentary, "In Search of Noah's Flood," narrated by Leonard Nimoy, and shown on scores of television stations across the country early in 1979.

As a result of such media exposure, in addition to all the direct influence of creationist literature and meetings, the public began to be more and more aware of the creation/evolution issue, including evolutionist control of the public schools. Furthermore, public opinion began to show up as strongly favoring creationist objectives.

So far as I know, the first actual polls of public opinion on the

---

1. "The Unanswered Challenge," in *Creation: Acts, Facts, Impacts,* Henry M. Morris, Duane T. Gish, and George M. Hillestad, eds. (San Diego: ICR Publishing Co., 1974), pp. 60–71. This was the only time I ever tried to arrange a debate by direct challenge. Dr. Mayer finally, in March 1984, agreed to debate Dr. Gish, in Evansville, Indiana. The results, predictably, were disastrous for the evolutionists.

subject were taken in California in 1973 and 1974. The first, in rural Del Norte County, found that 89% of the county's residents favored teaching creation in the schools (on a two-model, scientific basis, as ICR had proposed). The second, in the large metropolitan Cupertino Union district, showed that over 84% favored teaching both models and only 8% favored teaching evolution only. These were both based on random samples, with good statistical controls.

When the ICR Midwest Center was formed in 1975, one of its first projects was to begin a random telephone survey, not only in the Chicago area, but in many other places. This has continued for many years and, always, no matter where the survey was conducted (even on university campuses), it was found that well over 80% of the people desired to see creationism brought back into public school teaching.

Since these polls were all conducted by creationists, some evolutionists questioned their validity. However, a poll conducted by the *Tampa Tribune-Times* in Hillsborough County, Florida, in May 1980, found that 77% of the parents and 73% of the teachers wanted creation in the schools, with many of the rest undecided. Also, in March 1980, on page 52, the *American School Board Journal* reported that 67% of its readers (who are mostly school board members and school administrators) thought that creation should be taught in their schools. Then, in another unlikely group, *Glamour* magazine (August 1981, p. 29) found that at least 74% of its readers favored bringing creation back into the schools.

The most authoritative of all such surveys, however, was conducted on October 25-26, 1981, through a nationwide poll by the Associated Press/NBC News polling organization. The results were as follows:

"Only evolution should be taught"	8%
"Only creation should be taught"	10%
"Both creation and evolution should be taught"	76%
"Not sure which should be taught"	6%

Thus, nationwide, no less than 86% of our people in the United States believe that creation should be taught in their public schools. And this was in 1981, after generations of exclusive evolutionary indoctrination of themselves, their parents, and their children in the public schools! These were surprising statistics indeed.

It is also worth noting that a significant part of those who would like to see creation taught in the schools do not themselves believe in creation, but they do believe in freedom and fairness!

The Glamour magazine poll noted above also asked specifically whether its readers themselves believed in creation or evolution, and 54% indicated belief in creation. This is consistent with a 1979 Gallup poll, commissioned by the magazine *Christianity Today* and reported in its December 21, 1979, issue. This Gallup poll found that 51% of Americans believed in the special creation of Adam and Eve to start human life. Dr. Gallup found that, of the 20% of Americans who were "evangelicals," 88% believed in creation. This would mean that even 41% of non-evangelicals (Jews, Catholics, liberal Protestants, others) believe in creation.

An even more remarkable statistic, found in a 1982 Gallup poll, as reported in the San Diego *Union* on August 30 of that year, was that 44% of the American public agrees with this statement: "God created man pretty much in his present form at one time within the last 10,000 years." Atheists totalled 9%, theistic evolutionists or progressive creationists 38%, and undecided 9%.

Thus, in spite of over three generations of evolutionary brainwashing in the public schools, at least 51% of Americans now believe in special creation and 44% in *recent* creation! This is a remarkable development, and more recent polls continue to give similar results.

Evolutionists Sound the Alarm

It would seem right and reasonable for public schools and other public institutions to give at least equal consideration to creationism, in view of the creationist foundations of America and its original school system, the clear evidence that evolutionism is at least as much a religion as creationism, and the strong scientific case for creation. When the evidence of the polls is added to all this, demonstrating conclusively that an overwhelming majority of Americans want creation teaching restored to their schools, and that even a strong majority of school teachers and administrators think this should be done, then it is both amazing and frightening that the intellectual/educational establishment keeps resisting it, and doing it so successfully.

But this is not a simple question of democracy, or constitutionality, or scientific evidence—all of which would support creation if allowed to speak honestly. This is a spiritual battle, and the battle plans and tactics can only really be understood in spiritual terms. The primeval war against God the Creator still continues and may well be entering its final critical phases.[1]

Eventually the modern creationist revival had to be taken seriously. For a long time it was all but ignored; more recently it began to be ridiculed. Now it is being intensively and viciously opposed. At least we finally have their attention!

The first significant salvo in the current battle was fired by the American Humanist Association, in a 1977 Manifesto affirming that evolution is an accepted fact of science. This manifesto[2] was organized by Bette Chambers, president of the American Humanist Association, and sponsored by five famous evolutionary human-

---

1. See my book, *The Long War against God* (Baker Book House, 1989), for a fully documented account of the profound conflict of evolutionism against Biblical creationism that has been going on almost since the beginning of time.

2. "A Statement Affirming Evolution as a Principle of Science," *The Humanist* (Vol. XXXVII, January/February, 1977), pp. 4-5. Also, in the same issue, "Why a Statement Affirming Evolution," by Bette Chambers (p. 23). Dr. H. J. Muller had compiled a similar statement and list of signers, published in the *Bulletin of the Atomic Scientists* of February 1967, but it attracted little interest.

istic scientists: Isaac Asimov, Hudson Hoagland, Chauncey D. Leake, Linus Pauling, and George Gaylord Simpson. It was signed by 97 other leading scientists, and its main thrust was to insist on evolution and on "the fact that it is firmly established in the view of the modern scientific community." It also called on school boards, textbook publishers, teachers, and educational agencies to resist all efforts of creationists to have creation taught in the schools.

Among the signers were such well-known spokesmen as Preston Cloud, Edwin Colbert, Ernst Mayr, Barry Commoner, Norman Newell, Joseph Fletcher, Sidney Hook, Alfred Emerson, Nathan Horowitz, John A. Moore, Hampton Carson, and John T. Bonner. Their "Affirmation" was the lead article in an edition of *The Humanist* almost entirely dedicated to warnings against the "dangers" of creationism. It was sent to all the major school districts in the United States.

This special issue and manifesto of the American Humanist Association, which publishes *The Humanist,* seems to have propelled the AHA into a position of leadership in the anti-creationist cause. *The Humanist* magazine ever since has been devoting much space and emphasis to berating creationism in particular and Biblical Christianity in general.

Soon after this, there began a steady stream of attacks on creationism by the news media and evolutionary spokesmen in the schools and colleges. The first of a lengthy string of anti-creationist books appeared in 1977, written by Dorothy Nelkin,[1] a professor of sociology at Cornell University. Even though she had spent much time with us, and we had tried to show her every courtesy, and to explain as carefully as we could the ICR position, her book was still filled with factual errors,[2] as well as a badly distorted

---

1. Dorothy Nelkin, *Science Textbook Controversies and the Politics of Equal Time* (Cambridge, MA: M.I.T. Press, 1977), 174 pp.

2. For a listing of some of these and a brief critique of the Nelkin book, see my article, "An Inaccurate Critique of Creationism," in *Up With Creation,* D. T.

picture of ICR and the entire creation movement. These errors were then called to her attention, but she never acknowledged them nor did she correct them in a later updated edition of her book. Instead she has continued to combat creationism in papers, lectures, and testimonies, with the same old misunderstandings (if that is the right word). Nelkin acknowledged on the witness stand at the Arkansas creation trial that she is an atheist. At that, however, her treatment was less hostile than those of most writers whose articles and books were published after hers. Apparently a serious and concerted attack on creationism was beginning to be orchestrated.

Over the next few years, beginning about 1977, and still continuing, the number and virulence of anti-creationist articles accelerated rapidly. We have an extensive collection, far too many to discuss here. But just to give the flavor of these attacks, the following choice excerpts are taken from a few of these articles.

> But of all the recent manifestations of old-time religion, I can think of none more intellectually impertinent or socially and politically ominous than that of the Creation Research Society and its [sic] Institute of Creation Research, devoted to destroying the ideas of cosmic and organic evolution. The mischief that this organization is prepared to do to the life and earth sciences, particularly in elementary and secondary schools, staggers the scientific imagination.[1]

> These "creation-science" textbooks, if allowed in our schools, can only serve to increase that mental anguish by teaching that the *Genesis* gibberish is a legitimate scientific theory.[2]

Gish and D. H. Rohrer, eds. (San Diego: Creation-Life Publishers, 1978), pp. 130–134.

1. Delos B. McKown, "Close Encounters of an Ominous Kind: Science and Religion in Contemporary America," *The Humanist* (Vol. XXXIX, January/February, 1979), p. 4. McKown is Philosophy Department Chairman at Auburn University.

2. G. Richard Bozarth, "The Meaning of Evolution," *American Atheist* (February, 1978), p. 19.

Without a doubt humans and civilization are in sore need of the intellectual cleanness and mental health of atheism.[1]

Such questions are in one sense irrelevant because what is really in dispute is the effort of an aroused religious movement, whose leaders have made a deity out of a book, to make the larger society bow down before their totem .... The short answer is, yes, you're right, it is nonsense, and we are under no obligation to teach it in our schools.[2]

Creationism fails on all counts. It is biased, it is scientifically untestable, it is not predictive, and it is dishonest. Creationism does not qualify as science and should have no more standing in the scientific community or in the science classroom than does alchemy.[3]

The "scientists" in the movement do science as one does literary criticism, picking among facts and theories for ones that support a preexisting point of view—which in their case is a literal reading of Genesis—and either twisting whatever does not fit, or simply discarding it. Creationism is no more science than is astrology or palm-reading; it is William Jennings Bryan's know-nothingism in a lab coat.[4]

These quotations are essentially random samplings from a vast body of anti-creationist bombast published in recent years. It may be worth noting that only one of the authors of the five articles cited above is a scientist, and he was a graduate student. I didn't really notice this until after citing them, but it does seem to be a rule of thumb that non-scientist doctrinaire evolutionists tend to be

1. *Ibid.*, p. 30. This journal is published by Madalyn Murray O'Hair's American Atheist Association, headquartered in Austin, Texas.

2. John Skow, "Creationism as Social Movement," *Science 81* (Vol. 2, December 1981), p. 60. Skow is a free-lance journalist.

3. William Rogers, "Creationism is Not a Science," *Newsletter on Intellectual Freedom* (Vol. XXX, November, 1981). Rogers was a zoology graduate student.

4. Gene Lyons, "Repealing the Enlightenment," *Harper's* (April, 1982) p. 39. Lyons calls himself "an apostate English professor" (p. 74).

even more vitriolic in their anti-creationist polemics than evolutionary scientists.

There are plenty of both. In a remarkable bibliography of materials dealing with the creation/evolution question—almost all written from either an anti-creationist or neutralist point of view,[1] Lazar has the following totals:

Number of book citations	81
Number of monograph citations	50
Number of periodical article citations	697
Number of newspaper article citations	721
Number of debate citations	133
Number of directory citations	99

New books and articles attacking creationism seem to appear continuously these days. One of the most frustrating problems we face at the Institute for Creation Research is how to deal with this stream of anti-creationist literature. There's hardly a day's mail that doesn't bring at least one letter from some distant town, with an enclosed newspaper or journal article promoting evolution or fighting creation, urging us to write a reply.

We have, indeed, written many such replies, but we can't begin to answer all of them—the number is far too great. Furthermore, more often than not, the publication refuses to publish our reply even when we take the time and effort to write one. Not infrequently, even when the editors themselves offer us the chance to reply, they change their minds once the reply is written. Or they may condense it in such a way as to delete or distort its main arguments. Thus we have, with only occasional exceptions,

---

1. Emie Lazar, *Creation-A Critical Bibliography* (San Francisco: Privately published, 2nd ed., Nov. 1983), 145 pp. These totals appear on the final page (p. 145). See also an extensive listing (over 300 items) in "A List of Selected References on Creationism," *in Journal of Geological Education,* by James H. Shea, Vol. 32, 1984, pp. 43-49.

stopped trying to reply at all.[1] These articles almost never contain any argument or evidence that we haven't already dealt with quite adequately in one of our books, but of course the problem is getting people to read them.

Creationists have been under attack not only from evolutionist writers, of course, but also from radio and television producers and commentators. The number of local radio and television programs dealing with the creation/evolution issue, usually in an attempt to discredit creationism, is impossible even to estimate. ICR scientists alone have participated in hundreds of both.

Of greater significance have been a number of national television programs. Probably the most deceptively harmful attack was on Walter Cronkite's *CBS Evening News* on March 9, 1980. Cronkite and his staff smeared the creation movement, including ICR, as simply a fundamentalist pressure group trying to force their antiquated religious beliefs on the public schools. This was after we had spent two days with his film crew, trying to cooperate in every way possible. They took extensive footage in our classes and in the Museum, as well as of personal interviews with Dr. Gish and others—especially with me showing the scientific evidence for creation. None of this was included in the program, the whole purpose from the beginning having been merely to brand us as religious eccentrics.

Essentially the same experience was repeated with Sylvia Chase and ABC's 20/20 program, shown on February 5, 1981. More details of these two national television "exposes," are given in one of our biennial anthology volumes.[2]

---

1. I tried to deal with the most frequent and most hurtful of the false claims and charges found in these attacks in a small booklet, *Creation and Its Critics* (*San* Diego: Creation-Life Publishers, 1982), 31. pp. More recently (1993) ICR has published a 451 page book by Dr. Duane Gish, *Creation Scientists Answer Their Critics*, in which the main arguments of the more important critics have been refuted.

2. *Creation: The Cutting Edge*, Henry M. Morris and Donald H. Rohrer, eds.

An even more flagrant distortion was produced by the Public Broadcasting System in a program aired nationwide in July 1982,[1] For example, a series of segments were shown of Dr. Gish giving scientific arguments for creation, but interjected between them were segments with Dr. Richard Doolittle belittling Dr. Gish's statements, one after another. To the viewing audience, it looked as though the two were having a debate, but the fact was that Dr. Gish had no idea that Dr. Doolittle was on the program at all. This fraudulent presentation was—at least in effect, if not in intent—a transparent attempt to refurbish Dr. Doolittle's reputation after his devastating defeat in a formal debate with Dr. Gish at Liberty Baptist College the previous year, on October 12, 1981.[2]

There have been a few major television programs, however, that were more objective in their presentations. This was true in the case of the *CBS Sunday Morning Show*[3] and the British Broadcasting Corporation's *Man Alive,*[4] taped on the Christian Heritage College campus on May 26, 1982.

With a few noteworthy exceptions, however, the media coverage, both in the press and on the air waves, has been non-factual and distorted, almost always one-sided and often even sarcastic and insulting, in its attitude toward creationism and creationists in general, and to ICR in particular. And since we have not had either the time to respond to these hundreds of attacks, nor access to the media even when we do try to respond, it has been for us mostly a lesson in patience and faith.

(San Diego: Creation-Life Publishers, 1982), pp. 216–220.

1. "PBS Telecast Typifies Establishment Attack on Creation," ICR *Acts & Facts* (Vol. 11, September 1982), p. 1.

2. "5000 Hear Gish-Doolittle Debate in Virginia," in *Creation: The Cutting Edge* (San Diego: Creation-Life Publishers, 1982), p. 200.

3. "CBS Sunday Morning Show Gives Fair Treatment to ICR," *op cit.,* (November 23, 1980), pp. 218–219.

4. "Unique BBC Television Debate Features ICR," ICR *Acts & Facts* (Vol. 11, August 1982), p. 5.

Organized Anti-Creationism

In spite of the barrage of anti-creationist articles and programs that followed the *Humanist* affirmation of 1977, the creationist movement continued to grow stronger. Bills requiring a two-model approach in the public schools had been introduced in the legislatures of almost half the states and, since this was clearly what the public wanted, the academic establishment became more and more alarmed. All across the country, it had become obvious that the scientific creation/evolution debates were resulting in gains for the creationists, so it became increasingly difficult to find evolutionists willing to debate. But this very reluctance, when publicized on the many campuses where student organizations had tried unsuccessfully to get any of the local faculty to participate in a debate, also resulted usually in a victory-by-forfeit for creationism.

It was not until 1979 or 1980 that evolutionists really began to take the creationists seriously enough to try to develop an organized program of anti-creationist activities. Wayne Moyer, who was then Executive Secretary of the National Association of Biology Teachers,[1] began to prepare and circulate a regular anti-creationist newsletter, seeking to alert the NABT membership to the creationist threat.

Soon after this, a more formal quarterly journal entitled *Creation/Evolution* was initiated under the formal auspices of the American Humanist Association, particularly its San Diego representatives. Three of the latter—Dr. William Thwaites, Dr. Frank Awbrey, and Fred Edwords—have since achieved more eminence in this new field of anti-creationism than they had ever been able to reach in their own fields.

Why the San Diego Humanist Society became so active in fighting creationism I don't know, though it surely had something

---

1. In 1983, Dr. Moyer joined the staff of Norman Lear's ultraliberal "People for the American Way" organization, to carry on the anti-creationist and anti-fundamentalist agenda of Lear and his television media cohorts.

to do with the proximity of ICR and the need to try to discredit us on a regular basis. Drs. Thwaites and Awbrey are on the genetics faculty at San Diego State University, and we first heard of them when they, in effect, challenged Dr. Gish and me to a debate on the SDSU campus, in April 1977.

We had already held one debate there, in 1976, with two other evolutionary biologists, and it had proven such an embarrassment to the entire campus evolutionary establishment that some sort of rematch was needed. Thwaites and Awbrey proceeded to make a diligent study of the creationist literature and debate tapes and felt they could redeem the evolutionist cause through a second debate.

They did, indeed, make a better case, at least in our judgment, than any previous evolutionist debaters had done, but most people in the audience still felt the creationists had won. Still later, they participated in a debate with Dr. Gish and Dr. Parker,[1] and then for three years in a sort of prolonged classroom debate with the entire ICR science staff. They organized a regular semester course on "Creation versus Evolution," to be offered as an elective on the SDSU campus and invited us to participate in it, even asking us to provide questions for our part of the exam. The format would be to have a creationist speak on Tuesday, then Awbrey or Thwaites on Thursday. They attended our lectures but, with rare exceptions, none of us had time to attend theirs, so we did not hear their rebuttals.

This seemed to most of our staff to be a worthwhile project, although I didn't like the idea myself (the evolutionists would always get the last word, the class was small, it took much ICR staff time, and ICR received no stipend for this teaching service). Anyway, we did it for three years and apparently did get a few converts to creationism—one or two were even won to Christ as a result. However, Drs. Thwaites and Awbrey, of course, made the

---

1. For more detailed accounts of these and other ICR debates, see the book previously mentioned, *From Fish to Gish*, by Marvin Lubenow.

claim that most of the students became stronger evolutionists, and they got much national publicity when they later presented a paper making this claim at a national convention of the American Association for Advancement of Science.

As far as philosopher Fred Edwords was concerned, he also has made a sort of mini-career debating creationists. He was president of the San Diego Humanist Society when he and the Society's vice president, physicist Philip Osmond, challenged Dr. Gish and me to a debate. They clearly lost the debate, but Edwords has kept at it, debating Dr. Gish and others at various times and places since. He achieved national recognition of a sort and has moved to Buffalo, where he was made Administrator of the American Humanist Association, writing a regular anti-creationist column for *The Humanist* magazine.

The best evolutionist debater to surface to date, however, has been Dr. Kenneth Miller, biologist at Brown University in Providence, Rhode Island. The evolutionists claim that his debate with me in April 1981 was the turning point in the current evolution/creation warfare.

It was obvious that, unlike most of our opponents, he was exceedingly well-prepared, having read most of our books and studied our tapes. He had a multitude of slides and the most modern projection equipment. He is handsome in appearance, charismatic in manner, and very glib of speech. His most effective ploy, however, was evidently based on advice given in a then soon-to-be-published article by Dr. David H. Milne,[1] who had debated Dr. Gish some months previously and was profoundly convinced he had won his own debate. That advice was to parade as rapidly as possible a long series of evolutionary claims and anti-creationist charges, far too many for the creationist opponent to have time to answer. On a university campus, already brain-

---

1. David H. Milne, "How to Debate with Creationists—and 'Win,'" *American Biology Teacher* (Vol. 43, May 1981), pp. 235–245.

washed in evolutionary claims, such dogmatic assertions would sound convincing, even without evidence, whereas creationists necessarily would have to explain and document their assertions in some detail to be convincing.

Miller employed this oratorical device with great skill, and no doubt many in the audience thought he won the debate. The student paper, however, surprisingly wrote it up as more or less even. The real facts, of course, are that he neither gave any real evidences for evolution nor gave any real answers to my evidences for creation. But he was, indeed, an effective demagogue on the platform.

I have since debated him once more, and Dr. Gish has debated him twice. In addition, the two of us debated him and Dr. Milne at the University of Arizona, before what was probably the second most unruly audience we have encountered (I think the worst was at the University of Texas). Miller is today considered by most evolutionists to be their most effective champion in a debate, and many others started using his techniques, slide collections, etc. They still don't have any *real* evidence, of course, but at least they are taking the issue seriously and are collaborating with each other in attempting to stop the creationist revival.

Another important organizational step was taken by Dr. Stan Weinberg of the National Association of Biology Teachers. In December 1980, he initiated what are now called "Committees of Correspondence," local groups of committed evolutionists who will do battle for evolutionism whenever creationism appears in any kind of organized, local effort.[1] By 1982 many of these were well organized and quite active, and we began encountering their activities, both directly and indirectly, with increasing frequency. Among other things, Dr. Weinberg, who is President of the National Committees of Correspondence, began publishing another

---

1. Stanley Weinberg, "Committees Active against Creationism," *Transactions, American Geophysical Union* (Vol. 64, August 23, 1983), p. 514.

anti-creationist periodical, five to nine times yearly. There were 55 committees in 48 states and four Canadian provinces as of 1984.

Another very significant organizational step was taken in the fall of 1981, when most of the societies, organizations, and other groups most vitally concerned to oppose creationism all agreed to work cooperatively together to destroy the movement. Just before the Arkansas creation trial was scheduled to be held, leading evolutionists organized a number of important meetings for the purpose of planning future anti-creationist strategies. These were all high-level "invitation-only" conferences, and we have access only in limited degree to accounts of the proceedings. What we do have indicates the deadly seriousness with which these people view the issue (I only wish that Christian people could somehow be awakened to view it with the same seriousness!).

One of the meetings[1] was held at the John F. Kennedy Library in Boston, at a conference on the humanities sponsored by Northeastern University and the National Endowment for the Humanities. A panel deploring creationism featured such leading intellectuals as Stephen Jay Gould, the Marxist geology professor at Harvard, Dorothy Nelkin, the atheist sociologist at Cornell who had written the first modern anti-creationist book, Warren Hutchison, a Harvard Divinity School professor, and many others of similar fame and faith.

An even more significant gathering was organized by Wayne A. Moyer, then Executive Director of the National Association of Biology Teachers.[2] The meeting was held at the headquarters of the National Education Association (NEA) in Washington, and also included delegates from the National Council of Churches, the American Humanist Association, Americans United for Separation of Church and State, the American Association for Advancement

---

1. Patrick McQuaid, "Scientists are Chastised for Attracting Attention to Creationists' Ideas," *Education Week,* November 9, 1981, p. 6.

2. Alex Heard, "Educators, Scientists, Clergy Form Network to Get Out Message," *Education Week,* November 9, 1981, p. 6.

of Science, and various other key organizations.

This was an odd assortment—the atheists of the AHA, the "Christians" of the National Council, the "teachers" of the NEA, along with the evolutionary scientists of AAAS and NABT! The only glue that could bind such diverse groups together would have to be hatred of the doctrine of special creation.

A still more important meeting was held the very same week (week of October 19, 1981), also in Washington, at the headquarters of the most prestigious of all organizations of scientists, the National Academy of Sciences. The organizations represented at this auspicious convocation were as follows:

American Humanist Association
National Science Teachers Association
American Museum of Natural History
American Institute of Biological Sciences
Smithsonian Institution
American Association for Advancement of Science
National Association of Biology Teachers
American Society of Biological Chemists
American Geological Institute
Federation of American Societies for Experimental Biology
American Anthropological Association
Biological Sciences Curriculum Study
National Cancer Institute
National Academy of Sciences
University of California at Berkeley
University of California at Riverside
State University of New York
University of Massachusetts
University of Kentucky

The delegates to this convocation developed a long list of measures that should be taken to combat creationism. The Executive

Director of the Assembly of Life Sciences of the National Academy of Sciences prepared a report of the meeting for circulation to the various organizations involved,[1] but this is not generally available. I was able, through one of our supporters, to obtain a copy, however, and have prepared an analysis and discussion of it, as included in one of my books.[2]

There have been other such meetings, undoubtedly including many of which we are unaware. The American Civil Liberties Union, for example, seems to be rather closely involved with all anti-creationist activities, especially those which relate to public schools. In an emotionally charged fund-raising appeal for the ACLU, the prolific scientist-author, atheist Isaac Asimov, said:

> We must be prepared for the long and costly battle of challenging every creationist statute in every state in which it is introduced. . . . As a fellow advocate for science, I urge you to consider giving the ACLU the most generous contribution you can possibly afford to help it wage this most important, historic legal battle.[3]

In this, and in other anti-creationist tirades, Asimov, who boasted (literally) of having authored over 400 science or science fiction books (and even developed his own set of scientific terminology and principles for his fictional worlds) called creationists "an army of the night," among other colorful pejoratives. He persistently refused to debate any creationist scientist, however, except for one magazine debate with Dr. Gish,[4] in which he came in a distant second.

---

1. Alvin G. Lasen, "Summary Report: Meeting on Creationism-Evolutionism" (National Academy of Sciences, October 19, 1981), 6 pp.

2. Henry M. Morris, *Evolution in Turmoil* (San Diego: Creation-Life Publishers, 1982), pp. 135–139.

3. Isaac Asimov, *Fund Appeal Letter for the American Civil Liberties Union,* March 1982, 4 pp.

4. The Genesis War," Debate between Duane Gish and Isaac Asimov. *Science Digest* (Vol. 89, October, 1981), pp. 82–87.

In a later fund-raising letter for the ACLU, Asimov, who later served as President of the American Humanist Association until he died in 1992, had said in effect that they would fight any creationist action at any level.

> Now the movement to force sectarian religious doctrine into the public schools has taken a new and dangerous turn. Countless efforts are being made by creationists to push their fundamentalist textbooks and views on local school boards. There are 26,000 local school districts in the United States and it is an overwhelming responsibility to monitor them all and to be prepared to act when the assault comes.[1]

The strategy apparently agreed on was that, whenever creationism appears in a given community, the nearest Committee on Correspondence would go into action—pressuring the local news media, school board, even the churches—to repudiate it. If this fails, and a local creationist directive or ordinance is successful, then the ACLU would be prepared to challenge it in court.[2]

This intimidation tactic has been very successful, and any political approach that would force creationism to be taught in public schools has at present (1993) essentially been placed on "hold." The polls have clearly demonstrated that Americans want creationism back in their schools. In the meantime, however, legislation and litigation have not yet aided creationist efforts, and probably this situation will continue.

By no means does this mean, however, that the creation revival has stopped, with evolutionists winning the battle. Evolutionists

---

1. Isaac Asimov, *Fund Appeal Letter for the ACLU,* March 1983, 4 pp.

2. The most recent such threat, (1993) receiving national media coverage, was against the Vista, California, School Board, which was considering allowing scientific creationism to be discussed as a possible alternative to evolutionism. The ACLU and its cohorts vigorously objected even to allowing any negative evidence against evolution to be introduced with no reference to creation or intelligent design! Evolution has, indeed, become a sacred cow to these bigots.

themselves are well aware that creationism—as well as Biblical Christianity in general—is alive and healthy, growing stronger all the time.

> The creationist movement is gaining momentum in the United States. . . . With the emergence of national conservative religious groups, such as Moral Majority, as participants in the creationist campaign for equal time, local efforts have the potential of being very successful.[1]

Even if the public schools continue to bar creationism, the Christian school movement is burgeoning, and practically all of the new Christian schools (this would not usually be the case with the older parochial schools, however) are creationist schools. In fact, that is one main reason why they are being formed in the first place.

It should not be forgotten that President Reagan himself had gone on public record as favoring creation and believing the Bible.[2] And despite all the frantic efforts of the educational establishment, the message of creation is even reaching the biology teachers in the schools. A survey and statistical study by a Cornell University graduate student for her Master's thesis, discovered the following encouraging facts.

> 96% of all biology teachers have read some creationist literature;
>
> 16% of all biology teachers have attended an ICR seminar;
>
> 50% of all biology teachers have attended some creationist presentation.

The above figures, however, may be skewed to some degree, since 45% of the questionnaires returned and used in the analysis were from teachers in Christian schools, with 55% in public

1. Dean R. Fowler, "The Creationist Movement," *American Biology Teacher* (*Vol.* 44, December 1982), p. 542.

2. "Republican Candidate Picks Fight with Darwin," *Science* (Vol. 209, September 12, 1980), p. 1214.

schools.[1] With all necessary allowances, however, the figures are still surprisingly high. Other interesting results include the following:

> The two-model approach to teaching origins is actually being used by 29% of public school teachers and 93% of Christian school teachers;

> Man was specially created, according to 18% of public school teachers and 98% of Christian school teachers.

The above statistics need to be weighed into the balance lest Christians and creationists abandon too quickly the hope that even the public schools can yet be reached for God and the truth of creation. There are, in fact, now at least two[2] organizations of Christian teachers in the public schools trying to maintain a witness there for Christ and the Word of God.

In any case, it is clear that the battle lines are being drawn. Creationism is stronger than it has been for over a century, but evolutionary humanism is not about to give up. The humanists have even published another manifesto, following their two famous declarations of 1933 (when the American Humanist Association was formed) and 1973. This latest one was published in the first issue (October 1980) of *Free Inquiry,* a new humanist magazine edited by Dr. Paul Kurtz, a prominent AHA leader and philosophy professor at the State University of New York at Buffalo. Kurtz drafted the statement, which was signed by such atheistic stalwarts as Isaac Asimov, B. F. Skinner (the famous

---

1. Pamela Ramsay, *A Comparison of Christian and Public School Biology Teachers' Beliefs about the Nature of Science and Creation/Evolution Issues* (M.S. Thesis, Cornell University Graduate School, Ithaca, NY 1983), 170 pp.

2. These are: (1) National Association of Christian Educators, P. O. Box 3200, Costa Mesa, CA 92626; (2) Christian Educators Association, 1410 W. Colorado Blvd., Pasadena, CA 91105. Both organizations are firmly Biblical in position. Of the two, the first (NACE), under Dr. Robert Simonds, is the more aggressive in combating the teaching of evolutionism and humanism in the schools.

Harvard psychologist), Sir Francis Crick (co-discoverer of DNA), Kai Nielsen (Head of Philosophy at Calgary University), Dora Russell (widow of Bertrand Russell), Albert Ellis (sexologist and sex therapist), Joseph Fletcher (the famous situation ethics and "death-of-God" theologian), Ernst Nagel (Columbia University philosopher), Sir Raymond Firth (anthropologist at the University of London), Milovan Djilas (former vice-president of Yugoslavia), and many others.

The document was entitled "A Secular Humanist Declaration." Among its affirmations are the following:

> Secular humanism places trust in human intelligence rather than divine guidance;

> Human beings are responsible for their own destinies—they cannot look toward some transcendent Being for salvation;

> We deplore the efforts by fundamentalists . . . to invade the science classrooms, requiring that creationist theory be taught to students.

Also indicative of the coming battle is the following quotation (now well-circulated among fundamentalists) from a recent prize-winning humanist essay:

> I am convinced that the battle for humankind's future must be waged and won in the public school classroom by teachers who correctly perceive their role as the proselytizers of a new faith: . . . The classroom must and will become an arena of conflict between the old and the new . . . the rotting corpse of Christianity, together with all its adjacent evils and misery, and the new faith of humanism. . . .[1]

Lester Mondale, brother of the former vice-president, even says that the God of the Bible is a "false god."

> Although I sympathize with Elijah's zeal in exposing false gods, I must observe—and herein lies my dissent—that Elijah's

---

1. John J. Dunphy, "A Religion for a New Age," *The Humanist* (Vol. 43, January/February 1983), p. 26.

Yahweh is also false. . . . What holds for the typical godhead Father holds also for the Son. . . . I feel certain that, in holding fast to the standards, values, and culture by which we are driven to judge false gods as false, we are vastly closer to the moral character a real Supreme Being would be likely to exemplify were He(?) to overcome the world with an authentic First Coming![1]

Such blasphemy seems to look even beyond humanism and atheism. Mondale is waiting for a "god" who is the antithesis of the true God, and will no doubt be ready to believe his Lie when he comes.

Attack on the ICR Graduate School

The broad opposition to scientific creationism reached its greatest intensity thus far in a concerted attack on the ICR Graduate School (ICRGS) during the period 1987-1991. This school had been operating since 1980, with the "Approval" rating of California's Office of Private Post-secondary Education (OPPE) and its successor agency, the Private Post-secondary Education Division (PPED). In fact, officials of the agency seemed for the first seven years to regard ICRGS as one of the most deserving of its "Approved" schools. The "Accredited" rating is a step higher, but this rating is normally administered by one of the regional accrediting agencies rather than the state—in California, the Western Association of Schools and Colleges (WASC). Because of the fact that WASC is largely committed to a secular educational philosophy (as clearly shown in the experiences of Christian Heritage College with WASC), ICRGS had opted not to consider possible affiliation with WASC at all. For our purposes, the state's "Approval" rating was all we needed or wanted. This was adequate for the needs of our school, and the lack of accreditation with WASC has never

---

1. Lester Mondale, "False Gods," *The Humanist* (Vol. 44, January/February 1984), pp. 33, 34.

been a significant hindrance to our graduates.

However, the very existence of the ICR Graduate School, with its well qualified science faculty, was like a bone in the throat of the educational and scientific establishments, since it was the only science graduate school in the country teaching science entirely within the framework of full commitment to Biblical inerrancy and special creation as taught in the Bible.

Accordingly when anti-creationist forces got fully organized, as described in the preceding section, they soon began to aim especially at the ICR Graduate School. The nationwide network of Committees of Correspondence obtained financing from the Carnegie Foundation and other sources, and established what is now euphemistically called the National Center for Science Education, dedicated specifically to the eradication of scientific creationism, with Eugenie Scott as Executive Director. Dr. Scott was (and is) a staff member at the University of California at Berkeley. With the establishment of the NACE office at Berkeley, that campus became a stronger center of anti-creationism than ever.

About this same time Bill Honig, Superintendent of Public Instruction in California began his own anti-creation crusade. Honig had been first elected in 1982, then reelected in 1986. Honig was neither a scientist nor an educator by training, but had a J.D. from Berkeley and limited experience as a superintendent of a small school district in the San Francisco area. He was essentially unknown in the state when he ran for the office, but had heavy financial backing and somehow managed to win. Although he is Jewish, he does not practice that religion (or any religion, so far as we know). He was evidently much involved in the famous "Berkeley scene" as a graduate student in the Berkeley law school in the sixties, and seems at least amenable to the current New-Age emphasis there and in many California public schools.

Whatever the reason, he and his associates —both at Berkeley and in his department in Sacramento—began a strong push to saturate California's schools with evolutionism. They were soon able to get a new Science Framework adopted for all California's public schools, requiring evolution to be taught exclusively as a scientific fact and to permeate the curricula in all fields. ICR strongly opposed this, of course, and this may have incited him to try to destroy ICRGS soon afterwards.

A more obvious reason for this latter vendetta, however, was the strong campaign against ICRGS orchestrated by the nationwide Committees of Correspondence, through their newly formed National Center for Science Education. A national campaign of slander against us soon generated what one state official called a "two-foot stack of outrage" in his files demanding that ICRGS be closed.

In 1987-88, department officials began insisting that we cease calling our degrees by scientific names. When it was time for a "re-approval" evaluation, the State fielded a site visitation team in August 1988, hoping they would recommend denial of the "Approved" rating, even though the school was greatly improved over what it had been in 1981 when approval was first granted.

However, the team voted 3 to 2 in our favor. Normally that would have been sufficient. One member of the committee, however, was a strong anti-creationist and anti-ICR professor who had lobbied to get himself on the team, and a second was equally prejudiced against creationism. When he was outvoted, he sent a bitter "minority report" to Honig. This gave Honig the leverage to persuade one of the committee members (a Stanford University professor) to change his vote, thus producing a negative majority. The sole basis for the vote switch, as stated in the letter written by Honig's attorney and signed by the professor, was that it had been rendered unconstitutional (based on a misrepresentation of the 1987 Supreme Court decision on the Louisiana Creation law) to teach science in a creationist context. Honig's attorney stated that the State could not allow a creationist institution to grant science degrees even though it met all academic and other requirements.

This whole procedure was so unethical, however, and the constitutional issue so distorted, that the Honig clique knew they were on weak ground, and so resolved to find other means for closing the school.

Consequently a second evaluation team was sent out in August 1989, after careful screening to include the most doctrinaire anti-creationists, three of whom had been recommended by anti-creationist lobbyists. This one came back with a 4 to 1 majority for closing the school, the ostensible reason being that our programs were not "comparable" to other schools. Various weaknesses were cited (e.g., more faculty needed, more books in the library, better research theses by the students, more elective courses, bigger laboratories).

These criticisms (actually both wrong and irrelevant) should be placed in proper context, however. This is best done by citing the final conclusion of their report, which stated that, even if all weaknesses were corrected, the school still should be denied its approval as long as it taught its science courses in anything but an evolutionary context! It was also significant that all four of the men voting against us were notoriously anti-creationist professors from large state universities, obviously inappropriate selections to do a "peer review" on a small private school like ICRGS, but perfect for the hatchet job the establishment wanted. One had signed Humanist Manifesto II with its anti-creationist creed; one had written an article against creationism; one had disparaged ICR while debating an ICR educator; one had served a term as president of the Society for the Study of Evolution. Honig proceeded then to issue his intent to deny our reapproval.

Since this treatment was a flagrant denial of our civil rights, academic freedom, freedom of speech and freedom of religion, we decided to file a federal lawsuit against Honig and his department, to get his ruling reversed. Otherwise, if they could succeed in preventing ICR from teaching science in a creationist framework, they would undoubtedly proceed to do the same in other Christian schools and colleges. The precedent could eventually prove lethal

Figure 35.
Attorney Wendell Bird
The nation's top legal authority on creationism in relation to First Amendment law, Wendell Bird, J.D., was lead attorney in I.C.R.'s victorious legal battle against the California Department of Public Instruction.

to Christian education everywhere, if allowed to stand.

As one of the nation's top First Amendment attorneys, Wendell Bird was the obvious choice as our lead attorney. Loren McMaster, a California attorney experienced in education matters, was his associate. In addition to the constitutional violations, the entire procedure had been filled with administrative irregularities, and these were included in our complaint. The federal judge, however, required that the latter had to be adjudicated first in the state court system before he would hear the constitutional questions.

When our attorneys listed the long litany of constitutional violations, aggressively took the depositions of Honig and all committee members, and won the state court suit, Honig wisely decided to withdraw his denial action, and gave back our "Approval." He and his attorneys recognized that their serious procedural irregularities had in effect nullified their case anyhow, so hoped by this device to get the federal case dismissed. Also, a new law had gone into effect in 1991, giving a new commission authority over all private post-secondary schools in California, so that Honig could "pass the buck," as it were, to another agency. Our attorneys, however, refused to dismiss the suit until justice was done, despite Honig's pleas.

In the meantime, the Trans-National Association of Christian

Schools (TRACS) finally received U.S. Department of Education recognition as an approved accreditation agency for Christian, creationist post-secondary institutions. Since the ICR Graduate School had already been fully accredited (as of 1989) by TRACS, that meant that our school not only once again had full state "Approval" but also now had national accreditation by a federally recognized accreditation agency. This was, indeed, a significant victory by God's grace and power, not only for the ICR Graduate School but also for Christian education in general.

Although state approval is still under the jurisdiction of the new commission, it does appear that the latter will not seek to attack us on the basis of our creationism at least. However, our attorneys do warn us (and Christians everywhere) that we need to be careful and watchful. The educational establishment is still bitterly anti-creationist and will continue to oppose creationists in whatever ways appear feasible.

ICR's lawsuit against Honig and the California Department of Education was finally settled in ICR's favor early in 1992, via a Declaratory Judgment by the federal district judge in San Diego. Not only did the State have to pay most of ICR's legal costs, but also the State had to agree that it would not interfere in curriculum or course content in *any* private school in the future. So far as known, this marked the first real court victory for creationism.

The Problem of Christian Compromise

The most disconcerting aspect of the creation/evolution con-flict, however, is not the bitter opposition of the evolutionary humanists (one would *expect* this), but rather the willingness of professing Christians to compromise with the evolutionists (one would *not expect this!*). The truth is, however, that many Christians seem all too eager for approval from those on the side of the Enemy, and this has been true all through the ages. One could write a large volume on the history of Christian compromise with evolution. Such compromise often takes the form of so-called religious liberalism, with its "higher criticism" of Genesis, but more often the form of strained exegesis to accommodate evolution in the Genesis account of creation. Probably most often, however, it takes the form of pious apathy, professing belief in creation while staying fully occupied with more "spiritual" matters.

We have already recounted the distressing effects of such compromise in the Darwinian and post-Darwinian periods. First, Christian leaders compromised on the literal Genesis record of creation and the flood, interpreting Genesis in terms of the geological ages and a local flood. Very quickly, this led them into theistic evolution. Next came an errant Bible, religious liberalism, and the social gospel. Finally there was nothing left but humanism. This very sequence, in fact, was the experience of Darwin himself, as well as that of multitudes of others before and since.

God is never honored by compromise on this most basic of all issues. Evolution, in one guise or another, is the ubiquitous global religion which is "against God" (the precise meaning of atheism), since it is the only conceivable way of explaining things without a personal omnipotent Creator God. There are only two possible models of origins, or world views, creation and evolution, and trying to bring them together is like trying to equate God and Satan. Evolution is naturalism, limited to mechanistic processes in its operation. This necessarily means endless ages of random changes which, in the process, leave untold waste and pain and death in their wake. Theistic evolution is a contradiction in terms. The God of the Bible is a God of wisdom and power and love, and such a God could never be guilty of such an incredibly inefficient and cruel scheme of development as evolution.

Yet many leading Christian theologians and intellectuals still persist in trying to persuade Christian "laymen" that evolution is merely God's method of creation. We have already cited a number of sad examples of this in the past, even in the immediate past. The case of the rapid decline of the American Scientific Affiliation from its creationist foundations into theistic evolutionism, with its resultant baleful influence on evangelicalism for the past four decades, is a case in point. This decline was almost inevitable, of course, when its founders refused to take a stand on literal six-day creation and a worldwide flood.

This tendency to equivocate and accommodate has been felt most keenly in evangelical seminaries and liberal arts colleges, the institutions which should be providing intellectual leadership for the Bible-believing Christian community. The factor of peer pressure seems to be more intimidating among Christian academics than any other group. The desire for acceptance by their professional colleagues in the secular universities, the supposed necessity to earn advanced degrees in such secular universities (there are still no true Christian universities!), and the rush to attain institutional accreditation from secular accrediting agencies have all been powerful and effective compromise-generators!

But of course, "none dare call it compromise!" No evangelical would ever admit to *compromising* with evolutionary humanism. They simply call it "interpretation." From our point of view, however, any interpretation of Genesis which accommodates the standard system of evolutionary geological ages is a clear-cut compromise with atheistic evolutionism, and it is very sad that Christians who profess to believe the Bible as the Word of God will not acknowledge this. Not only is theistic evolution such a compromise, but so is progressive creation, the day/age theory, the gap theory, the poetical theory, the local-flood theory, and the tranquil flood theory.

The Bible clearly teaches the special creation of all things in six literal days (e.g., Exodus 20:8–11) and a worldwide cataclysmic destruction by the flood (e.g., II Peter 3:3–6), and it is only special pleading and strained exegesis that can force any other meaning into the Biblical record.[1] This teaching is so clear and definite in

---

1. For typical expositions of this Biblical evidence (unanswered and unrefuted as yet, though generally ignored by compromising evangelicals), see my

Scripture that it seems redundant even to have to discuss it. It ought to be considered a "given," like the deity of Christ, for all who profess to be Bible-believing Christians.

Furthermore, even if it wasn't clear in Darwin's day, the modern scientific creationist movement has made it abundantly clear in our day that all the *real facts of science* support this Biblical position.[1] Despite all the bombastic books and articles, both by secular evolutionists and compromising evangelicals, which have opposed the modern literature on scientific Biblical creationism/catastrophism, the evidence is sound, and more and more scientists are becoming creationists all the time.

Nevertheless, as noted above, the most disappointing aspect of the modern creationist movement is the opposition and/or indifference of so many who profess to be evangelical Christians. If the community of true Christians would somehow become concerned and unified on this issue, the evolutionists wouldn't have a chance! The evidence—historical, Biblical, moral, scientific—is so completely in favor of special, recent creation that the chief bulwark of evolutionism against creationism has become the compromising Christian. Therefore, I urge any reader who is still inclined to temporize on the question of the evolutionary geological ages, to consider carefully the following facts:

1. The Bible, if taken naturally (as the writers intended) clearly teaches the recent creation of all things in six literal days.
2. All *known* human history (i.e., written records) corresponds with the Biblical several-thousand-year history.

---

books *The Genesis Record* (Grand Rapids: Baker Book House, 1976), Chapters I–IV, VIII; and *The Biblical Basis of Modern Science* (Grand Rapids: Baker Book House, 1984) Chapter IV.

1. Two summary treatments of the scientific evidence are found in the ICR books, *Scientific Creationism*, Henry M. Morris, ed. (San Diego: Creation-Life Publishers, 1985), 281 pp.; and *What is Creation-Science?*, by Henry M. Morris and Gary E. Parker (San Diego: Creation-Life Publishers, 1987), 336 pp. There is, of course, a great amount of additional material now available in the broad field of scientific creationism.

3. The hypothetical geological ages are unverifiable scientifically, being based entirely on indirect evidence and unwarranted uniformitarian extrapolation (plus circular reasoning—fossils are dated by the rocks in which they are found, with the rocks dated from the assumed evolutionary stage of their fossils).

4. Vast geological ages are necessary for evolution (which is based on no real *scientific* evidence) to be feasible at all.

5. Evolution is a necessary prerequisite for the religious philosophies of atheism, humanism, pantheism, materialism, etc., as well as Buddhism, Confucianism, Taoism, Hinduism, etc., not to mention communism, nazism, anarchism, racism, etc.

6. There is no theological justification for God to use such a wasteful, inefficient, cruel process as evolution as His method of creation.

7. The geological ages are identified explicitly only by the fossil remains found in their corresponding strata, all speaking of worldwide, eon-long, suffering and death in the world, long before man and human sin.

8. There is no theological justification for God to create animals in brief spurts interjected between long ages of suffering and death, since man's creation and dominion was His ultimate purpose in creation. In fact, the Bible explicitly teaches that death "entered the world" only when Adam sinned.

9. The record of rocks and fossils can be better understood in terms of Biblical catastrophism—especially the Genesis flood—than in terms of evolutionary geological ages.

10. If the geological ages were nonexistent, then evolution is impossible, and all the deadly philosophies based on it have no foundation.

Therefore, why in the Name of Him who is absolute truth and holiness, should any Christian continue to compromise with such a system as this?

There is a great battle coming and "if the trumpet give an uncertain sound, who shall prepare himself to the battle?" (I Corinthians 14:8). As the prophet Elijah challenged the people of God long ago: "How long halt ye between two opinions? If the Lord be God, follow Him; but if Baal, then follow Him" (I Kings 18:21).

The Future of Creationism

I am certainly no prophet, but one thing does seem fairly certain: the situation will never revert back to what it was, say, at the time of the Darwinian Centennial in 1959, when evolutionism seemed to have triumphed completely and real creationism seemed dead, at least to the secular world. There are now thousands of scientists who are strict, young-earth, flood-geology creationists, plus multiplied thousands of young people; there are scores of Bible colleges and other Christian institutions that have returned to strict creationism; the Christian school movement is mushrooming vigorously, and these schools are almost all creationist; the creation movement is rapidly spreading worldwide, not just in the United States; there is far more sound creationist literature available than ever before in history; and it seems that the strength of the scientific creation model itself increases with every new scientific discovery. No, things will not go back like they were before!

At the same time, the strength of the anti-creationist opposition is growing (not the strength of the evidence, of course, but the opposition). This is not surprising, in view of the numerous Biblical prophecies concerning the apostasy and growth of organized opposition to God in the last days (Psalm 2:1–6; Daniel 11:36–38; Matthew 24:24; Luke 18:8; II Thessalonians 2:3–12; 11 Timothy 3:1–7, 12–13; 4:3–4; II Peter 3:3–6; Jude 14–19; Revelation 3:14–20; and many others).

Since the 1977 publication of the first full-fledged anti-creationist book by sociologist Dorothy Nelkin, already mentioned, there have been at least 40 others, not to mention the hundreds and hundreds of anti-creationist articles in conference proceedings, newspapers, and magazines. There is also the mobilized and organized opposition of the American Civil Liberties Union, the American Humanist Association, the Committees of Correspondence, and other such groups. All of this is absolutely without precedent in history.

Where all this will lead no one can predict with certainty. The decision by the Supreme Court to strike down the Louisiana creation law has certainly been hurtful in some ways, but the creation movement seems to keep growing stronger in spite of this setback, at least in terms of public interest in our seminars and books. The Court decision has encouraged the evolutionary educational establishment to increased pressure on both public and Christian schools, with resulting increased polarization of the Bible-believing Christian community against the secular humanist community, with the religious compromisers trying to decide whether they can still ride the fence.

I would hope that, if the Lord does not return soon, the younger creationists now in our schools—especially those coming out of our ICR Graduate School—will soon be in responsible scientific and educational positions and will fill leadership roles in gradually restructuring science and education in a creationist context. I still hope a true creationist university will eventually emerge, either through the Trans-National Association of Christian Schools, or through further expansion of the ICR Graduate School, or in some other way. A fully creationist, Biblical, Christian educational system—in all fields and at all levels—is a Scriptural ideal toward which I hope true Christians will continue to strive, until the Lord comes.

These may be dreams, rather than goals, and they are certainly not intended as predictions. But they can at least indicate the direction we should head. Regardless of what the near future may bring, of course, we can at least predict with confidence what the *ultimate* future will hold.

For after all, evolutionary humanists to the contrary notwith-
standing, God *is* the Creator and He cannot fail! He is
long-suffering, but the Day of the Lord will come. I think it would
be appropriate to conclude this book on the history of creationism
with just a few of the Biblical assurances of the final victory of
the Creator.

> The Lord sitteth upon the flood; yea, the Lord sitteth King
> for ever (Psalm 29: 10).

> And blessed be His glorious name for ever; and let the whole
> earth be filled with His glory; Amen, and Amen (Psalm 72:19).

> For all the gods of the nations are idols; but the Lord made
> the heavens. . . . For he cometh to judge the earth (Psalm 96:5, 13).

> Let them praise the name of the Lord; for He commanded,
> and they were created. He hath also established them for ever
> and ever: He hath made a decree which shall not pass (Psalm
> 148:4, 6).

> I saw in the night visions, and, behold, one like the Son of
> man came with the clouds of heaven, and came to the Ancient
> of days, and they brought him near before Him. And there was
> given him dominion, and glory, and a kingdom, that all people,
> nations, and languages, should serve him; his dominion is an
> everlasting dominion, which shall not pass away, and his king-
> dom that which shall not be destroyed (Daniel 7:13–14).

> And the Lord shall be king over all the earth: in that day shall
> there be one Lord, and His name one (Zechariah 14:9).

> For in those days shall be affliction, such as was not from the
> beginning of the creation which God created unto this time,
> neither shall be. . . . And then shall they see the Son of man
> coming in the clouds with great power and glory. . . . Heaven
> and earth shall pass away; but my words shall not pass away
> (Matthew 24:19, 26, 31).

> God that made the world and all things therein, seeing that
> He is Lord of heaven and earth, . . . hath appointed a day, in the

which He will judge the world in righteousness by that man whom He hath ordained, whereof He hath given assurance unto all men, in that He hath raised Him from the dead (Acts 17:24–31).

. . . until the appearing of our Lord Jesus Christ: which in His times He shall shew, who is the blessed and only Potentate, the King of kings, and Lord of lords (I Timothy 6:15, 16).

. . . by the word of God the heavens were of old, and the earth. . . . But the heavens and the earth, which are now, by the same word are kept in store, reserved unto fire against the day of judgment and perdition of ungodly men (11 Peter 3:5–7).

Thou art worthy, 0 Lord, to receive glory and honour and power: for thou has created all things, and for thy pleasure they are and were created (Revelation 4:11).

Fear God, and give glory to Him; for the hour of His judgment is come: and worship Him that made heaven, and earth, and the sea, and the fountains of waters (Revelation 14:7).

These shall make war with the Lamb, and the Lamb shall overcome them: for He is Lord of lords, and King of kings: and they that are with Him are called, and chosen, and faithful (Revelation 17:14).

Appendix A[1]

The Declaration of Students of the Natural and Physical Sciences

WE, the undersigned Students of the Natural Sciences, desire to express our sincere regret, that researches into scientific truth are perverted by some in our own times into occasion for casting doubt upon the Truth and Authenticity of the Holy Scriptures. We conceive that it is impossible for the Word of God, as written in the book of nature, and God's Word written in Holy Scripture, to contradict one another, however much they may appear to differ. We are not forgetful that Physical Science is not complete, but is only in a condition of progress, and that at present our finite reason enables us only to see as through a glass darkly; and we confidently believe, that a time will come when the two records will be seen to agree in every particular. We cannot but deplore that Natural Science should be looked upon with suspicion by many who do not make a study of it, merely on account of the unadvised manner in which some are placing it in opposition to Holy Writ. We believe that it is the duty of every Scientific Student to investigate nature simply for the purpose of elucidating truth, and that if he finds that

---

1. This Declaration was published in London in 1865 and contained the signatures of 717 recognized scientists of the day. Among these were included such prominent leaders of science as Sir David Brewster, Sir Henry Rawlinson, Philip Gosse, James Joule, J. H. Balfour, Thomas Bell, Robert Bentley, F. Le Gros Clark, James Glaisher, Robert Main, John Nelson, James Napier, John Henry Pepper, E. Renevier, Sir John Richardson, Henry Rogers, and Adam Sedgwick. There were 86 Fellows of the Royal Society on the list.

some of his results appear to be in contradiction to the Written Word, or rather to his own *interpretations* of it, which may be erroneous, he should not presumptuously affirm that his own conclusions must be right, and the statements of Scripture wrong; rather, leave the two side by side till it shall please God to allow us to see the manner in which they may be reconciled; and, instead of insisting upon the seeming differences between Science and the Scriptures, it would be as well to rest in faith upon the points in which they agree.

Appendix B

Doctrinal Commitment for Membership in Creation Research Society

(Voting, Sustaining, and Student Members)

1. The Bible is the written Word of God, and because we believe it to be inspired throughout, all of its assertions are historically and scientifically true in all of the original autographs. To the student of nature, this means that the account of origins in Genesis is a factual presentation of simple historical truths.

2. All basic types of living things, including man, were made by direct creative acts of God during Creation Week as described in Genesis. Whatever biological changes have occurred since Creation have accomplished only changes within the original created kinds.

3. The great Flood described in Genesis, commonly referred to as the Noachian Deluge, was an historical event, worldwide in its extent and effect.

4. Finally, we are an organization of Christian men of science, who accept Jesus Christ as our Lord and Savior. The account of the special creation of Adam and Eve as one man and one woman, and their subsequent Fall into sin, is the basis for our belief in the necessity of a Savior for all mankind. Therefore, salvation can come only through accepting Jesus Christ as our Savior.

Appendix C

List of Creationist Organizations

The following list contains the names and mailing addresses of known creationist associations and organizations whose *primary* purpose is apparently to research, promote, teach, and/or disseminate information in support of scientific and/or Biblical creationism and catastrophism, including the doctrine of a young earth and the cataclysmic worldwide Noachian deluge. Since new creationist organizations are being formed continuously, this list is bound to be out of date very quickly, but at least it is indicative of the worldwide interest in creationism that has surfaced in recent years.

I. National Organizations

Apologetics Press
3906 E. Main St.
Stockton, California, 95205

Associates for Biblical Research
P.O. Box 125
Ephrata, Pennsylvania, 17522

Bible Science Association
2911 E. 42nd St.
Minneapolis, Minnesota, 55406

Catholic Creation Minitries
P.O. Box 997
Jordan, New York, 13082

Center for Scientific Creation
5612 N. 20th Place
Phoenix, Arizona, 85016

Chronology History Research
  Institute
P.O. Box 3043
Spencer, Iowa, 51301

Committee on Openness as a
  Principle of Science
2115 N. Kansas Street
El Paso, Texas, 79902

Creation Education, Inc.
P.O. Box 40133
Mesa, Arizona, 85274

Creation Research Society
P.O. Box 14016
Terre Haute, Indiana, 47803

Creation Research Society Books
5093 Williamsport Drive
Norcross, Georgia, 30092

Creation Resource Foundation
P.O. Box 16100
South Lake Tahoe, California,
    95706

Creation Science Legal Defense
    Fund
P. 0. Box 78312
Shreveport, Louisiana, 71137

Creation Science Research Center
P. 0. Box 23195
San Diego, California, 92123

Creation Social Science and
    Humanities Society
1429 N. Holyoke
Wichita, Kansas 67208

Creation Truth Foundation
Route 10, Box 11
Florence, Alabama, 36533

Education Research Analysts
P.O. Box 7518
Longview, Texas, 75602

Films for Christ
2628 W. Birchwood Circle
Mesa, Arizona, 85202

Genesis Institute and Ark Project
7323 Morgan Avenue South
Richfield, Minnesota, 55423

Geoscience Research Institute
Loma Linda University
Loma Linda, California, 92350

Institute for Creation Research
P. 0. Box 2667
El Cajon, California, 92021

International Conferences on
    Creation
P.O. Box 17578
Pittsburgh, Pennsylvania, 15235

Master Books
P. 0. Box 26060
Colorado Springs, Colorado 80936

Origins Research and Information
    Service
137 Oak Crest Drive
Lafayette, Louisiana, 70503

Students for Origins Research
P. 0. Box 38069
Colorado Springs, Colorado,
    80937

II. Regional and Local Organizations

Creation Science Committee
Box 72282
Fairbanks, Alaska, 99707

Tucson Association of Creationists
P.O. Box 17292
Tucson, Arizona 85731

Creation Research of the North
  Coast
2450 Alliance Road
Arcato, California, 95521

Center for Creation Studies
12259 Oriole Avenue
Grand Terrace, California, 92324

Creation Science Association of
  Orange County
P.O. Box 4325
Irvine, California, 92716

San Fernando Valley Chapter,
  Bible Science Association
12001 Foothill Boulevard #88
Lakeview Terrace, California,
  91342

Riverside Chapter, Bible Science
  Association
10926 Hole Avenue
Riverside, California, 92505

Creation Conference Committee
2541 Borica Way
Sacramento, California, 95821

Silicon Valley Bible Science
  Association
13445 Harper Drive
Saratoga, California, 95070

South Bay Creation Science
  Association
22322 Harbor Ridge Lane, #2
Torrance, California, 90502

Creation Science Association of
  Ventura County
528 South Dos Caminos
Ventura, California 93003

Alpha Omega Institute
P.O. Box 4343
Grand Junction, Colorado, 81502

Citizens for Scientific Integrity
5620 N.E. 22nd Avenue
Fort Lauderdale, Florida, 33308

Compatriots for Academic
  Freedom
P. 0. Box 1121
Bradenton, Florida 33506

Creation Education Ministries
1345 Hill Drive
Largo, Florida, 34640

Midwest Creation Fellowship
7861 South Ramsgate
Hanover Park, Illinois, 60103

Indiana Creation-Science
Association
5210 N. Arlington Avenue
Indianapolis, Indiana 46226

Iowa Coalition for Education
Freedom
3701 E. 38th Street Court
Des Moines, Iowa, 50317

Louisiana Citizens for Academic
Freedom in Origins
P.O. Box 10010
River Ridge, Louisiana 70181

Citizens for Better Science in
Education
2721 Merrick Way
Abingdon, Maryland, 21009

Creation Science Association
18346 Beverly Road
Birmingham, Michigan, 48009

Lake Huron Bible Science
Association
101 North Superior
Oscoda, Michigan, 48750

Twin Cities Creation Science
Association
6120 First Avenue South
Minneapolis, Minnesota, 55419

Creation Science Association for
Mid-America
Route 1, Box 247-B
Cleveland, Missouri, 64734

Missouri Association for Creation
405 North Sappington
St. Louis, Missouri 63122

Billings Creation Evangelism
Committee
1702 Avenue F.
Billings, Montana, 59102

Missoula Creation Society
234 Barclay
Lola, Montana, 59847

Roswell Creation Science
Association
402 South Birch Avenue
Roswell, New Mexico, 88201

Creation Science Fellowship
P.O. Box 10550
Albuquerque, New Mexico, 87184

Triangle Association for
Scientific Creation
P. 0. Box 33222
Raleigh, North Carolina 27636

Creation Research Science
Education Foundation, Inc.
P.O. Box 292
Columbus, Ohio 43216

Institute for Scientific and
Biblical Research
3196 Thistle Drive
Lancaster, Pennsylvania, 17601

Creation Science Fellowship, Inc.
362 Ashland Avenue
Pittsburgh, Pennsylvania, 15228

Creation Study Group
19 Gallery Centre
Taylors, South Carolina, 29687

Creation Science Association of
Middle Tennessee
P.O. Box 972
Brentwood, Tennessee, 37024

Creation Research Centre
P.O. Box 281
Hartsville, Tennessee, 37074

Nashville Bible Science
Association
2805 Glen Oaks Drive
Nashville, Tennessee, 37214

Metroplex Institute of Origin
Science, Inc.
P.O. Box 550953
Dallas, Texas, 75355

Creation Evidence Museum
P.O. Box 309
Glen Rose, Texas, 76043

Texas Institute for Creation
Science
P.O. Box 335
Ore City, Texas

Utah Back-to-Genesis Committee
215 West 4850 South
Ogden, Utah, 84405

Center for Creation Studies
Liberty University, Box 20,000
Lynchburg, Virginia, 24506

Mountain View Bible Science
Association
101 Laurel Hill Drive
Stephens City, Virginia 22655

Origin Science Association
4141 Rainbow Drive
Virginia Beach, Virginia, 23456

Seattle Bible-Science Association
P. 0. Box 66507
Seattle, Washington 98166

Creation Outreach Association
West 4011 27th Avenue
Spokane, Washington, 99204

Lutheran Science Foundation
19545 102nd St.
Bristol, Wisconsin, 53104

Creation-Science Association
2825 Riva Ridge Circle
Cottage Grove, Wisconsin, 53527

Creation-Science Society of
Milwaukee
5334 North 66th Street
Milwaukee, Wisconsin 53213

Creation Education Association
Route 1, Box 161
Pine River, Wisconsin 54965

The Creation Report
P.O. Box 558

Plover, Wisconsin 54467

III. Foreign Creationist Organizations

Creation Science Foundation
P. 0. Box 302
Sunnybank, Queensland, 4109,
    Australia

Creation Research Center
P.O. Box 260
Capalaba, Queensland, 4157,
    Australia

Creatioisten Belgie
Meenselstraat 10
B 3461 Molenbeek
Wersbeek, Belgium

El Otro Lado de la Ciencia
Casilla 9864
La Paz, Bolivia

Associacao Brasileira de Pesquisa
    da Criacao
Caixa Postal 3511-CEP30012
Belo Horizonte, MG, Brazil

Creation Science Association of
    Alberta
194 3808 Calgary Tr S, Sta. 1136
Edmonton, Alberta, T6J 5M8,
    Canada

Creation Science Association of
    Canada
Box 39577 White Rock PO
Surrey, British Columbia, V4A

3P8, Canada

Creation Science Association of
    Ontario
P.O. Box 821 Station A
Scarborough, Ontario, M1K 5C8,
    Canada

Creation Science Association of
    Quebec
P.O. Box 10 Pierrefonds
Province of Quebec, H9H 4K8,
    Canada

Creation Science Association of
    Saskatchewan, Inc.
P.O. Box 26
Kenaston, Saskatchewan, S0G
    2N0, Canada

North American Creation
    Movement
1556 Arrow Road
Victoria, B. C., V8N 1C5, Canada

ORIGO
Hundborgvej 42
DK-7700 Thisted, Denmark

Creation Resources Trust
Mead Farm, Downhead, West
    Camel
YEOVIL, Somerset, BA22 7RQ,
    England

Greek Association of Scientists
  for Scientific Truth
43 Ellanikou St.; 39 Menandrov St
Athens, 10437, Greece

Schools for Christ Foundation
5, Tong Yam Street
Tai Hang Tung, Kowloon, Hong
  Kong

Creation Research and
  Apologetics Society of India
16A Saraswati Nagar-1
Mahalgaon PO, Gwalior, M.P.,
  474002, India

Bible and Science Society
1-4-41 Kaminito, Mito Shi
Ibaraki Ken, 310, Japan

Korea Association of Creation
  Research
P.O. Box 2122
Seoul, 135-621, Korea

Foundation for the Advancement
  of Studies Faithful to the Bible
Kampweg 106, Doorn 3941 HL
The Netherlands

Creation Literature Society
391 Cook St., Howick
Auckland, New Zealand

African Creation Science
  Foundation
P.O. Box 2905
Mushin - Lagos, Nigeria

Creation Science Society
P. O. Box 222
Sta. Mesa, Manilla 1008
Philippines

Puerto Rico Creation Society
P.O. Box 5099
Cagunas, Puerto Rico, 00626

Deus Dixit
P.O. Box 13816
0129 Sinoville, Republic of South
  Africa

Moscow Creation Science
  Fellowship
Menzhinski Str.
25-44 Moscow 129327 Russia

Coordinadora Creacionista
Apartar 92041
08080 Barcelona, Spain

Förening för Biblisk Skapelsetro
PI 5062 B, 69400 Hallsberg,
  Sweden

Centre Biblique European
Casa Postale 2386 En Chollet
CH 1418 Vuarrens, Switzerland

Biblical Creation Society
P.O. Box 22
Rugby, Warwickshire, CV22 7SV,
  United Kingdom

Creation Science Movement
50 Brecon Ave, Cosham
Portsmouth, Hanta, P06 2AW,
    United Kingdom

Torbay Christian Creation Topics
Lower Park 9, Courtland Road
Torquay, Devon, TQ2 6JV,
    United Kingdom

Creation Science for Catholics
19 Francis Ave., St. Albans
Herts, AL3 6BL, United Kingdom

Creation News
3 Church Terrace Penylan
Cardiff, Wales, CF2 5AW, United
    Kingdom

Appendix D

Formation of Evolution Protest Movement ˙

The incentives for the organization of the first significant creationist organization of the twentieth century are outlined in the initial promotional letter, reproduced here, of the Evolution Protest Movement, established in 1932.

EVOLUTION PROTEST MOVEMENT

TELEPHONE
CENTRAL 7914
ALL COMMUNICATIONS
SHOULD BE ADDRESSED
TO THE SECRETARY
Mr. O. R. ACWORTH
B.A. (Cantab.)

BANKERS—LLOYDS, 222, STRAND.
AUDITORS—READE, COCKE & WATSON

24, ESSEX STREET,
STRAND, W.C.2.

ADVISORY COMMITTEE.

CAPTAIN B. ACWORTH, D.S.O., R.N., F.R.A.I.,
(Chairman of the Liberty Restoration League).
DR. BASIL ATKINSON, Phil.D.,
(Under Librarian Cambridge University).
DOUGLAS DEWAR, Esq., F.Z.S., B.A
THE REV. DR. DINSDALE YOUNG, D.D.
SIR JOHN LATTA, BART.
THE REV. HUGH MILLER,
(Principal of the London School of Bible Studies).
DR. JAMES KNIGHT, M.A., D Sc., F.R.S E.,
(Vice-President of the Royal Philosophical Society).

Dear Sir (or Madam),

The public is conscious that the country is in a critical state and that subversive doctrines are undermining every aspect of our national life. There must, therefore, be some fundamental fallacy operating in the mind of the country as a whole.

We believe this fallacy to be the acceptance, as true, of the theory of Evolution and its employment as the spring of action in all spheres. Professor F. A. E. Crew, an Evolutionist, admits this when he says "The Evolutionary concept has been applied to religion and philosophy" and "has shaken the whole edifice of social tradition". Economics and politics now conform to the same concept.

Christianity sanctifies the individual and the home; Evolution glorifies the herd and is the parent of Socialism and Communism. In Russia the theory of Evolution has supplanted Christianity. Darwin is the new Messiah.

We feel the public are being deceived. Evolution propaganda does not present the facts impartially; it dwells upon those which favour the theory, while suppressing those which oppose it. Such are not the methods of true, but of false, science.

Few people realise that the tactics which evolutionists employ would be regarded as "special pleading" in a Court of Law; and that many scientists have declared that evolution is both unproved and unprovable.

It is significant that the preachers of the theory are reluctant to meet the objections of dissenting scientists, or to answer the challenge of leaders of traditional Christian thought.

The aims and methods of our Movement are set out overleaf. If you approve of our aim your active assistance is invited.

Yours faithfully,

BERNARD ACWORTH
BASIL F. C. ATKINSON
D. DEWAR
DINSDALE T. YOUNG
JOHN LATTA
HUGH MILLER
JAMES KNIGHT.

Appendix E

The Need for a Creationist Educational Center

(Letter to T. LaHaye, February 1970)

The following paragraphs, discussing the original goals and philosophy proposed for Christian Heritage College and the Institute for Creation Research, are excerpts from the first letter written to Dr. Tim LaHaye by the writer on February 12, 1970.

February 12, 1970

Dr. Tim F. LaHaye
Scott Memorial Baptist Church
2716 Madison Avenue
San Diego, California 92116

Dear Tim:

Thank you very much for your letter of February 2, and the enclosed booklet describing the ministry of your church. It is evident that the Lord is using you and your church in a positive and powerful way. It was a blessing to meet you and to share in the things of the Lord recently at Biola.

. . . (3 paragraphs omitted)

Now, if you don't mind reading a long letter, I would appreciate the opportunity to share with you a few thoughts of my own. Over the past 30 years, since I became seriously committed to Biblical

Christianity, I have been rather closely observing the various trends in evangelicalism and fundamentalism and have been in a great number of churches and schools, and numerous missions and associations of various types. Doctrinally, I am a strongly convinced Baptist and pre-millenialist, although I have also worked quite a bit with the Gideons and other interdenominational evangelistic organizations. But with all this heterogeneous background, I do believe that the issue of Biblical creationism is the most urgent issue confronting Christianity today. The evolutionary system is at the root of most of the spiritual and moral problems that have arisen to hinder the gospel and its proclamation today.

By God's grace, some have tried to do what they could to help meet this need, and the Lord has blessed, in spite of significant opposition. In recent years there has been an amazing revival of solid Biblical creation doctrine, evidenced especially in the formation of the Creation Research Society and now in the recent decision to include creationism as a viable alternative in California school science teaching. It seems we may be on the threshold of a sweeping movement back to faith in the integrity of God's Word, and its authority in every discipline of thought and life. Of course this will undoubtedly remain a minority position, and will be held and advanced only against powerful opposition, but it does seem that God may yet raise up one more strong witness to His Truth in these last days.

Now, it would be tremendous if somehow a great center of Biblical truth could be established as the nerve-center of this testimony. This could include a Bible college, but more importantly a Christian university, with a strong publications and extension ministry also, seeking to prepare and send out solid Christians in various strategic professional fields as well as in posts of full-time Christian service. And I believe the integrating principle in all these fields should be a strong emphasis on the doctrines of creation and redemption. These truths provide the necessary key to the most effective understanding and application of the data of any science or profession. Maybe this is a visionary and impractical dream, but God is not limited and it may be that He is waiting for just such an undertaking, one committed to uncompromising faith in the Holy Scriptures as the source of all truth, in order to demonstrate the full extent of His mighty power and abiding faithfulness. Perhaps it should take the form of a foundation, one of whose projects would be the establishment and operation of a university and training institutes of various kinds, another the publication and distribution of literature, another the operation of an extension ministry of lectures and evangelism, another the sponsorship of significant research, and so on.

If something like this could somehow be initiated, I would be thrilled to take part in it in whatever capacity I could best serve. From my contacts around the country over the past ten years, I believe that many other qualified people would likewise be ready to move into it as the Lord leads.

Well, all the above thoughts may seem far-out, but I felt maybe you, more than most others, might be responsive to them. In any case, we can surely pray for God's guidance concerning ways in which we can most effectively magnify His great Name in these closing days.

Sincerely, in Christ

Henry M. Morris

Appendix F

Christian Heritage College Doctrinal Statement

The original Christian Heritage College statement of faith for its faculty and students is of historical significance because of its unique commitment to recent literal creation and a global cataclysmic flood, vital issues strangely ignored by previous Christian liberal arts college founders and administrators. Unfortunately this statement was considerably shortened in 1984, but it still retains its commitments to recent creation and worldwide flood.

1. **The absolute integrity of Holy Scripture** and its plenary verbal inspiration, by the Holy Spirit, as originally written through men prepared of God for this purpose. The Scriptures, both Old and New Testaments, are inerrant in relation to any subject with which they deal and are to be accepted in their natural and intended sense as of full authority over Christian faith and life. No other religious writings or supposed revelations are to be accepted as divinely inspired or authoritative.

2. **The Triune God—Father, Son, and Holy Spirit.** There is only one God, who is the source of all being and meaning, and who exists in three Persons, each of whom is eternal, omnipotent, personal, and perfect in holiness.

3. **Direct creation and divine preservation of all things.** All things in the universe were created by God in the six days of special creation described in Genesis 1:1-2:3. The Creation account is accepted as factual, historical, and perspicuous, and is thus foundational to the understanding

of every fact and phenomenon in the created universe. Theories of origins and development which involve "evolution" in any form are thus recognized as false and sterile intellectually. Furthermore, all things which now exist are being sustained and ordered by God's providential care, and this fact also is essential to the proper understanding of any truth.

4. **Man, created in God's Image** and ordained as God's vicegerent over His creation. Although now marred by the Fall, man was originally given the authority and ability to exercise dominion over the created world. Even now, redeemed and regenerated men have the incentive and potential to reclaim in part the processes of nature and the institutions of society for the accomplishment of God's revealed purposes.

5. **The pervasive influence of sin and the Curse.** When the first man sinned, he brought himself and all his descendants, as well as his entire dominion, under God's curse. Thus the entire physical creation, the world of living organisms, and all of man's institutions are now under the same "bondage of corruption" which has afflicted man himself. This universal principle of decay and death must be recognized in all phenomena if those phenomena are to be fully understood and properly utilized.

6. **The redemptive work of Jesus Christ.** In order to redeem man and the creation, God the Son became man, through the miraculous conception and virgin birth of Jesus Christ. As the Son of Man, He lived a perfect and sinless human life and then yielded Himself up to die on the Cross, in substitution for all men. The great Curse finally reached its climax when the Creator Himself accepted and endured its ultimate and greatest intensity.

7. **The centrality of the bodily resurrection of Christ.** After the death and burial of the body of the Lord Jesus, He rose from the grave on the third day. The redemption price had

been fully paid, and man's justification before a holy God is now completely assured, as confirmed by His victory over the Curse and its universal law of decay and death. Not only can individual souls now be redeemed, but ultimately, the bodies of believers will likewise be resurrected and glorified, and even the Creation itself will be delivered from its bondage of corruption—all because Christ died and rose again.

8. **The imminent return of Christ.** Although the price has been paid and the victory is assured, the final consummation is to be realized only when Jesus Christ, now in heaven at the right hand of the Father, returns personally to the earth to destroy all rebellion and to establish His perfect and eternal reign. His second coming, like His first, will involve many events, including the rapture of His Church, the Seven-Year Tribulation Period, and the glorious appearing of Christ on the earth to set up His millennial kingdom. This will culminate in the installation of a new earth and a new heaven, which will last forever and in which His glorious purposes in Creation will finally be accomplished. In the meantime, His coming is imminent and may be expected momentarily.

9. **Personal salvation through faith in Jesus Christ.** All men are guilty sinners before God, both by heredity and by willful disobedience to the light received through nature and through conscience, as well as by the breaking of God's written commandments when known. No one can ever earn his own salvation, but Christ has graciously provided the free gift of salvation to all who will receive it, on the basis of His atoning death and resurrection. When a person's will and mind are submitted in repentance toward God and faith toward Christ, then God the Holy Spirit makes that person a new creation, with a renewed mind and converted will. This great salvation (assuming it is real and not merely a

superficial emotional or intellectual decision) imparts eternal life to the believer, and therefore, can never be destroyed.

10. **The real, though temporary, nature of evil.** Although God is not directly responsible for the existence of evil in the universe, He has allowed it to intrude for a time, in consistency with His creation of freedom and responsibility for all spiritual beings, and also in order to manifest Himself as both Creator and Redeemer. All present evil in the universe is headed up in the cosmic rebellion instigated by Lucifer, originally the highest of God's angels, who is now Satan, the head of a mighty host of fallen angels actively opposing God's purposes in Creation and Redemption. Ultimately, these will be confined forever to the lake of fire, along with the resurrected bodies of all men who died without accepting the Lord Jesus and His gift of salvation.

11. **The Biblical framework of history.** The true understanding of the present world requires correlation of all the data of science and history within the historical framework provided by the Bible, including the following major events:
    (a)   special Creation of all things in six natural days;
    (b)   the entrance of sin and the Curse into the world;
    (c)   the worldwide Flood, which cataclysmically changed the entire earth in the days of Noah;
    (d)   the origin of nations and languages at the Tower of Babel;
    (e)   the preparation of a special nation, Israel, through which to reveal God's Word to men;
    (f)   the incarnation, death, and resurrection of the Lord Jesus Christ, as the Surety of Redemption;
    (g)   the consummation of all of God's redemptive plans, as well as His purposes in Creation, through the events associated with the bodily return of Jesus Christ.

12. **The Christian's responsibility to society.** God has divided

mankind into nations, tribes, and languages in order to enable each unit more effectively to fulfill its own mission in the world, and to prevent a unified rebellion against Himself such as occurred at Babel. The institutions of the home, the church, and of government were established also with this end, all ideally to be directed toward the most effective ordering of society and history to implement God's purposes. The individual believer therefore is responsible for loyalty and obedience to these social institutions, including the civil government, which are faithfully fulfilling their ministries in accordance with God's Word. He is similarly responsible, as God leads and enables, to seek changes in these if they become disobedient to God's Word. In general, the constitutional government of the federal Republic of the United States, together with the individual state and local governmental systems, has proved an effective means of accomplishing these purposes in this country, and is deserving of the support and defense of its citizens.

13. **The Great Commission.** Until the return of Christ, it is the Christian's duty and privilege to seek the conversion, baptism, and full instruction of men in every tribe and nation, in accord with Christ's Great Commission.

14. **Primacy of the Local Church.** While recognizing and emphasizing the importance of the universal fellowship and cooperation of all true Christian believers, the Scriptures make it plain that local organized assemblies of such believers are of primary importance in the practical implementation of the Great Commission. The ministry of Christian Heritage College, as well as of all other Christian associations and institutions, should be considered, therefore, as an extension or supporting ministry of a local church or of a group of such churches. Similarly, all students and employees should be active members of a local church in the community where they live.

Appendix G

ICR Tenets of Creationism

The Institute for Creation Research Graduate School has a unique statement of faith for its faculty and students, incorporating most of the basic Christian doctrines in a creationist framework, organized in terms of two parallel sets of tenets, related to God's created world and God's inspired Word, respectively. Reproduced below are the ICR Educational Philosophy and its Tenets of Scientific Creationism and Biblical Creationism.

ICR EDUCATIONAL PHILOSOPHY

The programs and curricula of the Graduate School, as well as the activities of other ICR divisions, while similar in factual content to those of other graduate colleges, are distinctive in one major respect. The Institute for Creation Research bases its educational philosophy on the foundational truth of a personal Creator-God and His authoritative and unique revelation of truth in the Bible, both Old and New Testaments.

This perspective differs from the evolutionary humanistic philosophy which has dominated most educational institutions for the past century, providing the most satisfying and meaningful structure of a consistently creationist and Biblical framework, and placing the real facts of science and history in the best context for effective future research and application.

More explicitly, the administration and faculty of ICR are committed to the tenets of both scientific creationism and Biblical creationism as formulated below. A clear distinction is drawn between *scientific creationism* and *Biblical creationism* but it is the position of the Institute that the two are compatible and that all genuine facts of science support the Bible. ICR maintains that scientific creationism should be taught along with the scientific aspects of evolutionism in tax-supported institutions, and that both scientific and Biblical creationism should be taught in Christian schools.

Tenets of Scientific Creationism

1. The physical universe of space, time, matter, and energy has not always existed, but was supernaturally created by a transcendent personal Creator who alone has existed from eternity.

2. The phenomenon of biological life did not develop by natural processes from inanimate systems but was specially and supernaturally created by the Creator.

3. Each of the major kinds of plants and animals was created functionally complete from the beginning and did not evolve from some other kind of organism. Changes in basic kinds since their first creation are limited to "horizontal" changes (variation) within the kinds, or "downward" changes (e.g., harmful mutations, extinctions).

4. The first human beings did not evolve from an animal ancestry, but were specially created in fully human form from the start. Furthermore, the "spiritual" nature of man (self-image, moral consciousness, abstract reasoning, language, will, religious nature, etc.) is itself a supernaturally created entity distinct from mere biological life.

5. The record of earth history, as preserved in the earth's crust, especially in the rocks and fossil deposits, is primarily a record of catastrophic intensities of natural processes, operating largely within uniform natural laws, rather than one of gradualism and relatively uniform process rates. There are many scientific evidences for a relatively recent creation of the earth and the universe, in addition to strong scientific

evidence that most of the earth's fossiliferous sedimentary rocks were formed in an even more recent global hydraulic cataclysm.

6. Processes today operate primarily within fixed natural laws and relatively uniform process rates but, since these were themselves originally created and are daily maintained by their Creator, there is always the possibility of miraculous intervention in these laws or processes by their Creator. Evidences for such intervention should be scrutinized critically, however, because there must be clear and adequate reason for any such action on the part of the Creator.

7. The universe and life have somehow been impaired since the completion of creation, so that imperfections in structure, disease, aging, extinctions, and other such phenomena are the result of "negative" changes in properties and processes occurring in an originally-perfect created order.

8. Since the universe and its primary components were created perfect for their purposes in the beginning by a competent and volitional Creator, and since the Creator does remain active in this now-decaying creation, there do exist ultimate purposes and meanings in the universe. Teleological considerations, therefore, are appropriate in scientific studies whenever they are consistent with the actual data of observation, and it is reasonable to assume that the creation presently awaits the consummation of the Creator's purpose.

9. Although people are finite and scientific data concerning origins are always circumstantial and incomplete, the human mind (if open to the possibility of creation) is able to explore the manifestations of that Creator rationally and scientifically, and to reach an intelligent decision regarding one's place in the Creator's plan.

Tenets of Biblical Creationism

1. The Creator of the universe is a triune God—Father, Son, and Holy Spirit. There is only one eternal and transcendent God, the source of all being and meaning, and He exists in three Persons, each of whom participated in the work of creation.

2. The Bible, consisting of the thirty-nine canonical books of the Old Testament and the twenty-seven canonical books of the New Testament, is the divinely-inspired revelation of the Creator to man. Its unique, plenary, verbal inspiration guarantees that these writings, as originally and miraculously given, are infallible and completely authoritative on all matters with which they deal, free from error of any sort, scientific and historical as well as moral and theological.

3. All things in the universe were created and made by God in the six literal days of the creation week described in Genesis 1:1–2:3, and confirmed in Exodus 20:8–11. The creation record is factual, historical, and perspicuous; thus all theories of origins or development which involve evolution in any form are false. All things which now exist are sustained and ordered by God's providential care. However, a part of the spiritual creation, Satan and his angels, rebelled against God after the creation and are attempting to thwart His divine purposes in creation.

4. The first human beings, Adam and Eve, were specially created by God, and all other men and women are their descendants. In Adam, mankind was instructed to exercise "dominion" over all other created organisms, and over the earth itself (an implicit commission for true science, technology, commerce, fine art, and education) but the temptation by Satan and the entrance of sin brought God's curse on that dominion and on mankind, culminating in death and separation from God as the natural and proper

consequence.

5. The Biblical record of primeval earth history in Genesis 1–11 is fully historical and perspicuous, including the creation and fall of man, the curse on the creation and its subjection to the bondage of decay, the promised Redeemer, the worldwide cataclysmic deluge in the days of Noah, the post-diluvian renewal of man's commission to subdue the earth (now augmented by the institution of human government) and the origin of nations and languages at the tower of Babel.

6. The alienation of man from his Creator because of sin can only be remedied by the Creator Himself, who became man in the person of the Lord Jesus Christ, through miraculous conception and virgin birth. In Christ were indissolubly united perfect sinless humanity and full deity, so that His substitutionary death is the only necessary and sufficient price of man's redemption. That the redemption was completely efficacious is assured by His bodily resurrection from the dead and ascension into heaven; the resurrection of Christ is thus the focal point of history, assuring the consummation of God's purposes in creation.

7. The final restoration of creation's perfection is yet future, but individuals can immediately be restored to fellowship with their Creator, on the basis of His redemptive work on their behalf, receiving forgiveness and eternal life solely through personal trust in the Lord Jesus Christ, accepting Him not only as estranged Creator but also as reconciling Redeemer and coming King. Those who reject Him, however, or who neglect to believe on Him, thereby continue in their state of rebellion and must ultimately be consigned to the everlasting fire prepared for the devil and his angels.

In addition to a firm commitment to creationism and to full Biblical inerrancy and authority, the ICR Graduate School is committed to traditional education and to high standards of academic excellence. Each student's graduate program will consist predominantly of classroom lecture courses, with interaction between instructors and students, plus a research investigation and M.S. thesis. ICR's highly qualified and experienced faculty is in itself assurance of a rigorous and creative educational experience for its graduates, equipping them both for productive careers in their chosen fields and for making a significant contribution to the ongoing worldwide revival of theistic creationism.

Index of Names

Index of Subjects